The Lives of David Brainerd

Recent titles in

RELIGION IN AMERICA SERIES
Harry S. Stout, General Editor

SOME WILD VISIONS
Autobiographies by Female Itinerant Evangelists in 19th-Century America
Elizabeth Elkin Grammer

NATHANIEL TAYLOR, NEW HAVEN THEOLOGY,
AND THE LEGACY OF JONATHAN EDWARDS
Douglas A. Sweeney

BLACK PURITAN, BLACK REPUBLICAN
The Life and Thought of Lemuel Haynes, 1753–1833
John Saillant

WITHOUT BENEFIT OF CLERGY
Women and the Pastoral Relationship in Nineteenth-Century
American Culture
Karin E. Gedge

A. J. TOMLINSON
Plainfolk Modernist
R. G. Robins

FAITH IN READING
Religious Publishing and the Birth of Mass Media in America
David Paul Nord

FUNDAMENTALISTS IN THE CITY
Conflict and Division in Boston's Churches 1885–1950
Margaret Lamberts Bendroth

A PARADISE OF REASON
William Bentley and Enlightenment Christianity in the Early Republic
J. Rixey Ruffin

EVANGELIZING THE SOUTH
A Social History of Church and State in Early America
Monica Najar

THE LIVES OF DAVID BRAINERD
The Making of an American Evangelical Icon
John A. Grigg

John A. Grigg

The Lives of David Brainerd
The Making of an American
Evangelical Icon

OXFORD
UNIVERSITY PRESS
2009

OXFORD
UNIVERSITY PRESS

Oxford University Press, Inc., publishes works that further
Oxford University's objective of excellence
in research, scholarship, and education.

Oxford   New York
Auckland   Cape Town   Dar es Salaam   Hong Kong   Karachi
Kuala Lumpur   Madrid   Melbourne   Mexico City   Nairobi
New Delhi   Shanghai   Taipei   Toronto

With offices in
Argentina   Austria   Brazil   Chile   Czech Republic   France   Greece
Guatemala   Hungary   Italy   Japan   Poland   Portugal   Singapore
South Korea   Switzerland   Thailand   Turkey   Ukraine   Vietnam

Copyright © 2009 Oxford University Press, Inc.

Published by Oxford University Press, Inc.
198 Madison Avenue, New York, New York 10016
www.oup.com

Oxford is a registered trademark of Oxford University Press

Library of Congress Cataloging-in-Publication Data

Grigg, John A.
    The lives of David Brainerd : the making of an American evangelical icon / John A. Grigg.
        p. cm.
    Includes bibliographical references and index.
    ISBN 978-0-19-537237-3
    1. Brainerd, David, 1718–1747. 2. Missionaries—East (U.S.)—Biography.
    3. Mohegan Indians—Missions. 4. Delaware Indians—Missions. I. Title.
    E99.M83B734 2009
    266'.51092—dc22   2009000871

9 8 7 6 5 4 3 2 1

Printed in the United States of America
on acid-free paper

To my parents, Barry Charles Grigg and Deidre Grigg,
and in memory of David Charles Grigg (1964–2008)

Acknowledgments

Since there is no single repository for David Brainerd's documents, my research for this book has enabled me to meet a number of wonderful folks at archives in the United States and Scotland. I would like to specifically thank Will Garrison and the staff of the Mission House in Stockbridge, Massachusetts, who were kind enough to provide me with access to the leaf from David Brainerd's journal in their possession as did Sylvie Merian and her staff at the Pierpont Morgan Library in New York City. The Reverend Evans Sealand went to great lengths to make available to me eighteenth-century records of the Congregational Church in Connecticut. Martha Smalley at the Yale Divinity School Library was particularly gracious in allowing me to transcribe David Brainerd's manuscript sermon the day before the manuscript collection was closed for remodeling. Diana Yount and Jeffrey Brigham provided access to the papers of Jonathan Edwards held in the Trask Library at the Andover-Newton Theological Seminary. Danelle Moon and the staff at the Yale Archives allowed me to peruse the early records of Yale College, and Bette Dybick did the same with respect to the town records of Haddam, Connecticut. James Lewis, formerly at the New Jersey Historical Society, was most accommodating to my requests. I would also like to thank the archivists, assistants, and other staff members at the Beinecke Rare Book and Manuscript Library at Yale University, New-York Historical Society, Rare Book Department of the Library of Congress, Peabody-Essex Library, Yale Divinity School Library, Rare Books and Special Collections at the Princeton Library, Princeton Theological Seminary Library, Connecticut State Library, Connecticut Historical Society, National Archives of Scotland, Edinburgh University Special Collections, Spencer Library at the University of Kansas, New College Library at the Edinburgh Divinity School, National Library of Scotland, Historical Society of Pennsylvania, American Antiquarian Society, Moravian Archives, and Presbyterian Historical Society. My thanks also to the staffs in the town clerks' offices at Durham and East Haddam, Connecticut. I also appreciate the efforts of Patrick Frazier and Cindy Jungenberg, who provided a translation of one of the Moravian documents.

I never ceased to be amazed at the ability of interlibrary loan (ILL) offices to track down almost anything a historian might need, and I express my gratitude to the ILL offices at the University of Kansas and Johnson County Community College and particularly to Gerry Randall at Hampden-Sydney College and John Schneiderman at the University of Nebraska, Omaha.

A somewhat different version of chapter 4 first appeared at *History Compass* while an extended analysis of Brainerd's ordination sermon was published by the *New England Quarterly*. Thanks to both publications for permission to use the material here. Thanks also to Elizabeth Malloy of the Haddam Historical Society for the photo of the Brainerd home site, Stan Sherer for the photo of Brainerd's grave, and Marv Barton for the maps.

My thanks to the participants in the Early Modern Seminar at the University of Kansas for comments on an earlier version of chapter 3, to Dr. Ray Hiner for his helpful suggestions when this book was in its dissertation incarnation, and to the members of FLEA—the Fall Line Early Americanists—for comments on a much earlier version of chapter 1. My sincere appreciation also to Doug Winiarski for his comments on another version of chapter 1 as well as further input along the way, which helped me to conceptualize Brainerd's place in the revivals of the 1740s.

As I grappled with the best way to analyze Brainerd's life, I received invaluable encouragement and input from David Silverman, Jim Rohrer, Dan Richter, Mendy Gladden, Fredrika Teute, and Caleb Maskell. I also appreciate the support and encouragement of my colleagues, first at Hampden-Sydney College and then at the University of Nebraska, Omaha. The former institution provided funds for research while the latter provided funds for various tasks associated with finishing the manuscript for publication.

My thanks also to everyone at Oxford, especially Theo Calderara, Paul Hobson, Merryl Sloane, and Justin Tackett for all their support and wisdom. I am also grateful for the input from two anonymous readers at Oxford, whose suggestions helped me to produce a greatly improved final version. Appreciation also to Mary Brooks for the indexing.

My final and most important thanks go to Peter Mancall, advisor and mentor extraordinaire. He was co-leader of my first-ever grad school seminar and has continued to provide support and encouragement along the way. I remember standing at the door to his office when I first told him I was thinking of writing my dissertation on a guy he probably hadn't heard about called David Brainerd. The enthusiasm was immediate, infectious, and continual. (I learned later, to my chagrin, that Peter had mentioned Brainerd several times in his first book, which I at the time had not read.) He also made suggestions on the final format and has, thus, been involved in the whole process.

Despite all this input, any mistakes are my responsibility.

Last, in the spirit of no man being an island, my thanks to some folks who had little, if anything, to do with the book, but who kept me sane and grounded as a person during this project: the Straw Dogs from KU—the best part of grad school; my friends from two church homes, the Vineyard Fellowships in Overland Park and Omaha; and the Upstream Brewery crowd in Omaha.

I started making revisions for the final version in the fall of 2007 and finished in the summer of 2008. Along the way, I found time to watch some college sports, and my final thanks—completely unrelated to the book—go to Mark Mangino, Bill Self, Mario Chalmers, and the rest of the Jayhawks, for the greatest year ever.

Contents

The Lives of David Brainerd

Introduction

David Brainerd is one of the more ubiquitous figures in American colonial history. Scenarios from his life appear in academic works that focus on religion, literary studies, missions, colonial expansion, and theology.[1] For the most part, such studies cast Brainerd in one of two roles. In the first, he serves as an example of the conflict and division caused by religious revival in 1740s Connecticut. Responding to some of the more radical preachers, Brainerd challenges the conservative establishment, which reacts by expelling him from Yale, thus putting an end to his goal of becoming a typical Connecticut minister. In his second role, Brainerd has already been expelled from Yale. With his dreams in tatters, he is now compelled to serve as a missionary among Native Americans. Although diligent and self-sacrificial, Brainerd the missionary is generally ineffective, achieving little more than an early death. Since most scholars utilize Brainerd as an example of a broader argument, presenting such snapshots of his life makes a great deal of sense. However, these vignettes have two tendencies which obscure a more complete understanding of Brainerd. First, Brainerd's life is often irrevocably bifurcated between events that precede the expulsion and those that follow it, and second, he is understood only within the context either of the Great Awakening or of Indian missions. Because of this, the bulk of his life, the first twenty years or so, is erased, effectively cutting Brainerd loose from the culture in which he grew up. Any sense of continuity, of heritage, disappears and Brainerd becomes a fragmented abstraction, an example of discrete aspects of colonial America.

It is a central theme of this book that David Brainerd can be properly understood only by reconnecting these fragments into an integrated account and by restoring the abstraction to its proper context. To be sure, there are difficulties attending such an effort. The principal surviving autobiographical sources themselves tend to abstract and fragment Brainerd's life. All three of these sources were written—or constructed—to make a specific point, and so they lack any real context or depth. Brainerd moves across the pages of these accounts almost unencumbered by external events and without any real explanation of his decisions.[2]

Given the limitations of these sources, it is pertinent to ask whether it is actually possible to reconstitute Brainerd's life beyond the outlines that emerge from the autobiographical accounts. The answer to this is a qualified yes. Some of the context of Brainerd's life can be gleaned from a handful of letters, official records, and other accounts which have survived. More important, a greater understanding of David Brainerd can be developed by making use of the increasingly nuanced interpretation of colonial America that is emerging from more recent scholarship. In particular, insight into Brainerd's life is enhanced by the work of those scholars who have developed multifaceted interpretations of the period in contrast to earlier either-or dichotomies.

One example of this is scholarship on the religious revivals of the 1740s, which are collectively referred to as the Great Awakening. In traditional interpretations, New Lights promoted the revivals and Old Lights opposed them. This paradigm was replaced by a tripartite interpretation of the revivals, which divided the pro-revival forces into moderate revivalists and radicals. In this model, the conflict between moderate revivalists and radicals was often more intense than that between pro- and anti-revival forces.[3] More recently, even this tripartite model has proven inadequate as scholars have demonstrated that many pro-revival ministers swerved, or at least appeared to swerve, across the moderate-radical line as circumstances and experiences changed. Gilbert Tennent tore up the tranquility of the Yale campus with his revival sermons before the excesses of lay preachers moved him to a more moderate position. Even Jonathan Edwards, doyen of the moderate wing, preached at meetings where enthusiasm was on full display, but he then abandoned such meetings to become one of the most prolific defenders of the moderate awakening and an articulate critic of enthusiastic excess.[4]

Even analysis of such well-known ministers does not provide a full explanation of all the strands of the revivals. Historians have demonstrated that responses were far more individualistic than previously recognized. Ministers such as John Cleaveland and Daniel Rogers forged their own models of pastoral work as they grappled to find a place in New England society. Many laypeople refused to conform to their expected role and crafted their own experiences of Christianity, which borrowed from a number of sources and incorporated various aspects of their heritage.[5] David Brainerd was another individual who emerged from the religious upheavals of the 1740s seeking to combine distinct subcultures, in his case the traditional stability of Connecticut culture with the radicalism of the revivals. One of the arguments of this book is that Brainerd's work as a missionary was not a separate part of his life but flowed from his efforts to blend these two subcultures.

Brainerd's life among the Indians can be understood within the multifaceted model of Christian missions being developed by a number of scholars. David Silverman, Jane T. Merritt, and Rachel Wheeler are among the scholars who have produced studies that run counter to an either-or dichotomy of missions.[6] By reading Brainerd's writings alongside such scholarship, a more complex man emerges. While never escaping completely the cultural and racial stereotypes with which he grew up, Brainerd did develop substantial sympathy for his Indian charges. Moreover, as a solo missionary for most of his adult life, living in the midst of Indian culture, he could not help being changed himself.[7] And, it is important to note, the changes which Brainerd brought about, and those which he experienced, occurred over a period of less than four years. We are left to wonder what else would have happened had he survived even another ten years.

Of course, much of what makes Brainerd such a recognizable figure in colonial America is the extraordinary legend that developed after his death. Given the theological and ministerial luminaries who were his contemporaries or near-contemporaries—Joseph Bellamy, James Davenport, Jonathan Dickinson, Gilbert Tennent, Samuel Hopkins, Nathaniel Emmons, and others—it is remarkable that Brainerd is probably the second most recognizable American religious figure of the eighteenth century, behind only Jonathan Edwards. This reputation is owed, in the first instance, to Edwards's own *Life of Brainerd*. However, the legend was continued and expanded by new versions of Brainerd's life, especially that written by John Wesley, as well as by references to the inspiration his life has offered in the diaries, letters, and promotional literature of missionaries, mission organizations, ministers, and lay Christians from the eighteenth century to the present day. Many of those who have used Brainerd's life as an example did so in order to advance personal and/or corporate agendas. As such, Brainerd was first fragmented anew, abstracted again, and finally often used as little more than a starting point to create an argument out of whole cloth.

Because of the profound impact of this legacy, the work which follows is in two broad parts. The first part, chapters 1–3, chronicles Brainerd's life. Although the chapters generally flow in chronological order, at times I have collected certain events under one heading and slightly out of order, to make Brainerd's decisions and actions easier to follow. Chapter 1 begins with the events of the Great Awakening at Yale and then traces Brainerd's life from his birth in 1718 to his arrival at Easthampton on Long Island in 1743. It was during this period that the two major strands of Brainerd's life which informed his later decisions were woven together. Chapter 2 tells of his brief work at Easthampton, his ministry at Kaunaumeek, New York, and the first year of his work in the Delaware Valley. In addition to the details of Brainerd's activities, I seek to explain his final decision to forgo the traditional work of a minister in favor of the greater freedom available to him in the work among the Indians. This chapter also examines the important influence that his growing role as a revival minister among the Presbyterian churches of the middle colonies had on his work with the Indians. The third chapter examines Brainerd's life from his arrival in New Jersey in 1745 to his death in Northampton, Massachusetts, in 1747. Since this was the period during which he witnessed numbers of Indian conversions, this chapter also examines cultural reasons for these conversions and the way in which his growing congregation began to affect Brainerd's attitudes both toward Indians and toward other colonists.

There are some issues which I do not explore in great detail. In some cases, this is because my focus is on the way in which Brainerd interacted with the society in which he lived. Thus, for example, I eschew any detailed examination of Brainerd's well-documented melancholy.[8] In other cases, the limitation of the sources makes in-depth interpretation of some of Brainerd's attitudes impossible; in particular, little more than a cursory conclusion about his attitude toward issues of gender can be made.

The second section of the book, chapters 4–6, examines various aspects of Brainerd's legacy. Because of the importance of Jonathan Edwards and John Wesley themselves, and because of the impact of their versions of Brainerd's life, I devote a separate chapter to each man. Although I pay some attention to the editorial work of the two men, since it has been treated in detail elsewhere, I am more concerned with why each of them published their versions of Brainerd's life when they did.[9] The final chapter consists of several thumbnail sketches of Brainerd's legacy at certain points: the birth of modern Protestant missions in Britain in the late eighteenth and early nineteenth centuries; the development of missions in the United States in the antebellum period; the student mission movement roughly in the period 1880–1914. The chapter concludes with a brief overview of Brainerd's ongoing impact on evangelical Protestantism in the United States since 1945.

Brainerd's life has offered inspiration to Christians for over 250 years. This study endeavors to demonstrate that it can also offer insight to historians.

1

A Child of Two Worlds

It is only about thirty miles from New Haven, Connecticut, to the small town of Haddam nestled on the banks of the Connecticut River. But in the early 1740s, the cultural separation between the two was far greater than any geographical distance. Haddam was typical of many of the smaller towns located along the great river. Most of the people lived on family farms, although they were perhaps not quite as prosperous as those who lived in most other settlements in the Connecticut Valley. The town was home to a few artisans and some men who enhanced their wealth with commercial activity. It was a peaceful, stable community, not a place given to embracing practitioners of new beliefs, particularly those that might disrupt the unity of the town. In contrast, New Haven, home to Yale College, had become a place notorious for disruptions to the social order. Many of the students were determined to embrace a radical expression of their Christian faith. College authorities, used to dealing with a lack of dedication to the gospel, were now faced with a student body that declared those same authorities to be the ones not sufficiently dedicated to God.

In the late summer of 1741, as twenty-three-year-old David Brainerd returned to Yale to start his junior year, the relatively short journey from his hometown of Haddam must have seemed like a road connecting two very different worlds. In Haddam, he was but one younger son of a respected family in a town with a number of such men—a town that seemed little changed since its founding eighty years earlier. In New Haven, he was part of a small coterie of men who believed they were in the vanguard of ushering in a new and greater work of God. In the coming months and years, those two cultures would work together in Brainerd as he fashioned a life, and ministry, that was neither one nor the other but a hybrid of the two.

Yale Radical

Perhaps the response of conservative church leaders to the goings-on in New Haven during commencement in 1741 was best captured by Daniel Wadsworth (1704–1747), a Yale trustee and pastor of the First Church in Hartford. "Much Confusion this day at New-Haven," he wrote, "and at night the most strange management and a pretence of religion that ever I saw." Indeed, there was confusion for many during that week and in the tumultuous period both preceding and following it. But for those whom Wadsworth would have perceived as the perpetrators of this confusion, men like Joseph Bellamy (1719–1790), James Davenport (1716–1757), Benjamin Pomeroy (1704–1784), Jedidiah Mills (1697–1776), and Eleazar Wheelock (1711–1779), there was no confusion. In fact, supporters of the revival sweeping the colony saw the world with crystal clarity. True religion was awakening, false teachers were being exposed, and tumult was to be expected when God was at work. Had not Christ himself warned his disciples: "think not that I am come to send peace on earth: I came not to send peace, but a sword"?[1]

The men who spearheaded the revivals believed not only that they were doing God's work, but that the awakening of religion was itself an answer to the concerns of many ministers in the British Atlantic world in the decades prior to 1740. For years, Protestant clergy had decried what they saw as a decline in true religion. As early as 1700, Samuel Willard (1640–1707) had cautioned that, while there was a "*Form of Godliness* among us," there was "too much of a general denying of the power of it." Believing that earlier efforts to effect a civil transformation of society had failed, many ministers began to stress the need for revival—the sovereign pouring out of God's grace and spirit on a people. More and more clergy urged their audiences to move beyond intellectual assent to the Christian faith and to experience conversion as a personal, life-changing event. In New Jersey, Gilbert Tennent (1703–1764) warned readers that, while they had "often heard [their] Danger describ'd," they were "not awaken'd yet." For many ministers, the fault lay not so much with the people as with the clergy, who were failing to provide the right kind of preaching. Solomon Stoddard (1643–1729) had declared that "there is a great deal of Preaching that doth not much Promote [conversion], but is an hindrance to it." While only God could bring revival, ministers had a responsibility to conduct what historian Michael Crawford has described as a "conversionist, evangelical, Gospel ministry." In 1717, Solomon Stoddard had declared that the duty of ministers included making sure that "a good number of the People [were] Savingly Converted." Likewise, William Williams insisted that ministers were not just to take care of those already part of the church but also to be "Labourers in God's Harvest" and "not to Loyter."[2]

By the 1720s, those in the British Atlantic world anxiously awaiting revival began to hear reports which suggested that God's spirit was moving. In Teschen in Upper Silesia, the preaching of Johann Steinmetz attracted huge crowds every Sunday. From Teschen, preachers spread revival through Silesia—where, decades earlier, children had conducted open-air prayer meetings seeking a restoration of Protestant freedoms—then into the Habsburg lands of Bohemia and Moravia. In 1731, when the Prussians offered a home to Salzburg Protestants expelled by the Habsburgs, many continental Protestants construed this as a miraculous rescue brought about by the hand of God. The event was widely reported in Protestant literature as a sign that God was imparting his spirit to the world in new ways. Many such reports were initially spread by the pietists headquartered in Halle, and pietism itself became a powerful influence on revival-oriented ministers throughout the Protestant world. The teachings of pietist leaders such as August Francke and Philipp Jakob Spener were widely read. Their emphasis on personal conversion, an experiential knowledge of God, and the importance of private meetings between pastors and laity influenced pro-revivalists in England, Scotland, and Wales. Pietist writings also crossed the Atlantic—Cotton Mather and Jonathan Edwards were two of the New England clergy influenced by pietist teachings.[3]

Occasionally, ministers too crossed the Atlantic. The preaching of East Friesland émigré Theodorus Frelinghuysen (c. 1692–c. 1747) sparked local revivals in New Jersey in the 1720s. Combining strong Calvinism with pietist practice, Frelinghuysen also exuded the appeal to the heart that was central to the growing evangelicalism. In addition, he was willing both to itinerate and to challenge the spirituality of other ministers. Significant numbers of people in New Jersey were converted under Frelinghuysen's ministry, and he became close friends with the Tennent family of preachers. The Tennents began preaching the new birth conversion in various parts of the colony in the 1730s, and a series of moderate local revivals took place in Gilbert Tennent's church at New Brunswick and William Tennent's at Freehold. At roughly the same time, revival broke out in Jonathan Edwards's church in Northampton, Massachusetts, and spread up and down the Connecticut Valley. Although such local awakenings were not uncommon, Edwards transformed the way people interpreted them when he connected events in Massachusetts, New York, and New Jersey and argued that they were part of a single event brought about by the sovereignty of God. Edwards's account *A Faithful Narrative of the Surprizing Work of God* became a key document in inspiring revivalists in England, Scotland, Wales, and some of the German states.[4]

Although the American events quickly dissipated, there were glimmers of hope as word came of new revivals in Wales in 1735; in Bern, Switzerland, in 1735 and 1736; and among Polish speakers in parts of Prussia in 1736. Excitement among revivalists grew as accounts of the ministry of George Whitefield (1714–1770) began to spread. Whitefield had experienced a dramatic conversion and emphasized the need for this spiritual transformation in his preaching. Beginning in 1737, he drew large crowds to churches throughout England. After a three-month sojourn in Georgia, he returned to England and, in February 1739, gave his first outdoor sermon, believing that this "field preaching" would both draw large crowds and give him greater independence in the conduct of his ministry. Revival supporters in Britain and America eagerly devoured reports of Whitefield's ministry.[5]

More than likely, David Brainerd was one of those who read accounts of Whitefield's success. At about the time Whitefield was laying plans to begin field preaching, Brainerd was in the midst of his own conversion experience. Brainerd's description of his conversion was compiled some years later and, although presumably accurate in its general outline, is a constructed narrative, encompassing certain tropes and concepts common to the religious culture of which Brainerd was a part. Brainerd identified Solomon Stoddard's *A Guide to Christ* as "in the hand of God…the happy means of my conversion."[6] By the time Brainerd wrote his narrative in the early 1740s, Stoddard, who had died more than a decade earlier, was respected by the majority of New England clergy, and it seems likely that Brainerd's account follows the Stoddardean model because that model was considered acceptable across a great deal of the evangelical spectrum.[7] Stoddard spent most of his life as a pastor at Northampton, Massachusetts, was a prolific author, and played a crucial role in the development of ideas on conversion and church government in New England in the late seventeenth and early eighteenth centuries. He taught that conversion was preceded by a period of spiritual preparation that involved misery, humiliation, and repentance. Conversion itself was not a gradual progression but a single moment, rooted in an experiential conviction of sin and a very real fear of hell, when God swept away the sinners' fears and sins and brought them new life.[8]

Stoddard believed, "God leads men through the whole course of preparation, partly by fear, and partly by hope." Both were important, for to have one without the other was to be like a ship "in danger" of being "broken to pieces." A person undergoing preparation was "subject to many affrightments, and discouraging temptations." For Stoddard, the explanation of how much preparation and knowledge were necessary for conversion was deceptively simple. For true conversion, one must "know so much as is sufficient to bring them off from trusting in their own righteousness and their own strength." This was because, as Stoddard noted elsewhere, God was "wont to shew them that righteousness don't answer the law."[9] As people went through their preparations, they could expect moments of false confidence, which were rooted in their own righteousness and not in God's. In one sense, preparation was to teach sinners that their own works counted for nothing. Once they firmly grasped this, conversion would follow. The Stoddardean model was one where most of the process of salvation was located in the struggles of preparation while conversion was a single moment, almost lost in the preceding details.

In keeping with Stoddard's teaching, Brainerd began the story of his conversion with what he described as "The Beginning of Thorough Conviction" when, in a moment of terror, God gave him "such a sense of my amazing danger & the wrath of God & hell, as it were, under my feet." In Brainerd's Stoddardean world, this moment of terror had the desired effect. He had such a "view of my sin and vileness" that he was "much dejected & kept much alone & wondered how people could be so chearfull and unconcerned." He even "grudged the birds and beasts their happyness." The narrative was further punctuated by regular moments of holy terror. At one point, he recalled, "the Lord gave to me such a sense of my sin and danger that I feared the ground would cleave under my feet & become my grave."[10] In addition, Brainerd noted the moments of false confidence or false conversion against which Stoddard had warned. At times, he was "greatly encouraged and imagined that God loved me and was in some measure pleased with me and thought I should be fully reconciled to God," only to realize that this was "founded upon meer presumption." Further in keeping with Stoddard's model, he recognized that there was "no necessary connection between my prayers and the bestowment of divine mercy." And he remembered that when he "felt any melting of heart, I hoped now the work was at most done," only to be disappointed that it was "only the moving of the passion."[11]

However, there was another narrative embedded within this orthodox account of conversion. Interlaced with the conservative Stoddardean model were recollections of moments infused with emotionalism, enthusiasm, and esoteric expression. These were usually a result of Brainerd's inability, in his own mind, to cross over from death to life. On occasion, Solomon Stoddard was a target of Brainerd's frustrations, since he did not "tell me anything that I could do that would bring me to Christ." Furthermore, Brainerd wondered why, if Stoddard himself had found Christ, "he could not tell me the way." He conceded, in a marginal note, that at the time he had these thoughts, he had not yet been "effectually and experimentally taught, that there could be no means prescribed whereby a natural man could obtain that which is supernatural." More often, though, Brainerd's anger was directed at God. Thus, at one time, he believed God guilty of "cruelty and injustice & thought he delighted to oppress and crush poor mortals. I thought if God was once in my place as much afraid of hell as I was he would never make souls to damn 'em." On another occasion, he secretly wished for "another God equal in power with whom I might joyn and fight against the living God." Brainerd "longed to pull the eternal God out of his throne and stamp him under my feet." Sometimes, his anger was even more creative. He thought:

> Adam was a fool for being scared by that sword [of the angel of God]; &
> me thought if I could get there, I'd venture the sword to do its work
> if I could but suddenly leap and catch hold of the outside twigs of the
> tree of life before it pierced me through, or I contrived whether I could
> not evade the blow of it by means of some good defensive instrument
> and such other fruitless contrivances.[12]

One of the key moments in Brainerd's narrative came when he experienced a vision of a beautiful house against which he had been heaping rubbish and dirt. For Brainerd, the application was obvious, that he had "been heaping my devotions before God—fasting and praying and pretending and indeed really thinking that at sometimes I was aiming at his glory, when I never once intended his honour and glory but only my own happiness." The vision was a watershed in his conversion experience. He previously believed his efforts to be well intentioned but imperfect. Now, he came to see them as completely selfish with no intent to glorify God—the crux of the preparation period. Less than three days after this revelation, he experienced God as "a glorious divine being" and was now satisfied that "he should be God over all forever and ever."[13]

The Sunday following this vision, the entire conversion process reached its culmination. That day, as he attempted to pray, "'unspeakable glory' seemed to open to the view and apprehension of my soul" and "a new inward apprehension or view that I had of God; such as I never had before." For Brainerd, it was clear that God had "brought me to a hearty desire to exalt him," and he "continued in this state of inward joy, peace and yet astonishment till near dark." The way of salvation had "opened to me with such infinite wisdom, suitableness and excellency that I wondered I should ever think of any other way of salvation." "This happy season," he wrote, "was Lord's Day 12 of July as I remember, 1739."[14] Brainerd had prepared himself for, and then experienced, conversion. In the Stoddardean tradition, it was chronologically specific, memorable, and definitive. But, while orthodox in its trajectory, it was also shot through with esoteric events and emotional aspects that would be associated with the more extreme wing of the coming revival.

In the light of this experience, it is perhaps not surprising that, when he entered Yale a scant six weeks later, he did so with less excitement than when he had begun the process almost eighteen months earlier. Brainerd feared that his time at Yale would prevent him from leading "a life of strict religion in the midst of so many temptations." Although he may have remembered his concerns to be greater than they were at the time, there were at least some grounds for unease. In the first part of the eighteenth century, students at both Harvard and Yale suffered from a general lack of discipline and commitment in their studies. Jonathan Edwards had complained of the poor attitude and conduct of most of the students during his time at Yale while cases of drunkenness and thievery were not uncommon. As Yale historian Richard Warch observed, "the need for discipline was a dreary constant in Yale's existence."[15]

In addition to anxiety over the behavior of his fellow students, Brainerd was also in an awkward social situation. At twenty-one, he was four or five years older than the average freshman. Others may have been even younger: Jonathan Edwards was a month or so shy of his thirteenth birthday when he started his studies at New Haven in 1716 while Joseph Bellamy—a future confidant of Brainerd—was only twelve when he entered Yale in 1731. To make matters worse for Brainerd, the college hierarchy placed freshmen at the bottom of the pack. One can imagine his chagrin, and possibly even resentment, at having to clean the shoes of a senior who was a year younger than himself or having to ask permission from a seventeen-year-old sophomore before ascending a staircase. He hinted at such humiliations once in his memoirs when he noted being "much exposed on account of my freshmanship."[16]

On the other hand, the daily schedule did include plenty of opportunity for Brainerd to cultivate his solitary habits with ninety minutes of free time after lunch and another two hours after dinner.[17] In his account of his first two years at the college, Brainerd made repeated distinctions between true spirituality and his college training. It was during his solitary times that he often "enjoyed a sweet refreshing visit," an experience of the power of God. His first few months at Yale were enjoyable as "sundry passages of God's Word opened to my soul with divine clearness, power and sweetness," and he "enjoyed considerable sweetness in religion," but his earlier fears were realized during his second semester, when "ambition in my studies greatly wronged the activity and vigor of my spiritual life."[18]

Brainerd's struggles to come to grips with life as a student were further complicated by two serious bouts with illness which required him to spend considerable time in Haddam recuperating. In January 1740, having contracted

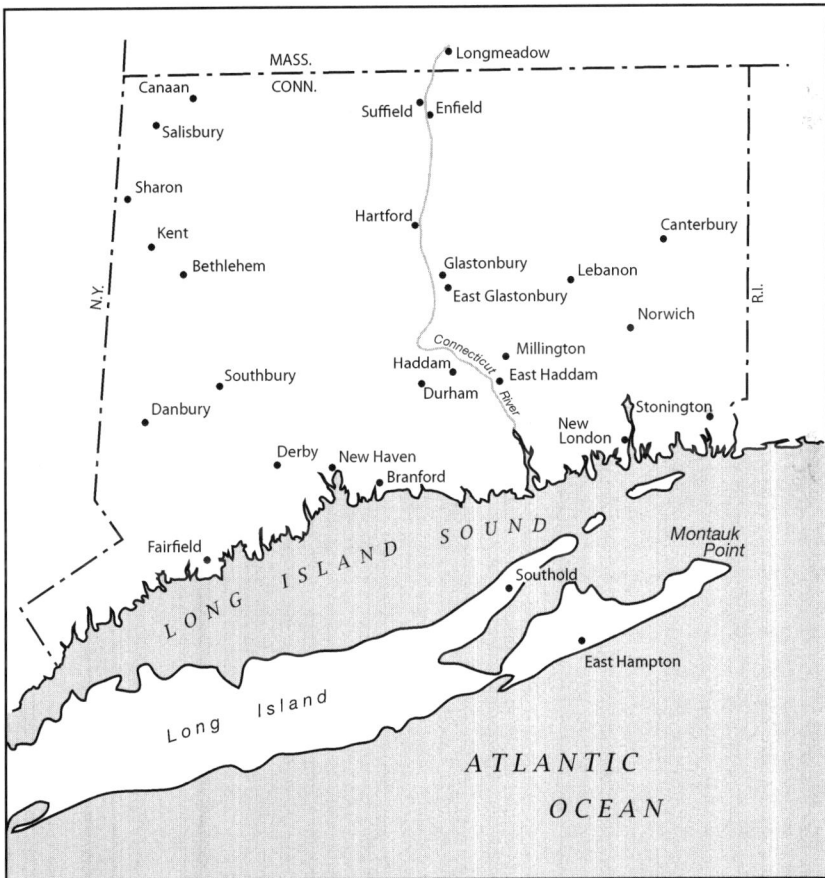

Connecticut in the mid-eighteenth century. Map by Marvin J. Barton; adapted from Bushman, *From Puritan to Yankee*, frontispiece: by Saml. H. Bryant, drawn from a map by Bernard Romans. Connecticut and Adjacent Parts, Amsterdam, 1777, and by Cóvens, Mortier & Cóvens, Jr.

a "distemper" and with measles spreading through the college, Brainerd went home. However, after two days in Haddam, he was "taken with the measles" and did not return to New Haven until the spring. Once again, "by reasons of hard and close studies," he had "little time for spiritual duties." Later in the spring and into the summer of that year, he "enjoyed more comfort in religion." His second illness-enforced absence from college came in the fall of 1740. Although Brainerd put it down to "too close application to my studies," he also remembered that he "had spit blood more than once," clearly marking the onset of the tuberculosis that would ultimately claim his life seven years later.[19]

At about the same time that Brainerd was going home to recuperate from his illness, George Whitefield was landing in Rhode Island. He had traveled throughout New York and New Jersey the previous year, but this was his first visit to New England. He spent several days in October 1740 at Yale, where he was introduced to the rector, Thomas Clap (1703–1767), who had been in office for less than a year but who, at least at this time, held an open mind toward Whitefield and his ministry. While Clap was a disciplinarian and a most orthodox member of the Connecticut establishment, during his own college days at Harvard, he had undergone his conversion experience and had been part of a group known as the "praying students." Furthermore, Clap was aware that Yale's charge was to operate as a "school of the prophets," entrusted with training young men who could become able preachers of the gospel. If Whitefield offered hope that this vision could be renewed, he should be welcomed in New Haven. Whitefield's first impression of the school was that there was "no remarkable concern among [the students] concerning religion." However, following his preaching, Whitefield noted, "[t]here were sweet meltings Discernible," and he "observed an especial Presence of God in the Assembly," although there was no full-blown revival as a result of his visit. Yale senior Samuel Hopkins (1721–1803), who "highly approved" of Whitefield, remembered that the meetings at which Whitefield spoke "were crowded and remarkably attentive."[20]

Although Brainerd missed hearing Whitefield speak, he was encouraged by the news of Whitefield's time in New England, and Brainerd felt his "soul was refreshed and seemed knit to him."[21] Brainerd returned to college during the first week of November 1740, fearful that he might be "getting away from God" at the place which had "proved so hurtful to my spiritual interest." However, his trepidation was alleviated somewhat when Yale granted him "liberty to board out of college at a private house," namely, the home of Isaac Dickerman (1677–1758). Although not necessarily the college's preferred option since it lost a degree of control over its students, lack of sufficient campus housing meant the administration had little choice but to allow some of its students to live off campus. Permitting Brainerd and others to live with Dickerman did not present much of a risk since Dickerman was a reliable member of the establishment (at least in 1740), having been regularly elected deputy to the Connecticut Assembly as well as serving in a number of town offices.[22]

From the time of his return to Yale through most of January 1741, Brainerd found that, in general he "felt much of the power of religion almost daily." He also seemed to commit himself irrevocably to some kind of intellectual career when he sold most of the land he had inherited or purchased from his family to John Camp of Durham for £600, seemingly closing the door to a return to the life of a farmer. The funds would have been more than enough to see him through his remaining years at Yale.[23] That winter, revival seemed to be at Yale's door; Samuel Hopkins recalled that "people in general appeared to be in some measure awakened."[24] At the end of January, Brainerd, however, struggled with growing "more cold and indolent in matters of religion by means of my old temptation, viz. ambition in my studies." Through the month of February, he felt things had become worse as he enjoyed neither time with God nor his studies. By late February, he had recovered somewhat and his spirits were lifted even further when a visit from fellow student David Youngs (1719–1752) led to an evening spent with "great satisfaction in Christian conversation and in relating what God had done for us respectively." The pair also "consulted to do something if possible for the interest of religion," and they considered setting up private meetings for groups of three or four students, but before they could bring their plans to fruition, "a great and general concern soon after spread itself over the college."[25]

Although Whitefield's visit the previous fall had indeed brought "sweet meltings," by all accounts it was the arrival of Gilbert Tennent in March 1741 which brought forth the full manifestations of revival. Tennent had begun his New England itineration the previous December with Whitefield's encouragement, and he preached a total of seventeen times in New Haven during March. Tennent informed Whitefield that "the Concern was general in both College and Town." Samuel Hopkins remembered that a "remarkable awakening had been produced" in New Haven because of Tennent, and the "members of the college appeared to be universally awakened." It also seems that it was Tennent's preaching, whether intentionally or not, which opened the door to actions by the students which challenged the college authorities.[26]

Tennent was obviously a charismatic speaker, and his insistence on making clear demarcations between converted and unconverted ministers had already drawn a great deal of attention. In his (in)famous sermon *Danger of an Unconverted Ministry*, Tennent had warned that "the Ministry of natural Men is dangerous, both in respect of the Doctrines, and Practice of Piety." Furthermore, such men were "poor Guides" to anyone seeking salvation since they "call it Melancholy, or Madness, or dawb those that are under [conviction], with untemper'd Mortar." Like Tennent, Brainerd had demonstrated a willingness to make judgments about the spiritual condition of his peers. On one occasion, after partaking of communion at college, he had "felt alone in the world like a stranger and pilgrim," since he believed that most of his fellow students lived "without God."[27]

Tennent's message also spoke to Brainerd's growing skepticism over the value of a liberal education, since Tennent believed that education that was not infused with the power of God was pointless. In *Danger*, Tennent declared that, since "publick academies [were] so much corrupted and abused," the solution was to "encourage private Schools, or Seminaries of Learning." To such private schools, "pious and experienced Youths, who have a good natural Capacity, and great Desires after the Ministerial Work" could be found and recruited. To a young man like David Brainerd who, apparently, hungered after an experiential ministry but was lukewarm about the practices at Yale, such an idea would have been very attractive. These kinds of unofficial schools proliferated throughout New England and the middle colonies in the decades following the revivals.[28]

Among those especially fired up by Tennent's preaching were Brainerd, David Youngs, and a third like-minded student—Samuel Buell (1716–1798). On the surface, the three were drawn together by their mutual dedication to spreading revival. Samuel Hopkins later recalled that all three were among a "small number" who had been truly converted before arriving in New Haven and that they exhibited "extraordinary zeal." However, it also seems likely that they were drawn together because of age. Both Youngs and Buell had entered Yale at an age above the average; in 1741, when Brainerd was twenty-three, Youngs was twenty-two and Buell twenty-five. Perhaps first drawn together by frustration over being made subordinate to seniors younger and less devout than themselves, the three gradually developed a common religious cause.[29]

Hopkins remembered that Brainerd and his friends had "concern for members of the college" and that without "regard to the distinctions of higher and lower classes they visited every room in college, and discoursed freely and with the greatest plainness with each one." Indeed, it was following one of Brainerd's visits to him that Hopkins began to question his own salvation. During this visit, Brainerd had "observed that he believed it impossible for a person to be converted and to be a real Christian without feeling his heart, at sometimes at least, sensibly and greatly affected with the character of Christ, and strongly going out after him; or to that purpose." This "struck conviction into my mind," wrote Hopkins, and convinced him that he was not truly converted.[30]

In April, New York clergyman Ebenezer Pemberton (1704–1777) preached at the college. A friend of Gilbert Tennent, he had been the first northern minister to open his pulpit to Whitefield and apparently came to New Haven at the direct invitation of the students. In his sermon published as *The Knowlege* [*sic*] *of Christ Recommended*, Pemberton conceded that conversion required an intellectual understanding of Christ and the doctrines of salvation. But he also insisted that salvation required a knowledge that was "not produc'd by the powers of human reason or the common methods of education or instruction." In a warning to his student audience, Pemberton noted that "men are apt highly to value themselves upon the account of their human knowledge and to look down with contempt upon others whom they esteem ignorant and unlearn'd." However, Pemberton went on, without "an experimental knowledge of Christ," such knowledge was "but specious ignorance, and is esteem'd by God no better than foolishness."[31]

If much of the exegesis in Pemberton's sermon was challenging, his application, directed in particular to those who were "candidates for the service of the sacred ministry," was revolutionary. Pemberton was aware that "Arts and Sciences, may advance your credit among men" and that the "study of other things may entertain and amuse you." However, he also had no doubt that his audience would recognize the "insufficiency of all human teaching." In light of this, he challenged them to make experimental knowledge of Christ the "design you have continually in view" while "all your other studies be managed in such a manner as may subserve this noble Intention." So phrased, Pemberton essentially challenged his audience to forgo their studies if it interfered with their experimental relationship with Christ, in a sense echoing Brainerd's own priorities. Not surprisingly, Brainerd purchased six copies of the sermon as did Samuel Buell and David Youngs. Samuel Hopkins, apparently now well within the awakened camp, purchased eight.[32]

Prepared by Whitefield, sparked by Tennent, and fueled by itinerant preachers, the revival at New Haven and throughout Connecticut continued to boil through the summer of 1741.[33] By that time, too, unease was rising in New England and other colonies over some aspects of the revivals. Critics were appalled at the prevalence of claims about esoteric experiences and incidents of physical manifestations among many supporters of the revivals. A letter from the anonymous "Querists" accused Whitefield of making "high Pretensions to immediate Revelation, in his professing to think and act by the immediate Guidance of divine Inspiration." They also identified the "Strange Fits, Convulsions, involuntary Raptures, horrid Noises, and Visions" of the revival as "Lying Signs and Wonders."[34] Likewise, the anonymous author(s) of *The Wonderful Wandering Spirit* lampooned the revival as consisting of "violent bodily Convulsions.... Sometimes, like *Balaam*, they fall into Trances, with their Eyes open."[35] Charles Chauncy (1703–1787), probably the most consistent and outspoken critic of the revivals, warned against an enthusiasm that "affects their bodies, throws them into convulsions and distortions, into quakings and tremblings."[36]

Of even greater concern to many in New England was the disruption to the social order already caused by the revivals along with the distinct possibility that things would get worse. Many critics were willing to stipulate that the revivals may have been started by the power of God. However, they could point to any number of religious movements which had also, ostensibly, sprung from the hand of God only to collapse into disorder and confusion. There were the Münster Anabaptists of the 1530s whose support for the common ownership of goods was as much feared by many Protestants as was their endorsement of polygamy. In England itself, from female prophets during the English Civil War to the Fifth Monarchists, women and men inspired by radical religious beliefs had threatened the good order and functioning of a godly society.[37] Preachers from the Family of Love had engaged in an anti-authority, anticlerical appeal to people whom T. Wilson Hayes has identified as "literate working people."[38] Of more recent vintage were the French Prophets, refugees from the failed Camisard Rebellion in southeastern France who were often invoked in anti-revival writings in New England. Once in England, the French Prophets recruited locals to their ranks, and some of their members claimed to possess charismatic gifts such as being able to speak in new languages or to predict coming events. As with the

New England revivals, religious services among the prophets and their converts featured outdoor dancing and singing. More threatening than this, however, was their challenge to the social order. One of their number, John Lacy, claimed that the prophets were not subject to civil courts. Nor was English society in general enthused over what historian Hillel Schwartz has described as the "ambiguous boundaries of the group." To most English people, Schwartz has observed, the prophets were a "confusingly diverse social group composed of a baronet, reputable gentlemen, physicians, merchants, artisans, shopkeepers, pie-vendors, laborers, and refugees without work or money," and thus threatened the stability and hierarchy of society.[39]

It is not surprising then that, as the revivals in New England—and in some areas of the middle colonies—became increasingly radical, members of respectable society were more outspoken in their criticism. The spread of itineration was of particular concern. The revival had been birthed through itineration, and its supporters, naturally, encouraged properly qualified ministers to continue to preach in different churches where possible. But just as it had in England, in Connecticut, itinerancy, as Timothy D. Hall has explained, undermined civil and ecclesiastical order, threatened status, and raised the specter of revolutionary chaos. In New England, itinerant ministers simply turned up uninvited in parishes other than their own and unleashed vociferous, public critiques on the inadequacies of the established minister. George Whitefield had often hinted that the responsibility for spiritual decline lay not with the laity but with the clergy. Gilbert Tennent was frequently far more open in his attack on the authority of established ministers as were many of the younger itinerants who set out to emulate him. These men preached, in Harry Stout's words, "a revival *against* the established churches," and "instead of augmenting regular preaching, the itinerancies of young evangelists…threatened to displace it."[40]

Critics did not hold back in their attacks on these itinerant evangelists, and the fear of disorder ran through their writings. The Querists accused pro-revivalists of "slander[ing] and misrepresent[ing] *pious* and *godly* Ministers" and of causing the "Confounding of Order, Disturbing of Peace, Banishment of Charity, Distracting of Communities, and Raising of Factions."[41] Charles Chauncy based much of his opposition to the revivals on the criticism of established ministers, lamenting that there was "not so MUCH AS ONE MINISTER IN THE WHOLE LAND, but the Minds of many are so *prejudiced* against them…that their Power to do good is hereby greatly lessened." But he also noted that some revivalists were "open disturbers of the peace of the world."[42] *The Wonderful Wandering Spirit* warned that the revival "hates Rules and good Order, or Bounds and Limits."[43]

While the itinerancy of ordained ministers such as Tennent and Pemberton was bad enough, the wild-eyed enthusiasm of lay preachers was an even greater threat to ecclesiastical, civil, and social norms. Chauncy condemned "private christians" who, "being moved by the Spirit," were "quitting their own proper station, to act in that which belongs to another." These practices would destroy order in the church and "may be followed with mischiefs greater than we may be aware of."[44] Here, the anti-revivalists were support by the majority of revivalists. Gilbert Tennent, for example, was aghast at the use of unordained ministers. Writing to Stephen Williams of Longmeadow, Tennent declared that, if laymen were allowed to preach, it would result in a "dreadfull consequence to the churches peace and soundness in principles."[45] However, the situation was more complex than it appeared, since the preaching of Tennent—and many other ordained itinerants—did empower laypeople. Tennent would go so far as to endorse laypeople separating from their established minister if they could find no alternative. To make matters worse, some ordained itinerants, such as James Davenport, openly supported lay preaching.[46]

Davenport, the minister, at least in theory, at Southold on Long Island, quickly became the favorite whipping boy of the anti-revivalists. One critic reported that Davenport had "travel'd from *Stonington* to *New Haven* about 80 Miles, and condemn'd almost *all* the Ministers." Apparently, one of Davenport's favorite practices was to pray in public against the local minister and then, declaring him to be "an unconverted Man, says, that Thousands are now cursing of him in Hell, for being the Instrument of their Damnation."[47] Itinerants had first been drawn to New Haven by simple logic. Many of them had graduated from Yale, and its student body, young men training to enter the ministry, was an obvious target for revivalists seeking adherents to their vision of a more vibrant Christianity. At the same time, many of the students were anxious, in Harry Stout's words, to "restore religion's preeminence to their generation." The support for the revival, even in some of its more enthusiastic forms, exhibited by many students and a large number of the townspeople kept the itinerants coming back.[48]

At the forefront of the anti-enthusiast forces in New Haven was Yale's rector, Thomas Clap. Although Clap had cautiously welcomed Whitefield a year earlier, it was his disciplinarian side which greeted Davenport and his followers when they arrived in time for commencement in September 1741. Even before his appointment to Yale, Clap had, in the words of Yale historian Franklin Dexter, "become somewhat conspicuous among the ministry of the Colony for the stringency of his church discipline."[49] Clap's biographer Louis Tucker noted that it was "the fanatic Davenport [who] was the catalyst that precipitated Clap's anti-revival tendencies and made him an inveterate foe of the Awakening," and Clap decided to confront Davenport directly.[50] Legally, however, Clap's authority extended only to the college, and so it was there that he looked to confront the excesses of the revival. There was no comprehensive code of conduct: Clap had begun working on one during his first year at Yale, but it was not complete in 1741.[51] Instead, he worked with the trustees and attempted to control the situation by adopting something of a carrot-and-stick approach with the students. The stick was defined at a meeting of the trustees on September 9, 1741, when it was determined that, if "any Student of this College shall directly or indirectly say, that the Rector, either of the Trustees or Tutors are Hypocrites, carnall or unconverted Men, he shall for the first offence make a publick confession in the Hall, and for the Second Offence be expelled."[52] The carrot was an invitation to Jonathan Edwards, a pro-revivalist, to give the commencement address.

Historian George Marsden has suggested that, despite Edwards's pro-awakening sympathies, Clap may have hoped that Edwards, a staunch advocate of order, would counsel sobriety to the students.[53]

At the time, however, Edwards was not the moderate pro-revivalist who would emerge in 1742, and later, with lengthy examinations of revivalism such as *Religious Affections*. In September 1741, Edwards was less than three months removed from participation in a series of revival meetings in Connecticut Valley towns. At one meeting, he first preached his famous *Sinners in the Hands of an Angry God*, while in another case, his ministry was accompanied by "Groans & Screaches as of Women in the Pains of Childbirth; but above these were Houlings and Yellings, which to Even a Carnal Man might point out Hell." Edwards was so exhausted that he "called in the Assistance of 4 or 5 private Xians."[54]

Although there is no surviving copy of the sermon Edwards preached at commencement, he enlarged it and published it as *The Distinguishing Marks of a Work of the Spirit of God*.[55] Opponents of the excesses of the revival would, no doubt, have been heartened when Edwards announced his text from 1 John, which reads in part, "believe not every spirit, but try the spirits whether they are of God." Further encouragement to the anti-revivalists was offered when Edwards noted that, even in the age of the apostles, counterfeit spirits "did also then abound." However, Edwards quickly challenged such opponents by arguing that bodily manifestations and undisciplined behavior did not demonstrate that the entire revival was *not* the work of God. As Edwards noted, God poured out his spirit to "make men holy, and not to make them politicians."[56]

After then laying out a number of positive proofs that the revival was "in the general, from the Spirit of God," Edwards came to his application. Probably to the horror of the Yale administrators, Edwards declared that all should be "warned, by no means to oppose, or do anything in the least to clog or hinder that work that has lately been carried on in the land." While conceding that some improprieties had occurred, this was mainly because it was "chiefly young persons that have been the subjects of it." Furthermore, the fault did not lie with these young people, since they probably knew that they needed instruction. But since they could "see plainly that their ministers have an ill opinion of the work," they could not approach such men for advice and were therefore "without guides: and no wonder that when a people are as sheep without a shepherd, they wander out of the way." Not only had Edwards pronounced a blessing on the revival as a whole, he had laid the blame for the disorders not on rebellious students but on the shoulders of biased ministers.[57]

In retrospect, it is unlikely that anything Edwards, or the administration, could have said would have reined in the enthusiasts. During commencement week, Davenport, who, like Buell, Brainerd, and others was in his mid-twenties, "held forth every day" accompanied by "some other Ministers and young gifted Brethren." Often, the meetings lasted until late at night, with perhaps "20 or 30 distinct exercises carried on by 5 or 10 distinct Persons" in each meeting. Some speakers would pray, some cry, some laugh, and they could be found all over the building from the pulpit to the gallery. Jedidiah Mills and Joseph Bellamy were among the ministers who preached alongside Davenport. Although none of the "young gifted Brethren" were identified, the fact that they were distinguished from those who were ministers implies they were laymen, and their number surely included some of the college students. Probably Samuel Buell, who was soon to embark on his own itineration, was one, and possibly Samuel Hopkins. While Brainerd was not mentioned by name, given his sympathies it is likely that he, too, was involved in the events. Even if he was not one of the exhorters, we can be fairly certain that he was present at the meetings that week.[58]

Such meetings were a far cry from a traditional New England church meeting where the minister spoke in a sedate fashion, with perhaps an occasional "Amen" from the congregation. In contrast, the revival meetings must have been home to a cacophonous turmoil. Since the meetings featured multiple speakers in different parts of the building, it seems unlikely that only one person spoke at a time. More likely, each spoke out as he felt led. This, in turn, may well have caused those in attendance to be moving around the building, seeking to hear all that God was speaking to his people. Given what we know of other such meetings, and taking into account the criticisms of the anti-revivalists and the defenses of the supporters of the revival, there were probably dozens of people, if not more, crying out in response to what they perceived to be the presence of God, while others groaned or collapsed on the floor. Perhaps some expressed a gift of tongues or spoke a word of prophecy. Probably, the celebrants paraded through the streets singing psalms as Davenport had done in New London. Certainly, this was nothing like a Sunday service back home in peaceful Haddam.[59]

The turmoil spilled over into the commencement ceremonies themselves. Samuel Johnson, a Yale alumnus, writing to a friend in England, lamented that "[m]any of the scholars have been possessed of" the new enthusiasm, noting that "two of this year's candidates were denied their degrees for their disorderly and restless endeavors."[60] Thomas Clap, writing nine months later, was still angry enough to fulminate against men who "think that religion is but promoted by commotions, separations, overturnings and the like, and who have done their utmost endeavour to bring the scholars over to them." As with other critics of the revivals, Clap believed that, in addition to their theological shortcomings, the disruptions were injurious to the good order of society.[61]

In particular, Clap was furious over the criticism that Davenport and his allies directed against the Reverend Joseph Noyes, pastor of the First Church and a friend and supporter of Thomas Clap. Davenport, apparently, was particularly vociferous in his attacks on Noyes, calling him a "Devil incarnate," an "unconverted Man," and a "Wolf in Sheep's cloathing." Although there had been no apparent discontent with Noyes prior to this time, Davenport's attacks opened some seam of discord in the congregation which, by November 1741, had precipitated a separation attempt in First Church. It was in the midst of this turmoil within what was the unofficial college church that Clap learned that David Brainerd, one of his students, had questioned the spiritual condition of tutor Chauncey Whittelsey (1717–1789). One can only imagine the scenarios that began to play out in Clap's mind when he heard the report.[62]

The only account of the subsequent process which led to Brainerd's expulsion from the college was furnished by Jonathan Edwards in his *Life of Brainerd*. However, Edwards's sources for this account are thin, as he realized when he sat down to compile the *Life*.[63] Brainerd's diaries covering the time of his expulsion were destroyed at his request shortly before he died, while there is no record of the expulsion either in Clap's own history of Yale or in the official college records.[64] Lacking first-hand knowledge of the incident, Edwards wrote to Brainerd's younger brother John in late 1747 (shortly after David's death), asking that when John came to Northampton the following spring, he "would come furnished to give me a just, exact and certain account of that affair [the expulsion], that the Rector may have no cause, nor find any room to complain of the least misrepresentation in any respect."[65] We do not know what information, if any, John Brainerd imparted to Edwards, but Edwards recounted the story as follows. At the conclusion of a chapel service where Whittlesey had prayed, Brainerd remarked that the tutor "has no more grace than this chair." One of the freshmen overheard the remark and, although not sure at whom it was directed, recounted it to a woman from the town, who reported it to Clap. Clap interrogated the freshman, who gave the rector the names of those with whom Brainerd was talking. Clap then, in Edwards's words, "compelled them to declare what he [Brainerd] said, and of whom he said it." Under the rules promulgated by the trustees, Clap demanded that Brainerd make a "public confession, and to humble himself before the whole college." When Brainerd refused, he was expelled, sometime around November 24, 1741.[66] As Edwards presented things, then, Brainerd was punished for a single careless remark over which he refused to apologize.

But evidence from other sources suggests that there was more to the expulsion than the single criticism of Whittlesey. Just days after Brainerd's expulsion, Jared Ingersoll, an anti-revivalist New Haven attorney, noted, "Brainerd, a Junior att College is expeled for going to the Seperate meeting att N. Haven contrary to the Rectors Command & also for uttering certain speeches concerning the Rector and one of ye tutors, yt. were judged unbecoming for all which he refused to make any acknowledgement of blame." Two years later, in 1743, when Brainerd made a final effort to be readmitted to Yale, he apologized for "going once to the separate meeting in New-Haven…tho' the rector had refused to give me leave." Clearly, Brainerd *had* attended the separate meeting, thus confirming a second charge against him by Clap.[67] Did he, in addition, utter "certain speeches concerning the Rector" that were "unbecoming"? At the 1743 hearing, Brainerd asserted that he could not remember ever having wished Clap would "drop down dead for fining the scholars that followed Mr. Tennent." He did, however, issue a blanket apology for any such statement that he had forgotten making—in itself at least a tacit admission that he was capable of such outbursts. Further evidence that Brainerd was capable of such behavior comes from the diary of Yale freshman John Cleaveland (1722–1799). In January 1742 (i.e., two months after Brainerd had been expelled), Cleaveland reported that he had heard "a horrable story concerning Brainerd how that people suggest that he got up a letter or paper upon a mans door and said we are men and the first time that we meet with you whether by night or by day we will pull your tongue out by your throte and brake every boan that you have in your body." At the time, Cleaveland was, at the least, a regular acquaintance of Brainerd, if not a close friend. However, Cleaveland noted no outrage concerning this charge nor is there any suggestion in Cleaveland's diary that Brainerd was incapable of this kind of intimidation. On the contrary, the entry could be read as Cleaveland regretting that a friend had committed a terrible, but not unexpected, indiscretion.[68] Thus, while the evidence is not conclusive, it strongly suggests that Brainerd's conduct went far beyond a single careless remark that was seized upon by Clap as a means to make an example of a supporter of the awakening. To the contrary, it is much more likely that Brainerd was neck-deep in the upheavals, joining Davenport and others in preaching to separate meetings, condemning the establishment leadership, and generally adding to the disorder roiling the town.

In addition to Clap's determination to move against instigators of disorder, it may well be that Clap and other anti-revival trustees saw Brainerd as betraying his social standing. Most supporters of the revivals were sons of poorer, more anonymous families who lived in newer towns on the periphery of Connecticut settlement. Brainerd, in contrast, came from a well-respected family which lived in one of the older Connecticut settlements. Rhys Isaac has detailed how class defections by elite Virginians in favor of the religious enthusiasm of the Baptists often brought vociferous, and even violent, attacks on the defectors. It may well be that Clap was particularly fearful that Brainerd's support for the revivalists signaled the beginning of a larger defection from the wealthier section of Connecticut society. And, indeed, Brainerd's former landlord, Isaac Dickerman, a man who had served multiple terms in the Connecticut Assembly, publicly demonstrated some sympathy for the revivalists later in 1742, although he continued to serve as a deacon at First Church. Since so much of the opposition to the revivals concerned the breakdown in order, Brainerd's background as a member of a well-regarded family probably presented an extra concern for Clap and his allies.[69]

Not surprisingly, Brainerd's expulsion did little to calm things on campus or in the town. It was less than a month later that the pro-revival group in First Church requested permission to form their own society, citing the ministry of Noyes which, they claimed, "has been in great measure unprofitable to us."[70] In response, on January 25, 1742, the conservative members of the New Haven church "voted a conformity to the Saybrook Platform" and, so, in the minds of the pro-awakening faction within the church, claimed an authority "contrary to the known, fundamental principle and practice of said church."[71] Apparently, Brainerd too remained in the thick of the unrest. At the end of January, John Cleaveland reported a "battle concerning religion" during which his landlord described the work of "Brainerd and many others of the same class" as being of the devil. Brainerd was still in New Haven at the end of February, helping to lead unsanctioned prayer meetings in private residences; Cleaveland and others listened to Brainerd as he "repeated a sermon." As late as the first week of March, Cleaveland reported that he and his friends were "very handsomely treated" by Brainerd and others.[72]

Brainerd was only one contributor to the chaos that continued to rock New Haven. Joseph Bellamy and Jedidiah Mills were both in town around the same time, preaching at separate meetings, as was, apparently, Gilbert Tennent who further contributed to the general chaos. James Davenport and Andrew Croswell were leading people in "singing thro' the streets to and from the house of God, and favouring exhorters of no gifts, or prudence for public speaking."[73] In an effort to promote the case for separation, "two young Women pretended to be in a Trance for a Week, to have been to Heaven and to have seen Glymps of it." Perhaps not surprisingly, "God had revealed to them that Mr. Noyes was unconverted," and "God had commanded them to separate from the Church in *New-Haven*."[74] In an attempt to rescue the situation at the church, Clap and other church leaders compelled Noyes to accept Aaron Burr (a moderate pro-revivalist) as a second minister. But Burr declined, and further efforts went unrewarded. In May, Bellamy, Samuel Cooke, John Graham, and Elisha Kent presided over a meeting wherein they formally recognized the dissenters as a Congregational church. For at least the next year or so, the church met in private houses.[75]

Nor was Clap having any success in restraining his remaining scholars, some of whom continued to "go about exhorting," while others had "fallen into the practice of Rash Judgeing and censureing others," even, in some cases, directing their ire against the "Gouernours, teachers & Instructors of the Colege." Even worse, for Clap, he had learned that the separatists were actively trying to recruit students from the college with promises of being licensed to "preach without any regard to a degree." It was even rumored that they planned to "license one to preach who has been expelled for plain breeches of the laws of Christianity as well as those of [the] college." Finally, Clap had to acknowledge at least temporary defeat. As the *Boston Evening Post* would put it, "the divisions are so great, that the students have all left." In early April 1742, Clap had been compelled to close the school. It would not reopen until June.[76]

Was Brainerd the expelled student who was to be licensed by the New Haven separatists? Perhaps. Although there were two other students who had been expelled, Brainerd had been in New Haven at least through late March. By the time Clap closed the college, and before he mentioned the rumors regarding licensing students, Brainerd had left town. Sometime in late March, he had traveled, not home to Haddam but to Ripton, Connecticut, to lodge with Jedidiah Mills, a member of the Yale class of 1722 who had been pastoring there since 1723. As one of those who disrupted the 1741 commencement, Mills was firmly inside the pro-revival camp. He was also a member of the Fairfield East Ministerial Association, a group which strongly supported the awakening. Its members included itinerant preacher Joseph Bellamy, now once again safely ensconced at Bethlehem, and Samuel Cooke (1687–1747), a minister at Stratford who had been dismissed from his position as trustee at Yale for his support of the separatists in New Haven. The Fairfield East Consociation had issued an invitation to Whitefield in October 1740, had rejected the idea that itinerant ministers were disorderly, and in January 1742 had endorsed the ministries of Whitefield and

Gilbert Tennent. While noting that "diverse humane weakness, Imperfections & Imprudencies" had sometimes been displayed by supporters of the work, the consociation had also attacked the "many false reproaches cast upon the good Work of the Lord."[77]

In addition to Mills's pro-revival credentials, he was also well known as a provider of post-college studies for Yale graduates, making it possible for him to supply the balance of the education Brainerd had lost through his expulsion. While we cannot be certain, there is a likelihood that Brainerd had gone to Ripton to receive further instruction from Mills in order to be licensed by the Fairfield East Ministerial Association as the separatist pastor of New Haven. However, while in Ripton, Brainerd gradually moved to a less radical position. Although the move was driven in part by events outside of his control, the shift also reflected Brainerd's own upbringing.

Child of the Establishment

Although David Brainerd embraced much of the radicalism of the revivals and was about the same age as many of its protagonists, in one important respect his background differed from those of many of his colleagues. The majority of the itinerants and radicals, such as Samuel Hopkins and Joseph Bellamy, had come from poorer, less well-established towns and families (Samuel Buell was an exception to this). Brainerd, on the other hand, came from the older town of Haddam, which lay closer to the colony's major centers, such as Hartford. His family was relatively well known in the colony, a reputation rooted in long-term residence in the same town and persistent service to the standing order.[78] Appeals to order and moderation mounted by both the authorities and erstwhile supporters of the revival resonated with the aspect of Brainerd's character, that had been shaped as a member of a respected, prosperous family that was very much a part of the Connecticut establishment. The Brainerd family's background was American myth brought to life. David's paternal grandfather, Daniel Brainerd, had arrived in Hartford, Connecticut, in 1649 as an eight-year-old indentured servant. He served the Wadsworth family of Hartford until he was twenty-one, at which time he became a member of a group which established in 1662 the town of Haddam, about thirty miles south of Hartford.[79]

In some ways, the original settlers of Haddam were an anomalous group. They were typical in that they were Connecticut natives who located their settlement near a major river—in this case, the Connecticut. However, the group seems to have been smaller than the norm, and it took Haddam, the last town established on the river in the colonial period, almost twice as long as average to be granted town privileges by the Assembly. The layout of Haddam resembled that of the agricultural villages in the open-field regions of England. Most of the early inhabitants settled on the west bank of the Connecticut River with so-called home lots lying between the river and the main road and other lots lying to the west of the main road. This settlement pattern meant that the families lived fairly close together around the village center. A common pattern in colonial Connecticut, it was adopted for its social utility since the compact nature of the home sites facilitated church attendance and community oversight by town leaders.[80]

Although Daniel Brainerd received a little more land than most of the original settlers, the range of sizes among them was small, suggesting it is unlikely that there was any real social stratification in the early years of the settlement. However, by the time Daniel Brainerd died in 1715, he had amassed a considerable estate. The Haddam town records note at least six separate land purchases by Daniel between 1672 and 1702, encompassing in totality hundreds of acres. Family tradition asserts that Daniel, in addition to his real estate activities, was the fledgling settlement's only merchant and that he built a wharf in the town to facilitate this role. Whether true or not, the town records make it clear that he was one of its leading men. Two years after he helped to found Haddam, in 1664, Daniel Brainerd married Hannah Spencer, and the couple had eight children, seven sons and a daughter, between 1666 and 1681.[81]

In 1707, Daniel's youngest son, Hezekiah (1681–1727), then aged twenty-six, married Dorothy Mason (1679–1731), three years his senior and the widowed daughter of the Reverend Jeremiah Hobart, Haddam's minister. Dorothy had an impressive family heritage. Her first husband had been Daniel Mason (d. 1705), grandson of Captain John Mason, a combatant in the Pequot War, while her maternal grandfather (Hobart's father-in-law), the Reverend Samuel Whiting, was a brother-in-law of Oliver St. John, Oliver Cromwell's chief justice. The couple's offspring numbered nine—five boys and four girls. The sixth child, and third son, born on April 20, 1718, was named David.[82]

By the time of David's birth, both the town of Haddam and the Brainerd family were fairly typical of early eighteenth-century New England.[83] Haddam was one of the older Connecticut towns and was located within the region of the colony whose residents made up a substantial portion of Connecticut's social elite. However, Haddam did not develop quite the same level of prosperity as most of the other older towns in the colony. Poor soil quality prevented the accumulation of widespread agricultural wealth. Over the course of the eighteenth century, numbers of Haddam farmers left the land and became artisans whose products probably served a fairly local market. Commerce, too, failed to provide substantial and widespread economic growth. Although Haddam supported a small amount of trade—including some from overseas—the relatively short distance to Middletown hampered Haddam's development as a substantial commercial center. The town probably supported a number of stores, a physician, and other accoutrements of a provincial town. Historians have generally viewed Haddam in the eighteenth century as a second-tier town: having a modest level of local manufacturing with a small number of wealthy local men, but not one of the growing commercial or manufacturing centers of the colony.

Hezekiah Brainerd was one of those local wealthy men. In 1716, when Hezekiah was thirty-five, Daniel Brainerd died, and Hezekiah, although the youngest son, received a substantial inheritance, including his father's house, farm buildings, orchard, and more than a hundred acres of land.[84] The inheritance did not breed complacency; indeed, Hezekiah improved his material condition markedly over the course of his life. The inventory compiled when he died in 1727 runs to three pages—two of land and one of other possessions. Since these other possessions included a "pair of Money Scales and weights," it is probable that Hezekiah owed at least some of his prosperity to commercial activities, an interpretation that is reinforced by the listing of large quantities of materials such as silk, mohair, and broad cloth among the inventoried items. Although not as substantial an inventory as that possessed by merchants in other New England towns, it would appear that Hezekiah Brainerd and his family were well and truly integrated into what T. H. Breen has characterized as an "empire of goods." Furthermore, Hezekiah's merchant activities would have strengthened his commitment to the structure and stability of Connecticut society.[85]

Other items in the inventory point to the relative personal wealth of Hezekiah, Dorothy, and their family: two looking glasses, assorted items of silverware, a substantial amount of pewter, pieces of furniture, numerous candlesticks, and "a pocket compass." In addition, Hezekiah owned two yoke of oxen, two dozen head of cattle, two horses, more than twenty sheep, and a few swine.[86] The increasing complexity of trade would also have connected Hezekiah to merchants in other parts of New England and perhaps even as far away as London. His commercial activities coupled with Haddam's location in the Connecticut Valley also means that the Brainerd family would have had regular access to the growing number of newspapers printed in Boston, which carried both American and British news. While David Brainerd and his parents and siblings may have lived in a small farming town, by no means did they live a marginal life in a colonial backwater. In contrast, the Brainerds were a prosperous family that enjoyed the growing availability of consumer goods, and they were increasingly connected to wider colonial and possibly even Atlantic society.[87]

Hezekiah's family connections and commercial success drew him into Connecticut's political circles. It seems likely that the Brainerd family was part of what historian Bruce C. Daniels has described as a "family-dominated oligarchy." Hezekiah served his first term as Haddam's deputy to the General Assembly in the same month that he turned twenty-one and repeated the role at frequent intervals in subsequent years. In later years, he served as clerk of the House of Representatives, the Speaker of the House, a member of the governor's council, and the town clerk of Haddam. Hezekiah's continual service to both the colony and the town further underlines both his prestige and wealth. Prestige led to his election to colonial and town offices while wealth enabled him to devote time and the upfront expenses of town service without suffering financial loss himself. Furthermore, the occasional appending of "esquire" to Hezekiah's name in the Connecticut records indicates that he served as a judge or justice, an office which required both knowledge of the law and prestige at the town level, but which also added to one's prestige. Of course, political service also brought its rewards: in 1716, the Assembly granted him a license to operate a ferry over the river near Haddam while shortly before his death he was awarded a substantial land grant in the western region of the colony, just then being opened up for settlement.[88] One reason for the prosperity of the Brainerd family was the absence of war in most of New England following the 1713 Treaty of Utrecht, which marked the end of Queen Anne's War. Although vicious guerrilla conflicts were fought between various Indian groups and English settlers on the Massachusetts, Maine, and New Hampshire peripheries, in the southern Connecticut Valley peace reigned from the mid-1720s until 1744.[89]

The Haddam records also suggest that the town was an example of what Michael Zuckerman has described as "peaceable kingdoms," New England towns which sought unity and compromise in their policy making.[90] Given the small number of wealthy families and the age of the settlement, it is probable that there were few major disputes or occasions for disunity. Indeed, the only issue that seems to have caused any serious conflict within the town revolved around access to worship. The original grant of land spread both east and west of the Connecticut River and, in 1697, a group of men from the east side of the river appeared before the Assembly, asking that "they might have liberty to embody themselues in church estate on that side of the river and to call and settle a minister among them."[91] Although the original petition was turned down for financial reasons, the dispute continued to fester for several years and involved a further representation to the Assembly. As was typical of other Connecticut towns, the request probably reflected a desire on the part of the petitioners to remove themselves from the authority of the older town leaders. This is implied by the one piece of extant personal communication that mentioned the dispute. In early 1699, Jeremiah Hobart wrote to the Reverend Timothy Woodbridge of Hartford: "we are outwardly quiet but observe, that on our day of fast, Not one of that side stopped, tho they had a copy of that order [for a joint meeting] sent."[92] Perhaps not surprisingly, at its next meeting, the Assembly decided to grant "liberty to the inhabitants of Haddum [sic] that dwell on the east side of the great river to imbody themselves in church estate," although East Haddam was not, at this time, incorporated as a separate town. The resolution of the dispute suggests that the residents, in keeping with Zuckerman's interpretation, agreed to the separation as a way to avoid more intense and protracted conflict.[93] Other than this, Haddam seems to have been a model town and seems to have been religiously conservative: Jonathan Edwards's 1734–1735 Northampton revival swept up and down the Connecticut Valley without, apparently, having an impact on Haddam, East Haddam, or David Brainerd. No itinerants recorded a stop there; and there is no hint of any separatist group in the towns.[94] This, then, was the world in which David Brainerd grew up: stable, orderly, peaceful, materially comfortable, and well connected to the outside world.

Of Brainerd's childhood, we know very little, with the only accounts coming from unsourced genealogies and town histories. According to these, Hezekiah Brainerd received little education as a child but, as an adult, took it upon himself to acquire "expansive knowledge." He underwent a conversion experience fairly early in life and practiced a deep personal faith. He also is supposed to have run his family with "rigid notions of parental prerogatives and authority."

Site of the Brainerd family home, Haddam, Connecticut. Photo by Elizabeth Malloy. Courtesy of the Haddam Historical Society, Haddam, Connecticut.

Dorothy Brainerd, the daughter of a clergyman, can be assumed to have instructed her children from infancy in the religious mores of Connecticut. Although we know little about the education of David and his siblings, the fact that he and three of his brothers gained entrance to Yale indicates solid instruction during their childhood. On the whole, it is reasonable to accept the broad outlines of a sober and religious domestic life as it is unlikely that Hezekiah would have been called into public service as frequently as he was had things been otherwise.[95]

David Brainerd's prototypical New England family was disrupted when Hezekiah Brainerd died when David was only nine years old. Hezekiah had been attending the Connecticut Assembly session in May 1727, but on May 18 he was taken ill and died less than a week later.[96] Five years later, when David was only fourteen, his mother died, the victim of a general outbreak of disease that was so severe and so widespread that, in May 1732, the Assembly promulgated "An Act Providing in Case of Sickness."[97] We can only conjecture as to the impact the deaths of his parents had on Brainerd since his own description of his childhood was not written as detailed autobiography but was meant to serve only as the opening act of his conversion narrative.[98] Daniel Shea has observed that spiritual autobiographies, especially those which dealt with the conversion of the narrator, were constructed according to cultural formulas. Most important, Shea notes that these narratives were written by the spiritually mature person looking back on the struggles of the "pilgrim." Thus, the narrator is "expert where the pilgrim was ignorant, composed and steady of view where the pilgrim was inconstant and vacillating in his self-regard."[99]

Although Brainerd's narrative of his life prior to his conversion is not exactly of the type addressed by Shea, it is clearly a constructed narrative. It is not that Brainerd's recollections were fabricated but rather that he invested in them certain terms and tropes which reflected the theological views he held as an adult. One of the most important of these was to emphasize the false religion—and thus the absence of salvation—that existed in one's life prior to the memorable, chronologically specific conversion experience, which set the true Christian apart from those who simply practiced the outward signs of devotion. Conversion narratives usually featured moments when the authors would become aware of their spiritual shortcomings, pursue God for a time, but then lose interest in their quest—terms such as "cold" and "dead" were common. This cycle may occur a number of times before the author's actual moment of conversion. Thus, in writing of his childhood, Brainerd recalled being "terrified at the thoughts of death," which led him to be diligent in his religious practices when he was seven or eight, but he lamented that because religious duties "destroyed [his] eagerness for play," his "religious concern was but short lived."[100]

Another aspect of these accounts is that they stripped away everything that had no direct bearing on the conversion process. Of course, if the accounts were written years later, this meant including only those things which the mature author *remembered* as being important. Thus, of his father's death, Brainerd writes nothing. His mother's contributed to him being "exceedingly distressed and melancholy" and was apparently one of the factors that led to his second period of religious concern. But this second period of concern, when he was once again "roused out of carnal security," he attributed mainly to the "mortal sickness in Haddam." This time, the "Spirit of God proceeded far" with him and he was almost "persuaded to be a Christian." But this, too, faded away. All we can conclude is that, when Brainerd compiled the account as an adult, he could not recall that the deaths of his parents had any significant bearing on his spiritual journey. He did remember, however, reading a seventeenth-century work by the English minister James Janeway (1636?–1674) entitled *A Token for Children.*[101] Janeway's work—a collection of stories about thirteen children who came to salvation in their preteen years—was extraordinarily popular and widely read in New England. Given that Brainerd still remembered reading it at least a decade later, we can safely assume that it did impact him at the time of his illness.

In particular, Brainerd may have found inspiration in Janeway's fifth example, which recounted the "pious Life, and joyful death, of a child which Dyed when he was about 12 years old, 1632" and who "had no sooner learned to speak, but he took himself to prayer."[102] The young boy in this account suffered from a "lingering disease" and, in an effort to comfort him, some of those at his bedside told him "of possessions that must fall to his Portion." Unimpressed, the youngster replied: "And what are these? said he. I had rather have the Kingdom of Heaven, than a thousand such inheritances." Writing in his late twenties, Brainerd thus emphasized the parallels between the accounts in Janeway's work and his own life. The young David Brainerd faced the inheritance of some of his father's property, the "lingering disease" which afflicted the town, and the real possibility that he would contract the same, so it is not surprising that the mature Brainerd would, years later, remember finding "delight in reading" Janeway's *Token*.[103]

However the loss of his parents affected Brainerd emotionally, materially his close-knit and prosperous family ensured that he and his siblings would not become destitute orphans. David's eldest brother, twenty-three at the time, retained control of the family house, and David lived there for about a year following his mother's death after which he moved to East Haddam, where he lived for four years, probably with the family of his father's sister, Joseph and Martha Spencer. Certainly, the Brainerd and Spencer families had a shared history, and this was not the first time orphans had traded households. In 1682, John Spencer, Joseph's grandfather, had declared that, on his death, his eldest son and eldest daughter should be "at the disposal of his Brother-in-law Daniel Braynard and his own sister Hannah the wife of Daniel Braynard."[104] Although he was the third son, his family's prosperity meant that David was reasonably well provided for. David Brainerd received less land than his older brother and no provision for an education as was willed to Nehemiah, the second son, but the will provided that David would receive enough land when he turned eighteen to provide at least a comfortable living.[105] Since the four years following David's move to East Haddam had no bearing on his spiritual progress, he simply glossed over them in his narrative. However, he must have been a witness to the final resolution of the decades-long argument between those residents on the east side of the river and those on the west. East Haddam was incorporated in 1734, when David was sixteen, while Haddam formally recognized the right of East Haddam to form a separate church society in 1736.[106] Brainerd picked up his own story in 1737 when, "being full 19 years of age I removed to Durham & began to work on my farm."[107]

But then, no more than a year after moving to Durham, he made the decision to go to Yale because, according to his conversion narrative, he had a "natural inclination" to earn a college education as, being "conceited," he "desired to devote myself to the ministry." Even allowing for Brainerd emphasizing his selfishness—and thus his unconverted state—for the purposes of his narrative, it tells us little about why he changed direction in life. In fact, we cannot even be certain that his original intent was to enter the ministry. As historian James W. Schmotter discovered, by the 1730s only about a third of the students who entered Harvard and Yale ended up in the ministry. Given the status of the Brainerd family and their connections to the colony's elite, David may well have been considering a professional career of some sort.[108] Although we cannot be certain of Brainerd's motivation, historians have observed that the general stability and orderliness of Connecticut was beginning to experience some mild tremors in the mid-1730s, triggered primarily by population growth. This, in turn, led to expansion onto new lands, the establishment of new towns, a rash of land speculation, and a moderate economic decline. There were related public arguments over the founding of land banks, the formation of trading companies, and the issuing of paper money. Many in Connecticut also expressed concern over the slow but steady growth of groups of religious dissenters—Anglicans, Baptists, and Quakers. In some towns, there was the whiff of separatism in the air. And, in the middle of the decade, there came the news of the revival in Northampton and other towns in the valley.[109]

We do not know to what extent these events affected Brainerd, but it is unlikely that they simply passed him by. In addition to the knowledge of the wider world that he probably acquired in childhood, his new status as a land-owner must have caused him to be more engaged with events taking place around him. Although he lived in Durham and went to church there, his land actually lay within the bounds of Haddam. In 1736, the Connecticut Assembly had ordered certain "persons and estates in Haddam" to pay a "ministerial charge" for the sup-port of Durham's minister, Nathaniel Chauncy, a ruling that must have included David Brainerd.[110] In addition to paying taxes, however, being a landowner also made him more attractive as a potential husband, and there is a hint that he was actively seeking marriage during this period. In his diary introduction, Brainerd claimed he was not "exceedingly addicted to young company or frolicking," the practice of groups of young people socializing together, particularly after sun-down on Sunday. Exactly how loose was the behavior at "frolics" is not exactly clear—and it probably varied markedly—but it certainly did not accord with the standards of Connecticut society. And despite Brainerd's disclaimer, he clearly attended a number of them as he also noted that he "never returned from a frol-lick in my life with so good a conscience as I went with. They always added new guilt." Whether he felt guilt at the time, or he glossed this when he edited the introduction, it does not change the reality that the young landowner, having moved away from his family and attending church where few knew him was also socializing with members of the opposite sex while removed from parental supervision.[111]

In these outlines of the year he spent in Durham may be seen a possible reason for his decision to go to Yale. Although the amount of land he owned was probably sufficient to shield him from the general economic decline of the period, the land around Durham and Haddam was relatively poor in quality so it may not have been adequate to maintain the kind of comfortable living he had enjoyed as a child. Coupled with the prestige his father had enjoyed and David's knowledge of the changes that were taking place around him—both in Connecticut and farther afield—it may well be that he longed to make some kind of mark in life, that his ambition drove him to seek a future that was big-ger than that of an anonymous Connecticut Valley farmer. And one way to open the door to that kind of future was to earn a college degree. Brainerd's later life strongly suggests that he was not content with being one face among many but sought that which was out of the ordinary. As Jackson Turner Main observed of eighteenth-century Connecticut, "the sedentary and conformist stayed at home and bore adversity quietly; the ambitious left."[112] Whatever his reasons, having made the decision to seek an alternative to life as a farmer, in April 1738 Brainerd moved in with Haddam's minister, Phineas Fiske, a not unusual action for those preparing for college.[113] Since 1713, Fiske had been at Haddam, whence he had come from his position as tutor at Yale.[114] Evaluations of Fiske are mixed. Samuel Johnson, a convert to Anglicanism and, later, president of King's College, described him during his time at Yale as "a prompt man and apt to teach in what he knew, but it was nothing but the scholastic cobwebs of a few little English and Dutch systems."[115] Haddam town historian David D. Field, writing in 1814, described Fiske as a man "rather solid than brilliant" who was "regarded as a sound rather than a popular preacher."[116] On the other hand, Ezra Stiles warmly endorsed Fiske's abilities, declaring him to be one of the "pillar tutors and the glory of the College," an assessment that was shared by Benjamin Trumbull.[117]

Certainly, Fiske seemed to have had some ability to prepare men for the ministry. In addition to his work in this regard at Yale, during his time at Haddam, at least four other men—Fiske's own son, two of David Brainerd's brothers, and one of Brainerd's cousins—all entered the ministry, while a third Brainerd brother entered Yale but died before graduating.[118] Fiske set about developing in David Brainerd that proper, undemonstrative, and serious approach to life which one associates with New England ministers. As Brainerd recalled, Fiske advised him to "abandon young company & associate [himself] with grave elderly people." Beyond this, he diligently read his bible, paid close attention to sermons, and developed a "regular" life that was "full of religion."[119] As part of this regular life, he spent "much time every day in secret prayer & other secret duties," composed "prayers suitable for all seasons," and made efforts to memorize sermons to which he listened.[120] When Fiske died late in 1738, David continued his studies under the direction of his brother Nehemiah. Nehemiah had graduated from Yale in 1732, had married one of Fiske's daughters, but had not yet found a pulpit.[121] It was during this time of preparation that Brainerd underwent the conversion experience that, in large part, shaped his actions at Yale and eventually led to his arrival in Ripton in April 1742.

By that time, in addition to his establishment upbringing, events in Connecticut were having an impact on Brainerd. A number of ministers who had favored the revivals from the beginning were now expressing reservations over some of the more extreme practices. In January 1742, the Fairfield East Consociation had conceded:

> [D]iverse humane weakness, Imperfections & Imprudencies have
> attended this great & good work, both in some of the Instruments
> who have appear'd zealous to promote it, & in some who, we hope,
> are wrought upon Sincerely to believe in the Lord Jesus Christ; as
> well as in those under Awakening & Concern.—And there are diverse
> Strategems & Devices of Satan & Endeavours of his to deceive unwary
> souls and impose upon them & thereby throw a Blemish & reproach
> on the work of God.[122]

Jonathan Dickinson in New Jersey had concluded, "Satan has found the means to turn mens minds from their greatest concern," and Dickinson had helped to convince Joseph Bellamy that things had gone awry. Benjamin Colman believed that Davenport and Andrew Croswell had "often preached under actual fevers." In April 1742, Jonathan Edwards warned his Northampton congregation to be sure their "experiences don't gradually degenerate," and later that year, in *Some Thoughts Concerning the Present Revival of Religion in New-England*, he frankly acknowledged that some "errors of the friends of the work of God, and especially of the great promoters of it, give vast advantage to the enemies of such a work."[123]

Opponents of the revivals were also taking steps to deal with the disorder that had been caused. At the urging of the New Haven Ministerial Association, the Connecticut Assembly had called a general consocation of churches, which met at Guilford in November 1741. The Guilford meeting focused on the issues of itinerant preachers and the demands for separation based on the unconverted nature of the settled minister in a given parish. With certain specific exceptions, the Guilford Resolves declared, "for a minister to enter another minister's parish, and preach, or administer the seals of the covenant, without the consent of, or in opposition to the settled minister of the parish, is disorderly." On the issue of separation, the consocation "earnestly Advise[d] ye Ministers of Christ and all Serious Christians" to unite together to advise those who were dissatisfied to "avoid Such Seperations & Divisions."[124] Although the resolves did not carry the weight of law, the Assembly had already asked the consocation to report on its deliberations at the legislative session the following May, suggesting that some more legally binding action would be taken.

Thus it was that in the spring of 1742 at the Ripton home of Jedidiah Mills, twenty-four-year-old David Brainerd contemplated a future which was at the least murky, if not completely impenetrable. Personally, he was not the same man who had arrived at Yale in 1739. Brainerd's recent experiences in the fires of revival had burned a permanent mark on his soul. Child of the establishment he may have been, but he had also been a part of something that was far from ordinary, and he was not willing to let go of that so easily. However, the stability and certainty of his upbringing could not be put away either. He was unable, or unwilling, to completely separate himself from his respectable background in the way that men like Davenport and Croswell had done. And, with friends of the revival like Bellamy now voicing some opposition and the authorities contemplating legal constraints, his options were diminishing. However, if he were to be licensed by the Fairfield East Association and invited by the New Haven separatists, he would possess an imprimatur of legitimacy that might protect him from persecution by men of authority, such as Thomas Clap. And pastoring a separate church held the promise of continuing, at least in part, the radical nature of the revivals while at the same time being a respected member of the establishment.

Before taking that step, Brainerd made an effort to find another way out of the constricted place in which he found himself. In May 1742, at about the same time that the Connecticut Assembly was meeting in Hartford, Brainerd went there and "[w]aited on a council of ministers," hoping they would intercede on his behalf with the Yale administration. Tellingly, he "spread before them the *treatment I had met* with from the Rector and tutors of Yale College" (emphasis added). Thus, Brainerd hoped he would be readmitted to the school, but construed the situation in such a way that he was the one who had been wronged. His case persuaded the men in question, who "thought it advisable to intercede for me with the Rector and trustees." The ministers sent a letter to the trustees, who were also meeting in Hartford that month, to accompany one written by Brainerd.[125] Unfortunately for Brainerd, as the Fairfield East Association later noted, "the said letters were delivered into the hands of the Rector at Hartford in May last when & where the Trustees were sitting but never communicated to them."[126] Not surprisingly, as Jonathan Edwards dryly noted, "the application which was then made on his behalf had not the desired success."[127]

One need not attribute smallness of spirit to Clap on this occasion. In a speech delivered early in the Assembly's session, Governor Jonathan Law, speaking of Yale, had observed, "for youth there to be trained up in Disobedience" to the law would "lay a foundation for Sedition and Disregard to all humane laws." In response, the Assembly had appointed a special committee to look into the situation at Yale and that committee had tendered its report on the same day Brainerd arrived in Hartford. It began with a catalog of problems, among which were students who had "fallen into the practice of Rash Judgeing & censureing of others, even Some of the Governors, teachers & Instructors of the Colege, as being unconverted" and students who had "made it theire practice by day & night, & Some times for Several days together, to go about…before greate Numbers of people, to teach & Exhort, much after the same maner, that ministers of the Gospel do."[128]

In light of these problems, the committee recommended that the rector and trustees be "verry carfull to Instruct the Students in the true principals of Relegion" and to "keep them from all Such errors as they may be in danger of Imbibeing." Any students who "contumatiously refuse[d] to submit to the Laws, orders & Rules thereof" should not "Injoy the preveledges of it." Given such strong language from the legislature, it is not surprising that Clap decided to give no consideration to Brainerd's petition. While the committee had recommended that "all proper meanes be first used…before they be dismissed [from] the Colege as Incorageable," Brainerd had already been dismissed and there is no evidence that his request to be reinstated carried a strong sense of remorse. Readmitting him would further undermine the authority of Clap and the trustees and could even be interpreted as an affront to the Assembly and to the governor.[129]

At the same session of the Assembly, a combination of the Guilford Resolves, Clap's decision to close Yale early, and criticism of aspects of the revivals by some of their proponents had led the deputies to take legislative actions to deal with the disorders. The resulting Act for Regulating Abuses and Correcting Disorders in Ecclesiastical Affairs is a lengthy document, but there are two sections that are particularly pertinent to understanding David Brainerd's subsequent actions. The first, probably to no one's surprise applied stiff penalties to anyone who "shall enter into any parish not immediately under his charge, and shall there preach or exhort the people." Violators would be compelled to post a bond of

£100 against a future repetition.[130] Even more important for Brainerd, the act also prohibited "any association of ministers" from undertaking to "examine or license any candidate for the gospel ministry, or assume to themselves the decision of any controversy, or as an association to counsel or advise in any affair" that was "properly within the province and jurisdiction of any other association." If Brainerd had been counting on being licensed by the Fairfield East Association, this provision effectively cut off any hopes he entertained of returning to the New Haven separatists, since New Haven lay outside the bounds of Fairfield East's jurisdiction.[131]

Nor were the authorities reticent about making use of the new law. Just days after its passage, James Davenport was convicted by the Assembly and deported from Connecticut. In July, four others were imprisoned for holding a separate meeting in the town of Colchester. Other itinerants, separatist ministers, critics of anti-revival ministers, and even lay supporters of separatism were either expelled from the colony, fined, or both. Within months of the passage of the act, it must have been clear to Brainerd that, while dreams of an itinerant ministry had not been completely removed—he could, for example, minister in churches in the Fairfield East Association, which had issued him an invitation—they had been severely curtailed.[132]

Not surprisingly, the uncertainty over his future and the conflict with Yale was much on Brainerd's mind during the spring of 1742 and appears to have had an impact on his spiritual well-being. At times, he found that "the Lord was pleas'd to lift up the light of his Countenance upon me," while at others he felt "very heartless and dull."[133] But the Yale issue was clearly an open wound, which he interpreted through various prisms. On occasion, he attempted to construe the whole episode as a test of his faith, describing it as his "great Trial at College" and finding it a challenge to "forgive all Injuries done" to him. Here, Brainerd is the victim, the radical preacher, persecuted for the sake of God's kingdom. In speaking out for the truth of the gospel, Brainerd had been brought low by those who opposed it. But there is also a glimpse of that other part of Brainerd's character: the child of a respectable family who mourned because of the "Disgrace I was laid under at College."[134]

Perhaps of more immediate concern, however, was his future. Having sold his land the previous year, he could not easily return to the life of a yeoman farmer. He probably still had funds left over from the sale but would have had to move out into the western areas of New England, not a particularly attractive option. And, even had he wanted to return to farming, it is likely that his poor health may have precluded any kind of steady physical exertion. Lacking his degree closed off avenues that were available to fellow radicals like Joseph Bellamy, who could return to his own pulpit, or Samuel Buell, whose degree enabled him to hold out the hope of some kind of gainful employment. Finally, the provisions of the Assembly's act had removed the New Haven option. Faced with this impasse, Brainerd cast his lot with the men of the Fairfield East Association, established ministers who, no matter that they now rejected some of the excesses of the awakening, had also been touched by the real work of God.

Working under their protective authority, he began to seek a way to forge his own path out of the dilemma in which he found himself.

Establishment Itinerant

Upon his arrival in Ripton, David Brainerd spent most of his time in studies, ministerial preparation, and personal devotions, all designed to fit him for the work of ministry. After several months of instruction at the hands of Jedidiah Mills, on July 29, 1742, he was "examined by the Association met at Danbury," which issued him "a license to preach the gospel of Christ."[135] The members of the association, although overwhelmingly supportive of Brainerd, entered a lengthy statement into their records at the time, probably to preempt any criticism that might be forthcoming from New Haven or other anti-revival bastions. The association noted that Brainerd had made legitimate efforts to be reinstated by Yale but that he had been "effectually prevented redress at that Board [the trustees]; and so utterly incapacitated to fill out his time at College to a Graduation." Furthermore, it was the "proper business of an Association to judge for themselves who (especially within their own proper district) they may examine and license for the ministerial improvements." They also observed that Brainerd's conduct among them had been "very agreeable to the Character of a Christian."[136] All of these factors made him an acceptable candidate for the ministry and so, in their view, eligible to undergo the association's examination.

The association's rules for examination had been laid out in 1735 and required that a candidate be able to read Greek, Hebrew, and Latin and be able to translate all three orally. He also needed to have "a General Idea of Theology & Philosophy," be a man of high character, and show a desire to win souls to Christ.[137] Finally, candidates needed to "offer a sermon composed by themselves of a Text given to them by the minister, unto whom they move for Examination & shall be opposed therein, that so their Ability to defend the truths of the Gospel may thereby be discerned."[138] Neither Brainerd's diary nor the association minutes recorded the biblical text from which Brainerd preached at his licensing, but it is quite possible that a manuscript sermon attributed to Brainerd and now held at the Yale Divinity Library is the sermon he preached on the day he was licensed by the association.[139] The manuscript in question takes as its text Romans 8:2, a verse that would provide ample grist for a candidate to demonstrate his ability to defend the truths of the gospel. Furthermore, the sermon is didactic in nature with little attention given to personal application as would be expected if it had been delivered to an audience of laypeople.[140]

The only surviving Brainerd sermon, the opening section affirmed Paul's teaching that while the law of Moses brought knowledge *of* sin but not salvation *from* sin, the law itself was still "Holy, just and good." In the much longer second section of the sermon, Brainerd addressed what he called the "principle of spiritual life." When compared with the law, Brainerd argued, this principle was "engag'd to free the soul from the power of indwelling sin." Thus, unlike the law,

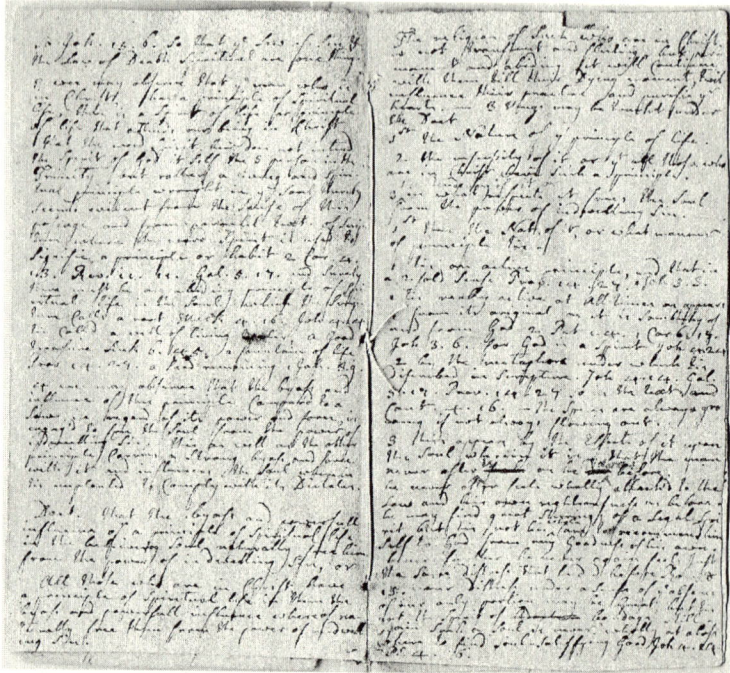

A page from David Brainerd's licensing sermon, 1742. Used by permission of the Yale Divinity School Library.

the principle of spiritual life, which was present in a believer, freed him or her from sin. For Brainerd, while this principle was "forceable," "strong and powerful," it did not "offer violence to any man's understanding or will." Rather, it "captivate[d] the whole soul and so gain[ed] its consent or sweetly constrain[ed] that man to be governed by its dictates." It altered the character of Christians so that of the "carnally-minded it makes men spiritually-minded: of proud it makes men humble: it changes the Lyon into a Lamb." Furthermore, the true faith that flows from this spiritual principle is a "living faith" that "works by love" and "purifies the heart." In fact, this living faith was so dynamic that it caused one to "fulfill the Great Commission." In sum, for Brainerd, this principle was a "spirit of great comfort," rather than condemnation, and was a sign that a believer was "concurring with the influence of the divine spirit."[141] Brainerd's sermon, then, was a celebration of the new life that was available to a believer. This new life was bestowed by a benevolent God and led the recipient to want to live a godly life based on a desire to be close to God rather than a fear of punishment. This was the sermon of a man who understood the role of the compassion and love of God in salvation.

That Brainerd would pass his examination was probably never in doubt. The meeting was moderated by Samuel Cooke, and Brainerd's friends John Graham and Joseph Bellamy were both present as was his teacher Jedidiah Mills. Their formal examination found:

> [Brainerd is] a person of such natural and acquired abilities of such orthodoxy in the Faith & hopefull experimentall acquaintance with the Lord Jesus Christ; that we judge him worthy to be improved in the Gospel Ministry, & as such, commending him & his Labours to the Grace & Blessing of God, we recommend him to any people among whom God in his Providence may call him to labour.[142]

The problem was that, in July 1742, God still didn't appear to be calling him to labor anywhere in particular, although there were many opportunities to preach and otherwise be involved in the work of ministry. Right around the time of his licensing, he had moved to Joseph Bellamy's house in Bethlehem, where he functioned as a sort of unofficial second minister. Although, at times, Brainerd preached when Bellamy was at home, he most often preached at Bethlehem when Bellamy, who was in fairly heavy demand as a revival preacher, ministered in other churches. However, there can also be no doubt that the association had simply been waiting for Brainerd to obtain his license before releasing him to something of an itinerant ministry. The day after his successful examination, he rode to Southbury, where he preached with "Power to get hold of the Hearts of the People." That week, he rode to Kent, where his audience included a number of Indians, and once again "spake with power." Over the next few months, he spent a significant amount of time preaching in various parts of the colony, including Simsbury and West Suffield, although the list may well be longer.[143]

Despite his being able to function, at least marginally, within the boundaries of the anti-itinerancy law, it is also clear that Brainerd could not, or would not, abandon the ministry he had developed during his Yale days, as he continued to make regular visits to New Haven. In fact, he had gone there twice before he was licensed although we don't know with whom he met. He may have visited John Cleaveland and other Yale students, but Edwards noted that the visits to New Haven included times of "joining in prayer," which makes it likely that he was meeting with the separatists at New Haven and was participating in and probably preaching at informal services being held in private homes. One of his prelicensing visits came only days after Joseph Bellamy and three other ministers officially organized the separatists as an independent church.[144]

His first visit to New Haven after being licensed was toward the end of August 1742 for about ten days. Although things had cooled off in the town a little since the halcyon days, ecclesiastical affairs continued to be in a state of turmoil. Although the county court allowed the separatists to hold worship services in private residences, the anti-itinerancy law prohibited ministers from preaching at these separate meetings. When Brainerd arrived in August, he visited a number of friends in and around the town where he spent time in "Family-Prayer" or "pray'd privately with a dear Christian Friend or Two." On his last night in New Haven, he "sung and pray'd with a Number of Christians." While this sounds relatively innocent, events which took place when he returned to New Haven a week later give the lie to this sanitized description.[145] On that subsequent trip, he was compelled to stay with someone who lived "at a distance from the Town," as he had learned that "they only waited for an Opportunity to apprehend me for Preaching at *New-Haven* lately." It becomes obvious that, in August, when he had "sung and pray'd," he had actually been conducting a service for the separatists, not only violating the anti-itinerancy law, but simultaneously twisting his thumb in the eyes of Clap and the Yale administration. Furthermore, upon learning of the plan for his arrest, rather than leaving town, he ended up spending another ten days in the area, going at least once "very privately into Town" where he met with a number of friends.[146]

Whatever sense he had of the "disgrace" that he was under regarding his expulsion, it clearly did not extend to obeying the law when it clashed with his own views on the necessity of itinerant preaching. He avoided New Haven for two months as he continued to preach at Bethlehem and a number of other towns, but was back in mid-November. By then, the mood of some supporters of the revival had turned decidedly pessimistic. John Maltby, stepson of pro-revival itinerant Eleazar Wheelock and son of Wheelock's wife, Sarah (the widow of Captain William Maltby), lamented that he had gone "without Preaching 2 or 3 months" and that "the opposers Rise and the Children of God sink." As he put it, "this lital flock of Christ has no Pastor to lead and guide them." The same day he wrote this, Maltby had seen Brainerd and Samuel Buell, who was also in town.[147] Brainerd's relationship to the "lital flock" at New Haven epitomizes the two worlds he was seeking to reconcile. On the one hand, he could not abandon these saints, so desperately in need of a pastor, who repeatedly welcomed him. On the other, he would not force a confrontation with the establishment as Davenport, Croswell, or Samuel Finley would have.

But the day after meeting with Maltby, a new option was finally opened to Brainerd, when he received a letter from Ebenezer Pemberton, pastor of the First Presbyterian Church in New York, asking him to come to New York to "consult about Indian affairs in those parts; and to meet certain gentlemen there that were intrusted with those affairs." Not surprisingly, on receipt of the Pemberton letter, Brainerd's "mind was instantly seized with great concern," and he retired to pray with some friends, then rode to Ripton to speak with Jedidiah Mills, before setting out for New York the following day.[148]

Peacemaker

The men with whom Brainerd met in November 1742 were the Correspondent Committee of the Society in Scotland for Propagating Christian Knowledge (SSPCK), which had operated irregularly in the colonies since 1731.[149] Based in Edinburgh, the society conducted its American affairs by appointing local committees which were empowered to recruit local ministers to fill missionary posts.[150] Pemberton, along with Jonathan Dickinson, had first written to the SSPCK in 1738, asking it to consider supporting one or two men who could serve as missionaries to the Indians as well as to new European settlers, who were "almost in a state of heathenism." The SSPCK had responded favorably to this request and authorized Pemberton and Dickinson to commission correspondents in New York to oversee the planned work. In October 1740, the two men had formed their first committee, whose numbers also included Aaron Burr and Gilbert Tennent. Why and how the SSPCK committee in New York had settled on Brainerd as a potential candidate is unknown. Pemberton and Dickinson were probably the key figures. Pemberton, of course, had spoken at Yale in that tumultuous spring of 1741, while Dickinson had traveled to Connecticut and probably knew of Brainerd's situation from discussions with other ministers in the colony.[151]

Brainerd arrived in New York "still much concerned about the importance of my business; put up many earnest requests to God for his help and direction." Like many visitors to Gotham before and since, he was "confused with the noise and tumult of the city." The following day, November 25, 1742, he was examined by the committee, a process which made him "sensible of my great ignorance and unfitness for public service." The examiners, he believed, were "deceived in me" and would be miserably disappointed "if they knew my inside."[152] The committee did not agree with Brainerd's self-assessment. On December 8, Pemberton wrote to the SSPCK to inform it that the committee had, "at last, found a young candidate" who gave them "an encouraging prospect, that he will engage in the work with zeal and fidelity." The committee decided to send Brainerd, early the next spring, "among the Indians that are settled upon the banks of the rivers Delaware and Susquehanna" and also decided "to send an interpreter with him."[153] At the SSPCK general meeting in March 1743, the meeting accepted the recommendation of the committee to employ Brainerd and to allow up to £20 per year for an interpreter.[154]

Immediately following his examination, Brainerd returned to Connecticut. Not all of his stops are known, but they did include Haddam, where he stayed for a number of days, and Southbury, where he met with Nehemiah Greenman. Brainerd committed himself to providing financial support to enable Greenman to go to college, support which continued until Brainerd's death by which time Greenman had completed three years at Yale. By December 11, 1742, Brainerd was back at Joseph Bellamy's house in Bethlehem, and he preached twice the following day. Over the next few weeks, he visited old friends throughout Connecticut and preached at Derby, Ripton, Canterbury, and Haddam. He also paid a visit to New Haven where, in a poignant scene just before he left, he "kneel'd down and pray'd with a Number of dear Christian Friends in a very retired Place in the Woods," casting himself as the fugitive shepherd in a final, dramatic farewell to his erstwhile flock.[155] The day after he left New Haven, he traveled to Branford, where it seems that he and Samuel Buell held a revival meeting in the home of the local minister, Philemon Robbins. Brainerd remembered that there was "sweet Power and Pungency: The Presence of God attended our meeting." Apparently, some of the members of the local church were less impressed. As a result of the meeting, the permission the church had given to Robbins in July of that year to "invite and call in any ordain'd Minister or licensed Preacher" was rescinded the following year, and division over the ministry of Brainerd, Buell, and James Davenport, who had also preached in Branford, continued for at least another four years.[156]

The SSPCK commissioners had not wanted him to start his work in the winter and, instead, directed him to spend a brief period as a supply minister at Easthampton on Long Island. His path to the island led him through much of the eastern portion of Connecticut, where he spent most of his time seeking to bring about reconciliation between various factions spawned by the revivals and challenging some of what he saw as false expressions of true faith. Whether Brainerd went there as a free agent or at the behest of someone else is not known. Immediately prior to the trip, he had spent some time with Solomon Williams, the pastor at Lebanon and a supporter of the more moderate aspects of the revival. Since men like Williams, Edwards, Pemberton, Dickinson, Bellamy, and Burr were in reasonably close contact with one another and since they all supported the revival in general but opposed its more radical and judgmental aspects, there may have been a consensus to send Brainerd to these troubled towns to try and heal the growing rifts and moderate the more outrageous events. Given Brainerd's expulsion and subsequent reputation, he would have had tremendous cachet with more radical revivalists.[157]

Even before he set out on this trip, he had been weighed down by distress for "the interest of Zion" because of "false appearances of religion, that do but rather breed confusion." As early as September, he had been discouraged by having to "correct some Disorders among Christians." At Southbury in December, he tried "with tenderness, to undermine false religion"; in Canterbury in January, two days before he met with Williams, he had "exhorted the people to love one another" and "not to set up their own frames as a standard to try all their brethren by."[158] No doubt, his fear that religious arguments were producing division was rooted in the establishment part of his character; he had grown up in an atmosphere of considerable unity. So, regardless of whose idea it was to have him make the trip into eastern Connecticut, he was clearly sympathetic to its goal.

On January 24, 1743, he arrived at Joseph Fish's church in Stonington. Fish was a friend of the revivals who opposed the more extreme methods of some of the radical itinerant preachers. Eventually, he would, by his own count, lose more than two-thirds of his congregation to separatist churches. Shortly before Brainerd came to town, James Davenport had preached there and drawn many away from Fish's church to a separatist meeting.[159] Two days after his arrival, Brainerd preached "to a pretty large assembly" at Fish's church, where he "insisted on humility and steadfastness in keeping God's commands, and that through humility we should prefer one another in love." He hoped that something good would come from the meeting, that the people would be freed from "Party-Zeal, and censuring one another."[160] Despite this, as Brainerd wrote to Joseph Bellamy several days later, "there was much false zeal among them," but God "helped me to love them all to death."[161]

The next day, Brainerd traveled to New London, another hotbed of revivalism and an embarrassment for the pro-revival forces. In addition to the extremism of men like James Davenport and Andrew Croswell, who had been widely supported in the town, Timothy Allen—who had been removed from his West Haven pulpit by the New Haven Consociation—had set up the New Light ministerial school known as the Shepherd's Tent in New London. These kinds of unorthodox training schools had their roots in the dissenting academies in England but enjoyed little toleration in Connecticut during the revivals. As early as October 1742, the Connecticut Assembly had declared that no one was to "erect, establish, set up, keep or maintain, any college, seminary of learning, or publick school," except those specifically "allowed by the laws of this colony." Brainerd was probably also motivated by personal reasons to go to New London: his brother John had dropped out of Yale and had begun attending classes at the Shepherd's Tent. Right around the time of David's visit, John left New London, humbled himself before Yale's administration, and was readmitted. Whether David's visit encouraged John to leave New London or John's decision motivated David's visit is not known, but it seems likely that the two events were connected.[162]

Brainerd's impression of the situation at New London was that it was even worse than that at Stonington. He found "some fallen into some extravagances, too much carried away with a false zeal and bitterness." He spent the evening talking with some of these people on issues of conduct but "did not agree with them."[163] Brainerd's efforts had no appreciable impact on the goings-on in New London. A month after his visit, Timothy Allen informed Eleazar Wheelock, the pastor at Lebanon Crank (the second parish of Lebanon), that, for the previous two weeks, there had been a "sweet season also in the school" and the number of students was now at fourteen. However, contrary to Allen's expectations, the Tent had less than a month of life left. A week after he wrote to Wheelock, Allen joined James Davenport and the students of the Tent in the notorious book burning and clothing bonfire on the New London waterfront. Faced with increasing legal action and abandoned by all of the moderate pro-revivalists, the Tent folded permanently.[164]

Brainerd's journey through eastern Connecticut had not been easy for him personally. He had preached to people who had been divided by the ongoing revival activities in the region. At Stonington, there was "much false zeal among them," while in New London he found "much wild confusion—too long to mention." He believed that only "God can keep us from running into the wildest confusion." Brainerd found his own thoughts confused: at one point, he thought that "calling sinners to Christ," which had been "blest of God in the late glorious Revival of Religion," was little more than "foolishness." But then, God let him feel that he could "rend heaven down upon their heads if they would not come to God." In turn, he understood that he was "warring against wildfire," which could, in turn, cause him to "fall into an extreme."[165]

Brainerd's trip brought him face-to-face with his own past, and an exchange of letters with Joseph Bellamy opens an important window onto his thinking. Although he had moved away from his more radical Yale days and considered some more esoteric activities to be false religion, there are hints that he had not completely abandoned all of his radical opinions. The letters were shot through with emotion and passion; at times, he lamented that he felt "so hellishly vile that [I] cant but think that God will let loose mankind upon me to destroy me";

at others, there was a "dawn of divine light," so that he "could love even a close refin'd hypocrite, in the midst of all his most nautious actions." On one occasion, he seemed to invoke some kind of modest esoteric experience, describing himself as being "in the midst of an immense vacuum or empty space, void of any thing soul-satisfying."[166] We also catch his radical side when he refers to James Davenport's celebrated New London bonfire. Although Brainerd was distressed when he learned that Davenport had included the Old Testament in the works turned over to the flames, he did not express any regret over nor condemnation of the bonfire in general, unlike many other moderate pro-revivalists.[167]

Brainerd's main concern with the "false religion in sundry of those Eastern towns" was the increasing sense of polarization that radicals were imparting.[168] He had hinted at this as early as October when, preaching at West Suffield, he encountered some "Noise and Tumult in the Assembly." He attempted to "bear publick Testimony" against this with "Moderation and Mildness."[169] The implication is that what disturbed him was not so much the content of the words coming from some in the Assembly, but the disruption and disunity that resulted. His increasing concern over the polarization in the pro-revival ranks seems to have been triggered by time he spent with Samuel Buell during his trip through eastern Connecticut. One of Brainerd's fellow radicals from Yale, Buell too, by this time, was backing away from his conduct of the previous year. Following their time together, Brainerd concluded that, while his love for Buell was undiminished, "the Lord has not dealt with him just as he has with me." From this, Brainerd wondered whether he and Bellamy "hant been too dogmatical with regard to our own frames and feelings." He did not believe, necessarily, that all that he and Bellamy had done was wrong, but he was concerned that they had "set [their beliefs] up as standards," by which they could "try others." He had come to see "more and more that God dont deal with all his children as with me."[170]

While Brainerd was concerned with some manifestations of the radicals, he was at least equally concerned with something that was at the heart of his establishment upbringing: disorder and confusion. And it also seems that he believed that much disorder sprang from efforts—from any direction—to impose a single way of doing things. Even in commenting on his fear of antinomianism, he counseled Bellamy to be "very cautious in thinking and treating with other[s] that don't feel as we do." Since each person's "frames of feelings alter & vary almost every day," they should, instead, "put on utmost tenderness, love, meekness, humility, & candor & love our enemies to death, for that's a weapon they can't withstand & let us love all that don't think as we do even our enemies, so we shall be the children of our Father." While Brainerd recognized antinomianism as error, he sought to confront it in such a way so as to not cause division and strife. But just as Brainerd was counseling Bellamy not to apply their standards to everyone, it seems reasonable to assume that he did not wish others to apply their standards to him. As he crossed over to Long Island, he was still seeking a way in which he could reconcile the stability of his establishment background with the spontaneity and experiential nature of the religion which had first come alive to him in the months before his entry to Yale and which had been fanned by the revivals.[171]

2

Sojourner

Although David Brainerd had cast his lot with the SSPCK in late 1742, it took some time for him to come to grips with the new purpose in his life. One has the sense that, for the next eighteen months or so, he was a young man somewhat adrift, not entirely sure that the work he was doing was, indeed, what God had called him to. Even when he did commit himself irrevocably to working among the Indians, he still remained uncertain regarding his effectiveness and frequently worried over his "unfitness for publick Service."[1] In part, Brainerd's restlessness stemmed from his physical surroundings. For a great part of the twenty-eight months which followed his departure from Connecticut in early 1743, he operated on the periphery of the society of which he had been a part. In both New York and Pennsylvania, he was a considerable distance from the main colonial settlements. More important, he was no longer in the midst of religious happenings. While he welcomed the time he had to devote to introspection and meditation, he surely missed the fellowship with like-minded people, regular prayer meetings, and the opportunity to preach to those who understood both his language and his spiritual concerns. The clamor of revival, the cries of those seeking salvation, the singing of the saints were all signs that God was at work. They were replaced by the relative quiet of the New England backcountry, its very silence and isolation seemingly marking the absence of God at work.

Apprentice

After leaving Connecticut, Brainerd spent about a month in early 1743 as a temporary minister at the Easthampton church on Long Island. The pastor, Nathaniel

Huntting (1675–1753), had served the church since 1696 but was now in his late sixties and needed assistance in his work. Several other pro-revival ministers had preached in the town, including James Davenport and, possibly, Jedidiah Mills. Davenport had come to Easthampton from his own Long Island parish of Southold but had, apparently, spent more time attacking Huntting than helping him. It seems that part of Brainerd's mission in the town was to attempt to restore some kind of unity to the church, just as he had attempted to do in eastern Connecticut. We know nothing of Brainerd's work in the town although, as subsequent events would suggest, something of a bond formed between Brainerd and at least part of the congregation.[2]

While serving as minister at Easthampton, Brainerd also had the opportunity to observe the work of Azariah Horton (1715–1777), the only other missionary then supported by the SSPCK. Horton was officially appointed in 1741 to serve on Long Island, where he worked among the Montauk Indians until 1752.[3] This was Brainerd's first opportunity to witness missionary work, and, on several occasions, he was invited to preach to Horton's Indian congregation. On one such occasion, Horton noted that Brainerd's preaching was "attended with Power for enlivening the Children of God, and the further awakening such as were under Conviction. He spent the evening in giving them Instructions, Encouragements, Admonitions, according to their circumstances."[4] Brainerd described his own preaching during a second visit to the Indians as starting with "flatness and deadness," but after a time of prayer he "had some assistance; and I trust something of the divine presence."[5]

On March 14, 1743, Brainerd "took leave of the dear people of East Hampton," noting that his "heart grieved and mourned, and rejoiced at the same time." Brainerd traveled to New York and preached at Aaron Burr's church in Newark on March 20. The next day, he met with the SSPCK correspondents in Woodbridge, New Jersey, and discovered, once again, that his move to Pennsylvania had been put on hold. The commissioners in New York had decided not to send him to the Delaware Indians since they were "suspected of contention with the English," and instead the commissioners decided to take advantage of a new opportunity which had presented itself. As Brainerd wrote to Joseph Bellamy, "Div. providence has strangely & unexpectedly changed my course for the present." Instead of going to Pennsylvania, Brainerd was directed to a small settlement "about 18 mile northeast from Albany," where he would be part of the expanding work of John Sergeant among the Mahican Indians.[6]

Sergeant's—and Brainerd's—work was part of a growing interest in mission work in a number of the northern colonies. Although one of the ostensible goals of British colonization had been to convert the Indians to Protestantism, such efforts had rarely been sustained. In New England, mission efforts had a checkered past. John Eliot's work in the praying towns had led to several churches being gathered among Indian peoples, but the mutual distrust engendered by King Philip's War had eroded most of the limited support for mission work. More long-lasting was the work begun by the Mayhew family on Martha's Vineyard: the church established there in the 1640s endures to the present. While colonist-Indian relations on the Vineyard survived King Philip's War, and the Indian churches continued to flourish, few in New England looked to the island as a model for the rest of the region.[7]

Nonetheless, a few individuals continued to push their fellow colonists toward renewed support for Indian missions. In New England, interest was most commonly fanned by the members of the New England Company for the Propagation of the Gospel. Cotton Mather, inspired in part by accounts of pietist missionaries in India, urged that similar work be conducted among Native Americans. In Plymouth, John Cotton and his son Josiah preached in Indian settlements for almost four decades. Richard Billings worked among the Indians near Little Compton, Rhode Island, for more than twenty years beginning in 1705. Other, less successful efforts were made to establish works on the Maine frontier and among the Pequot and Mohegan peoples of Connecticut. The Anglican Society for the Propagation of the Gospel (SPG) had placed its first Indian missionary in the Mohawk community at Tiononderoge in 1704, but the work there persisted, in an on-and-off fashion, only until 1718. Farther afield, the SPG had maintained a missionary among the Yamasee Indians of South Carolina from 1702 to 1715.[8]

By the 1720s, with the Anglo-French peace established by the Treaty of Utrecht generally holding, many ministers, looking at New England's place on a larger stage, increasingly turned their attention to Indian missions. These ministers were developing the concept of a unified transatlantic Protestantism, which historian Thomas S. Kidd has identified as the "Protestant interest." It emphasized both a British consciousness and an aggressive anti-Catholicism, and leading ministers on both sides of the Atlantic identified French successes among the Indians as a major problem for the Protestant interest. Thus, while the goal of converting Indians for the good of their souls remained, added to it was the geopolitical benefit that would accrue to British colonists since converting Indians to Protestantism would deny their military strength to the Catholic French. Whether consciously or not, promoters of this idea were moving along traveled paths: almost a century earlier, the triumphant parliamentary forces had embraced the idea of using missions to achieve political loyalty following their subjugation of Wales.[9]

The concept of mission as diplomacy was captured in Solomon Stoddard's *Question: Whether God Is Not Angry with the Country for Doing So Little toward the Conversion of the Indians?* (1723). Published when Father Rale's War was ravaging parts of eastern New England, Stoddard's *Question* contained tropes that would have been familiar to those who had lived through King Philip's War: death and destruction had come upon New England because of the sins of its inhabitants. But whereas Puritans in the 1670s had identified the length of men's hair or the behavior of children as causes of God's wrath, Stoddard asserted that divine anger was being poured forth because "we have little care of the Heathen." The efforts of New Englanders paled when compared to that of German and Danish missionaries in East India, and even the "Activity of the Papists for the spreading of their Religion" should give New Englanders pause to consider their own sorry record. Stoddard evoked the commands of Christ and the love of humanity as being among the reasons to evangelize the Indians, arguing that preaching the gospel to them would be "a means to make them live more comfortably in this World." Finally, Stoddard insisted that conversion would be better than a peace treaty because if the Indians signed a treaty but stayed heathens, "they will be apt to fall in with the Papists" and would be ready to "avenge themselves by making War." In contrast, if Indians became Protestants, this would open the door to "Hopes of a Durable Peace." And this, for Stoddard, was a far better option than the one being pursued by men with a "Bloody Spirit" who "meditate nothing but utter destruction."[10]

Stoddard's essay was one of the factors that eventually prodded clergymen and mission organizations to turn their attention to Native Americans as a potentially fruitful mission field for both geopolitical and spiritual reasons. Among these organizations, the SSPCK, although a latecomer to American missions, was committed to the goals inherent within the concept of a greater Atlantic Protestantism. Founded by well-to-do lowland Scottish Protestants in 1701—the same year that the Act of Succession excluded the Catholic Stuarts from the throne—the society was determined to bring enlightenment to the highlands, that region where "the whole religious knowledge…was reduced to a few Popish legends and ceremonies" and politics consisted of a "blind, but furious, attachment to the…House of Stuart."[11]

The society's strategy was to establish schools in the remote highland parishes that would provide free instruction to local youth in such subjects as "should be thought suitable to their circumstances" as well as a healthy dose of the "Christian Reformed Religion." Essentially, the SSPCK schools, open to the children of "Papists as well as Protestants," were designed to supplement the work of the kirk by providing English-language instruction so that, the society hoped, a "little light might be diffused" to those "dreary and dark regions of their own Country." As Margaret Connell Szasz has observed, the SSPCK's definition of education was broad and its "ultimate goal was to change the worldview of the Highlanders." Closely affiliated with the Scottish kirk, the society used the kirk's connections to obtain funding and royal support. By 1732, the SSPCK, with the full support of the Church of Scotland, had established more than 100 schools in the highlands, a number which would increase to 176 by 1758.[12]

Spurred by a bequest from English dissenter Daniel Williams, in the early 1730s the society began efforts to support missionaries among the Indians of New England, under the aegis of both Governor Jonathan Belcher and one of the key advocates of transatlantic Protestantism, Benjamin Colman. Although the society eventually placed three men in New England and a fourth in Georgia in the 1730s, none of the efforts were productive and all came to an end after a few years. Following these first disappointments, the society was less willing to work with official representatives of colonial governments, but it did, however, maintain its clerical contacts with representatives in New England. Only months after learning of the dismissal of its three missionaries in the region, the society first heard of the work of John Sergeant among the Mahican Indians at Stockbridge.[13]

The work among the Stockbridge Mahicans had started in 1734 when the interests of a number of western Massachusetts clergy, political leaders in the colony, and the Mahicans themselves coincided. By the 1730s, the Mahicans had suffered through a century of European contacts. The introduction of new tools and weapons and the incorporation of market-based economics into Indian commodity exchanges had altered hunting, settlement, and trade patterns. The Mahicans suffered from the effects of alcohol, disease, war, and the loss of game. Although they retained a sense of cultural unity, the Mahicans were compelled to disperse their population through a large number of villages and settlements in western Connecticut, western Massachusetts, and eastern New York. Increasingly, many Mahicans turned to the production of goods such as brooms, mats, and canoes in order to trade with colonists for European goods and food staples. Others harvested sugar from maple trees or worked as laborers on colonial farms in order to earn enough to buy food to supplement, or supplant, the diminishing supply of game. Forced further to the margins of survival, the Mahicans also turned to land sales as a means to generate income in order to survive. The Mahicans believed that both epidemics and a decrease in game animals indicated a problem in their relationship with spiritual beings. At the same time, the increasing wealth and lower losses to disease experienced by colonists suggested that the power held by the Christian God was important. As Mahicans had done in the past when threatened by Indian neighbors, they now sought an alliance with the English.[14]

From the colonists' perspective, the work among the Mahicans combined both the religious and political aspects of the Protestant interest. It was first proposed to the New England Company in 1734 by Samuel Hopkins (1693–1755), the pastor at nearby Springfield and the uncle of David Brainerd's Yale colleague. In a series of meetings in the spring and summer of 1734 among several local ministers and the Mahicans, the Indians agreed to receive an English missionary. It seems likely that the Mahicans were further motivated by the prospects of receiving instruction in reading and writing, which would make it possible for them to read and understand the treaties and land sale documents that had affected them so profoundly. Having heard that Yale tutor John Sergeant (1710–1749) was more interested in working among Indians than being called to a regular parish, Hopkins and Nehemiah Bull, the pastor at Westfield, traveled to New Haven to meet with him. There, they presented to Sergeant a "very encouraging Account of the good Inclination of those *Indians*, and of their Desire to be instructed in the Principles of the *Christian Religion*." Yale agreed to release Sergeant for about three months in order for him to begin mission work. He would then return to Yale to see his current crop of students through to the end of their studies, then return to the Mahicans full time. While Sergeant realized that he would "lose a great many agreable Amusements," he insisted, among other things, that since "so much Pains [were] taken by those of the *Romish* Church" to convert Native Americans, Protestants should seek to emulate their efforts.[15]

Sergeant arrived in western Massachusetts in early October 1734 and seemed to quickly develop a rapport with many of the Mahicans. Sergeant preached, prayed, and taught reading through an interpreter, while the Mahicans built a meeting hall, "both to meet in on the *Sabbath*, and to keep the *School* in." Sergeant proved to be an adept preacher, while Timothy Woodbridge, hired as the schoolmaster, was a favorite among the Indians; the children in particular were "fond of him," and the mission became a magnet for both Mahicans and other Indians who lived in the region. In August 1735, with the full approval of the Stockbridge Mahicans, Sergeant was ordained as their minister. In a classic representation of the Protestant interest, the ordination was subsumed within a treaty negotiation at Deerfield involving Governor Jonathan Belcher, local elite leader Colonel John Stoddard (son of Solomon), and the Caughnawagas, a group of Catholic Mohawks. In addition to the ordination, the four-day conference involved agreements of mutual support, pledges of allegiance among the groups involved, and treaty signings. As Sergeant noted in his journal, "His *Excellency's* Treatment of our *Indians* was exceeding grateful to them, and they have conceiv'd the highest Opinion of the *Governor*." Belcher met with the Indians again the following year and, as a result, urged the Massachusetts Assembly to appropriate more funds in order to help construct the school building and purchase farming equipment.[16]

The Mahicans continued to respond to Sergeant's preaching, and the missionary found himself called on to preach in a number of the scattered Mahican settlements, which made it increasingly difficult to devote sufficient time to the central work at Stockbridge. Sergeant first preached at Kaunaumeek in September 1737. Although only a small group lived there, they invited other Indians from nearby, who came to hear the minister. Sergeant spoke there several times over the next six months, and a number of Kaunaumeek residents came to Stockbridge to hear Sergeant and others preach. However, the increasing demands on Sergeant's time at Stockbridge meant that, by 1743, there was a need for at least one additional worker to support the efforts at Kaunaumeek.[17]

Although the SSPCK admired Sergeant's efforts, the terms by which they had obtained the funds to support American missionaries precluded funding an already established missionary.[18] Nothing prevented them, however, from adding new missionaries to an existing work conducted by another mission agency. In fact, there was often a close relation between the SSPCK and the New England Company; in 1740, for example, John Sergeant had been appointed a member of the SSPCK committee which was developing a plan for new missionaries in Pennsylvania and New York. As Ebenezer Pemberton informed the SSPCK, the correspondents had learned that the Indians at Kaunaumeek were "desirous of having a missionary sent [to] them." With Brainerd's venture to Pennsylvania on hold, the New York correspondents saw this as "too favourable an opportunity to be neglected" and dispatched him to western New England. On March 31, he arrived at Sergeant's house in Stockbridge, and the next day he made the eighteen-mile trip to his first solo missionary assignment at Kaunaumeek, just across the border in New York.[19]

Brainerd's shock upon arriving at Kaunaumeek, located about halfway between Albany and Stockbridge, is almost palpable in his diary. Echoing Sergeant's initial judgment that the region was "a most doleful Wilderness,"

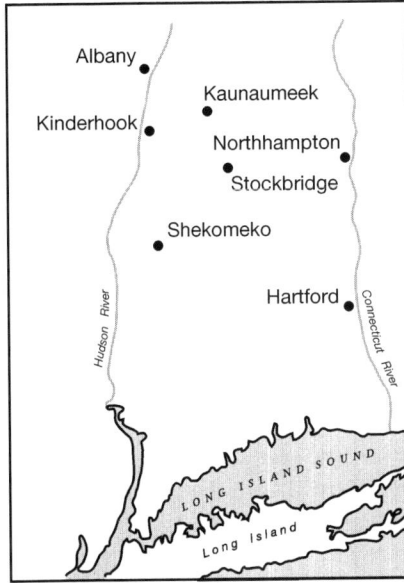

Western New England and eastern New York. Map by Marvin J. Barton; adapted from Patrick Frazier, *The Mohicans of Stockbridge* (University of Nebraska Press) frontispiece.

Brainerd described it as "sufficiently lonesome, and unpleasant" and a "lonesome desert." Brainerd was based twenty miles from the closest English village and six or seven miles from the nearest Dutch. He initially lived with a family of Scots highlanders who had settled in the area two years previously. Only the husband spoke fluent English. Brainerd, writing to his brother John, observed that his diet consisted "mostly of hasty-pudding, boil'd corn, and bread." His bed was "a little heap of straw, laid upon some board, a little way from the ground." Further adding to his difficulties was that he lived about a mile and a half from the Indians, a distance he walked most days.[20]

Perhaps not surprisingly, Brainerd's first two months at Kaunaumeek were a time of struggle and adaptation, made worse by an overwhelming sense of loneliness. He had spent much of the previous year ministering in churches before generally welcoming congregations, which would respond to his preaching and which would, in all likelihood, engage in activities such as the singing of hymns and public prayer. Even when he traveled alone, he could be assured that almost every night would include the companionship of pastors and friends. In contrast, Kaunaumeek must have seemed to be the end of the earth: his task was the conversion of a small group of Indians, and there seemed little potential that this would grow into a large congregation or any kind of more dynamic work. Adding to Brainerd's depression was the lack of, in his mind, Christian company. When he wrote to John, he noted how much he longed to see his brother and complained twice of the lack of English company (the Scots and the Dutch, apparently, did not suffice). In his diary, he noted that what he most missed was a "fellow Christian to whom I might unbosom myself, and lay open my spiritual sorrows." In addition, the work did not provide the same degree of autonomy he had enjoyed in the previous months. Although he was on his own at Kaunaumeek, this was still Sergeant's mission, and Brainerd was, in many ways, Sergeant's apprentice. There is also some evidence that Sergeant was perhaps less demanding than Brainerd when it came to evidence of thorough conversion and may have taken a dim view of the exuberant nature of the revivals.[21]

Brainerd was also concerned over his initial lack of success in converting the Indians. Although, as he wrote to John, they "seem[ed] generally kind" and were "mostly very attentive to my instructions," there was "little of the special workings of the divine spirit," which gave Brainerd "many a heart-sinking hour."[22] Since many revival preachers had consistently emphasized that a common reason for the lack of a work of God was the spiritual condition of the preacher, Brainerd may well have believed that his lack of success was at least partly attributable to his own personal failings. In light of this, it is not surprising that Brainerd worried that he was "altogether unequal to [the] work," and he feared he would never "have any success among the Indians."[23] He began to look inside himself for those failings and shortcomings which, he believed, were keeping God from working through him. In addition to the regular whipping boys of pride and selfishness, he also recognized what he described as "party-spirit" or "party-zeal," an attitude which caused division within the church. No doubt, his experiences in New London and Stonington several months earlier had brought this particular sin into sharp focus. In his diary, he noted that this divisiveness had arisen in "time past, when I attempted to promote the cause of God." He believed that "poor souls stumbled over it into everlasting destruction." In response, he spent much of his early weeks at Kaunaumeek praying, repenting, and asking God to "deliver me from my blood-guiltiness."[24]

Despite his struggles, Brainerd plunged into his work with the Indians. The SSPCK expected its missionaries to instruct the Indians in the "principles of the Christian reformed Protestant religion." In order to accomplish this, men such as Brainerd were to "preach and catechize" on a regular basis.[25] Since Brainerd initially lived about a mile and a half from the Indian village, he did not spend every day with the Indians, instead visiting with them and preaching several days a week. The rest of the time, he was engaged in personal prayer, frequent fasting, and study. Brainerd would later note that the Indians, because of Sergeant's earlier work, were "in some good degree, prepared to entertain the truths of Christianity." He was also fortunate to have the services of an interpreter, John Wauwaumpequunnaunt, an Indian who had been taught by both John Sergeant and Stephen Williams, the pastor at Longmeadow, Massachusetts. Although Brainerd himself was often wracked by a sense of guilt over his own sin, in preaching to the Indians he decided to emphasize both the "sinfulness and misery of the estate they were naturally in" and "the fulness, alsufficiency, and freeness" of redemption.[26]

As time went by, he was also, on occasion, asked to preach to European settlers in the area. However, as he learned more about these colonists, their presence was often problematic to him. He was continually afraid that the Indians would be "prejudic'd against Christianity, and their Minds imbitter'd against me" because of the "Insinuations of some who (although they are call'd Christians) seem to have no concern for Christ's kingdom."[27] John Sergeant had targeted the Dutch in particular, noting as early as 1734 that local traders made a "vast Profit by selling them Rum, and making bargains with them when they are drunk." For this reason, Sergeant believed, the Dutch had been "very industrious to discourage the *Indians* from being *Christians*."[28] Brainerd, too, singled out the Dutch as people who had "no regard to the souls of the poor Indians" and who were trying to "drive them off" their land. Indeed, Brainerd believed that Dutch traders were actively working against his efforts, hoping that the Indians "should remain Heathens, that [the settlers] may with the more ease, cheat, and so enrich themselves." As Brainerd later recalled, his fear of European efforts to undermine his work was "much more pressing to me, than all the difficulties that attended the circumstances of my living."[29]

At the end of May, Brainerd journeyed to New Jersey to meet with the SSPCK correspondents. Along the way, it is likely that he paid a visit to the Indian-Moravian settlement at Shekomeko. Christian Heinrich Rauch had been the first Moravian to arrive in Shekomeko when he made the journey there from New York in 1740. After initially facing determined opposition, Rauch won an audience among some of the people of Shekomeko and counted his first converts in late 1741. Gradually, a small but vibrant community developed both in Shekomeko and in nearby Pachgatgoch. In March 1743, Joseph Bellamy wrote to Brainerd about a lengthy discussion he had had with a Moravian preacher named John Mae. Bellamy feared that Mae was "not as sound in his principles" since he seemed to believe in "universal redemption, free will" and he "seemed to be more taken with the blood & wounds of Christ than with Christ himself." Nonetheless, Bellamy hoped that Mae was a Christian and concluded by declaring, "the Moravians puzzle me more than any other people I ever met with."[30] The letter from Bellamy may have sparked Brainerd's curiosity about a group which was still fairly new to the colonies. In June, Moravian missionary Heinrich Senseman wrote to a friend about an "English minister" who, having heard much about the Moravians, had come to visit Shekomeko. Although Senseman did not mention the man's name, he noted that the minister was of the Church of Scotland and that he was preaching in a "savage place, called Kaunaumeek," making it all but certain that it was Brainerd who had come calling. According to Senseman, the visitor had come to visit some of the Christian Indians living with the Moravians since, he claimed, many of them had "been made to believe by him." But, Senseman wrote, the Indians "didn't make much of him, however, and he went only into a few houses."[31]

The Indians whom Brainerd wished to visit were not any of those from Kaunaumeek, to whom he had only been preaching for two months, but those to whom he had preached near Kent in August 1742 and again on his way to

Kaunaumeek in March 1743. Rather than being "made to believe" by Brainerd, it seems more likely that Brainerd meant that they had been awakened to their spiritual condition by him—a distinction that may well have been lost in translation. One of the people awakened by Brainerd was a young Indian woman named Rachel who, after being baptized by the Moravians, married one of their number, a Prussian immigrant named Christian Frederick Post. Despite the somewhat dismissive tone of Senseman's letter, Brainerd's visit must have generated some interest on the part of the Moravians. Two months later, at least one and probably more Moravians visited Brainerd at Kaunaumeek, and he invited them to spend the night. As he had in eastern Connecticut, Brainerd was willing to offer hospitality to people with whose theology he may have disagreed. He apparently enjoyed their companionship, and after they departed in the morning, he was "enabled to raise my soul to [God] with desire and delight."[32]

Once Brainerd arrived in New Jersey, his discussions with the SSPCK correspondents centered on working out the details of the school which was to be set up at Kaunaumeek. As in the Scottish highlands, missionaries were instructed to "keep a school for teaching the foresaid heathens to read the holy Scriptures of the Old and New Testament, and other good and pious books, writing, and arithmetick, and to understand and speak the English language and to direct them how to pray, and to carry as becometh the gospel."[33] Of course, the idea of education as a way to "civilize" the Indians went back to the earliest days of English colonization and had been attempted in almost all of the colonies by a number of different civil and religious groups. Even the colony of Connecticut, which had longed dragged its feet on Indian missions, had funded four Indian schools between 1725 and 1735; during part of this time, the father of the young David Brainerd had been serving in the Assembly.[34]

In Massachusetts, John Sergeant, too, was a strong advocate of placing schools among the Indians. In 1743, he had forcefully proposed education for Indian children as a way to change the Indians' "whole Habit of thinking and acting; and raise them, as far as possible, into the Condition of a civil industrious and polish'd People; while at the same Time the Principles of Vertue and Piety shall be carefully instilled into their Minds."[35] The school at Kaunaumeek began operations in June 1743 with John Wauwaumpequunnaunt, at Brainerd's request, serving as schoolmaster. He may have been one of the first, if not the first, Indian officially on the payroll of a British mission society. The New York correspondents had approved a salary of £24 per annum, an amount that was agreed to by the SSPCK when news of it reached them. Eventually, the society would pay Wauwaumpequunnaunt £13.16 for about four months of service. Brainerd's own records indicate that he was confident enough in the young man's ability to leave the day-to-day running of the school in the hands of his interpreter, although he would visit often so as to "give the Children and young People some proper instructions, and serious exhortations suited to their age."[36]

In July, Brainerd also decided to resolve the problems that were created by living so far from the Indian village. In particular, having to journey on foot meant he could not be with the Indians "in the evening and morning, which were usually the best hours to find them at home." He thus relocated to the Indians' village where, for about a month, he "lived with them in one of their wigwams" before he "built me a small house, where I spent the remainder of that year intirely alone." Moving into his own home also meant that he could "at any hour of the day lay aside my studies and spend time in lifting up my soul to God for spiritual blessings." During this time, with the assistance of his translator, he also wrote prayers and psalms in the Indian language. This meant he could "pray with [the Indians] in their own tongue" and "sing in the worship of God" in their own language. Brainerd's emphasis on singing was another practice of the revivals which he applied to his mission work. Although not uncommon before the 1740s, public singing became one of the defining activities of the revivalists.[37]

In public preaching, he found "much more freedom" and also recorded that "God was pleased to give me some assistance." He became more ambitious in his teaching goals and, since the Indians had "gained some acquaintance with many of the Truths of Christianity," he began to systematically teach them "an historical account of God's dealings with his ancient professing people, the Jews," followed by an account of the life of Jesus. Having thus sought, as he put it, to "prepare the Way," he turned to almost nightly explanations of the book of Matthew, in order to offer more specific insight into salvation. On the evenings he did not preach to the Indians, he traveled to Stockbridge to "learn the Indian language with the Rev. Mr. Sergeant." He also had to spend a significant amount of time in everyday tasks, spending most of one day, at least, trying to "procure something to keep my Horse on in the winter." And providing for himself was also proving difficult since he was "forced to go or send ten or fifteen Miles for all the Bread I eat." And even then, "sometimes 'tis mouldy and soure, before I eat it." Fortunately, on at least one occasion, he had some "Indian Meal, of which I made little Cakes, and fried them."[38]

At the end of August, he set out for New York, for reasons which are not noted in the text. On the way back from New York, he visited friends and preached in various churches. He continued to focus on trying to heal divisions within the churches, basing his efforts on appeals to members of congregations to exhibit Christian character toward each other. At Stanwich, he tried to "establish Holiness, Humility, Meekness etc., as the Essence of true Religion" as well as to "moderate some noisy sort of Persons, that appeared to me to be acted by unseen spiritual Pride," while at Horse-Neck, he identified signs of false religion, including "Wild-fire Party-Zeal, spiritual Pride." As he had implied in his letter earlier in the year to Joseph Bellamy, he did not try to find a single theology that was acceptable to everyone but sought to heal division, which he believed came from a "confident, dogmatical Spirit" and sprang from "Ignorance of the Heart."[39]

After spending almost two weeks preaching through parts of Connecticut, he arrived in New Haven in time for commencement—the graduation of the class of which he should have been a part. He apparently attended the ceremony, visited with friends, and met with a number of ministers while in town. He also offered a written apology to the college administration for his behavior more than two years earlier. It was part of a coordinated effort, involving a number of sympathetic ministers, to have Yale grant him his degree but, as with earlier efforts, it too failed. After spending almost a week in Bethlehem laid low by illness, he returned to Kaunaumeek in early October.[40]

Brainerd continued at Kaunaumeek from October 1743 to March 1744. He did continue to hold private conversations with the Indians from time to time as well as preach to them most Sundays, but they do not figure as prominently in his accounts as they had in previous months. In part, this is due to the hand of Jonathan Edwards. Of the approximately five months between Brainerd's return from New Haven and his departure from Kaunaumeek, Edwards summarized about half of the period. However, Brainerd was also desperately ill for a great deal of this period—over the five months, he was virtually immobilized by illness for at least four weeks. As he wrote to his brother John at the end of December, he had spent "most of the Fall and Winter hitherto in a very weak State of Body."[41] He also continued to travel a great deal on various errands, such as the day he rode to Kinderhook and back (about forty miles round trip), where he "performed some business."[42] He visited Samuel Hopkins at Housatonnic at least twice—the first time to be present at Hopkins's ordination. Since there is nothing to indicate an unwillingness on Brainerd's part to minister to the Indians, it seems likely either that translators were not regularly available or that many of the Kaunaumeek Indians had dispersed further during the winter as was traditional.[43]

What is clear from the scattered diary entries of this period is that he was continuing to conduct something of an itinerant ministry in the region, and once again, he did not seem to shy away from working among more radical pro-revival groups. Whereas the previous year he had used Bethlehem as his home base, now it was Kaunaumeek. In mid-January 1744, he traveled to Salisbury, Connecticut, where he preached and may have also administered communion. The town had been settled only two years earlier, and its congregation had existed essentially as a separatist group from that time. When the members installed Jonathan Lee as pastor later in 1744, all of the ministers who participated were expelled by the New Haven Association. Later in the month, Brainerd rode to Canaan, New York, where he was "unexpectedly visited by a considerable Number of people." In the course of his conversation with them, he particularly emphasized the "Difference between a regular and irregular *Self-love.*" The people at Canaan were so few and scattered that a church was not formally organized until 1770, after which it quickly took on a Baptist confession.[44] Assuming that neither of these groups had moderated their attitudes toward the revival, it would seem that, once again, Brainerd's fundamental concern was not with particular expressions of Christianity but with the divisiveness that often resulted. If the people were of the same mind, he was far more accommodating to a range of views than were ministers such as Edwards, Bellamy, Hopkins, or perhaps even Gilbert Tennent.

By March, according to Edwards, Brainerd had decided that since the Kaunaumeek Indians were "but few in number," he "might now do more service for Christ among the Indians elsewhere" and set out for New Jersey to seek permission from the SSPCK commissioners to commence the work in

Pennsylvania.[45] While there is no reason to doubt this as a primary motivation, there were likely other factors at work. Since there was little visible evidence of a work of God among his audience (although they did seem somewhat responsive to his preaching), he probably took this as a sign that this was not the place where God wanted him to minister. Again, there is restlessness behind the diary entries—a man on a mission from God who is not quite certain where that mission is supposed to be taking place. In addition, if we assume that Brainerd was still engaging in more demonstrative preaching, there may have been some unease between him and Sergeant, who was probably not a supporter of some of the more extreme methods of the revival.[46] Finally, as King George's War came closer to this part of New England, Brainerd may have decided that the safety of his charges, and himself, might be served by moving. Residents of Kaunaumeek had been advised as early as October 1743 that, in view of the "utmost Danger of a Rupture with France," they should take "prudent measures for [their] safety."[47] Taken together, all these factors probably played a role in,Brainerd deciding to move to Pennsylvania. He thus informed the Indians that he would probably leave them in the near future and advised them to relocate to Stockbridge, where land had been set aside for them and they could come under Sergeant's ministry. Although Brainerd thought they were "very sorrowful" on hearing this news, he spent some time reasoning with them, until they seemed "disposed to comply with" his advice. He then set off for New Jersey to meet with the SSPCK commissioners.[48]

Alternatives

Since David Brainerd never explained why he chose to spend most of his adult life among Native Americans, historians, quite reasonably, have not usually addressed his motivation directly, although a tone of resignation seems to lie behind most descriptions—that is, Brainerd became a missionary because there were no other realistic options. Actually, Brainerd did not make his decision to work among the Indians final until this March 1744 trip to New Jersey when it was only one of several options available to him. The first option had been presented to him six months earlier during commencement week at Yale and was the culmination of a process that seems to have begun in early 1743. In May 1743, Aaron Burr wrote to Brainerd advising him that he (Burr) would "write to Rect & Mr. W—lsey" and that Burr "doubt[ed] not of your having a degree; but whether in this class, is a question."[49] The implication is that Burr had already been in discussion with someone at Yale (although, from the phrasing, probably neither Clap nor Whittelsey) and had won unofficial support for Brainerd's reinstatement. However, at the same time that some members of Yale's board were holding out hope for a reconciliation, Brainerd, it seems, changed the terms of the debate. Rather than requesting readmittance to Yale, Brainerd wanted the college to simply grant him a degree when the rest of his class graduated, presumably based on the training he had done with Jedidiah Mills and his subsequent work as a preacher and missionary. As Burr had pointed out to him, this seemed unlikely.

When Brainerd journeyed to New York in early June 1743 to discuss the appointment of a schoolmaster at Kaunaumeek, he spent a night at Burr's house in Newark where, no doubt, Yale was one of the topics of conversation. In his May letter, Burr had insisted that commencement in the fall "must be the time for your affair to be issued when the trustees are all together." Burr probably hoped that the trustees who already supported the petition to grant Brainerd his degree, or to reinstate him, could convince the rest of the trustees when they were together, but he seems to have felt that there was less chance of success if the trustees were approached individually.[50] Despite Burr's advice in his May letter, on Brainerd's way back to Kaunaumeek from the trip to Newark in early June 1743, he spent a week in New Haven, where, according to Jonathan Edwards, "he attempted a Reconciliation with the Authority of the *College*." We have no way of knowing whether Burr and Brainerd agreed on this approach during the evening they were together, or whether Brainerd went against Burr's advice. The tone of Edwards's comments suggests that Brainerd met privately with Clap, who was still clearly the key person. Perhaps Brainerd hoped that a personal appeal would evoke a degree of mercy from the rector. If so, he was once again disappointed.[51]

About a month later, in early July 1743, Brainerd again traveled to New Haven. Edwards claimed that this was because he was "so much exercised" with regard to his "past Errors and misguided Zeal at *College*." Edwards attempted to paint a picture of a penitent sinner offering repentance to those he had wronged and seeking their forgiveness. Once again, however, his efforts were "still in vain." Furthermore, it is unlikely that Brainerd was as conciliatory as Edwards attempted to paint him. In a diary fragment that Edwards did not include in his account, Brainerd noted that he was "still occupied with some business depending on certain grandees for performance. Alas! how much men may lord and tyrannize over their fellow countrymen.... Like the Holy Court of Inquisition, when they put a poor innocent to the rack, they tell him that what they do is all for the benefit of his soul!"[52] Clearly, this confrontation at Yale had involved more than a rejected apology. Given that, at this time, Brainerd was highly exercised over the issues of division and party zeal, it seems likely that he had apologized for causing division—but not for his other actions—and then asked the college to grant him his degree at the commencement which was to take place two months later.

These failures led, then, to a coordinated effort, involving a number of ministers including Edwards and Aaron Burr, at the time of the September 1743 commencement, to bring about a favorable—for Brainerd—resolution to the situation. The day after commencement, Brainerd presented a written apology to Clap and the trustees that was, he claimed, "for Substance the same that I had freely offered to the *Rector* before." He first acknowledged his criticism of Whittelsey, declaring he had "no right to make thus free with his character" and acknowledging that he had "long since been convinced of the falseness of those apprehensions." He then responded to an allegation from an unnamed person that he had wished Clap would "drop down dead for fining the scholars that followed Mr. Tennent." Brainerd declared that he could not remember saying this and, instead, offered a blanket condemnation of all such statements. Finally, he apologized for "going once to the separate meeting in New-Haven…tho' the rector had refused to give me leave." Aaron Burr took the lead among Brainerd's supporters in making "Earnest Application" that Brainerd "might have his Degree then given him." Although Brainerd was not sure whether he would be readmitted to the college or not, he noted that he could "cheerfully forego [*sic*]" what he believed to be his right.[53]

What was perhaps most surprising about this entire process was that it succeeded—in Edwards's words, the college was "willing to admit him again." But, at this moment of apparent triumph, Brainerd turned down the opportunity. The problem was that Yale would not award his degree " 'till he should have remain'd there, at least a Twelve-Month." This, Brainerd would not agree to since, according to Edwards, it was "contrary to what the [SSPCK] Correspondents" wanted.[54] It was not Yale, but Brainerd who prevented the reconciliation. Edwards's statement that the requirement of returning to New Haven for a year was not in accord with the desires of the SSPCK is less than wholly plausible. True, Burr, an SSPCK commissioner, had asked that the degree be granted immediately, but he had also warned Brainerd several months earlier that this was questionable. This should not have surprised any of the parties involved. Although some students were graduated in less than four years, Brainerd had completed only two years before his expulsion, so to require him to take another year of classes, especially given the circumstances of his leaving, must have seemed a reasonable compromise.

If it was so important—to Brainerd, to Burr, to the SSPCK—that Brainerd get his degree, why not go back to college for a year (or nine months, really)? It seems that the decision to turn down the offer was Brainerd's alone and that it was for reasons other than those that Edwards presented. More likely, Brainerd had no interest in returning to the place which, he would write several years later, had "proved so hurtful to my spiritual interest."[55] Yale, for Brainerd, had not been a place where he had found God. In contrast, it had hampered him spiritually, frustrated him, and finally driven him away. He had no interest in returning to college, he simply wanted its stamp of approval. When that was denied, the issue was dead and buried for him.[56]

Of course, his determination to win his degree from Yale does not necessarily mean that he was considering options other than the mission field, but events which took place on his way to New Jersey in the spring of 1744 do. Remarkably, in the space of three days while on his way to New Jersey to meet with the SSPCK commissioners, he was met by not one, but two messengers bearing offers from churches to settle, or to come on trial, as pastor. The first came from Easthampton while the other came from Millington, the second parish in East Haddam, where he had lived after the death of his mother. The offer from Easthampton points to one of the shortcomings that arose from Connecticut's attempts to clamp down on ecclesiastical disorder: radicals could simply move out of the colony if they received an attractive offer elsewhere.

John Cleaveland also ran afoul of Rector Clap and was expelled in 1744. After pastoring at a separatist church in Boston for about eighteen months, he was ordained by the separatist parish of Chebaco in Ipswich, Massachusetts, where he served for more than fifty years, challenging the predations of both Redcoats and Unitarians.[57]

We know little about the specifics of the offer from Easthampton apart from Brainerd's own assertion that it had come by "the unanimous Vote of that large Town." However, accounts by nineteenth-century historians of the town suggest that this claim is not entirely true. According to those accounts, the divisions in the town caused by Davenport's ministry had not been healed by 1744 and so prevented the people from uniting behind any candidate until 1746, when they agreed upon Brainerd's Yale friend Samuel Buell. Brainerd's own words tend to bear this out as he noted the "great difficulties of that Place," about which he was "much concerned and grieved." And more than a year later, when Brainerd was living in Pennsylvania, he traveled to Easthampton as part of a ministerial council invited by the church to "advise in Affairs of Difficulty in that Church." Taken together, although there is no reason to doubt that some kind of call was made to Brainerd, these other accounts raise questions as to whether it was truly unanimous or unanimous only on the part of one of the factions. It may have been that one faction at the church issued the call to Brainerd in hopes that he might serve in a peacemaker role as he had done in eastern Connecticut the previous year. Regardless of the full story of the call from Easthampton, Brainerd initially "felt some Desires to comply with their request."[58]

The vacancy at Millington had been caused by a disagreement between the minister and some, but not all, of the members. The minister resigned in May 1743, but the resignation was protested by a number of the members, including a Daniel Brainerd, who was probably one of David's cousins.[59] It was not until February 1744 that any kind of consensus developed, at which time the members agreed to hire a new minister and designated two of its members "to go to New Haven and inquire into and get what light they can about a difficulty that we understand has arisen between the Doctor of the College and Mr. David Brainerd." Clearly, Brainerd was their first choice, but there was a need to address some of the rumors then abounding. With doubts apparently assuaged, the following month, the Millington parish voted to "give Mr. David Brainerd a call to preach the Gospel to the people of the . . . parish," an offer which Brainerd received on March 18.[60] Following his receipt of this offer, Brainerd noted he was "something exercised in Mind with a Weight and Burden of Care."[61]

It is hardly surprising that Brainerd did not reject either offer out of hand. Here, in a sense, was his great opportunity. Each invitation gave him the opportunity to receive a regular salary, give up the drudgery of language instruction, and settle down to the kind of life he had known in Haddam. Three weeks after receiving the offer from Easthampton, and after meeting with the SSPCK correspondents in New York, Brainerd decided to "go on still with the *Indian* affair" even though he "felt some Inclination to go to

East-Hampton." He wrote those words while still in New Jersey, and subsequent events suggest that, even at that point, he had not completely resolved the issue. His return journey to Kaunaumeek took almost three weeks. In addition to visiting friends in New York and Haddam, he also visited Easthampton and made at least one, and possibly two, trips to Millington. On April 17, a Tuesday, he preached the midweek lecture there and spent the evening at his brother's house, where there was a further time of fellowship. Although he was, perhaps, simply providing a service to a congregation in need, the visit also resembles that of a candidate for the ministry preaching a trial sermon. To this speculation should be added the observation that for two messengers to find him within three days, while he was traveling, with similar messages is hard to accept as a coincidence. Rather, it conveys the impression that either Brainerd or someone close to him had suggested that he might be interested in a regular pulpit.[62]

He spent at least another day in Millington, perhaps longer, before making his way back to Kaunaumeek. It is not until May 1, the day he set out from there for his new posting in Pennsylvania that his diary entries reflect any determination to carry on working with the Indians, and it may well be that it was not until he made it back to Kaunaumeek that he made his final decision. So why was working with the Indians the choice Brainerd finally made in the spring of 1744? Edwards suggested in a footnote to this episode that Brainerd did so because he was "determined to forsake all the outward comforts" in order to "endure the Difficulties and Self-Denials of an *Indian Mission.*"[63] But this claim owes much to what Edwards was trying to accomplish with his own congregation at the time that he was compiling the *Life* in 1747 and 1748. The length of time involved in the decision-making process along with Brainerd's surviving notes suggest that the decision was not as straightforward as either Brainerd or Edwards made it appear. It is true that Brainerd had commented on the need for Indian missions prior to being sent to Kaunaumeek. In April 1742, just after moving to Ripton, he recalled, "Some time past, I had much Pleasure in the Prospect of the *Heathens* being brought home to Christ, and desired that the Lord would improve *me* in that Work." Several days later, he was willing "if God should so order it" to go "among the Heathen." In August of that year, he had "Thoughts and Hopes of the Ingathering of the *Heathen.*"[64] But none of these seem to imply a ringing endorsement of the idea of being a missionary. In fact, such expressions were not without precedent as implying more a sense of complete resignation to the will of God rather than an announcement of a specific call. In writing of the 1735 revival in Northampton, for example, Jonathan Edwards noted that some of those who had been awakened were "far more concerned for others' conversion" and had declared that they could "freely die for the salvation of any soul, or the meanest of mankind, of any Indian in the woods."[65] Brainerd's experience at Montauk does not seem to have provided any inspiration that his calling lay among the Indians. However, his two brief preaching sessions at Scaticoke near Kent in Connecticut in August 1742 and March 1743 may have given him cause for some optimism.[66]

Even if Brainerd's time at Kaunaumeek kindled (or rekindled) an interest in Indian missions, certainly Easthampton, and quite possibly Millington, still tempted him. So, when Pemberton and his fellow correspondents offered Brainerd an appointment as a missionary-pastor, Brainerd must have been attracted by something more than a determination to endure its accompanying difficulties. Here, historian John Van Engen's studies of conversions in early fifteenth-century Europe offer a useful tool for understanding why Brainerd made the choice that he did.[67] Van Engen sought to explain how conversions within an already religious society were interpreted. As he pointed out, prior to about 1350, European Christians who wanted to live a life of deeper obedience to God usually expressed such conversions corporately, typically by joining a religious order. However, in the period between about 1350 and 1450, a substantial number of people looked to express their religious conversion in an individual fashion. Since such converts often left the regular worship of the parish church, deeming it to be inadequate, their actions constituted "a repudiation, a rejection, implicit or explicit, of surrounding society." Because these converts believed both society and the church to be inadequate to express their devotion to God, they sought comfort directly from God, an "experiential return or blessing" known as the *consolacio*. The convert, in Van Engen's words, "had to carve out a distinct space, in some ways a new space, between the world and the religious, the parish and the cloister, at the risk of provoking both."[68]

This mirrors much of what Brainerd had been attempting to do since his experiences during the revivals. His motivations were a little different than those of the converts in Europe, but his objective was largely the same: "to carve out a distinct space." For Brainerd, that distinct space borrowed not from the parish and the cloister, but from traditional Connecticut society and the radical edge of the revivals. Unable to find any place in colonial society that allowed such a hybrid ministry, he found it in Indian missions, particularly as he looked at possibilities in Pennsylvania. In going to Pennsylvania, he would be out from under the Connecticut authorities, with whom he would have had to deal if he accepted the position at Millington. Furthermore, as a missionary-minister, he would be able to operate in a far more independent fashion than even the members of the local presbytery. It was unlikely that any ministers from settled towns would be paying regular visits to ensure that he was not becoming too excessive in his practices. Since pastoring among Indians would not carry the same social responsibilities as in a colonial town, Brainerd would be free from the materialism with which he was becoming uncomfortable and would have a great deal more time in which to engage in solo activities, such as prayer and study, which he enjoyed.[69] At the same time, remuneration would come not from his congregation, but from the SSPCK; thus, he would not be required to please powerful members of the congregation. It was also unlikely that he would have to deal with factions within an Indian church. This was still an important issue to him and probably a key reason that he turned down the offers from Millington and Easthampton. In the Delaware Valley, in contrast, since he would be building a church from scratch, he could assume that there would be a higher degree of unity.

The attitude of the Pennsylvania government added one more attractive feature to the plan. Unlike the work at Stockbridge or Natick, the SSPCK was not working with a colonial government, nor was the Pennsylvania government looking to establish or sponsor an Indian town. So, not only was Brainerd not dependent on keeping a congregation happy, neither did he need to work under any direct government constraints. Thus, accepting a role as a missionary, which in the mid-eighteenth century essentially meant being a missionary-pastor, provided him with guaranteed income; little, if any, congregational factionalism; and a very loose, almost nonexistent, accountability for his day-to-day preaching style and other activities. It provided him a unique opportunity to create a distinct space where he could serve God in a way that accorded with his individual concept of conversion and devotion. None of the other opportunities presented to him between September 1743 and April 1744 could offer a similar set of circumstances.

While Brainerd was in New Jersey in April 1744, the SSPCK commissioners agreed that the time had come for him to move on from New York and to take up the twice-delayed move to the Delaware Valley. By the time he arrived back at Stockbridge, the Indians from Kaunaumeek had already relocated there.[70] On April 27 and 28, he spent "most of the day" with the Indians, "instructing them and giving them serious advice."[71] In reflecting, several months later, on his time at Kaunaumeek, Brainerd seems to have been content with his efforts. He believed that the "truths of God's word" were, at times, "attended with some power upon the hearts and consciences of the Indians." Some, indeed, "with tears, enquired what they should do to be saved." While he could not attest to any conversions, he believed God was "preparing his way into their souls." As proof of this, he cited a change in their conduct. "Idolatrous sacrifices" were "wholly laid aside," and the "Heathenish custom of Dancing, Halloing etc." seemed "in a considerable measure broken off." And, perhaps most pleasing to Brainerd, the Indians "manifested a regard to the Lord's Day."[72]

On Sunday, April 29, he preached and took leave of his people, noting that he was "affected at parting." On May 1, he "disposed of my affairs here" and "set out for Delaware River."[73] On the way, he spent a day with some Indians at Minissink, New York. One of them, on learning of Brainerd's mission, asked Brainerd why he "desired the Indians to become Christians, seeing the Christians were so much worse than the Indians are in their present state. The Christians, he said, would lie, steal, and drink more than the Indians." This man added that "if the Indians should become Christians they would then be as bad" as the colonists. Refusing to defend the ungodly colonial society, Brainerd agreed with the man's argument and condemned the "ill conduct of some who are called Christians." He asserted that he did not "desire the Indians to become such as these" and won a grudging invitation to return to this group of Indians again, but only if he came as "a friend, if I would not desire 'em to become Christians." He then resumed his journey and, on May 12, 1744, arrived at a small Dutch-Irish settlement not far from the Forks of the Delaware. For almost the next three years, Brainerd would work among the Indians and colonists who lived in the Delaware Valley, in nearby areas of New Jersey, and at several locations along the Susquehanna River.[74]

The Peoples of the Delaware Valley

By the eighteenth century, Europeans identified most of the Indian peoples who inhabited the Delaware River Valley and its broader drainage region as Delawares. This term encompassed a large number of Algonquian-speaking groups which, prior to European contact, spread from west of the Delaware River through most of present-day New Jersey, western Long Island, southern New York, and into the northern part of Delaware. Although the Delawares, or Lenape as they referred to themselves, represented the coming together of a number of diverse groups, by the 1740s, they embraced a shared tradition.[75] According to the account that some Delawares gave Moravian missionary John Heckewelder in the eighteenth century, in ancient days the Delawares began a long eastward migration until they reached the Mississippi River. There, they negotiated passage across the lands of the Alligewi people but, when the Alligewi saw the size of the Delaware nation, they attacked them. Assisted by the Mengwes, the Delawares battled the Alligewi people for many years before driving them off to the south. Delaware hunters then forayed further east, returning with accounts of a land full of abundant produce that also lacked enemies. The Delawares, Heckewelder concluded, believed "this to be the country destined for them by the Great Spirit, [and] they began to emigrate thither, as yet but in small bodies." Finally, the people settled in the area they occupied when Europeans arrived and made "the Delaware [River], to which they gave the name of *Lenapewihittuck* the center of their possessions."[76]

The first permanent settlements in the Delaware Valley were probably established about 11,000 years ago. Originally hunter-gatherers, the peoples whose descendants became the Delawares continually adapted to the changing natural environment of the region, developing new tools and new methods for capturing game. About 1,000 years ago, inhabitants of the region began to practice horticulture. Corn, in particular, became a key part of their diet, and its importance is reflected in their legends. These ancestors of the eighteenth-century Delawares lived in a number of different community structures, which were probably connected to the main food supply on which a particular community was dependent. Thus, groups which devoted much of their energy to cultivation may have lived in longhouses which, while smaller than contemporary Iroquois buildings, were larger than single-family units. Other groups lived as hunting bands or around known fishing locales. Settlements associated with such activities were probably smaller and less permanent than the agricultural groups and may have been made up of single-family dwellings. Sites with good supplies of the materials needed for making tools were also occupied on a seasonal basis. Trade networks formed both between groups that lived in the valley and with groups outside it in order to obtain materials and goods unavailable in a particular location.[77]

Within the family structure, there was a gender division of labor with men responsible for hunting and women responsible for agricultural and domestic activities. Divorce, while not the norm, was not uncommon and suggests, but does not prove, that loyalty to one's matrilineage outweighed loyalty to one's spouse. The matrilineage was a kin-based group which traced its descent through the female line. Although evidence is not conclusive, it appears likely that the oldest women within a matrilineage had some responsibility in selecting new leaders. The kin-based nature of the leadership exercised by these sachems meant that when Indians lived in smaller groups, members of those groups may have recognized different leaders. Sachems were expected to offer hospitality to strangers and travelers and to circulate goods among their group.[78]

The peoples of the region shared their world with spiritual beings. The Delawares, Heckewelder noted, believed they were "highly favoured" by the Great Spirit, Kishelëmukòng, who had created the world. Because of this, they were entitled to their share of the bounty of the natural world, but they also understood that they were intimately linked to the creation, being "only the first among equals, the legitimate hereditary sovereigns of the whole animated race, of which they are themselves a constituent part." Kishelëmukòng was not intimately involved with his creation and so a great deal of power had been apportioned to lesser spiritual beings, who governed such things as the four seasons, Mother Corn, and the earth itself. While the Delawares did not believe in an evil antithesis to the Great Spirit, they did believe in evil spirits who wrought mischief in the world. For example, where Kishelëmukòng had made edible berries, evil spirits put thorns on the bushes. Other spirit powers controlled the seasons, the weather, and the actions of animals. The various spirits had to be honored or appeased through the correct practice of rituals, usually performed by sachems and which often centered on specific sacred sites. Religious ceremonies could also be conducted by shamans (often referred to as *powwows* in Brainerd's writings) who possessed personal spiritual power, which enabled them to interpret dreams, change the weather, influence hunting prospects, and inflict witchcraft or cure its effects. Moravian missionary David Zeisberger noted that the Indians "believe also in the immortality of the soul." The souls of good people remained in the vicinity of their bodies for a number of days before they began a journey to the home of the Creator. Once there, a person was reunited with parents and children and dwelt in a place without hardship. The Delawares were more circumspect on the fate of the wicked except they were certain that they did not enter into the home of the Creator. Some legends held that evildoers stayed on earth and were forced to visit all the places where they committed their deeds. Others taught that the souls of evil people went to where the evil spirits dwelled and were there subjected to the annoying pests and insects associated with these spirits.[79]

Individually, Delawares interacted with the unseen world through dreams, visions, and, in many cases, spirit guides. The personal spirit guide of a Delaware was of critical importance. The Great Spirit and the spirits who controlled things like the weather were too removed to be concerned with each individual, so the spirit guide functioned as the connection between the everyday life of an individual and the supernatural world. As Swedish explorer Peter Lindestrom noted in 1691, when an Indian dreamed about his *Pååhra* (i.e., spirit guide), "he will at once the following day be able to shoot as much game and catch as much fish as ever he wants to." A relationship with a spirit guide was, thus, of critical importance to a happy and healthy life. David Zeisberger noted, "If an Indian has no *Manitto* [spirit] to be his friend he considers himself forsaken, has nothing upon which he may lean, has no hope of any assistance and is small in his own eyes. On the other hand those who have been thus favored possess a high and proud spirit." Delaware parents were anxious that their sons be contacted by a spirit guide. Parents would push boys, sometime between the ages of twelve and fourteen, to embark on a solitary vision quest. The process was quite an ordeal as the boy was compelled to go without food and sometimes drank some kind of medicine to induce vomiting. The Delawares believed that this process would create a state of spiritual purity. Thus prepared, the boy was dispatched by the tribal leaders into the forest. If he was properly prepared and purified, he would hear a voice from part of the natural world, a sign that spiritual power had been conveyed.[80]

The exact nature of these spirit guides is complex and hard to define. Although they manifested themselves in a single animal, they represented an entire species. Moreover, it was not the animal itself that was divine but a spirit power that was, in some way, associated with the animal. Brainerd himself was careful to note that the Delawares did not "suppose a divine power essential to, or inhering in these creatures, but that some invisible beings, not distinguished from each other by certain names, but only notionally, communicate to these animals a great power."[81]

While the relationship between people and their spirit guides was an individual one, it also had a community component as people were frequently called upon to recount a successful vision quest. Accounts of spirit visions also featured in the Big House Ceremony, the most important of the Delawares' religious ceremonies, which was designed to offer thanks for provisions. The central figure in the Big House Ceremony was Mësingw, who functioned in something of a mediatory role between Kishelëmukòng and the Delawares. But the central moment each night was the recitation of spirit visions by members of the community.[82]

The spiritual, social, and physical world to which the Delawares had adapted was shattered in the decades after European contact.[83] Their fate followed the tragic trajectory common in the eastern woodlands: initial cautious cooperation, followed by disease, war, and dispossession. The first permanent European settlement in the region was the Dutch trading post on Manhattan. Despite being primarily interested in trade, the Dutch sought control over increasing amounts of territory, and successive directors purchased Manhattan, Staten Island, large portions of western Long Island, and parts of the mainland both north and west of Manhattan. Although the surrender of lands caused problems for native peoples, a greater impact came from their participation in the fur trade. Hunting for trade rather than for food led to the virtual exhaustion of beaver in the territories closest to Manhattan, and the focus of the trade moved north up the Hudson Valley. The fur trade also upset traditional relationships between the Algonquians, who lived near the Dutch, and the Mahicans, who lived farther up the Hudson Valley. From time to time, small-scale conflict over resources broke out between various groups. The presence of the Dutch also brought disease, loss of forest lands, invasion of farm lands, and the debilitating impact of alcohol. In 1639, a Dutch attempt to extort a corn levy from a number of Indian settlements led to a brutal war which wreaked devastation on Native American communities in the region. Fighting was ended by treaty in 1645, but fresh waves of violence erupted in the mid-1650s and early 1660s, bringing further destruction.

English control of the region after 1664 opened the door to increasing numbers of European settlers in the region. The first permanent English settlement in New Jersey, the village of Elizabeth-town, was established in that same year of 1664. The founding of Pennsylvania in the 1680s, followed by the establishment of Trenton, New Jersey, early in the eighteenth century meant that the Delaware Indians were now being pressured along both banks of the Delaware River from the south and by the expanding settlements to their east in New Jersey.

The establishment of new colonies meant that, in addition to resisting encroachment on their lands by individual colonists, Indians also had to deal with rivalries among the various English colonies. Pennsylvania and New York, for example, were often at odds with one another. Finding themselves subjected to conflicting demands, the Delawares utilized traditional diplomatic approaches to resolve these issues. Beginning with Edmund Andros in 1676, the governors of New York created a situation where they looked to the Iroquois Confederacy to speak for all of the Indians in the region. Making use of this, the Delawares, without surrendering control over their own affairs, allowed the Five Nations to speak for them when dealing with New York. At the same time, it seems likely that the Delawares acted as mediators between the Five Nations and other Algonquian peoples. As such, the Delawares took on a symbolic role as "women." Although a source of strength in the late seventeenth century, both the English and the Iroquois would use this symbolic understanding in the eighteenth century to badger and threaten the Delawares into conceding vast tracts of land.

In their relationships with Pennsylvania, however, the Delawares spoke for themselves. The Quaker settlement grew rapidly and, by 1750, numbered 150,000 people. Despite this growth, at least in the early decades there were fairly peaceful relations between colonists and Indians. In 1698, colonist Gabriel Thomas reported that the Indians were "very kind and civil to any of the Christians; for I myself have had Victuals cut by them in their Cabbins, before they took any for themselves."[84]

Of course, peaceful conditions did not mean a lack of tension as the population growth exerted tremendous pressure on the proprietary government to increase the amount of land available for settlement. In addition, William Penn and his representatives were determined to assert control over the Susquehanna River valley in the face of attempts by New York to do the same, even though there was no immediate demand to settle colonists in the region. The influx of Europeans and the sale of lands compelled the Delaware people to form new settlements and new relationships. Many moved northwest along the Schuylkill River while others moved farther north along the Delaware. In most cases, Europeans followed them into these regions, and Delawares frequently encountered small groups of colonists even near their new settlements. By the time of Penn's death in 1718, Delaware occupation of their land of Lenapehoking was concentrated in three scattered areas: the Tulpehocken Valley in the upper Schuykill drainage, the Brandywine Valley, and a region near the confluence of the Lehigh and Delaware rivers, which was known as the Forks of the Delaware. The English also permitted a handful of "Indian towns" to remain within the land ceded to them. In addition, there were smaller, isolated groups living in New Jersey while an increasing number of Delawares had moved to the Susquehanna Valley. Some of these people, apparently unhappy with conditions there, moved farther west to establish Kittanning on the Allegheny River.

Even the three small remnants of Delaware ancestral land were under threat from European expansion. In 1722, William Keith, the deputy governor of Pennsylvania, gave permission for a group of Palatines to settle on the Tulpehocken lands. The Delawares were forced out as these settlers poured in and, in 1732, following violence which led to the death of several people, Sassoonan, the Delaware leader on the Tulpehocken, relented and signed an agreement with Thomas Penn and his representatives that formally surrendered the last Delaware land on the Schuylkill to the colony of Pennsylvania. The Delaware lands on the Brandywine were lost to them by the 1730s. The Delawares believed that William Penn had reserved for them the land one mile to either side of the watercourse. Contrary to this, whites were settling on the land, and English settlement brought with it dams, which caused fish to disappear. The foraging by the Englishmen's cattle left little, if any, feed for the game hunted by the Delawares. In response to the Delawares' complaints, James Logan—the main architect of Indian affairs in the colony following William Penn's final departure in 1699—told them he could not find a copy of the treaty to which they referred. When the Indians could not produce their copy—it had been destroyed in a fire, they reported—Logan ordered the land surveyed and then formally sold it to the settlers. Faced with a choice of acquiescence or conflict, the Delawares along the Brandywine relocated again, some to the Susquehanna and some as far as the Ohio Valley. They took with them stories of Logan's fraudulence and the futility of trusting in agreements with the Europeans.[85]

The Delaware settlement at the Forks of the Delaware proved to be more resilient.[86] The Delawares there, under the leadership of Nutimus, knew that they had an agreement with William Penn that the boundary between his land and theirs was Tohickon Creek. This boundary, gradually established by a series of complex purchases and deeds over a period of time, was finally agreed to by 1718. However, the growing colonial population continued to exert pressure on the boundary. The Delawares steadfastly refused to concede more territory unless they could meet with one of William Penn's descendants. Despite this setback, William Penn's sons, saddled with debts and living in England, continued to sell the land without meeting with the Indians.

Finally, frustrated by the lack of progress, Thomas Penn arrived in the colony in 1732 and was joined by his brother John in 1734. Several weeks later, the two met with the Delawares, who refused to give up their land in the Forks for the token payment the Penns were offering. Determined to have the land, but unable to pay the asking price, the Penns looked for a means to get it cheap (or, even better, for free) without offending the legal sensibilities of the Quaker colony. In May 1735, Logan met again with the Delawares and brought before them what he claimed was a copy of a 1686 deed. This deed ostensibly ceded to William Penn all of the lands on the west bank of the Delaware, including the Forks. Although the Delawares refused to recognize the legitimacy of the deed, the Penns had the legal cover they needed. They continued to survey the land and proceeded with arrangements for its sale.

However, neither surveyors nor Logan's threats broke Nutimus's resistance, so Logan played his Iroquois card. In 1736, the Iroquois came to Philadelphia to meet with Logan. At this meeting, they willingly ceded to Pennsylvania control of lands that they themselves claimed on the Susquehanna, but refused to lay claim to the land owned by Nutimus's Delawares. Logan, ever the opportunist, went to work on the Iroquois. He sought to convert the Iroquois' refusal to lay claim to title to the land into a release of title to the colonial government. There can be little doubt that the Iroquois understood what Logan was trying to do. Lacking material offerings to win Iroquois support, Logan resorted to something less tangible but very desirable. He offered the Six Nations exclusive rights as agents between the colony of Pennsylvania and all Indians within its boundaries, essentially granting them political ascendancy throughout all of the territory claimed by the colony. It was too much for the Iroquois to resist. They agreed to surrender title to the west bank of the Delaware—a title which they had never possessed.

Betrayed by their allies, the Forks Delawares signed a copy of the 1686 deed, which called for a "walk" of a day and a half to take place to determine the northern extent of the land sale. The walk, which the Indians expected to be done at a normal walking pace, move up the west bank of the Delaware, and then follow Tohickon Creek, was instead completed at a pace just short of a run and went straight up the west bank of the Delaware. By the time it was finished, all of Nutimus's people's land belonged to the Penns. Publicly benevolent, Logan allowed the Delawares to keep the land north of the Kittatinny Mountains (which he did not want) and set aside ten square miles for them at the Forks.

Still, the Forks Delawares refused to move off the land. In response, Logan utilized the relationship created with the Iroquois in 1736 to negotiate a settlement that would suit the interests of the colony's proprietary government. In July 1742, Logan called a new conference in Philadelphia to which he summoned the "Chiefs of the Six Nations. Sassonan & Delawares. Nutimus and the fork Indians." At the meeting, Governor George Thomas called on the Six Nations to "cause these Indians to remove from the Lands in the fforks of Delaware and not give any further Disturbance to the Persons who are now in Possession." Three days later, Canasatego, as the representative of the Six Nations, rose to address the council. Playing upon European rather than Indian concepts of the symbolic role of women, Canasatego declared that the Delawares had been reduced to women after they had been conquered by the Confederacy and had lost all right to control their land. The Iroquois' betrayal of the Delawares was complete. Canasatego charged them to remove themselves from the Forks of the Delaware to either Wyoming or Shamokin, both located on the Susquehanna. With no one on their side, the majority of this last band of the eastern Delaware was compelled to move westward. Delaware occupation of their territory of Lenapehoking was all but extinguished. Having lost the Six Nations as protectors and allies, the Delawares who remained on their ancestral lands did so only at the sufferance of the colonial governments.[87]

By late 1742, only a handful of Indians remained at the Forks. In November of that year, "Titami, Captain John and sundry other Delaware Indians, setting forth that they have embraced the Christian Religion," appeared before the Pennsylvania Council, requesting permission to stay on their lands. Governor George Thomas decided that both Tatamy and Captain John, whose Indian name was Tishcohan, as well as Tatamy's wife and three children, could stay at the Forks although Tishcohan had to move off the land upon which he was living since he had no clear title. Tatamy, a landowner of substantial means, was allowed to keep his 300 acres at the Forks. A handful of Indians, whose exact affiliation is not entirely clear, also lived within the broadly defined area called the Forks of the Delaware but outside the area claimed by the Walking Purchase. Among these was Teedyuscung, a future Delaware leader. These small remnants, together with perhaps a handful of others who had lost their lands but not joined the move west, remained in the Forks region for at least another four years.[88]

Historian Steven Craig Harper has observed that the process of dispossession in the Forks "left strange wounds. No Delawares died as an immediate result of the Walking Purchase." Furthermore, since the Iroquois and Pennsylvania had conspired to deprive the Delawares of their land, there was a joint effort to silence or ignore subsequent Delaware protests. But such efforts cannot, in retrospect, hide the depth or longevity of Delaware fury over the scam: as late as the 1750s, Delawares took advantage of French victories in the Seven Years' War to avenge themselves on Pennsylvania settlers.[89]

In a legend recounted by Delaware Indians to white settlers, they told of twelve women who dwelled in caves near a river protected by a great ocean-dwelling serpent, which would swallow anyone who threatened the women. One day, a young man killed the serpent and destroyed the houses and possessions of the women. Looking upon the ruins of their lives, the women declared, "if you had left us in peace, we would have taught you many things, taught you to do what white-eyed people do who live over this great water here. A hundred years from now they will come here and drive you away, and you will have no land. You will be poor, no people."[90] By 1744, the Delawares who remained in their homelands were certainly "poor, no people." Most of the surviving Delawares had abandoned their traditional lands and headed west, many of them to the Susquehanna Valley. A handful remained in Pennsylvania and New Jersey, the majority of these living as isolated groups in Indian villages or in areas not yet claimed by Europeans. Most of these survived by subsistence farming and fishing. Many suffered from alcohol both by abusing it themselves and by being exploited in its use by colonial traders.

The systematic removal of the Delaware peoples had opened more land for the successive waves of European settlers. Since both the New Jersey and Pennsylvania governments welcomed colonists regardless of their ethnic or religious backgrounds, both colonies quickly became home to a heterogeneous mix of peoples. Scotch-Irish, English, Germans, Swiss, Dutch, Welsh, Swedes—all flooded into the Delaware Valley and gradually made their way into the Forks and other surrounding regions. In some cases, they settled in homogeneous groups, while in other cases, ethnically diverse communities formed. At first, this new influx of settlers was generally welcome but later, and particularly in Pennsylvania beginning in the late 1720s, doubts were raised in some quarters over the pedigrees of some of the arrivals. Specifically, concern focused on the changing conditions in the backcountry, which one member of the colony's elite judged was being "fill'd [by] vast numbers of Strangers and foreigners settling in it without order or method," while another judged many of them to be "Idle worthless people." In particular, colonial officials were concerned that many of these new immigrants had a tendency to occupy and use land they had not paid for, while the Scotch-Irish, in particular, developed a belligerent attitude toward Native Americans.[91]

For most of the immigrants, their faith was a key part of their lives, and religious diversity mirrored the ethnic diversity. Among the immigrants could be found Lutherans, Catholics, Anglicans, Baptists, Presbyterians, Quakers, Huguenots, and a mosaic of Protestant splinter groups among the Germans.[92] In some cases, religious belief formed the basis of new communities as in the case of the Moravians, who settled in the Forks of the Delaware not far from where Brainerd began his work. They had arrived in the region in 1740 and began the construction of Nazareth and Bethlehem the following year. These settlements quickly became one of the focuses of Moravian work in the colonies. The following year, the Moravians divided their work at the Forks into two groups, one of which focused on prayer, building construction, and farming, while the other dedicated itself to evangelism among both colonists and Indians. The Moravians baptized their first Indian converts in 1742, although systematic work among the Indians did not begin until several years later. Originally welcomed by most Protestants, theological differences caused these bonds to unravel. By the time Brainerd arrived in 1744, the Moravians had laid the foundations for a thriving community, but the breach between them and Protestants in the region was complete.[93]

Some Scotch-Irish immigrants also attempted to create like-minded communities on arrival in the region. Families who had attended the same church in Ireland often traveled to the colonies together and thus formed the nucleus of a church. While some groups succeeded in establishing themselves as communities with a common religion, many were thwarted by a chronic shortage of pastors. The leaders of the Presbyterian church in New Jersey and Pennsylvania encouraged settled pastors to act in a kind of semi-itinerant role to neighboring communities that lacked their own minister. But, in newly settled regions, such as the Forks of the Delaware, there really weren't any nearby ministers. Thus, when itinerant ministers did come to preach in a particular area, they often found themselves ministering to a multiconfessional audience as settlers of varying theological backgrounds took the opportunity to hear the word of God. This, in turn, fostered the growth of ethnically and linguistically diverse communities.[94]

In the longer-settled regions of New Jersey and parts of Pennsylvania, Presbyterianism was the preeminent denomination, especially among New English, Scots, and Scotch-Irish settlers. Confessionally very similar to the orthodox Calvinism of New England, there was an essential unity of faith among pro-revival ministers in the two colonies and their brethren in New England. This was exemplified by the close personal relations among ministers like Aaron Burr, Jonathan Dickinson, Jonathan Edwards, Stephen Williams, Ebenezer Pemberton, and Joseph Bellamy. Further, the Scottish heritage of many of the New Jersey Presbyterian churches meant that they embraced a model of preparationism and revivalism with which Brainerd and others from New England were familiar. These churches were also particularly receptive to Whitefield and other preachers who fired the awakening in the region. As in New England, not all ministers welcomed the events of the Great Awakening, and in Pennsylvania and New Jersey, the awakening exerted pressure on already existing tensions. Adding to the ministerial disagreements, as historian Marilyn Westerkamp has demonstrated, the Scotch-Irish laity were strongly supportive of the revivals and allied with like-minded ministers. Eventually, the tensions would erupt into schism with the pro-revival, or New Side, New Brunswick Presbytery leaving the Synod of Philadelphia in 1741 (or being ejected, depending on who was telling the story). This presbytery attracted a number of other ministers from the Synod of Philadelphia who were supportive of the revivals. From 1741 onward, in competition with the Synod of Philadelphia, the New Brunswick men also ordained newly qualified ministers, including Richard Treat and Samuel Blair, who would both become close friends of Brainerd.[95]

The Presbytery of New York, which included SSPCK commissioners Ebenezer Pemberton and Aaron Burr as well as Jonathan Dickinson, tended to be somewhat supportive of the revival although wary of its extremes. It was this Presbytery of New York which welcomed Brainerd to the region and which would ordain him later in 1744. No doubt, the relative proximity of Pemberton, who had been inspirational when he spoke at Yale in 1741, and Burr, who had provided so much support during Brainerd's struggle with Yale, was welcome to Brainerd. In 1745, the Presbytery of New York joined with those of New Brunswick and Londonderry to form the Synod of New York. David Brainerd operated under the authority first of the Presbytery of New York and then under the synod of the same name.[96]

Foundations

Brainerd did not arrive at the Forks at a particularly fortuitous time as relations between the Delawares and the colonists, which had been tense since the 1742 conference, had been brought to a boil by recent events. Only weeks before

Brainerd arrived in May 1744, news had filtered into Philadelphia from the upper Susquehanna that an Indian trader named John Armstrong and two of his servants had been murdered by "three Delaware Indians" sometime in February.[97] What might have been seen as an isolated incident two or three years earlier was magnified in April when Governor Thomas warned the Pennsylvania Assembly that "it is not to be Doubted but that a Warr against France is declared" (war had actually been declared in Britain in March). Thomas scheduled a conference with the Iroquois to take place at Lancaster in June. Was the murder of Armstrong an isolated incident or the first act of Indians determined to bring death and destruction to the colony at the behest of the hated French? Pennsylvania authorities promptly dispatched veteran negotiator Conrad Weiser to the Susquehanna town of Shamokin to demand that Indian leaders hand over the guilty parties, although the Indians did not immediately respond to this demand. Although the Armstrong murders were discussed at Lancaster, the issue of the French war was of far greater concern. After a number of land disputes was resolved, the Iroquois assured Thomas of their loyalty to the British cause. However, troubled by the absence of the Shawnees, Thomas made inquiries and learned that the Shawnees had "been endeavouring to draw the Delawares from Shamokin to Ohio," where the Delawares might join the Shawnees as opponents to the Six Nations.[98] In the end, in 1744, both the French crisis in Pennsylvania and the Armstrong murders were resolved without resort to conflict. Pennsylvania was able to ignore the French threat for almost two years simply because no fighting took place in the colony. The Armstrong case was brought to a conclusion when a Delaware named Musha Meelan was identified as the murderer and handed over to the colonial authorities by the Delawares. Musha Meelan's trial began in October 1744. He was found guilty and executed for the murders in November. The whole incident required several meetings between the governor and the Delaware deputies and eventually required a formal renewal of the chain of friendship between the two. Despite the absence of conflict, the two issues created a turbulent atmosphere in the colony at the very time Brainerd was arriving at the Forks of the Delaware.[99]

In the days following his arrival at the Forks, Brainerd came to realize the magnitude of the task facing him. Unlike the situation at Kaunaumeek, where the Indians had formed a settled community, in Pennsylvania, he reported, the "number of Indians in this place is but small; most of those that belonged here are dispersed and removed to places further back in the country. There are not more than ten houses hereabouts that continue to be inhabited."[100] While the remaining Indian settlements in the region were fairly dispersed by nature, the uproar that had begun in April probably had made the Indians wary about gathering in large numbers where colonists could see them. Also unlike the situation at Kaunaumeek, where John Sergeant had laid a significant foundation and where the Indians had requested a missionary, there is no evidence that Christianity made any significant inroads among the Delawares prior to the 1740s.[101] Despite the difficulties which confronted Brainerd on his arrival, he was happy to note that God was "pleased to support my sinking soul" so that he "never entertained any thought of quitting my business among the poor Indians."[102]

Brainerd had little time to contemplate his work among the Delawares before preparing for his own ordination. This had been insisted on by the SSPCK in Edinburgh, which had noted that, while the New York correspondents were pursuing "the best method in [their] power for…spreading the everlasting Gospel among the Indians," the rules of the society required that "whoever is sent among the Indians, must be an ordained Minister of the Gospel." The correspondents set June 1744 as the time and, two weeks after arriving at the Forks, Brainerd headed to New Jersey. While preparing for his ordination, Brainerd spent time in Newark, probably with Aaron Burr, and New York, where he certainly met with Ebenezer Pemberton. However, most of the time he was at Elizabeth-town, where he would have stayed with Jonathan Dickinson (1688–1747), pastor there since 1708. Dickinson and Brainerd developed a deep personal friendship in the three years that Brainerd ministered in the Delaware Valley. Brainerd devoted his efforts while at Elizabeth-town "chiefly in studies preparatory to his ordination."[103]

The ordination process, which took place on June 11 and 12, 1744, consisted of two separate examinations before the presbytery, one of which concerned Brainerd's "experimental acquaintance with Christianity," as well as the preaching of a "Probation-sermon" from Acts 26:17, 18. Particularly well suited to a man called to preach to the Indians, this verse reads, in part, "Delivering thee from the people, and from the Gentiles, unto whom now I send thee, to open their eyes, and to turn them from darkness to light." Although Brainerd did not feel well, "God carried [him] thro' comfortably." Ebenezer Pemberton advised the SSPCK that Brainerd "appeared uncommonly qualified for the work of ministry. He seems to be armed with a great deal of self-denial, and animated with a noble zeal to propagate the gospel among those barbarous nations."[104]

At 10 a.m. on Tuesday, June 12, 1744, Brainerd was ordained, with Pemberton preaching the ordination sermon from Luke 14:23: "And the Lord said unto the servant, Go out into the high-ways and hedges, and compel them to come in, that my house may be filled." Pemberton outlined the desperate state of the lost, the kindness of God in providing salvation, and the duty of ministers to attract sinners. The latter section occupied much of Pemberton's time as he noted the various methods by which ministers could "compel sinners to come in." Ministers needed to remind sinners of their "guilty and perishing condition" by setting the "terrors of the Lord in array against the sinner, and let him hear the thunder of divine curses." But, warned Pemberton, such preaching of terror could "only give the knowledge of sin." In addition, preachers had to "preach the unsearchable riches of Christ" and "exhibit the unspeakable advantages, that will attend a compliance with the gospel-call."[105]

Pemberton also directed part of his message to Brainerd in particular, noting that "greater degrees of prudence, humility, and meekness, mortification to the present world, holy courage and zeal for the honour of God our Saviour, are necessary where any are called to minister the gospel unto those who, through a long succession of ages have dwelt in the darkness of Heathenism." And yet, declared Pemberton, dependence on God made such a task possible and transformed the "lonely huts of savages into more delightful habitations than the palaces of princes." Little wonder that Brainerd commented in his diary that he "was affected with a sense of the important trust committed to me; yet was composed, and solemn, without distraction."[106] His return to the Forks was delayed several days, first by his writing a report of his activities from the time of his move to Kaunaumeek, then by illness.

Once he returned to the Forks, he set about reaching the Indians with determination. He had actually preached to them the day after he first arrived there and, the following Sunday, he had preached to the Indians twice more, focusing on an effort to "remove their prejudices against Christianity." He also had an opportunity to witness an Indian funeral. He was "affected to see their Heathenish practises" and longed that they "might be turned from darkness to light!" On his return from his ordination, he spent his first Sunday back at the Forks visiting and instructing a number of Indians individually. Over the next week or so, he devoted large portions of his prayers to the conversion of the Indians. In particular, he noted that he "[h]ad more freedom and fervency in prayer than usual of late; especially longed for the *presence of God in my work that the poor Heathen might be converted*" (emphasis added). He preached to the Indians several times over the next few days, frequently noting how the attitude of his heart impacted the way in which he addressed his audience. One Sunday morning, he "preached to the Indians without my heart." His afternoon preaching began the same way, but he soon "found in myself a spirit of love, and warmth, and power to address the poor Indians." He finished believing that "the Lord touch'd their consciences." By July, he was preaching fairly regularly to both Indians and colonists and had also begun to translate prayers into the Delaware language, but the

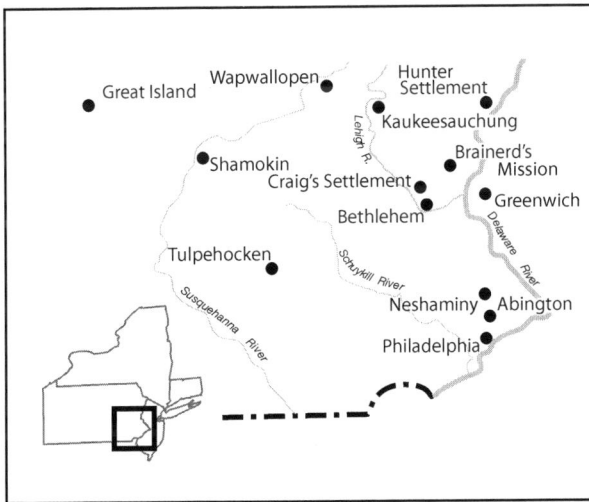

Eastern and central Pennsylvania. Map by Marvin J. Barton; adapted from Merritt, *At the Crossroads*, 35, 133.

going was tough because his "interpreter was altogether unacquainted with the business." He had also had one conversation with a young man who spoke some English and who was "much concern'd about his Spiritual state," asking "what he might do to be sav'd."[107]

In the middle of that month, Brainerd learned that a religious ritual, in his words "an *idolatrous Feast and Dance*, was to take place."[108] Since most of the feasts common to the native peoples of this region occurred outside the summer months, it seems likely that this was a local ritual perhaps associated with a nearby sacred space.[109] Brainerd determined that he "must in conscience go and endeavour to break them up," but he "knew not how to attempt such a thing." He thus returned to prayer, which lasted through a great part of the night, slept, and then rose to pray again. He emerged from this time of prayer with the sense that "nothing could discourage me from this blessed work" and a "strong hope that God would bow the heavens and come down, and do some marvellous work among the heathen."[110]

With this mindset, he rode out to the Indians and "found them engaged in their *Frolick*."[111] Brainerd did not record exactly what he did or said when he reached them, but his brief diary notes suggest a fairly passive approach. He was probably not cut from the same cloth as the French Jesuit Paul Le Jeune. Traveling with a group of Montagnais in the winter of 1632–1633, Le Jeune spent much of the time in verbal warfare with the group's shaman, Carigonan. Le Jeune attempted to undermine Carigonan's credibility by disparaging his religious practices as falsehoods and superstitions.[112] In contrast, Brainerd noted only that "through divine goodness I persuaded them to desist and attend my preaching." Nonetheless, he observed "nothing of the special power of God among them." He preached to them again in the afternoon when they were "more sober than before but still saw nothing special among them."[113] However, it seems that this experience sharpened his awareness of the struggle for spiritual authority in which he was involved. By early September, he had come to understand that some members of his audience were "afraid to hearken to, and embrace *Christianity*, lest they should be inchanted and poison'd by some of the *Powows*." Although he did not immediately challenge the Indian spiritual leaders directly, he did tell the Indians that he was "a Christian, and ask'd them why the *Powows* did not Bewitch and Poison me."[114] He believed this had an effect since some of the Indians had been "brought to renounce *Idolatry*, and to decline partaking of those *Feasts* which they used to offer in Sacrifice to certain supposed unknown Powers."[115]

Shortly after this, he went to New England for three weeks and, upon his return, he began to make plans for a trip to the Susquehanna.[116] The region had been on the minds of the SSPCK correspondents and the SSPCK in Edinburgh for some years. In 1738, Ebenezer Pemberton and Jonathan Dickinson had written to Scotland, seeking a missionary to serve both Indians and colonists in New York, New Jersey, and Pennsylvania. After some debate in Edinburgh and the colonies, Pemberton, writing on behalf of the Synod of New York, suggested that a place on the "banks of the River Susquehanna, seems to afford a large prospect of success." In March 1741, the SSPCK agreed to the request from New York "to employ two missionary ministers among a large tribe of Indians on Susquehanna River." The SSPCK had also written to John Sergeant, seeking his input on the matter, and in 1741, Sergeant took a trip out to the Susquehanna River valley to assess the situation. Sergeant's assessment was not a rosy one; he described the Indians in the region as "averse to the reception of Christianity."[117]

Given the focus on the Susquehanna by the Synod of New York and the support for this plan on the part of the SSPCK in Edinburgh, it seems likely that the correspondents had initially sent Brainerd to the Delaware Valley hoping that he would make contacts among Indians that would open the door for him to move his work to the Susquehanna.[118] If this was the hope of the commissioners, it proved, in its initial stages at least, to be well founded. As early as July 1744, he had ridden "about 30 miles westward" from the Forks to the village of Kauksesauchung, to preach to about thirty Indians. Most of these people "seem'd glad of being instructed or at least, pleased with the novelty of the thing." However, he also discovered that they were only temporary residents there and were "going home to Susquahannah where they belong'd and desir'd that I would visit them there."[119] As he informed Ebenezer Pemberton, this gave him hope that "God designed to open an effectual door to me for spreading the Gospel among the heathen farther westward." With this invitation and the likely encouragement of the correspondents, Brainerd prepared for his first trip to the Susquehanna Valley.[120]

The Delawares and other Native Americans who relocated to the Susquehanna River had at first fared a little better than those who remained in Lenapehoking. The Susquehanna settlements lay beyond the line of the European advance. There was an abundance of fish for food and deer for trade to which was added the fertility of the river land for growing crops. The Iroquois encouraged various groups to move into the valley in hopes that their subsequent submission to the Iroquois would solidify Iroquois claims to sovereignty over the region. By the 1740s, Delawares, Shawnees, Tutelos, Tuscaroras, and others called the Susquehanna Valley home. The relative stability and prosperity of the residents increased the attraction of the Susquehanna for those Indians still living among colonial settlers. Furthermore, the Six Nations, which claimed nominal domination of the Susquehanna, were determined to keep white settlers out. Although they were not completely successful in this attempt, Pennsylvania found it harder to acquire lands in this region than it had to the east.[121]

Brainerd set out eastward on October 1 accompanied by Eliab Byram, the pastor at Rockciticus; his interpreter, Moses Tatamy; and two unnamed "chief Indians" from the Forks of the Delaware. Much of the trip was through a "wilderness almost unpassable by reason of mountains and rocks." It was the "most difficult and dangerous traveling, by far, that any of us had seen." Along the way, Brainerd's horse broke her leg, and he was obliged to continue the journey on foot. It took the party the better part of four days to make the trip to a village Brainerd identified as Opeholhaupung, but which was also known as Wapwallopen.[122]

Brainerd asked permission of a man he identified as the "king" to address the people. This was granted, and Brainerd preached to the residents at various times over the next three days. There seemed to be some interest in his message since the men delayed a planned hunting trip for several days, and Brainerd and his companions visited a number of them in their houses. Curiously, the women did not attend his preaching at first, "supposing the affair we were upon was of a publick nature, belonging only to the men."[123] Brainerd preached to an audience that "mostly heard with attention, but yet seemed to have very little notion of the soundness and solemnity of the business." Shortly after he finished preaching, one of the men prepared and offered a sacrifice to one of their "supposed deities." Brainerd learned that the offering had been made for the "Spirits of the dead," and he informed them of the "evil and folly of their sacrifices." He encouraged them instead to turn to the one God, who could feed everyone.[124]

He even took the opportunity to encourage them to get the women to come to his preaching since everyone had a soul that would be "happy or miserable"; if only the "men were made happy, that would do the women no good." He noted that, "after much pains," some "few [women] ventured to come and stand at a distance." Some of the men informed Brainerd of their objections to Christianity but gave him a "fair opportunity for using my best endeavours to remove from their minds those scruples and jealousies they labored under." Since it seems that the men were anxious to start their hunting trip, Brainerd asked if he could return the following spring, a request met with enthusiasm by most of those present. Brainerd and his companions spent almost eight days in travel in order to spend three and a half days preaching to the Susquehanna Indians, but he "could not but rejoice that I had taken that journey among them, altho' it was attended with many difficulties and hardships."[125] Despite this optimism, the approach of winter meant that he had to wait until the following year to return to the region.

On his return to the Forks, he oversaw the construction of his house into which he moved by December 1744, a "happy Opportunity" which allowed him to spend time in "secret Fasting and Prayer." This move did not make his work any easier among the scattered Indian settlements, an issue that was increasingly of concern to him.[126] One Sunday in January, although he had spoken with "some Freedom and Concern," he had had to do so at "two of their settlements." He believed that this *Manner of their living*," so that they were "continually roving from Place to Place," was a key reason for the difficulties attending the work. He provided the example of a group of two or three families that he believed were open to hearing his message but were at a "vast disadvantage, [in] that they live so dispers'd, and remote from each other, that they can seldom have an opportunity of being instructed."[127]

Lest one thinks that Brainerd was exaggerating the problems, he was not the only person to make note of the difficulties of travel through the region. In contrast to New England with its broad river valleys and roads worn clear by more than a century of European occupation, Pennsylvania presented unique challenges. As James H. Merrell has noted, most journeys through Pennsylvania were "more ordeal than lark." Nor was this a cultural problem: the ritual of the Pennsylvania Indians known as "At the Woods' Edge" opened by describing the travails of travel. Roads tended to run through swamps and over fallen trees and other obstacles, and required the traveler to cross streams—sometimes at easy fords but at other times at what appeared to be virtually nonexistent crossings. It was not uncommon for horses to eat poisonous plants, break a leg, be bitten by a snake, or simply give up. This, of course, added to the price of travel. It cost Brainerd £50 to replace the horse which had broken her leg on his journey to the Susquehanna the previous fall. And these everyday problems were compounded in the winter. Little wonder that both colonists and Indians viewed the forests of Pennsylvania with trepidation.[128]

Brainerd did not encounter this problem to the same extent when he ministered among the colonial settlements in the region since the colonists settled in larger groups than did the Indians and travel tended to be along shorter, more identifiable trails. Brainerd devoted a substantial amount of effort to working with the settlers in the surrounding region. His most consistent work was with the nearby "Irish Settlement" (probably Hunter's Settlement), references to which appear frequently in his journal. Brainerd first preached there on the day after he arrived in the Forks, and by late July, he had begun to notice that, as Jonathan Edwards summarized events, "[t]here was a considerable appearance of awakening in the congregation."[129] Brainerd's rapport with the people there grew over the months and extended to other settlements in the region. On the way back from his first visit to the Susquehanna, he and Eliab Byram spent several days at another "Irish settlement." Although they had just completed an arduous journey, the day after they arrived both "he and Mr. *Byram* preached there to the people." By December 1744, the circle of settlement to which he ministered had extended. He spent several consecutive days preaching at Greenwich, New Jersey, a vacant parish which had placed itself under the pro-revival New Brunswick Presbytery.[130]

By February, the response to his preaching in some of the colonial settlements began to approach the experiences with which he had been associated during the revivals in New England. With his interpreter absent for most of the month, he was unable to preach to the Indians and spent successive Sundays instead ministering to "*white* People." On February 17, he held forth to a "considerable Assembly," which had gathered "in the Wilderness upon the sunny side of a Hill." He spent most of the day preaching to them, basing his discourse on the appeal of Jesus from John 7:37, that any who were thirsty should "come unto me, and drink." He observed that there were "many Tears in the Assembly," and he was sure that "the Spirit of God was there."[131]

Brainerd rarely, if ever, mentioned the ethnicity of the congregations before which he spoke. But, given his affiliation with the Presbyterians and the fact that he does not mention translators, it seems that most of the people were probably Scotch-Irish. However, it would not be surprising if Germans, Dutch, and other people had gathered for the novelty of an ordained preacher in their isolated area. Even among such a diverse group of people, Brainerd probably had some natural advantages. The style of preaching he had learned from men like Gilbert Tennent, James Davenport, and others was a pietistic, emotional style that appealed to the Scotch-Irish settlers of the region. Many of these people were open to more emotional displays and were quite happy to spend long periods outside listening and responding to preachers. In addition, the revivalist style of preaching would also have been welcomed by many of the Dutch and Germans, who were heavily influenced by pietism.[132]

Despite his effectiveness among the colonial settlements, Brainerd's goal still remained the Indians, particularly those along the Susquehanna. As part of this plan, he spent five weeks traveling through New Jersey, New York, and New England preaching in a number of churches and visiting friends. His primary goal was to "raise some Money among Christian Friends, in order to support a colleague with me in the Wilderness, (I having now spent two Years in a very solitary manner)."[133] Regardless of how this quest turned out, he was determined to return to the Susquehanna as soon as possible. As he wrote to John Sergeant in late March 1745, he wanted to "spend most of the summer in those parts, if a door opens for it." The one obstacle to his Susquehanna plans, as he had told Sergeant, was that the Indian lands in the Susquehanna "belong to the Six Nations i.e. the Mohawks, and tis something doubtfull whether they will suffer a missionary to come among their tributaries, and on to their lands. Yet this difficulty, we hope, may be removed by the influence of the Governor of Pennsylvania, who maintains a strict friendship with the 6 Nations."[134] Accordingly, in mid-April, just a few days after he returned from New England, he traveled to Philadelphia to see if the governor would use his influence to get permission for Brainerd to live at the Susquehanna, at least for the summer. It is probable that Brainerd was seeking a written endorsement from the governor, something that would have added substantial weight to an attempted mission on the Susquehanna.[135] Since he left for the Susquehanna a few weeks later, it is likely that he received official approval for the trip.

As it turned out, April was an important month for Brainerd as, just before setting out for the Susquehanna, he learned of the conversion of his interpreter, Tatamy.[136] Although an isolated event at the time, it would prove to have important ramifications. Moses (Tunda) Tatamy (c. 1695–c. 1760) was, by 1745, about fifty years old. He had been one of the Delawares at the center of the land disputes at the Forks of the Delaware, where he had kept his land by convincing the authorities he was a Christian. Prior to those events, sometime in the summer of 1742, Tatamy had met the Moravian leader Count Nikolaus Ludwig von Zinzendorf, who recognized Tatamy as a fellow believer although not a Moravian. Under what circumstances and ministry Tatamy had first embraced Christianity is not known, but it was fortuitous for Brainerd as Tatamy was one of the few people in colonial Pennsylvania who possessed both the necessary language skills to act as a translator and a theological knowledge sufficient to grapple with the more abstract concepts of the Christian message.[137] Brainerd presented Tatamy, prior to his conversion, as someone who had a "head" knowledge of Christianity but not an "experimental" knowledge, that is, he was in the same state as an unconverted colonial churchgoer, just as Brainerd believed he had been before his conversion experience.

Brainerd's account of Tatamy's spiritual pilgrimage follows the standard progression of preparation, conviction, and conversion that was part and parcel of the theology of both preparationists, such as Solomon Stoddard, and the revivalist preachers. Shortly after he began work as Brainerd's interpreter, Tatamy "behaved soberly" and "appeared especially desirous that the Indians should renounce their heathenish notions" but "seemed to have no concern about his own soul." Then, in the late summer of 1744, "divine truth took hold of him, and made deep impressions on his mind," and it was now "his great enquiry, *what he should do to be saved.*"[138] Brainerd was clearly aware that Tatamy was undergoing some kind of spiritual struggle at the time. In December 1744, he prayed for "converting grace for my *Interpreter*," and a week later, he observed that Tatamy was "amazingly assisted" and "encouraged and exhorted [him] to *strive* to *enter in at the strait Gate.*"[139]

As Tatamy's preparation struggle continued, he had what can only be described as a vision experience. Although couched by Brainerd in a symbolic form by the use of words such as "seem'd," one is still left with the unmistakable impression that Tatamy was describing a more esoteric moment in his spiritual journey. The key element of this experience was what Tatamy perceived to be "an impassable mountain before him." Tatamy spent time looking "this way and that Way, but could find no Way at all." After he had "labour'd for a Time, but all in vain," he realized it was not possible "for him ever to help himself." He then "gave over striving," realizing that "his *own* Power" would be forever "vain and fruitless."[140]

Two things immediately jump out as profoundly significant about this passage. First, as already noted, among the eastern Indians, visions and dreams were extremely important measures of spiritual consequence. Brainerd would later note the critical role that dreams played in the lives of the Indians. Since Tatamy received the revelation of the pointlessness of his own striving in such a way, it carried more weight than hearing it through the words of a preacher. Second, although expressed in a different metaphor, Tatamy's story parallels Brainerd's vision of the "stately mansion," which had convinced him of the pointlessness of his own striving after righteousness. Brainerd added some editorial comments after Tatamy's account, probably as a sop to potential readers, noting that he (Brainerd) was "not without fears" that this was Tatamy's own imagination rather than the "Effect of any divine Illumination." But clearly, Brainerd believed it was "divine Illumination" (or, at the very least, he believed that Tatamy believed it was) or he would not have included the story. He must have experienced some emotion himself on hearing an echo of his own journey to salvation.[141]

After all these travails, Tatamy explained to Brainerd, he reached a point where "his soul seemed to rest and be in some measure satisfied." Although Brainerd harbored some concerns because Tatamy could not "remember distinctly any views of Christ, or give any clear account of his soul's acceptance of him," he declared that there was a "very great change in the man, so that it might justly be said, he was become another man, if not a new man." The reference to becoming a new man was a clear evangelical statement of conversion. More important, Brainerd described both Tatamy and his wife as "having some *experimental* Knowledge in Religion," that is, it was not simply an intellectual assent to Christian principles.[142]

The conversion and baptism of Tatamy was an important moment for Brainerd for a number of reasons. As his account of the event, written at the time of Tatamy's baptism in July 1745, shows, it was, for Brainerd, first and foremost a great encouragement. Tatamy was his first convert in Pennsylvania, and this came at a time when he was seeing God use him to reach colonists but not Indians. His lack of success among the Indians weighed heavily upon him. Even as late as July, he was having thoughts of "giving up my *Mission*" because of a combination of "Dejection of Spirit, pressing Discouragement, and an Apprehension of its being unjust to spend Money consecrated to religious Uses, only to...bring [the Indians] to an *external* Profession of Christianity."[143] While Tatamy's conversion obviously did not completely ease his discouragement, it did give him the strength to persevere a few more months.

But Tatamy's conversion had another, more measurable impact on Brainerd's work. Some of his previous interpreters, he lamented, had caused him to "labour under a vast Disadvantage," and "divine Truths would unavoidably loose [*sic*] much of the *Energy* and *Pathos*...by reason of their coming to the Audience from a *Second Hand*."[144] Not so with Tatamy. When revival broke out in New Jersey several months later under Brainerd's preaching, he noted that God inspired Tatamy with "longing Desires for the Conversion of the *Indians*." More remarkable, when Brainerd was "favoured with any *special Assistance* in any Work, and enabled to speak with more than common *Freedom, Fervency* and *Power*," Tatamy was "usually affected in the *same Manner* almost instantly, and seem'd at once quickened and enabled to speak in the same *pathetick Language* and under the same Influence that I did." Furthermore, Tatamy "took Pains Day and Night to repeat and inculcate upon the Minds of the *Indians* the Truths I taught them daily."[145]

It is hard to know, from this distance and from the surviving records, exactly how important Tatamy was to the future course of Brainerd's work. Solo missionaries such as Brainerd did not have a military as the Spanish Franciscans did in New Mexico to destroy native worship and enforce Christian practices on Indians. They had to win souls by persuading Native Americans to abandon long-held beliefs and adopt new ones. The importance of Indian converts in this process is being increasingly noted by historians. David Silverman has emphasized that Christianity did not take off among the Indians of Martha's Vineyard until the first convert, Hiacoomes, was able to convince his brethren of the truth of the claims of the Mayhews. Although an important part of this was Hiacoomes's decision to confront tribal powwows, also critical was the ability of Hiacoomes to, in Silverman's words, "filter Christian teachings through Wampanoag religious ideas," something Silverman identifies as "religious translation."[146] Brainerd did not note any specific speeches or actions of Tatamy's, but he did acknowledge that Tatamy was capable of "communicating, without mistakes, the *Intent and Meaning* of my Discourses, and that without being confined *strictly* and oblig'd to interpret *verbatim*," which makes it highly possible that Tatamy was doing his own "religious translation." It is clear that Tatamy was key in the future course of Brainerd's ministry.[147]

In May 1745, at just about the time that he learned of Tatamy's conversion, Brainerd embarked on his second trip to the Susquehanna. We know very little about this trip, since Edwards reduced the diary entries covering it to a one-page summary. However, we do know that Tatamy again accompanied Brainerd, that they traveled 100 miles up and down the river, and that they visited a number of towns and settlements, including the Delaware town of Shamokin. Probably founded around 1728, by 1745 Shamokin was a remarkably cosmo-politan location; in addition to Delawares, Tutelo and Seneca Indians called the town home, and it served as the location of an Iroquois council fire as well as being a way station for trappers, traders, and war parties. Conrad Weiser, the Indian-Pennsylvania negotiator, and Moravian leader Zinzendorf were among its visitors.[148]

Originally established as a refuge for Delawares migrating from their former homelands farther east, Shamokin's peaceful origins were lost by the 1740s. Traders who passed through the town depleted the food supply which, coupled with occasional floods which destroyed the fields, meant that the residents were frequently confronted with famine. The Indian settlements in the valley were relatively concentrated, and both smallpox and influenza struck in 1746. In addition, the residents of Shamokin were afflicted by the even greater scourge of alco-hol. Not only was it consumed there in large amounts, the town also came to be a supply base for Indians who traded in alcohol with other Indians. Brawls, vio-lence, and murder were not unknown in the town.[149] Not surprisingly, the town developed an unsavory reputation among most people who traveled through central and western Pennsylvania. Veteran Indian agent Conrad Weiser was tem-porarily at a loss for words on his arrival there. Moravian missionaries Martin and Anna Mack, who settled in Shamokin in 1745, described the town as "the very seat of the Prince of darkness." Indians, too, saw the town as a place of spir-itual darkness.[150]

We know of Brainerd's visit from the Moravian leader Bishop A. G. Spangenberg, who passed through the town only a few weeks after Brainerd. While at Shamokin, according to Spangenberg, Brainerd had "assembled the Delawares" and told them that on Sundays they should "assemble as the whites do, and pray as they do." If they did, Brainerd would "build a house for that purpose, and stay with them two years." To which Shickellamy responded that the Indians did not want to be "transformed into white men. The English are our Brethren, but we never promised to become what they are."[151] Behind Shickellamy's decla-ration was the Indian insistence that colonists wishing to work in Shamokin had to offer some kind of practical service to the community. The village had resisted Moravian efforts to establish a work there until they agreed to settle a blacksmith in the town to repair guns. Brainerd's inability to offer any such practical aid mit-igated against the likelihood that he would be welcomed to settle there.[152]

On his way back to the Forks, Brainerd had one of the most remarkable expe-riences of his career. He encountered one of the Indian prophets then active in

Pennsylvania, someone whom Brainerd portrayed as a "restorer of what he supposed was the ancient religion of the Indians." He was dressed in what Brainerd described as "his pontifical garb, which was a coat of bears' skins," "a pair of bearskin stockings," and a mask "painted the one half black and the other tawny." Brainerd declared that, of all the sights he saw among the Indians, "none ever excited such images of terror in my mind."[153] Visions and prophecies were, of course, not new to Native Americans. But the man Brainerd met was the beginning of a new wave of Indian visionaries. Conrad Weiser had heard reports of an Indian having visions in 1737 in the Susquehanna town of Otseningo. Unlike the Indian visionaries who would become more common in the 1750s and 1760s, neither the Otseningo seer nor the man Brainerd met used their religious calling to preach political action. This man claimed that "God had taught him his religion" during a period of solitary living in the woods. To Brainerd, it was obvious that the man "had a set of religious notions that he had examined for himself, and not taken for granted upon bare tradition." Although the man rejected the notion of a devil or hell, Brainerd was forced to concede that "there was something in his temper and disposition that looked more like true religion than anything I ever observed among other heathen."[154]

It is hard to be sure exactly why Brainerd was unwilling to dismiss this Indian's spirituality. Historian Richard Pointer has noted that there were similarities in the personal spiritual pilgrimages of the two men and has also suggested that the man's willingness to treat Brainerd with courtesy was proof of the "genuineness of [the] preacher's kindness and hospitality."[155] However, Brainerd's attitude may well have been rooted in a sense that the man's spiritual journey was a legitimate quest for God. As Brainerd had written to Joseph Bellamy several years before, "God dont deal with all his children as with me." Perhaps, in Brainerd's view, God was leading this man to himself down a different pathway that would eventually reach the same destination.

Although Brainerd's overall evaluation of the trip was somewhat ambivalent, two events did imbue him with a sense of optimism concerning future work on the Susquehanna. One was a meeting with some of his former charges from Kaunaumeek, now relocated to the Susquehanna, who, according to Edwards, "saw and heard him again with great joy." The other was time spent at Juniata, an island at the confluence of the Susquehanna and Juniata rivers, "where there was a considerable number of Indians who appeared more free from prejudices against Christianity than most of the other Indians." However, he arrived back at the Forks on May 30, 1745, "under Dejection of mind" and had to come to grips with the reality that God had still not used him to bring any Indians—apart from Tatamy—to salvation.[156]

In contrast with his lack of success on the Susquehanna, he was heartened by responses to his preaching from colonial congregations. On his way west in April, he and Charles Beatty, the minister at Neshaminy, Pennsylvania, preached and celebrated communion with Richard Treat at Treat's Abington church. Being modeled on the "Method of the Church of Scotland," the communion season lasted for several days, and Brainerd preached a total of three times over a three-day period. He used texts that spoke of the invitations of God: Matthew 5:3 ("Blessed are the poor in spirit"), noting that the "Assembly was sweetly melted, and Scores were all in Tears"; Revelation 14:4 (a reference to the redeemed of the Lord); and John 7:37 ("If any man thirst, let him come unto me, and drink").[157]

A week after returning from his second trip to the Susquehanna, in early June 1745, he traveled to Neshaminy at the invitation of Beatty and his congregation. As had been the case at Abington prior to going to the Susquehanna, it was a "Sacramental Occasion." He preached on Saturday, again choosing a text of encouragement, this time Isaiah 40:1. Then, on Sunday, he ministered with Beatty during the communion and then "discoursed to the Multitude *extempore*," which address was "attended with amazing power; many scores, if not Hundreds, in that great Assembly…were affected." He preached one final time the following day.[158]

He spent most of Monday enjoying "Conversation with dear Christian Friends," and the day following traveled to Maidenhead, New Jersey, where he visited a number of nearby ministers. It was also a time of reflection on the state of his work so far. There had been some hints of interest among Indian groups at both the Forks and the Susquehanna, as well as some positive response among some of the colonial population. But his ministry at Beatty's church, and probably his time at Treat's church several weeks earlier, had taken him back to the successes of the Great Awakening. Clearly, God was still using him to preach the gospel in a fashion that awakened people to their need for salvation. Since God *was* using him, but the Indians at the Forks and on the Susquehanna were not responding, the rhetoric of the awakening suggested that this must mean that those Indians were not willing to hear the voice of God. It was thus time to seek out those who *were* willing to hear from God and who would therefore respond to his calling.[159]

In June 1745, Brainerd recorded in his public journal that he had spent the bulk of his time, for more than a year, "amongst the Indians in the Forks of the Delaware in Pennsylvania" and had also made "two Journeys to Susquehannah River, far back in that Province, in order to treat with the Indians there, respecting Christianity." Despite these efforts, there was no "considerable appearance of special success" in either place, which had "damp'd my Spirits, and was not a little Discouraging to me." In keeping with the idea of looking for the audience which was responsive to God, he had heard of an Indian settlement at Crossweeksung (present-day Crosswicks), New Jersey. He "determined to make them a visit and see what might be done towards the Christianizing of them."[160] This decision would prove to be one of the most serendipitous of Brainerd's life.

3

Pastor

At their March 1747 meeting in Edinburgh, the members of the SSPCK, after perusing the journals of David Brainerd, noted that "his labours among the Indians have been blest with surprising success." Word of Brainerd's success had actually begun to move through the evangelical network the previous year. Jonathan Dickinson had advised Thomas Foxcroft that, if he "had now time I should give you some account of a most wonderful work of Grace making a triumphant progress among the *Indians* in this Province under Mr. Brainerd's ministry—you gain some particular account from the bearer [of this letter]." Similarly, Jonathan Edwards informed Scottish pastor John McLaurin about the missionary's "very remarkable and wonderful...success, among these, poor, ignorant people."[1] The subject of all this excitement was Brainerd's descriptions of a revival that had broken out among the Delaware Indians with whom he was working in New Jersey. From there, the revival had impacted settlers in the surrounding area and traveled with Brainerd and some of his Indian converts back to the Forks of the Delaware. Brainerd also tried, but failed, to duplicate his success in the Susquehanna Valley.

Brainerd interpreted the events at Crossweeksung not in terms of cross-cultural mission work but as the revival or awakening of religion among a local congregation. His account of this period follows the pattern of revivalism he had witnessed in New England: a godly preacher declares the word of God; some people are moved by this message; God responds to these people by sending his power among them, and revival breaks out; other people are drawn to the work of God; those converted then become witnesses to others of what God is doing. But the events at Crossweeksung included a dimension not usually commented on by the ministers who described such events in their churches. Just as Brainerd's words brought change to the Indians, so the response of the Indians brought change to Brainerd. Although he never was completely free of the cultural baggage of his colonial background, the events during those eighteen months did enable him to transcend, to some degree, concepts of race and culture then inherent in the European colonial world.

Revival

Our knowledge of the revival in New Jersey comes primarily from Brainerd's public journal, which was originally written to comply with SSPCK rules.[2] These required its missionaries at "least twice every year" to "report an account of your diligence and success to the foresaid Society's correspondent meeting."[3] Outside of this rather general guideline, the format of these reports was left entirely in the hands of the missionary. Although the SSPCK minutes indicate that most missionaries did send reports as required, none seem to have survived in the SSPCK's archives, although we know that copies of at least two different journals—one of Brainerd's and one of Azariah Horton's—arrived in Edinburgh. Unfortunately, another was "sent off in a ship bound hither [to Scotland]," but that vessel was "taken by our enemies."[4] The only other substantial report which appears to have survived is one by Azariah Horton, which is essentially a day-by-day record of his work among the Montauks.[5] While Brainerd's journal is, in large part, also a day-by-day record, it differs in some important respects. What Brainerd prepared for the SSPCK was not so much a missionary diary as it was a revival narrative of a particular type then common in the American colonies.

As historian Frank Lambert has explained, the origin of the revival narratives which proliferated in the 1740s can be traced to a 1743 circular letter issued by Thomas Prince, a Boston minister and editor of the *Christian History*, the main pro-awakening newspaper published in the colonies. He was one of the many ministers who found inspiration in Jonathan Edwards's *Faithful Narrative*, the account of the 1734–1735 Northampton revival. Using that work as a model, Prince asked pastors whose churches had been awakened to send to him as "cautious and exact an Account as may be, of the Rise, Progress and Effects of this work among you to the present Day." Prince included specific suggestions regarding the contents of such narratives. In particular, he wanted to know the impact of the revival on the young, the immoral, and those who had opposed the work; he suggested leaving out the names of people still alive; he also encouraged minister-authors to include "Attestations" from "some creditable Persons." The letter was published in Boston in 1743 and was also sent to a number of ministers.[6]

Historian Michael Crawford's analysis of these narratives has identified other common factors. Most narratives included a brief history of the town, a description of the spiritual condition of the people before the revival, the beginnings and progress of the revival, subsequent moral reformation in the town, comments on disorders and steps taken to correct them, some individual conversion narratives, and attestations from persons outside the town as to the genuineness of the work. Whether or not David Brainerd knew of Prince's original letter, he was certainly aware of the general format of such narratives. Given the widespread circulation of Edwards's *Faithful Narrative*, we can be fairly certain he had read it. Of the New Jersey and Pennsylvania ministers among whom he now worked, William Tennent, Gilbert Tennent, Samuel Blair, and Jonathan Dickinson all published such narratives in the first part of the 1740s. Most were published in the *Christian History*, but at least one—Samuel Blair's—was published separately in 1744.[7]

Brainerd's account of the revival among the Indians in New Jersey was written very deliberately to fit this model. In keeping with Prince's call for accounts describing the "Rise, Progress, and Effects" of revivals, Brainerd published the "Rise and Progress" of his work. The narrative is replete with descriptions of the revival, moral reformation among the Indians, and individual conversions. Apart from Tatamy, no other convert is mentioned by name. Historian Richard Pointer has suggested that this may have been because of Brainerd's inability to accurately spell the names or due to the Indians' reluctance to reveal their names. While this is certainly possible, the lack of names also complies with Prince's requirements and follows the pattern of other revival accounts.[8] Finally, the narrative concluded with a number of attestations from nearby ministers and respected church members. In constructing the events at Crossweeksung as a revival narrative, Brainerd was presenting himself as the minister of a local congregation which had experienced an awakening.

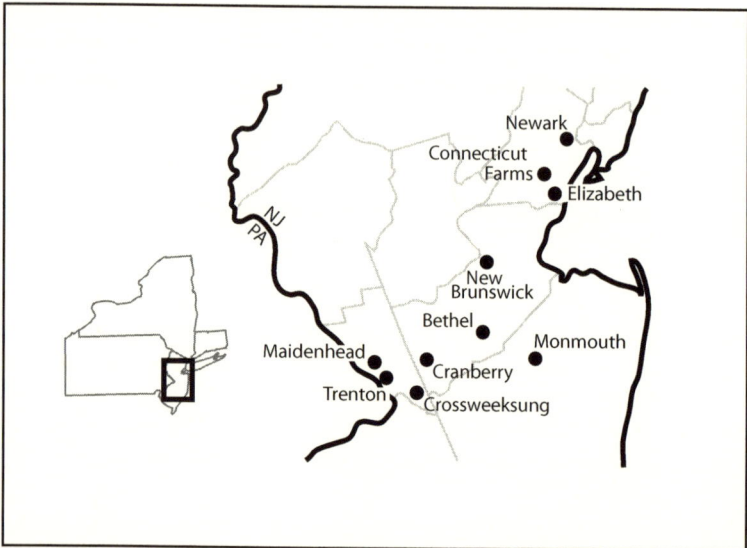

Northern and central New Jersey. Map by Marvin J. Barton.

Brainerd arrived at Cranberry (present-day Cranbury) on June 18, 1745, and lodged with "a serious minister" named Charles McKnight (1720?–1778).[9] The next day, he rode to Crossweeksung, seeking out the Indians of whom he had heard. Even more so than the people at the Forks, Delaware Indians in New Jersey were hemmed in by colonial society. Although they occasionally supplemented their diet by hunting, they mostly subsisted on what they could produce from small fields, perhaps on some domesticated animals, and on fish and other marine animals from rivers and streams. Their poor access to food meant they could not maintain village-sized settlements and, as Brainerd discovered, they were "very much Scatter'd, there being not more than two or three Families in a Place."[10] Some may have made traditional goods—brooms, mats, bowls—in sufficient number to sell to nearby colonists.[11] The disruption of their lifestyle had also led to less tangible problems. The migration of so many Indians meant that large-scale religious rituals became more difficult to celebrate. And, since colonial land hunger had forced so many Indians off their traditional lands, it seems likely that they had lost access to most of their local sacred sites. While Brainerd's account mentions powwows among the converts, he does not mention Indian feasts, or "frolicks," which suggests that even small-scale practices may have been difficult.

As a number of historians have observed, Indians in such a position were more likely to respond to Christian preachers. James Axtell has noted that an openness to new beliefs was "kept at bay initially by the conservative inertia of habit." But for these Indians at Crossweeksung, that "inertia of habit" had been shattered beyond repair. With their traditional lifestyle destroyed, one of the barriers to resisting new teachings was gone. "Settlement Indians," as historian James H. Merrell has identified them, with their own culture and religion so severely challenged, were "more susceptible to the missionary's method." And, reduced to an essentially sedentary lifestyle, these Indians were a stationary target for men like Brainerd. Missionaries did not need to worry about hunters leaving camp or the further dispersal of Indians into isolated winter quarters.[12]

Brainerd's initial foray to Crossweeksung was also attended by some favorable circumstances, although his account tells us that he missed their significance. On his first day, he was concerned that he found only a handful of Indians at home, but, when he preached to them, he observed they were "very serious and attentive."[13] He also noted, in an off-hand fashion, that his audience was "none but a few women and children," but this was probably a key factor in what happened over the next few days. After he finished preaching, Brainerd observed that a number of the women set out on journeys of ten or fifteen miles to invite others to hear him preach the next day, and "like the Woman of Samaria, seem'd desirous that others might see the Man that told them what they had done in their Lives past, and the Misery that attended their idolatrous Ways."[14] What Brainerd did not, in all likelihood, understand was the importance that women held as bearers of spiritual messages. While Delaware women could not, themselves, be shamans or powwows, they often assisted the men in their work. Moreover, women played an important role in Delaware religious ceremonies, and it seems to have been accepted that women could experience religious visions. Most important, in the context of Brainerd's first New Jersey sermon, women also acted as the keepers of spiritual practices within their families, entrusted with passing on religious knowledge. One can imagine that people would pay attention to a woman who traveled fifteen miles to urge them to come and hear a spiritual messenger.[15] Subsequent events support this conclusion: within several days, Brainerd reported, his audience "was now increased to near thirty." He noted that "not a word of opposition was heard from any of them against Christianity," and on at least one occasion, he "preached to the Indians at their own desire."[16]

Within ten days of his first sermon, he counted about forty persons now in the immediate area. While a welcome increase, the larger numbers probably put a strain on resources, especially food. It was at this point that a second favorable event took place. When some hunters "killed three deer, which was a seasonable amount for their wants," not far from the daily meeting place, Brainerd believed it to be an example of divine providence as it meant that the Indians could stay together "in order to attend the means of grace."[17] It is likely that the Indians, too, saw this as a spiritual sign. We know from Jesuit records that other eastern Indians became more open to the Christian message when it seemed that the Christian God provided for them. In 1650, a party of Kennebec Indians traveling with Jesuit Gabriel Druillettes ran out of provisions. Druillettes held a mass for the express purpose of asking God to provide for them, and, as he was concluding, a hunter returned to the camp having killed three moose.[18] While we don't have as much information about the state of provisions in New Jersey, it is reasonable to conclude that the taking of the deer may have enhanced Brainerd's credibility. In addition to these events, Brainerd as a solo missionary posed less of a threat to the Indians' land. Larger groups of missionaries, such as the Moravians, were sometimes treated with suspicion by Indians since it was assumed that they would want land on which to build a settlement.[19]

After two weeks at Crossweeksung, Brainerd decided he had to return to the work at the Forks, but the Indians in New Jersey "of their own accord, agreed that, when I should come again, they would all meet and live together during my continuance with them." Brainerd left the embryonic work at Crossweeksung under the supervision of William Tennent (1705–1777), the minister at nearby Freehold.[20] Tennent was one of a number of ministers who, practicing a Scottish revival and conversion model, believed that a legitimate revival required at least six months to develop and that anybody claiming a conversion experience required close supervision over an extended period of time. This closely paralleled the preparationist model that Brainerd used and so provided continuity in style for the Indians.[21]

Brainerd spent two or three weeks at the Forks, during which time he perceived a spiritual change to have come upon the Indians there as they "appeared concerned," and "Divine Truth seemed to make considerable impressions upon several of them." This initial openness was given further impetus when Brainerd baptized Tatamy and his family, "the first," he noted, "I baptized among the Indians." Two days after baptizing Tatamy's children, Brainerd preached a public message to the Delawares and observed that some of them were "more thoughtful than ever about their soul's concerns." They indicated "that seeing my interpreter and others baptized made them more concerned than anything they had ever seen or heard before." And he further noted that there was "a considerable appearance of divine power among them at the time the ordinance was admitted." Tatamy's conversion also served as a great encouragement to Brainerd, who noted on the day of the second baptism that "God was pleased to help me in prayer, beyond what I have experienced for some time. Especially, my soul was drawn out for the encouragement of Christ's kingdom, and for the conversion of my poor people; and my soul relied on God for the accomplishment of that great work."[22]

In early August, Brainerd made his way back to Crossweeksung. He discovered that the Indians had frequently visited Tennent in his absence, and Brainerd credited Tennent with the fact that some of the Indians were "under deep concern for an interest in Christ." Following in the pattern that had brought such overwhelming responses at Hunter's Settlement, Abington, and Neshaminy, Brainerd's first sermon on his return to New Jersey was invitational in nature, taking as its text Revelation 22:17, which reads, in part, "whosoever will, let him take the water of life freely." As he noted, God had "enabled [him] in a manner somewhat uncommon to set before them the Lord Jesus Christ as a kind and compassionate Saviour, inviting distressed and perishing sinners to accept everlasting mercy," and, as a result, "a further surprizing concern soon became apparent among them."[23]

Brainerd was so convinced that God was at work among the Indians that the following day when he went to a nearby church to assist with communion, he took almost fifty Indians with him, no doubt providing something of a surprise to the regular congregation. Although the church was not named, it was certainly one of the Scottish churches of the region (probably Freehold), since the communion "season" lasted several days. On the second day of the celebration, Brainerd preached, again bringing out his effective John 7:37 sermon, "come unto me, and drink." Even at this early stage of the revival, the work among the Indians was moving from preparation to conversion with Brainerd, following the revival narrative model, describing some specific, but anonymous persons who had "obtain'd Relief and Comfort."[24]

Once he returned to Crossweeksung, he continued to preach sermons which focused on the image of a compassionate savior. His texts included Isaiah 53:3–10, where Jesus is characterized as the suffering servant, and Luke 14:16–23, where Jesus portrays the kingdom of God as being open for the outcasts of society.[25] The latter passage, in particular, may have resonated with people who were treated as outcasts by those around them. Certainly, it was this sermon that unleashed a religious movement at Crossweeksung that carried all the hallmarks of the New England revivals of which Brainerd had been a part. His description is worth quoting at length:

[T]he Power of God seemed to descend upon the Assembly *like a rushing mighty wind*, and with an astonishing energy bore down all before it.

> I stood amaz'd at the Influence that seiz'd the Audience almost universally, and could compare it to nothing more aptly than the irresistible Force of a mighty Torrent or swelling Deluge, that with its insupportable Weight and Pressure, bears down and sweeps before it whatever is in its Way! Almost all Persons of all Ages were bow'd down with Concern together, and scarce one was able to stand the *Shock* of this surprizing Operation. Old Men and Women, who had been drunken Wretches for many Years, and some little Children, not more than Six or Seven Years of Age, appear'd in Distress for their Souls as well as Persons of middle Age.[26]

Brainerd's language was circumspect, telling his readers that people were "bowed down with concern" and "scarcely…able to stand the shock." But, for those familiar with some of the stories which had emerged from New England at the peak of the revivals, there were subtle allusions to some of the more "enthusiastic" events of those days. For example, at Suffield, Connecticut, in 1741, Jonathan Edwards had seen people faint and fall down under the power of God while he was preaching.[27] Given Brainerd's involvement in such events during the revivals and his continued association with radical groups while at Kaunaumeek, his account is probably sanitized, carrying the general sense of what happened, but shying away from explicit descriptions of enthusiasm.

He spent most of the next day meeting with people privately but preached again in the afternoon, using Matthew 11:28, yet another text which speaks of the simple availability of God's love and salvation. Once again, "a divine Influence seemed to attend what was spoken," causing those present to "cry out in Anguish of Soul," which in turn brought others to the area. Brainerd continued in the "same Strain of Gospel-Invitation" until almost all those present were "melted into Tears and Cries."[28]

The awakening continued the next day, and then the next. By the time Brainerd preached on the subsequent Sunday, news of what had happened had spread. In addition to the Delawares that Sunday, he noted the presence of "numbers of careless spectators of the white people, some Quakers and others," who came, apparently, to see what all the fuss was about. Some of these people were likewise awakened and "could no longer be idle spectators, but found they had souls to save or lose as well as the Indians." Brainerd took no credit for the revival, noting that he had never seen "the work of God appear so independent of means as at this time." In fact, he "seemed to do nothing, and indeed to have nothing to do, but to *stand still and see the salvation of God.*"[29] Over the succeeding days, he continued to visit with the Indians, counsel them, and preach publicly. He diligently noted the scripture passages from which he preached in order, he later wrote, to demonstrate his emphasis on one "continued strain of Gospel-invitation." His texts during this time included the parable of the prodigal son from Luke 15, the account of the Roman centurion Cornelius from Acts 10:34–48, and the story of the conversion of the Ethiopian eunuch Philip from Acts 8:29–39. All of these passages describe a merciful God reaching out to express his love to a repentant sinner, and none contain any sense of judgment or terror.[30]

By now, Brainerd counted seventy or more Indians as having "concern for their souls." On Sunday, August 18, he preached first to an "assembly of white people, made up of Presbyterians, Baptists, Quakers," and then to the Indians, this time from John 6:35, wherein Jesus portrays himself as the freely available bread of life.[31] The next day, August 19, after preaching to the Indians in the morning, he traveled to Freehold, New Jersey, and preached to "a considerable assembly," presumably at William Tennent's church. Instead of returning to Crossweeksung, Brainerd traveled from Freehold to Elizabeth-town to meet with Jonathan Dickinson, and he was "refreshed" by recounting to Dickinson and others "what God had done and was still doing among my poor people."[32]

Upon his return to Crossweeksung, Brainerd began to prepare for the baptism of a group of Indians. Just before traveling to Freehold, he had taken "occasion to treat concerning baptism," so that the Delawares could be "instructed and prepared to partake of that ordinance." The day after he returned, he "spent the forenoon in discoursing to some of the Indians, in order to [prepare them for] their receiving baptism." He explained in detail the "nature of the ordinance, the obligations attending it, the duty of devoting ourselves to God in it, and the privilege of being in covenant with Him." In response, several of the Delawares "delighted with the thoughts of giving up themselves to Him in that solemn and public manner."[33]

The baptism, Brainerd's first in New Jersey, took place the next day, Sunday, August 25. In some ways, the setting was not ideal. In the morning, there was a "multitude of white people," to whom he tried to speak, but the colonists "kept walking and gazing about, and behaved more indecently than any Indians I have ever addressed." Nonetheless, in the morning, he preached to the Indians from Luke 15:3–7, the story of the good shepherd, while in the afternoon his text was Revelation 3:20, in which Christ represents himself as knocking on the door of man's heart. Following the sermon, he baptized fifteen adults and ten children and then reminded them of "the solemn obligations they were now under to live to God" and saw that "their hearts were engaged and cheerful in duty."[34]

The day after the baptismal service, Brainerd again preached to the Indians, this time from John 6:51–55, where Jesus identifies himself as the living bread of God, given to bring life to humanity, another presentation of God as offering opportunity rather than judgment. The number of Delawares now regularly hearing his message was about ninety-five, and, once again, the meeting was impacted with a "tender, affectionate, humble delightful melting, and appeared to be the genuine effect of a spirit of adoption." This continued success convinced Brainerd that it was now his "duty to take a journey far back to the Indians on the Susquehanna River, (it now being a proper season of the year to find them generally at home)." As the first step in what would become a more dynamic partnership, Brainerd asked his New Jersey converts if they would be "willing to spend the remainder of the day in prayer for me, that God would go with me, and succeed my Endeavours for the Conversion of those poor Souls," a request with which the Indians were eager to comply.[35]

Brainerd traveled via Philadelphia, where he obtained a recommendation from the governor, then continued on to the Forks. He spent a week at the Forks preaching to and meeting with the Indians. During this time, he found the Indians there even more receptive to his message, including "two stupid Creatures that I could scarce ever before keep awake while I was discoursing to them." By now, Brainerd also saw changes among the white residents at the Forks, preaching, for example, at an Irish settlement where "the People of God seemed to melt, and others to be in some Measure awaken'd." On another instance, the changes among the Indians had a direct affect on the Europeans. On September 8, Brainerd recorded that "sundry of the careless white People now present were awakened, (or at least startled) seeing the power of God so prevalent among the Indians." With the hand of God so apparently on his ministry, Brainerd was at peace with himself and concluded, "God was both able and willing to do all that I desired, for my self and Friends, and his Church in general." His time of prayer that night was a "blessed evening."[36]

On September 9, 1745, he set off for the Susquehanna, arriving at Shamokin on September 13. Several days later, Moravian missionaries Martin and Anna Mack arrived in town. Brainerd visited the Macks at least once, and the couple remembered him as being "very friendly," noting also that he stayed at the home of Indian leader Shickellamy, in whose house he had preached in May.[37] The character of the local Indians, in Brainerd's eyes, was far different from that of the Indians at Crossweeksung. The Shamokin Indians were "counted the most drunken, mischievous, and ruffianly of any in these parts," and Brainerd thought there was little "human probability" that "these miserable, wicked Indians" could be brought to salvation in a place where "the devil now reigns in the most eminent manner."[38]

Despite his pessimism, following a positive welcome from the Indians' leader (probably Shickellamy), Brainerd spent several days going from house to house and preaching public sermons. Although he did not see the same kind of response as in New Jersey, he did record that "one or two seemed to be touched with some concern for their souls." He spent only four days at Shamokin before most of his audience went on a hunting trip, and Brainerd moved on to Juniata Island. There, he was further discouraged by the response of the Indians he had met on his previous trip. He had believed they would welcome his return, but they "now seemed resolved to retain their pagan notions, and persist in their idolatrous practices." While at Juniata, he observed a "great sacrifice and dance," which prevented him from gathering them together for a public meeting. He tried to speak with several of the Indians privately but without success. That evening, "near a hundred" of the Indians gathered together and "danced around a large fire, having prepared ten fat deer for the sacrifice." The ceremony continued most of the night, and Brainerd stayed and watched the entire event.[39]

The following day, a Sunday, the Indians resumed their rituals, this time in an attempt to discern the cause of an endemic illness on the island. Some of the men spent several hours "singing, sometimes howling, sometimes extending their hands to the utmost stretch, spreading all their fingers." Brainerd sat about thirty feet away, "undiscovered, with my Bible in my hand, resolving if possible to spoil their sport, and prevent their receiving any answers." Eventually, the ritual came to an end without, in Brainerd's opinion, the Indians "appearing to receive any answers." Nonetheless, he was forced to conclude that the Indians who lived along the Susquehanna were in a "deplorable" state.[40]

Not surprisingly, as Brainerd began the trek back east, his inability to effectively preach to the Indians in the area "greatly sank my spirits, gave me the most gloomy turn of mind imaginable." He was, he wrote, "much exercised with a sense of my barrenness" and felt that no other Christian "made so poor a hand of living to God as I." However, by the time he reached the area of the Forks, he was reminded that, despite his barrenness, "God had accounted me faithful, putting me into the ministry."[41] He stopped at the Forks briefly to invite the Indians there "to accompany, or, if not, to follow me down to Crossweeksung as soon as their conveniency would admit."[42] He arrived back in New Jersey on October 5, more than happy to be among those who were responding to God.

By now, the ministry at Crossweeksung was a source of encouragement to him, especially since the Indians were able to pursue God without him. The day after he returned was a Sunday, and he preached morning and evening but then, exhausted, went to bed. Nonetheless, "the Indians continued praying among themselves for near two hours together; which continued exercises appeared to be attended with a blessed quickening influence from on high." "What a difference," he exclaimed, "is there between these and the Indians I had lately treated with upon Susquehanna!" Brainerd was beginning to make a distinction between Indians who responded to the gospel and those who rejected it. As a consequence, the New Jersey Indians were becoming his brethren in God, while the Indians on the Susquehanna still lay outside that relationship.[43]

Just a month after his return from the Susquehanna, he prepared the first portion of his public journal for publication.[44] As much as possible, given the somewhat different circumstances, Brainerd followed the Prince form of the revival narrative. Rather than presenting a history of the decline of religion in the "town," as Prince had suggested, he instead described his own situation. The revival among the Indians began when he had the "least hope" and the "least rational Prospect of seeing a Work of Grace propagated among them." In fact, he had come to see himself as a "burden to the *Honourable Society*" and was having "serious Thoughts of giving up my *Mission*." But, at this low point, "God saw fittest to begin this glorious Work."[45] Brainerd then began to describe how the work had started. When he first arrived at Crossweeksung, he found only a handful of listeners, but then people "gathered from all Quarters," such that it "seem'd as if God had summoned them together" solely to "deliver his Message to them." Brainerd also described the hand of God at work in the conversion of Tatamy, as he had since become so vital to the work.[46]

Brainerd informed his readers that he thought it "remarkable" that God had brought about this revival by "one continued Strain of Gospel-Invitation," which his readers could guess "from a View of the *Passages* of *Scripture*" he used in his sermons. As one example, he cited his use of the parable of the great supper from Luke 14, which led to "so general an awakening," the likes of which he had never seen before. The revival, he noted, "always appear'd most remarkable when I insisted upon the *Compassions of a dying Saviour*."[47]

Brainerd assured his readers that he had definitely "instructed the Indians respecting their fallen State." While he conceded that the "preaching of *Terror*" was "perhaps God's more usual way of awakening Sinners," he reminded readers that when this had been done (for example, in New England), some observers had objected that those so awakened were only "*frighted* with a *fearful Noise* of *Hell* and *Damnation*," and there was "no Evidence that their Concern was the Effect of a Divine Influence." But, in the case of the awakening of the Indians, "God has left no room for this Objection."[48] While God had definitely moved among the people, they had not been scared into salvation; rather, the compassion and love of God had made them aware of their sinful nature and had, in turn, called forth the only rational response, a heartfelt quest for forgiveness.

Brainerd's decision to focus on emphasizing the "Compassions of a dying Saviour" was rooted in both personal experience and pragmatism. Although he had experienced moments of terror during his own conversion process, it had also been built on offers of a compassionate God, something he had also stressed in the sermon he preached at his licensing exam in Connecticut. At his ordination, Ebenezer Pemberton had emphasized, among other factors, that missionaries needed to preach the "compassionate care, which the Blessed Redeemer takes" of the lost. Pemberton had also insisted that preachers should not be "perpetually employed in the language of terror," because it was their "peculiar business to preach the unsearchable riches of CHRIST." Pragmatically, Brainerd turned to this style because it worked. Preaching compassion had brought responses from colonial audiences so why not preach the same message to the Indians? Once such an approach began to have an impact at Crossweeksung, it would have made no sense to change it; Brainerd simply continued doing that which was effective. And, as noted in the previous chapter, Brainerd also paid tribute to the efforts of Tatamy. Although we know nothing of the specifics, it can be assumed that the interpreter was presenting Brainerd's message in a way that made it most attractive to his Delaware audience. As proof of the sincerity of the converts, Brainerd completed a final portion of the Prince model by noting the moral reformation that had taken place among the Indians. Among the changes he had observed, their "*Pagan* Notions and *idolatrous* Practices seem to be entirely abandoned"; they appeared "regularly disposed in the Affairs of *Marriage*" and "generally divorc'd from *Drunkenness*."[49]

Despite the success of the work, Brainerd was careful to point out to his readers that difficulties remained. As at Kaunaumeek, one of his biggest initial obstacles came from colonists in the area. Some had told the Indians that there was "no need of all this *Noise* about Christianity," while others told the Indians that Brainerd was a "*Knave*, a *Deceiver*, and the like," who had "no other Design but to impose upon them." When these fairly mild invectives failed to work, they suggested to the Indians that Brainerd's goal was to "gather together as large a Body of them as I possibl[y] could, and then sell them to *England* for Slaves." However, Brainerd pointed out that these particular colonists were the Indians' "old Acquaintance, who had frequent Opportunities of gratifying their *thirsty Appetites* with strong Drink, and consequently, doubtless, had the greatest Interest in their Affections." Given the depredations by these settlers against Indian land and customs, it is not surprising that Brainerd observed that their accusations "only serv'd to engage the Affections of the *Indians* more firmly to me."[50]

There were other significant issues which had the potential to make the work more difficult or even to bring it to a premature halt. First, from a somewhat personal perspective, Brainerd was eager to find a "*Colleague*, or *Companion*, to travel with me." Although he had had "some Encouragement," he had not, to date, "found any Person qualified and disposed for this good Work." In fact, in a letter to Eleazar Wheelock, Brainerd intimated that the publication of his journal might help in finding someone to assist him in his work. He also lamented again the great distances which separated the various Indian groups as well as the language problems. In addition to the Indians at Crossweeksung, he still felt he was responsible for those at the Forks of the Delaware and at the various settlements on the Susquehanna.[51]

However, even with these reservations, Brainerd believed it was important to marshal more resources for the purposes of aiding the awakening. In particular, he informed his readers that it was necessary to have an "*English-School* speedily set up among these *Indians*," especially since the Indians were now "willing to be at the Pains of gathering together in a Body for this Purpose." To this end, the SSPCK correspondents had agreed to raise funds for the "Maintenance of a School-Master," a financial burden which was to be taken up among the churches under the pastoral care of the SSPCK commissioners. Up until this point, Brainerd had mainly been concerned with winning converts among the Indians. But now, he wanted to grow a church, a congregation of mature Christians, and for this, he needed more than simple converts.[52]

Disciples

For the majority of evangelical pastors, conversion was not an endpoint, the destination of the spiritual life. It was, instead, a gateway, the beginning of the authentic Christian life. Part of this meant growing in rational understanding of the Bible, developing a deeper relationship with God, and learning to be more obedient to God's revealed will. However, for many Christian leaders, it also meant that Christians should learn how to do God's work by serving the church, bearing witness to their faith, and performing other tasks suitable to the lay believer. While eighteenth-century Protestants did not usually endorse the levels of lay ministry seen in many churches today, they did expect some level of involvement. David Brainerd would seek to inculcate this type of spiritual growth among his Indian converts.

Brainerd opened the second part of his public journal on November 24, 1745, and recorded a further month of God working through both public preaching and private meetings. But, in late December, he decided that, since the Indians had "attained to a considerable Degree of Knowledge in the Principles of Christianity," he now "thought it proper to set up a Catechetical Lecture among them." The need for instruction was made more urgent by some Indians newly arrived at Crossweeksung, who had begun to introduce what he held to be poor doctrine, including "some of the Quakers' errors, especially this fundamental one, That if men will but live soberly and honestly, according to the dictates of their own consciences, or the light within, then there is no danger or doubt of their salvation."[53]

Brainerd used the Shorter Catechism of the Presbyterian church as the basis of his instruction. This contained 107 questions and answers (compared with 196 in the Larger Catechism), outlining the basics of the Christian life, as well as the Ten Commandments, the Lord's Prayer, and a version of the Apostle's Creed.[54] Other missionaries in the colonial period had found formal questions and answers to be a useful tool in developing religious understanding after an initial conversion experience. Jesuit priests in Julí, Peru, used a specially for-matted volume, the *Doctrina Christiana*, to systematize their instruction of the Aymara people.[55] The Mayhews and their coworkers on Martha's Vineyard relied heavily on catechetical instruction to help Wampanoag converts develop a fuller understanding of Christianity, as did John Sergeant at Stockbridge.[56]

Brainerd provided a list of the questions he used at the end of the second volume of his public journal, noting in some cases where he used a particular wording to help him overcome linguistic and conceptual difficulties. Although Brainerd provided very few details of the responses of his people, he was pleas-antly surprised to find the Indians' "doctrinal knowledge to exceed [his] own expectations." He also noted that his people answered his questions with "surpriz-ing Readiness and Judgment" and to his "great Satisfaction." However, this does not mean that all was smooth sailing. Sometimes, the Delawares, in keeping with Indians at other locations, used catechetical instruction to come to grips with their own doubts about Christian doctrine. Brainerd noted that he did have to deal with a number of thorny questions, "particularly the doctrine of *Predestination*" as well as the "proper *Method* as well as proper *Matter* of Prayer." In addition, Brainerd faced the problem of trying to explain concepts for which no Delaware words existed, "Justice, Condemnation, Faith, Repentance, Justification," among others. And we can imagine that the presence of those who had acquired Quaker doctrines must have led to some interesting exchanges. However, by late April 1746, Brainerd was satisfied that the Indians were "advanced in their Knowledge of the *Principles* of Christianity."[57]

Brainerd's move to a more methodical form of instruction did not slow down the awakening; it simply served as a different means by which it took place. On one occasion, as he "discoursed to my people in the Catechetical method," God "granted a remarkable influence of His blessed Spirit to accompany what was spoken, and a great concern appeared in the Assembly."[58] Nor did Brainerd allow his own schedules to interfere in the ways of God. One Sunday, as he preached to a mixed audience, he saw "some tears among the white people as well as the Indians." He went back to his house, intending to preach again in the afternoon, but the Indians crowded in almost immediately. At this point, a fresh response broke out among the people, and Brainerd "could not pretend to have any formal religious exercise among them." For the next two days, he both received Indians in his house and visited them in theirs. As 1745 drew to a close, he reported that "more than twenty families live within a quarter of a mile of me. A very convenient Situation in Regard both of publick and private instruction."[59] It is not hard to see why he would tell his brother John that he was "in one continued, perpetual, and uninterrupted hurry; and divine providence throws so much upon me, that I don't see it will ever be otherwise." Nonetheless, he did not wish for things to change, only that he could have "more strength and grace to do more for God."[60]

Through the month of January, Brainerd continued his work among the Indians, using all the methods now at his disposal: public sermons, private meetings, and catechetical instruction. And all three methods produced the desired results. During a sermon from Isaiah 55:6 ("Seek ye the Lord while he may be found"), the "Word of God seem'd to fall upon the Audience with a divine weight and Influence." The following day, he was "visited by divers Persons under deep Concern for their Souls." And all the while, he instructed them from the catechism, noting that his fears that the method would "tend only to enlighten the *Head*, but not to *affect the Heart*" were unfounded.[61]

Brainerd's ability to instruct the Indians was enhanced at the end of the month when the man chosen to be the schoolmaster commenced his duties. The importance of education in Indian mission work has already been noted. Brainerd, of course, participated in the schooling of the Indians at Stockbridge and, no doubt, subscribed to John Sergeant's motivations. As Sergeant had noted in his letter to Benjamin Colman, which was published during the time Brainerd was at Kaunaumeek, an appropriate education would "in the most effectual Manner change their whole Habit of thinking and acting; and raise them, as far as possible, into the Condition of a civil industrious and polish'd People," and would "instill into their Minds" the "Principles of Vertue and Piety." But while the goal of education was plain in the minds of missionaries such as Brainerd and Sergeant, Indians, too, often welcomed schools. At Crossweeksung, Brainerd recorded that the arrival of the schoolmaster was "heartily welcom'd" by the Indians, leading him to promptly distribute primers among some of the children. Clearly, like many other Native American groups that saw literacy, in James Axtell's words, as "a powerful tool of survival," the New Jersey Delawares were also anxious for an education.[62]

By April 1746, Brainerd had come to the conclusion that the spiritual growth displayed by some of the Indians as a result of their instruction made them "proper Subjects of the Ordinance of the *Lord's Supper*." For Brainerd and other ministers, the sacrament of communion was not something to be taken lightly, so much so that, before making a final decision on communion, Brainerd waited until he had "taken advice of some of the Reverend Correspondents in this solemn affair."[63] After all, question 97 in the Shorter Catechism, from which his flock was being taught, asked "What is required to the worthy receiving of the Lord's supper?" to which the reply was "It is required of them that would worthily partake of the Lord's supper, that they examine themselves of their knowledge to discern the Lord's body, of their faith to feed upon him, of their repentance, love and new obedience; lest coming unworthily, they eat and drink judgment to themselves."[64] By administering communion, Brainerd would be making a statement that he believed that "his people" had experienced true salvation.

Brainerd's organization of communion for the Delaware converts reflected the Scottish sacramental tradition then being practiced in many of the nearby Presbyterian churches in addition to replicating the solemnity with which communion was treated in many colonial churches. In Scotland, communion services were often community rituals, great religious festivals which included preparatory services, times of personal reflection, and controlled access to the elements. At Cambuslang, Scotland, in 1742, of an estimated 20,000 people who attended the preaching, about 1,700 partook of the communion. A month later, a second communion service attracted anywhere between 30,000 and 50,000, at a time when the population of Glasgow, which lay five miles away, was estimated to be about 17,000. Three thousand people took communion and many others wanted to but were unable because not enough bread and wine had been provided. These sacramental seasons were duplicated in the colonies, and people recognized communion as a time when God was likely to visit his people with his presence, and they prepared for it with due solemnity. This was magnified if some were preparing for their first communion, as all of Brainerd's charges were.[65]

For two days, Brainerd prepared the Indians—through preaching, prayer, and repentance—to receive communion. The day before the service, he baptized two converts, and that night, he instructed those who planned to partake in communion. As though to reassure his readers, he wrote that he had "abundant satisfaction respecting their doctrinal knowledge and fitness in that respect for an attendance upon it," and, furthermore, the Delawares were "earnestly concerned that they might be duly prepared for an attendance upon it." The following day, he preached from a straightforward text, Titus 2:14: "Who gave himself for us, that he might redeem us from all iniquity, and purify unto himself a peculiar people, zealous of good works." He then administered communion to twenty-three Delawares and noted that the "ordinance was attended with great solemnity, and with a most desirable tenderness and affection." He also assured his readers that the service was completed "without any boisterous commotion of the passions." The inference in Brainerd's journal is that, as at Cambuslang, many more attended the service than actually took communion. Also following the Scottish model, the communion season did not end with the sacrament itself but the next day, when Brainerd "concluded the sacramental solemnity" with a final sermon. As was the experience with communion celebrations in colonial churches, Brainerd noted that this "appeared to be a season of divine power amongst us."[66]

In the midst of all this instruction and communion preparation, the Indians and Brainerd were also in the process of relocating their settlement to some land not far from Cranberry which they also owned. The primary goal was to create a single settlement which was large enough to support all of the people now associated with the work. Brainerd had raised the possibility of centralizing the work in New Jersey as early as August 1745, just weeks after the revival started there, when he had spoken with Jonathan Dickinson about developing a plan "for the Settlement of the Indians together in a body."[67] The establishment of the school at Crossweeksung had, in Brainerd's mind, made centralization more imperative. Although there were "generally about thirty children and young persons in [the] school in the daytime," only about "fifteen married people [came] in the evening." The smaller evening attendance was due to the adults spending so much time away from Crossweeksung in order to provide food for their families, with Brainerd noting that the "number of the latter sort of persons [was] less than it would be if they could be more constantly at home."[68]

Although the problems caused by travel and dispersal motivated Brainerd to seek to centralize the Indian work, the idea of concentrating Indians into European-style nuclear settlements was, of course, neither new nor unique to him. Spanish Jesuits in Sinaloa in New Spain used a technique known as *congregación de Indios* to resettle isolated hamlets into a more central location to make evangelization more viable. Jesuits in New France also attempted to establish mission settlements although, lacking the military support available in New Spain, these efforts were less successful. In Brainerd's New England, the "praying towns" of Massachusetts were well established by the middle of the eighteenth century, although their role in protecting Indian rights was diminishing. A similar policy of establishing central locations for Indians was part of Sergeant's policy at Stockbridge, where he, too, noted that their "living in two Places, remote from each other...laid them under Disadvantages, as to attending upon the publick Worship, and the School." Brainerd, of course, had supported this policy when he encouraged his Kaunaumeek charges to relocate to Stockbridge and had considered similar actions while at the Forks of the Delaware.[69]

In addition to making instruction easier, centralized settlements also made it more likely that Indians could be persuaded to adopt European-style work practices. Instead of relying on hunting, which Europeans saw as a less civilized lifestyle, Indians, especially Indian men, living in static villages could learn to farm, an activity which befitted civilized persons. As John Sergeant had once argued, "perhaps the *Neglect of promoting Industry* among them is the chief *moral Reason* of so *little* being done to Purpose them in forming their Manners." But, whereas Indians welcomed some aspects of European culture—such as schools—they were often far less enthused about settling down in European-style villages to practice farming, frequently seeing it for what it was: an attempt to destroy their traditional lifestyle. Thus, although Indians in various parts of North America did move to new settlements, they did not always change their lifestyles in accordance with the wishes of Europeans. Indians who moved to Jesuit-run villages in Quebec frequently refused to take up farming, using the villages as bases to conduct hunting expeditions. And in Mashpee, in Massachusetts, although the Indians did maintain a centralized village, they retained control over the appointment of pastors to their church, insisting, for example, that any minister had to be able to conduct services in the Wampanoag language.[70]

In a similar vein, the Crossweeksung Indians exhibited some resistance to Brainerd's efforts to develop the new settlement, evoking some of his few criticisms of his charges. Prior to one of their first work days at the new site—about fifteen miles from Crossweeksung—Brainerd warned them to not be "*slothful in Business*, as they had ever been in their *Pagan* State." A week later, he again brought them together and "discours'd to them again on the Necessity and Importance of their labouring industriously," a tacit admission that his first effort had not brought the desired results. This time, Brainerd noted that "numbers of them (both Men and Women) seem'd to offer themselves willingly to this Service, and some appear'd affectionately concern'd that God might go with them, and begin their *little Town* for them." Noting the pattern of resistance at other Indian settlements, Richard Pointer has argued that what Brainerd saw as laziness was actually a way for the Indians to avoid being conformed to English cultural mores and so avoid becoming more dependent on the colonists.[71]

While Pointer is undoubtedly correct, it is important to keep in mind that the dynamic taking place at Crossweeksung and Cranberry was somewhat different to that which had occurred at other Indian-colonial settlements. In most such cases, some degree of coercive force was used. Jesuits and Franciscans in New Spain and New Mexico were backed by military force. Missionaries who established the praying towns in Massachusetts and the *reserves* of New France were protected and supported by colonial governments. But the sole outside catalyst for developing the Indian community at Crossweeksung was Brainerd's preaching. Furthermore, once the decision was made to relocate to Cranberry, it took the Indians only about six weeks to complete the process. While the majority of the Indians at the settlements were there to partake in Brainerd's ministry, it is also clear that there were other dynamics at work.

Unlike Natick, or Sillery, or the Sinaloa *congregación de Indios*, the settlement at Crossweeksung was growing not because Indians were being asked, or forced, to settle in the area but because they were coming there of their own volition. Brainerd himself was aware of this, frequently noting the arrival of new groups of people. In early November 1745, there were "sundry…persons lately come here from remote Places"; in January 1746, he reported that he "Visited some Persons newly come among us" and noted that there were "Strangers from remote Parts almost continually drop[p]ing in among us"; in March, there were "Fifteen *Strangers*, adult Persons, come among us in the *Week* past." Indeed, by the end of that month, he estimated that the little community had swollen to about 150.[72] Brainerd did not speculate on why this was happening, surely believing that the work of God was drawing these people in. But the growing settlement at Crossweeksung was also serving an important cultural purpose for the Indians. Historian Richard White has noted that, in the wake of the shattering of the *pays d'en haut*, the regions west of the Huron Indians, villages became the dominant

social structure in the region. With the fragmenting of the larger sociopoliti-
cal units, villages became a source of belonging, strength, and refuge. It seems
apparent that the settlement at Crossweeksung was serving a similar purpose.[73]
However, whereas in the *pays d'en haut*, the villages were what remained after the
breakdown of the larger structure, at Crossweeksung, the settlement was created
by the Indians to provide greater strength than the small two- or three-family
settlements which had existed after the rupture of the Delawares' world. Thus,
while the Indians may have been motivated, in part, to relocate in order to facilitate their instruction, they also supported the relocation since it provided them
with the ability to create a larger community from which they could draw greater
strength than was possible in the smaller, scattered locations.

However, this changing situation was about to bring the Indians and Brainerd
into conflict with colonists and landowners in New Jersey. The proximate cause
was the debt some of the Delawares owed for liquor purchases, a debt that had
been incurred some time before Brainerd's arrival. But, in January 1746, some of
the creditors arrested a number of the debtors with the presumed goal of obtain-
ing title to "a great Body of [the Indians'] Hunting Lands." Immediately aware
that for this to happen would mean that the Indians "could not subsist together
in these Parts," Brainerd took action. He went to the SSPCK commissioners, seeking permission to use money collected in their churches for the "Discharging of
[the Indians'] Debt, and securing of these Lands." Permission was granted, and
he made a payment of "Eighty two Pounds five Shillings" and so "prevented the
Danger of Difficulty in this Respect." However, in addition to paying the debt, he
also apparently complained of the "horrid Practice of making the Indians drunk,
and then cheating them out of their Lands and other Properties."[74]

Probably as retaliation for this, just five days after he recorded paying
off the Indians' debt, he learned that rumors were being spread that he was a
Catholic "sent by the *Papists* to draw the *Indians* into an Insurrection against the
English, that some were in fear of me, and others were for having me taken up by
Authority and punish'd." This was a particularly astute strategy by his opponents
in the midst of King George's War. Brainerd immediately suspected that the reason for the allegations was the complaints he had leveled against the liquor merchants. He remembered that he had made these charges with "too much Warmth
of Spirit" and so conjured up his old fears of division and discord. Up until this
point, during his time in New Jersey, he had been "enabled to mind my own business, in these parts, as well as elsewhere; and to let all Men and all Denominations
of Men alone, as to their Party-Notions."[75] Having escaped the divisions which
had so disturbed him while in New England, he now faced the threat of being
dragged into the kind of public divisiveness he wanted to avoid.

But financial machinations and character slurs were just the beginning of the
problems which surrounded the move to Cranberry, as the Indian settlement was
about to be pulled into a series of boiling land controversies that were creating
upheavals across parts of New Jersey. Coming, as they did, on the heels of a series
of disputes and tensions between Governor Lewis Morris and the Assembly, the
situation in the colony was extremely volatile for much of the 1740s. The New

Jersey land disputes grew out of a number of overlapping and mutually exclusive claims to ownership based on multiple land grants. Essentially, in the middle of the eighteenth century, the arguments took place between proprietors and their agents and tenants, on the one hand, who claimed ownership based on royal and proprietary grants, and smaller freeholders, on the other hand, who claimed legitimacy by right of purchase from Indians. The first violence occurred in 1745, when anti-proprietary settlers carried out a jailbreak. More violence followed in 1746 and would continue, off and on, for ten years fueled by a loss of faith in the judicial system by the smaller freeholders.[76]

In addition to the division between types of landowners, the dispute also featured religious divisions, which had their roots in the revivals of the 1730s and early 1740s. Anglican ministers and members of their churches had publicly opposed George Whitefield and the revivalists. In one infamous incident, two elite Anglicans, Robert Hunter Morris—son of the New Jersey governor— and James Alexander, had trumped up a charge of horse stealing against William Tennent and a friend of his. It is thus not surprising that when local Anglican ministers and men employed by the Anglican Society for the Propagation of the Gospel supported the proprietors, many Presbyterian ministers took the side of the freeholders. In addition, many of the freeholders were members of the Presbyterian churches. Among the leaders of the Presbyterians were Brainerd's confidants Jonathan Dickinson and Aaron Burr.[77]

Proprietary interests attempted to assert their claims by using the court systems and by appealing to imperial authorities in England. In contrast, smaller freeholders frequently appealed to land titles gained by purchases from Indian inhabitants. It was when the legal system began to favor the proprietors that the freeholders frequently turned to extrajudicial actions—and violence—to protect their lands. Given the competing approaches to land rights, the Indian lands at Cranberry took on added importance. If Indian ownership of the land was accepted, it might well have provided legal support for freeholder claims. Proprietors James Alexander and Robert Hunter Morris took the lead in attacking the claims of the Crossweeksung-Cranberry Indians. In a lengthy document ostensibly directed to the Lords of Trade, they laid out the proprietary case against the small freeholders—whom they held to be responsible for all of the violence taking place. As Alexander and Morris described events, the riots had broken out in September 1745, when about 150 men appeared at the Newark jail in "a riotous manner," armed with "Clubbs, Axes and Crowbarrs," in order to effect the extrajudicial release of one Samuel Baldwin. The crux of the rioters' claims, according to "State of the Facts," was that no men should be imprisoned for allegedly trespassing on lands when those men claimed legal title based on "Indian purchase Right." Although Alexander and Morris disputed the validity of this reasoning, their representation of their opponents' arguments was fairly accurate. While clearly operating from self-interest, the rioters recognized at least a de facto Indian claim to original ownership. The claim of Indian primacy in ownership galled Morris and Alexander, and they further alleged that the rioters had promised that future jail breaks would be "assisted by *One hundred Indians.*"[78]

As Alexander and Morris explained things, this threat was at first considered "ridiculous and impossible because the whole province of New Jersey had then Scarcely half that Number of Indian men belonging to it, or residing in it." In fact, the only Indian men they claimed to know of within fifty miles of Newark were two who lived near Cranberry. However, Alexander and Morris were shocked, or so they claimed, when they learned that by April 9, 1746, "*forty fighting men of Indians*" had arrived at Cranberry and that a total of 300 people were expected to make their homes there. This would result, in the view of Alexander and Morris, in at least attacks on the property of nearby colonists, if not worse. The two proprietors noted that the "Cause pretended" for this gathering was that the Indians in question were "to be taught the Christian Religion, by one Mr. Braniard [sic], and for that purpose they are to build a Town, a Church, and a School House." The authors declared such claims to be a "pretence" for they were "well assured that the said Mr. Braniard [sic] has never made any application to this Government, for leave to gather those Indians there," nor could they locate any legal title to the land in their records. They could only assume that the Indians gathering there were the fulfillment of the promise made by the rioters the previous September.[79]

It was all a fraud, of course. Alexander and Morris must have known that there were more than two Indians living within fifty miles of Newark. Their appeal to the idea that Brainerd had "never made any application to this Government" for the Indian gathering was of a part with their attempt to assert proprietary control over all the land. If Alexander and Morris recognized the right of the Crossweeksung Indians to the land at Cranberry, logic demanded that they recognize the right to all freehold titles based on purchases from the Indians. The allegation of 300 Indians relocating to New Jersey, with the further allegation that at least one of them claimed to be in receipt of gifts from the governor of Canada, at a time when the middle colonies felt an increased threat from the French in the middle of King George's War, was politically astute. When they compiled their report in late 1746, with no end to the war in sight, they may well have imagined that the apparently imminent threat posed by a large group of allegedly French-allied Indians halfway between New York and Pennsylvania would have brought a quick response in their favor from the London authorities or, at the very least, scare the New Jersey Assembly into taking action.[80]

Although the document was not sent to London until late 1746 or early 1747, it clearly presaged an effort to use legal means to seize the Indians' land. Although Brainerd left no clear record as to the steps he took to prevent any attempt to seize the land, it is possible to trace the outlines of his efforts, keeping in mind that Dickinson and Burr, along with other Presbyterian ministers, were heavily involved in the opposition to the proprietors' actions. On Tuesday, April 8, Brainerd journeyed to Elizabeth-town for a meeting of the presbytery. He stayed in the area until at least Thursday of the following week and "spent some Time in Conversation with several dear Ministers." He returned to Crossweeksung on April 20 and spent the next week or so preparing his people for the communion service described above. On the day he began preparing them for the sacrament, he also led them in a time of prayer for "the peaceable *Settlement* of the Indians together in a Body," asking God to "blast and defeat all the Attempts that were or might be made against that pious Design."[81] Appended to the diary entry where this prayer was recorded was a footnote wherein Brainerd observed that a "terrible Clamour [was] raised against the Indians in various Places in the Country," which included the claims that they were being trained to rise up and "cut People's Throats," probably referring to charges such as those made by Alexander and Morris. Brainerd dismissed these claims as attempts to "fright and deter them from settling upon the best and most convenient Tract of their own Lands" by people "pretending a Claim to their Lands themselves, altho' never purchased of the Indians." The phrasing is a strong indication that Brainerd was very much aware of the language and principles of the disputes taking place in the colony. On Tuesday, April 29, just two days after the great communion service, he went back to Elizabeth-town for another meeting of the presbytery and remained there for four days before traveling to Cranberry, where his people were now settled.[82]

There can be little doubt that Brainerd understood the verbal and legal assaults on the Indians' land development as being part and parcel of the broader dispute then taking place. During his trips to Elizabeth-town, he must have discussed the issue with Dickinson and Burr, who recognized him as an ally in their arguments with the proprietary party. Moreover, the strategy of the Elizabeth-town group would have appealed to Brainerd's sense of order. With people like Burr and Dickinson involved, this group, while opposing the proprietary interests, was not willing to embrace violence, relying instead on legal means to thwart the proprietors' plans. Since the second meeting of the presbytery was only two weeks after the first, the second meeting may have been called for the specific purpose of dealing with the land issue. Although Brainerd may not have raised a flag of rebellion in the midst of his people, he had certainly gone to work on their behalf. Whether he, as historian Brendan McConville has argued, "accepted the idea of the Native Americans as New Jersey's original owners" is less clear. It is not that he accepted or denied this premise, but rather that it was not something he really considered. What was important to Brainerd was that God was at work among the Indians, and the proprietary party, by opposing Indians' possession of the land, was opposing the work of God. Furthermore, his own desire to create a distinctive spiritual place was largely dependent on the perpetuation of the work in New Jersey. If that were to collapse, he would be drawn back into the normal currents of society. In the end, the decision was made to go ahead with the move to Cranberry, and much of the opposition to it seems to have passed on when Governor Morris did the same in June 1746.[83]

The dispute over the lands at Cranberry is also something of a counterpoint to the normal confrontations between colonists and Indians over land. In many cases, smaller landholders and newly arrived colonists seeking more land found themselves opposed by both colonial elites and Indians. More than one colonial leader worked closely with Indians to protect Indian lands from new settlers, not out of an abstract sense of justice but from a desire to buy the lands themselves and then resell them at a considerable profit.[84] New settlers and smaller land-holders perceived Indians as obstacles and often badgered Indians to sell land or simply settled on Indian land without permission. Making these situations worse, such colonists often took delight in humiliating Indians but then over-reacted when they themselves were the brunt of a practical joke perpetrated by Indians.[85] In these types of disputes, religious organizations and missionaries were often seen as allies of the Indians and, to a lesser extent, large landholders, since they frequently joined in efforts to defend Indian land claims against set-tler encroachments. John Wood Sweet has argued that missionary efforts were often opposed by ordinary colonists for fear that they would succeed and endow the newly converted Indians with the same rights as Europeans, which would include the right to keep their land.[86] But circumstances in New Jersey altered the equation. Since small freeholders held their land by dint of purchases from the Indians, then Indian possession had to be defended. As Brendan McConville has explained, the freeholders in New Jersey called on Lockean natural rights philos-ophy to bolster this claim. Since Native Americans had possessed and improved the land, they held a natural right to it and could legally—even in British eyes—sell it to colonists. The colonists, too, had improved the land, thereby cementing their right to it.[87] This argument virtually compelled freeholders to support the rights of the Crossweeksung Indians. Jane T. Merritt has noted a somewhat par-allel situation in Pennsylvania, suggesting that the chaotic nature of land deeds and overlapping grants in these two colonies combined to create an alternative paradigm and alliances which differed from the colonial norm.[88]

Approximate location of Brainerd's mission near Cranberry, New Jersey. Presbyterian Historical Society, Presbyterian Church (U.S.A.), Philadelphia, Pennsylvania. Photo by Mrs. William Kerwin.

Gaining secure occupation of the land was not, of course, an end in itself. For Brainerd, it was a means to further the instruction and spiritual growth of the Indians, in order to strengthen the nascent church which was taking shape. A key element in this was allowing the Indians a certain degree of freedom in ministering, counseling, and praying with one another. In so doing, Brainerd was not just creating a congregation, he was creating a congregation very similar to the one he had experienced at New Haven prior to his expulsion: directed by an experienced or ordained minister, but that also allowed public expression by suitably gifted laypeople. As the revival continued at Crossweeksung, the Indians there were increasingly initiating group activities, meeting "together of their own accord," where they "pray'd, and discours'd of divine Things among themselves." On one occasion, when Brainerd was absent for several days, his "People generally met together of their own Accord in order to spend some time in religious exercises." Toward the end of March, when a number of strangers joined the small community, some of the converted Indians had attempted to preach to them, whereupon the newcomers had got up and gone to another house. In response, some of the "serious Persons" had "agreed to disperse themselves into the several Parts of the *Settlement*. So that wherever the *Strangers* went, they met with some instructive Discourse, and warm addresses respecting their Souls Concerns."[89]

Beyond sharing ministry responsibility with Indian converts, Brainerd made other efforts to increase the role and opportunities for some of his people. Reminiscent of his efforts to have John Wauwaumpequunnaunt, his Indian interpreter, appointed as the schoolmaster at Kaunaumeek, in January 1746 Brainerd made a recommendation to the commissioners that one of the New Jersey converts, "a promising genius of upwards of twenty years old," should be trained for the ministry along with the fifteen-year-old son of Tatamy, who was "pious, has a good capacity, and is willing to be educated for the same design." The SSPCK approved the first request, but not the second; the commissioners in America eventually dismissed the young Indian candidate for the ministry, however, since he had "not taken his learning so well as expected."[90]

Brainerd was also looking for ways to increase the involvement of other converts. As early as August 1745, as he prepared to travel to the Susquehanna, he had asked his New Jersey converts if they would be "willing to spend the remainder of the day in prayer for me, that God would go with me, and succeed my endeavours for the conversion of those poor souls."[91] Then, in February 1746, noting that "divers of the *Indians*" at the Forks of the Delaware were "obstinately set against *Christianity*," he decided to pay them a visit. In so doing, he thought it might be "proper and beneficial" to "have a number of my religious People from *Crossweeksung* with me, in order to converse with them about religious Matters." Taking six of the New Jersey Indians, he met with those at the Forks. Some of the Forks Indians who had opposed Christianity "now behaved soberly, and some others laugh'd and mock'd. However the Word of God fell with such Weight and Power, that sundry seem'd to be stunned." The following day, after Brainerd had preached, his "People from *Crossweeksung* continued with them Day and Night, repeating and inculcating Truths I had taught them: And sometimes pray'd and sung Psalms among them." He noted that, several days later, "Divers of the *Indians* here seem'd to have their Prejudices and Aversion to Christianity remov'd."[92]

Although we know that the Delaware converts preached to their fellow Indians and played an important role in persuading some who, up until that point, had resisted the Christian message, we know even less about them than we do about Tatamy. In his case, we at least have some record of his own experiences even though they were filtered by Brainerd. In the case of these other Indian assistants, not even that record exists. There is no solid way to come to grips with the personal experiences of either these native evangelists or those to whom they spoke. As historian Peggy Brock has observed in analyzing Christian converts who became preachers in Africa, "we can know what they did, but remain removed from their lived experiences." We do know that the role of indigenous preachers was even more difficult than the role of outsiders. When men like Brainerd preached in colonial churches, they often called on their audiences to abandon their sinful ways—but not their culture. However, indigenous evangelists—such as Brainerd's Delaware preachers—stood in judgment of their own cultures. They were frequently demanding that their hearers abandon all, or most, of the cultural and spiritual practices which connected them to their own pasts and to those who had gone before them.[93]

Despite or perhaps because of this, indigenous evangelists played an important role in the evangelization of their own people. Wampanoag preachers from Martha's Vineyard were instrumental in spreading the Christian message to their brethren on the mainland and on the Vineyard, while Wampanoag converts did a great deal of preaching in Plymouth well into the eighteenth century. When John Sergeant first preached at Kaunaumeek in 1737, he took with him a number of the Stockbridge Indians, who "took pains to persuade [the Kaunaumeek Indians] to embrace the *Christian* religion." From these parallels, it seems likely that the Delaware converts played a vital role in convincing the previously resistant Indians at the Forks of the Delaware to listen anew to the claims of Christianity.[94]

In late July, Brainerd decided to make another attempt to bring the gospel to the Indians on the Susquehanna River. He again asked for his congregation's prayers but also "chose divers persons of the congregation to travel with me." On August 12, he set out west, accompanied by six of the New Jersey Delawares. This time, he traveled west from Philadelphia, a longer route but one which avoided the more mountainous regions. On the way, he preached at Treat's church on two occasions, presumably with the six Delaware converts present. On August 18, 1746, he arrived at Paxton on the Susquehanna. The New Jersey Indians separated from him for several days and rejoined him on August 22. The previous night, Brainerd had lodged with a family of unconverted colonists, but that night, he and the Indians slept in the open. His growing attachment to these people was revealed in his comment that he rested with "more comfort than while among an ungodly company of white people."[95]

The party arrived at Shamokin on Saturday, August 23. After visiting some of the Indians and speaking briefly the following day, Brainerd then developed something of a team approach to reaching the Shamokin Indians. On the second day, he sent his converts out among the local Indians to "contract a friendship and familiarity with them, that I might have a better opportunity of treating with them about Christianity." The next day, he preached in public but also "called out my people, who were then present, to give their testimony for God." He was, to an even greater degree, replicating the model that had been used in New Haven and other towns during the Great Awakening. Brainerd persisted at Shamokin for the next few days but was hampered both by his health and by the disappearance of most of the local Delawares. On September 1, he attempted a journey to Great Island, about fifty miles northwest of Shamokin, but his increasing illness made travel difficult. He did visit a "Delaware town" and a "small town of Shauwaunoes" but then became so ill that he returned to Shamokin. He spent two days there, virtually bedridden, before beginning the long trek back to Cranberry on September 8, 1746. Brainerd could only "entertain a strong hope that the journey should not be wholly fruitless."[96]

This account of what proved to be Brainerd's final trip to the Susquehanna did not make it into the second part of his public journal, which concluded with the entry for June 19, 1746, a year to the day since he had opened the account. The construction of the journal as a revival narrative has already been discussed. However, Brainerd, the son of a merchant, also wrote his journal with an eye to the marketplace. Following in the footsteps of George Whitefield, Brainerd and other ministers tapped into the growing demand for accounts of God at work in the world. Like Whitefield, Brainerd sent his journals to William Bradford of Philadelphia for publication. Brainerd retained a substantial degree of control over the process, writing to Bradford in September 1746 to give him instructions on small details of the finished product. As late as April 1747, while Brainerd was recovering from a serious illness in Elizabeth-town, he wrote again to Bradford, this time offering marketing advice. Brainerd advised Bradford that one contact could "find a market for fifty more" while another person "would take two dozen and carry [them] down" to Long Island. Unfortunately, someone else was apparently reprinting the journals in Boston, and Brainerd hoped that Bradford's "might sell first." As with Whitefield, Edwards, and other ministers, Brainerd saw no contradiction in using the power of the marketplace to promote the work of God.[97]

As for the text itself, the bulk of it narrated the revival just as accounts in colonial churches did. Brainerd was again careful to describe aspects of moral reformation which had taken place. As he noted on the day of his last entry, the Indians' "Drunken and *Pagan* Howlings, [were] turn'd into devout and fervent Prayers and Praises to God!"[98] The concept of moral reform was more fully introduced in a lengthy summary at the end of the daily accounts. The truth of the gospel, Brainerd recounted, had affected the Indians so that there was "now no Vice unreform'd. Drunkenness, the darling vice, was broken off from, and scarce an Instance of it known among my Hearers for months together." But it was not just alcoholism that had been dealt with. The "abusive Practice of *Husbands* and *Wives* in putting away each other, and taking others in their Stead, was quickly reform'd." Indeed, several couples who had voluntarily broken up their relationships "now live together again in Love and Peace." Most important, this "Reformation" of morals came from the "*internal* Influence of divine Truths upon their Hearts; and not from any *external* Restraints."[99]

The account was also replete with stories of individual conversions. None were as long as that of Tatamy, but there were many others, although, in keeping with Prince's model, no other names were given. Some appeared to be people with no particularly special standing among the Indians, such as a woman whose journey to salvation began around mid-December 1745, when she was "brought to such an *Agony* in seeking after Christ, that the Sweat ran off her Face for a considerable Time." Several days later, although not apparently as yet converted, she had received "Relief and Deliverance from the spiritual Distresses she had lately been under." Then, in early January, she was baptized, having discovered, "a very sweet and heavenly frame of Mind, from time to time."[100]

Other conversion accounts were of more notorious individuals, such as one man who was baptized in early May. While this particular conversion account was included for its own intrinsic interest, it also filled another of the requests made by Thomas Prince in his original circular, which asked ministers to include accounts of "opposers" of the work.[101] Although this man had murdered a fellow Indian, what "was worst of all" to Brainerd was his "*Conjuration*. He was one of them who are sometimes call'd *Powwows*." When Brainerd had preached of the miracles of Christ, other Indians had downplayed them, referring to the "Wonders of that Kind which this Man had perform'd by his *Magick Charms*." He had become such a thorn in Brainerd's side that the missionary had "often thought" that it would be most helpful if "God would take that Wretch out of the World." But, instead, God had been "pleased to take a much more desireable Method with him." He had first come under spiritual conviction when Tatamy and his wife were baptized and had then moved to Crossweeksung. He had "continued under Convictions of his sinful and perishing State," confessing to Brainerd at one time that he was going to hell since "*The Devil has been in me ever since I was born.*" His time of preparation and conviction continued until early February, when he had a "lively, Soul-refreshing View of the Excellency of Christ," and from that time on, "he has appear'd to be a humble, devout and affectionate Christian."[102]

This was not the only time that Delaware religious beliefs impinged on Brainerd's account of the revival, but it seems that he tried to downplay these in order to avoid accusations of enthusiasm or excessive emotionalism. Indeed, he made a point of noting that there had been no "*Prevalency*, nor indeed any considerable *Appearance* of *false Religion*," nor any "*Prevalancy* of Visions, Trances and Imaginations of any kind; although there has been *some* Appearance of something of that Nature since the Conclusion of that Journal."[103] However, it seems that Brainerd was willing to allow more space for esoteric experiences than this disclaimer would allow. In the account of the conversion of the powwow just discussed, Brainerd related how the man had accompanied him on a trip to the Forks of the Delaware. At the time, the powwow had been awakened but not converted. There, Brainerd was confronted by another powwow, who "threatened to *be-witch*" him. In response, the original powwow challenged the other to "do his worst, telling him; that himself had been as great a *Conjurer* as he," but, as soon as he felt God's word in his heart, "his Power of conjuring immediately left him." The same thing, he declared, would happen to his rival but, regardless, "you have no power to hurt [Christians], nor so much as to touch one of them." Brainerd concluded that, like Paul the apostle, the former "*Conjurer*" now "*preaches the faith which he once destroyed*."[104]

While the account lends itself to the correct interpretation—the power of God bringing enlightenment to a sinner—it has another aspect. Brainerd nowhere seems to deny that Indian powwows possess some kind of power. In a lengthy discussion of powwows in an appendix to his journal, Brainerd could only conclude by leaving it to his readers to "fathom" these "Depths of Satan," rather than denying that powwows wielded power and experienced visions. Indeed, in order to try to overcome their influence, Brainerd decided to issue a "challenge to all their powwows and great Powers to do their worst on me." He did this not because he believed that the powwows had no power, but in order to demonstrate to other Indians the "evidence of the power and goodness of God." The distinction is important: unlike the French Jesuit Paul Le Jeune, who mocked the Montagnais shaman Carigonan, Brainerd claimed that God would protect him from the power wielded by the powwows.[105]

Although Brainerd left his readers in no doubt as to what he thought of the origins of the powwow's abilities, he was less definitive when it came to other aspects of Delaware religion. He had also informed his readers that they "give much heed to dreams," which he, apparently, dismissed as "superstitious notions and traditions" and a "kind of ridiculous worship." And yet, he also admitted that he was "sometimes almost nonplussed" with the Indians over such things.[106] It is not surprising that he would make such an admission, as we have already seen that Tatamy's conversion involved an apparent vision that Brainerd was not willing to dismiss out of hand.

Among other conversion accounts Brainerd recorded was that of an elderly woman who came to him on the day after Christmas 1745, telling him that "*her Heart was distressed and she fear'd she should never find Christ*." Her crucial experience came the evening before Christmas, when she "felt as if she dream'd, and yet is confident she did not dream. When she was thus gone, she saw, she says, two Paths, one appeared very broad and crooked," while the other appeared "strait and *very narrow*." She followed the narrow way for some time but, just before she was about to enter into a gate at the end of the road, "she came back again, as she term'd it, meaning that she came to herself." In relating this story, Brainerd immediately noted that he was "sensible that *Trances* and *imaginary* Views of Things, are of *dangerous* Tendency in Religion," so he spent a great deal of time asking the woman questions to establish her understanding of Christianity and came to the conclusion that it was "next to impossible" that a "*Pagan*" should "gain so much Knowledge by any meer human Instruction." Furthermore, the woman seemed to be "really convinc'd of her Sin, and Misery, and her need of a Change of Heart." Brainerd concluded by noting that he couldn't "pretend to determine" how much "God may make Use of the *Imagination* in awakening some Persons," or whether her experience was "from a divine Influence," but "its Effects hitherto bespeak it to be such."[107]

It seems that, in dealing with such accounts, Brainerd was attempting to forge a path between two extremes. He may well have abandoned the more extreme manifestations of revivalism he had seen in New England and, in fact, denounced claims by some of the Delawares that they were having visions of Christ as "fanciful notions" and "vigorous attempts" by Satan to cause "turbulent commotions of the passions."[108] But, with his knowledge of Delaware beliefs, as well as his own experiences during his conversion journey, he simply could not or would not categorically declare conversion experiences which included dreams to be unacceptable. Instead, he fell back to the position that a changed life was the best sign that a dream or vision was from God. Indeed, even among the Indians, his concern continued to focus on the spiritual pride and self-aggrandizement that came from such experiences.[109] Ultimately, as with so much else about Brainerd, the editing of the remaining records and the absence of first-hand accounts by the Indians makes a definitive conclusion impossible. But enough evidence remains to suggest that Brainerd's abandonment of the radical aspects of the New England revivals was not as complete nor as definitive as people such as Jonathan Edwards sought to imply.

However, what cannot be doubted is that Brainerd wanted to present an account of a revival that was deeply rooted and not just transitory: God had "gather'd himself a *Church* in the midst of" the Indians. This work was authenticated by accounts of moral reform, conversion stories, and Brainerd's baptism of seventy-seven persons who had given "comfortable Evidences" of having "pas'd a saving Change." Furthermore, other people were willing to attest that the work at Crossweeksung came as the result of a genuine move of God. In June 1746, he had taken two of the SSPCK correspondents with him to visit the Indians, and they had witnessed first-hand what God was doing. And, in accordance with Prince's model, he appended a number of formal attestations to the published journal. William Tennent affirmed the "saving Conversion of a considerable number of Indians," noting that they usually met at his church for worship when Brainerd was absent. Tennent's elders and deacons added their support, based on "personal Acquaintance" with the Indians, which included having "joined with them at the Lord's Supper." Finally, Charles McKnight from nearby Crosswicks also supported Brainerd's claims, since he had had "frequent Opportunities of being present at their religious Meetings."[110] The manner in which Brainerd crafted his account of the *Rise and Progress of a Remarkable Work of Grace among a Number of the Indians* was unmistakable. Few supporters of religion in the northern colonies would have missed its intent: this was the story of God visiting his people with power in order to bring them into salvation. No doubt, many readers struggled to come to grips with the concept that God would work among the Indians in the same way he worked among the colonists, but they could have had no doubt that the minister to these Indians believed that God had worked in their midst. Some colonists may have had another question, too: why had these Indians responded to God's offer of salvation when so few in the past ever had?

Delaware Christians

Before offering some possible answers to that question, a word is necessary on the issue of religious conversion as a historical event. Historians, ethnohistorians, sociologists, and scholars of religion continue to grapple with the concept of conversion, particularly in the context of relations between colonizers and colonized, where the term usually describes a decision to move from one belief system to another. Within this context, James Axtell has suggested that conversion is a "personal, voluntary act of individuals, a decisive act of reason, faith, and will that no one can make for them."[111] Seen this way, conversion is a decision that, while made within the subject's cultural and community milieu, is essentially individualistic in nature. Further, in Axtell's interpretation, the components of that decision are themselves different in nature. Reason and, to some extent, will can be analyzed and understood; faith cannot. That is, there is at least a part of each conversion experience that is metaphysical in nature, beyond the ability of scholars to dissect and explain.

Kenneth M. Morrison has argued, using a critique of Axtell's work as a starting point, that one of the reasons that scholars have difficulty coming to grips with conversion is that the term itself "poorly describes the complex process of religious change." Morrison, using French-Algonkin relations as his field of study, argues that conversion is a "dehumanizing reification" that "dismisses Algonkins' historical agency." In effect, for Morrison, the concept of conversion suggests a situation where Native Americans abandoned their ancient beliefs to adopt a system that "offered them a morally superior, and intellectually more effective, way of understanding the world." In opposition to this, Morrison argues that Algonkins gradually accepted those aspects of Christianity which "intersected" with their own beliefs and which enabled them to "bolster traditional truth, ensure the survival of tradition, and affirm tribal solidarity."[112] In a parallel fashion, Neal Salisbury has argued that Christianity provided some North American Indians with a means "for reordering their lives materially, politically, and spiritually" in order to "sustain and reinforce" their own cultural identity.[113] Morrison and Salisbury seek to explain religious change from a communitarian perspective, where individual responses, while not rendered meaningless, are voluntarily submitted to the needs of the larger group. In a further disagreement with Axtell, Morrison does not see a "decisive act" or, indeed, any singular decision at all, but rather a process of cultural adaptation. In considering these competing approaches, we need to keep in mind that Axtell was generalizing across all Native Americans for the entire colonial period, while Morrison considered a specific group in a specific period to present his case.

When it comes to the Delaware (and other) Indians at Crossweeksung, Cranberry, and (to a lesser extent) the Forks of the Delaware, combining the two positions outlined above provides a basis for evaluating their responses. First, although the Indians in New Jersey still lived in small groups, their sense of cultural unity had been severely damaged following more than a century of European contact. Although they were probably not as individualistic in their thinking as their colonial neighbors (or Brainerd himself), they were no longer in a position where they could come to a community agreement on how to respond to the missionary's message. They could not, for example, meet together in council, as the Mahicans had done for John Sergeant to decide whether or not to allow Brainerd to preach in the area. Further, with their traditional culture in tatters, it was no longer a question of borrowing from Christianity in order to "bolster traditional truth." Thus, while Delawares may have discussed Brainerd's message in small family groups, as his diary documents, they largely responded as individuals.

However, for individuals to respond to a religious message, they have to be willing to listen to that message. Here, Morrison's argument that the process of religious change, or conversion, takes time is extremely valuable. Although Brainerd preached the need for a singular, decisive moment of conversion, his model insisted that people had to be prepared over a period of time before they could experience that moment. That is, he expected his audience to listen to him on repeated occasions before God would move them into salvation. While Brainerd may have interpreted that time period as God preparing a person's soul, it is much more likely that the Indians were measuring the content of Brainerd's message against their own beliefs. But why did Indians at Crossweeksung grant Brainerd multiple hearings? Here, we return to the importance of Tatamy. As Brainerd reported, Tatamy was able to translate Brainerd's words in a way that reflected not only Brainerd's content but his style of preaching.

William S. Simmons has argued that southern New England Indians responded to New Light preachers because those preachers incorporated bodily movements, speech patterns, songs, and other mannerisms which bore some resemblance to the behaviors of Indian spiritual leaders.[114] One has to be cautious here: we do not know to what extent Brainerd used the techniques of James Davenport or other radicals. But almost certainly, he did not completely abandon the more demonstrative techniques of the revivals. So, it seems likely that Brainerd was instantly attractive to the handful of women who first heard him preach because, in some way, he represented what they looked for in a man with spiritual powers. Furthermore, traveling alone, rather than as part of a group, he conformed still more to the Indian idea of a solitary holy man while, at the same time, representing little threat to Indian land. At that point, the role of women as communicators of spiritual teaching enabled them to draw other Indians to hear Brainerd teach.

Having attracted an audience, it is likely that Brainerd's message resonated with his listeners because it provided some common ground between Christianity and the Delawares' religion. Historians are increasingly recognizing the importance of cultural commonality in providing a platform for the transmission of beliefs. On Martha's Vineyard, it was sometimes explicitly developed out of discussions between Thomas Mayhew, Jr., and Hiacoomes. In other cases, it came about inadvertently as in Mayhew's use of small meetings of Indians to teach them Christian fundamentals—a practice which paralleled Wampanoag spiritual instruction. The Jesuit instructional manuals used in Julí presented a concept of God in the Lord's Prayer which paralleled the Andean concept of a deity, while the prayers to Mary bore a rough parallel to invocations to Andean divinities which took human form. In a similar fashion, Viviana Díaz Balsera has noted that Catholic conceptions of God presented by the Franciscans in New Spain were similar to Nahua beliefs, while both religions "encouraged the representation of the sacred in stone and wood." Ramón A. Gutiérrez has argued that the actions of the Franciscans in New Mexico unconsciously mirrored the Pueblo concept of "Inside Chief[s]," who were powerful spiritual leaders and would, like the Spanish, enforce their spiritual system after using force to triumph over their opponents.[115]

Brainerd's message also provided a common ground by which the Delawares could grapple with the content of his preaching. Delawares were used to frequent and lengthy discourses—such as those employed by Brainerd—as a means of instruction. In Delaware culture, listeners were required to sit and wait until the speaker was finished.[116] Furthermore, portions of Brainerd's theology may well have spoken to, or echoed, the Delawares' traditional beliefs. The willingness to emphasize the goodness of God's mercy carried overtones of the way the Delawares' Great Spirit provided good things for his people. Perhaps more important, Brainerd's preparatory model of conversion provided a rough parallel to the spirit quests of their traditional religion. Delaware teenage boys were required to enter adulthood, a new life, and embark on a spiritual quest leading to enlightenment. Although the quest usually took place over a shorter period of time, it required them to give up the things of their childhood and adopt the ways of an adult. This was a more serious, sober, and reflective period of their life. Although they prepared themselves the same as others did, each person embarked on his own quest. His spirit guide revealed himself when he was ready, and the Delaware male then followed his own individual guide for the rest of his life. In a parallel fashion, Brainerd's model required a period of preparation followed by a specific spiritual experience. Furthermore, conversion was wrought by an irresistible God rather than through a formal ecclesiastical structure, all of which has parallels to the spirit quest. For those Delawares who retained a more individual approach to spirituality and a dynamic interaction with the spiritual world, Brainerd's teaching would have resonated. This is not to suggest that the Delawares adopted Christianity as an updated form of their spirit quest. But in the period of preparation and in the idea of individual salvation through direct spiritual intervention, Brainerd's preaching may have provided an intercultural connection sufficient to open the possibility of at least listening to the message of the young missionary.

Brainerd also presented a God who was frequently the initiator of communication between himself and his creation. He moved according to his own plans to bring conviction of guilt, relief from distress, and judgment on sin. Although

a person could prepare, in the end it was God who controlled the communication. This, again, provided a parallel, a common ground with Delaware beliefs
that Indians could prepare themselves, but the spirits determined whether or
not communication would take place.[117] Thus, we find that there are important
commonalities between the revivalistic style of Christianity taught by Brainerd
and some of the Delaware beliefs. What most likely made these commonalities viable conduits for some Delawares to embrace Christianity was Tatamy.
Although Brainerd persisted in his attempts to acquire some fluency in the
Indian language(s), his journals indicate that he never did. Thus, when cultural
common ground came through in his sermons and instructions, it must have
done so first through Tatamy and then, possibly, through the other lay preachers. It was these men (and women?) who took Brainerd's concepts and presented
them in cultural containers that were understandable to their fellow Indians.

In the end, it is impossible to be certain as to exactly why conversions took
place, but there can be little doubt that many of the Delawares to whom Brainerd
preached themselves believed they had entered a new spiritual dynamic. The
willingness of Crossweeksung converts to accompany Brainerd on trips to the
Forks and to the Susquehanna in order to preach to other Indians offers proof
that they believed they had discovered a new truth. Furthermore, there is no
indication that they were attempting to restore a traditional lifestyle that had
been lost. On the contrary, the decision, in early 1746, to establish a permanent
agrarian lifestyle and the willingness to take formal school lessons indicate a realization that they needed to abandon some of their traditional practices. One is
compelled to accept the distinct probability that those Delaware Indians who
responded to the preaching of David Brainerd encountered something that they
recognized as truth and, accordingly, adopted it.

"Arrived among My Own People": Brainerd among the Indians

The Delawares responded to Brainerd, but how did Brainerd respond to the
Delawares?[118] There can be little doubt that Brainerd inherited the standard
colonial view of the Indians as lazy, savage, uncivilized people who resisted both
the true gospel and the blessings of English civilization. Having said that, it is
also possible that his perspective was modified somewhat because of the time
in which he grew up—the period of relative peace between Queen Anne's and
King George's wars. Without regular reports of Indian depredations against
"innocent" and unsuspecting colonists, it is possible that his concept of Indians
was more abstract than those who had grown up in the era of Deerfield and
Schenectady. We have already noted that his father was sitting in the Connecticut
Assembly when it voted funds to support education among the Indians still res-
ident in the colony.

In any event, during his time at Yale, Brainerd developed his own concepts
of good and evil, right and wrong, innocent and guilty. On the right side of the

ledger were those who were obedient to God: ministers who preached the gospel, laypeople who lived sober lives, and the lost who realized their need and sought salvation. True, as we have seen, Brainerd was not always willing to make a judgment over issues of doctrine and ecclesiastical practice, preferring, instead, that people avoid division and party zeal. However, it is also important to note that people on both sides of those divisions were attempting to be obedient to what they believed to be God's law or will—probably one of the reasons that Brainerd sought to tamp down divisiveness. Keep in mind the Indian reformer whom Brainerd was unwilling to dismiss out of hand or judge as a heathen or a savage. The only people Brainerd regularly placed on the other side of the ledger were those who actively opposed the work of God.

Gradually, Brainerd came to apply this criteria to the Indians among whom he ministered. He had been discouraged after his brief contact with the Montauks in early 1743, but his perspective on Native Americans began to change during his time at Kaunaumeek. Although his diaries do not demonstrate the same degree of warmth toward his charges as would become common during his time in New Jersey, his attitude did alter a little. Ten days after he arrived at Kaunaumeek, he noted that some of the Indians "behaved soberly" when he preached to them and that "two or three in particular appeared under some religious Concern." The next time he referred to his audience, they were not "the Indians," but rather "my people."[119] A minor point to be sure, but perhaps indicative of a change that was beginning in Brainerd's heart.

If it did begin at Kaunaumeek, it bloomed fully during his time in New Jersey. The pages of *Mirabilia* and the *Life* are replete with references to "my people" and to the joy he felt when ministering among them. At the time of the great communion season in April 1746, Brainerd rejoiced that "such Tokens of brotherly Love and Affection" existed among the Indians, concluding, "*Lord, 'tis good to be here, 'tis good to dwell where such an heavenly influence distills!*"[120] It is true that Brainerd was never able to see the Indians as friends—even Brainerd's effusive praise for Tatamy never stopped him seeking a fellow European to help him in his work.[121] But, while the Indians may not have been friends, they had become brothers—his equals in God's kingdom. And that relationship became increasingly important to Brainerd's emotional and spiritual well-being. We have already noted that he was much more content to sleep in the open with some of his godly converts while on the way to Susquehanna than under a roof with an ungodly colonial family. But his relationship with the Crossweeksung Indians went further than that. On one occasion after a public meeting, a number of the Indians went with him to his house. There, they enjoyed a "sweet Union of Soul: My Heart was knit to them." He had not experienced "such a sweet and fervent *Love to the Brethren*, for some Time past: And I saw in them Appearances of the same Love. This gave me something of a View of the heavenly State; and particularly that Part of the Happiness of Heaven, which consists in the *Communion of Saints*."[122] We should keep in mind that, although Brainerd made frequent trips to Elizabeth-town, Freehold, and New Brunswick, it was his Indian congregation that sustained him on a daily basis. It is also helpful to remember that

Brainerd's affection for his Indian charges had developed in only a few short years. One wonders how much more his thinking might have changed had he worked among the Delawares for twenty or thirty years.

What is also remarkable about Brainerd's interactions with the Indians is that it was frequently colonists who provided the counterpoint to the godliness of the Indians. In his first report to Pemberton, in 1744, he asserted that Indians were frequently prejudiced against Christianity because of the "*vicious* Lives and *unchristian* Behaviour of some that are call'd *Christians.*" And he saw this behavior for what it frequently was on the part of whites: "*the Hope of*...unlawful *Gain.*" He repeated this charge in the appendix to the public journal, written sometime in the middle of 1746, noting that the Indians "observe that horrid Wickedness in nominal Christians."[123] Further, the Indians had pointed out to Brainerd that the English had introduced to them "strong Drink," with which they had made the Indians "quarrel and kill one another," as well as to other vices, which meant that the Indians were "much more miserable than they were before the coming of the *white* People into the Country." Even worse, some declared, "the *white* People have come among them, have cheated them out of their Lands, driven them back to the Mountains, from the pleasant Places they us'd to enjoy by the Sea Side." How then could they believe that "*white* People are now seeking their Welfare[?]"[124]

Confronted with this new dichotomy—ungodly colonists and godly Indians—Brainerd began to use "white" to distinguish between the two. Thus, in August 1745 at Crossweeksung, he wrote of "careless Spectators of the white People" and "Several of the *white Heathen*" who "were awaken'd." On another day, it was "white people" who "kept walking and gazing about, and behaved more indecently than *any Indians* I ever address'd."[125] In fact, it was the Indians who "being awakened to a solemn concern for their souls" observed that these whites were "altogether unconcerned about their own souls," and the Indians thus concluded that the whites had no real concern for the souls of the Indians.[126] There were even occasions when the Indian response positively affected the colonists. After preaching one day at the Forks, Brainerd noted that "pious people of the English...seemed refreshed with seeing the Indians worship God."[127]

As Nancy Shoemaker has explained, the use of "white" as a racial category only emerged in northeastern America in the 1730s and was most often used, at least in diplomatic situations, to make distinctions between colonists and Indians.[128] Writing in the relatively early days of such distinctions, Brainerd was using white, English, Indian, and "my people" to make another kind of distinction. Whenever the term white entered his usage, it almost always described colonists who were not Christian, or at least not living demonstrably Christian lives. On the other hand, "my people" were Indians who had either been converted or were in some kind of preparatory stage prior to conversion. Thus, Brainerd was once again invoking the dividing line that had been so important during his Yale days: on one side stood those who were responding or had responded to the gospel, while on the other stood those who had not. And, just as had happened in Connecticut, creating such a dividing line caused social disruption. While it would be presumptuous to suggest that Brainerd had abandoned a Eurocentric world view, it is not far-fetched to suggest that his world view had been substantially modified by both the response of the Indians and the opposition to his work exhibited by many of the colonists in the area.

None of this is to suggest that he accorded all Indians equal treatment. In his judgment of Indians who had rejected the preaching of the gospel, he pulled no punches. Their minds, he noted were "extremely attach'd to the Customs, Traditions and fabulous Notions of their *Fathers*." Of his experiences on the Susquehanna in September 1745, he declared that the Indians there were "*led, captive by Satan at his Will*." When he returned to Crossweeksung, he was struck by the differences between the two groups, remembering that his time on the Susquehanna was "like being banished from God and all his People," while being in New Jersey was "like being admitted into his Family, and to the Enjoyment of his divine Presence."[129]

This divide between those who responded to the gospel and those who rejected it goes a long way toward explaining Brainerd's final addendum to the public journal: running some fifty pages, an appendix explained the methods and difficulties associated with instructing the Indians. The section describing "Difficulties Attending the Christianizing of the Indians" is the most difficult to place within Brainerd's surviving writings.[130] Unlike the compassionate accounts describing converts and awakened Indians in his daily entries and in the summary of the public journal, these pages are replete with negative, vicious observations on the Indians. Where does this divergence come from? To suggest that this appendix reveals Brainerd's true feelings is to suggest that his diary entries are a fraud, something that beggars belief. Instead, the explanation seems to lie in the distinction Brainerd made between those who had responded to God and those who had not. Toward the end of the critique contained in the appendix, he noted that "those who appear to have a sense of divine things, are considerably amended in this respect, and 'tis hopeful, that time will make a yet greater alteration upon them for the better." And, just several paragraphs later, he also noted that the Indians had sometimes been placed "in the way of Temptation" by "*white* People more horribly wicked" than unconverted Indians.[131] Thus, these negative views obviously refer to the unconverted, unresponsive Indians, not the ones he constantly referred to as "my people."

Brainerd's sense of fulfillment in his mission went beyond merely the response of dozens of Indians to the gospel message. The willingness of the Delawares to be gathered as a Christian church enabled Brainerd to construct a hybrid, a church composed of various components of Brainerd's experiences and beliefs. Functionally, it borrowed greatly from Brainerd's experiences during the revivals in Connecticut. Brainerd, as the ordained minister, exercised initial leadership and took on the bulk of the teaching just as James Davenport and Gilbert Tennent had done in New Haven. However, as circumstances warranted, Tatamy and other converts were encouraged to share their own conversion stories, counsel those under conviction, and lead the prayers and singing, just as Brainerd, Samuel Buell, and others had done several years earlier. And, in taking on responsibility for the colonial settlements as well as for the Indians on the Susquehanna, Brainerd also incorporated the itinerancy which was so important to the New England revivals. At the same time, however, the work in New Jersey did not exist only on the experiential, emotional basis that had characterized so much of the revivals. Between his own catechetical work and the efforts of his schoolmaster, the Indian converts were also receiving solid instruction both in Christian principles and in practical subjects. The church members and their minister did not want for food, shelter, or clothing, nor did they exhibit the materialism that was an increasing part of colonial life. Furthermore, by creating a central settlement, Brainerd had circumvented the transient nature that had afflicted so many of the centers of the revival. The church at Cranberry was traditional, radical, colonial, and missionary, combining aspects of all these worlds to form something new. Brainerd had essentially succeeded in his efforts to "carve out a distinct space."

Requiem

The September trip to the Susquehanna demolished what little was left of Brainerd's health. Five days after leaving Shamokin, he made it as far as Richard Treat's house, about twenty-five miles west of Philadelphia. There, his illness compelled him to rest for four days before setting out for Cranberry, a journey which took him another four days. He arrived there on September 20, 1746, and, from that date onward, his diary entries began to decline in both frequency and length. On the first Sunday in October, he once again celebrated communion, this time with a mixed congregation of Indians and whites. Later that week, he traveled to Elizabeth-town to attend a synod meeting but became so ill that he spent a further week recuperating at a friend's house. He returned to Cranberry on October 23, but found it increasingly difficult to conduct his ministry. Nonetheless, on those occasions when he could preach, there was still a response from his audience.[132]

The last week of October was spent visiting various ministerial friends in the area, but in early November his sickness was such that he was unable to preach the Sunday sermon to the Delawares, and he decided to make a trip to New England. In part, he hoped that "much riding" might cure his illness, apparently the best medical advice at the time. However, since he also harbored "little hope of recovery," he felt it his duty to visit friends in New England, some of whom he had "not seen for a long time." Before he left Cranberry, he visited his people "in their respective houses and discoursed to each one, as I thought most proper and suitable for their circumstances," describing these visits as "my farewell addresses to them." He departed on his trip the same day and made it as far as Elizabeth-town before an "extraordinary turn of disorder" confined him there until the end of February. Nonetheless, his mental state had improved so that, despite this illness, he was "enabled thro' mercy to maintain a calm composed and patient spirit, as I had been before from the beginning of my weakness."[133] Toward the end of December, he wrote to his brother Israel, then a student at Yale, telling him that death no longer frightened him. Instead, he was "much delighted with a view of its approach. Oh, the blessedness of being delivered from the clogs of flesh and sense."[134]

His illness continued into the new year, and it was not until February 24 that he was well enough to ride to Newark. He returned to Elizabeth-town the next day and, on February 28, one of the Delawares visited him and brought "letters and good news of the sober and good behavior of my people," which "refreshed [his] soul."[135] On March 11, he went to church for the first time in almost three months. But this temporary improvement in his health could not hide the fact that his time in New Jersey was over. A week later, he managed to pay one last visit to his people at Cranberry. He spent several hours in the morning talking with them of their spiritual state and answering some of their concerns. At ten o'clock in the morning, they joined together for prayer. An hour later, he departed Cranberry for the final time on March 20, 1747.[136]

The work at Cranberry was continued by his younger brother John, who had graduated from Yale in 1746. The correspondents summoned John to Elizabeth-town, where he met with them and David on April 10, 1747, and John began his work at Cranberry three days later.[137] In June, John counted 160 residents at the settlement, of whom 37 had been baptized and took communion. Fifty-three children were attending the school, of whom 27 could read the New Testament. The community had almost eighty acres planted with crops.[138] Unfortunately, during the subsequent months, a lethal disease "carried off a considerable number" of the Indians.[139] In the winter, John was visited by Elihu Spencer of Haddam and Job Strong of Northampton, who had been approved by David to go as missionaries to the Iroquois the following year. They were sent to New Jersey as a means to get accustomed to Indian customs before traveling to Iroquoia.[140] Job Strong reported that many of the Cranberry Indians were "growing Christians…in doctrinal as well as in experimental knowledge." He was also impressed that many of the Indians worshipped not only in public but also in private, noting that it was "a difficult thing to walk into the woods in the morning without disturbing persons with secret devotions."[141] In March 1749, the SSPCK was informed that the Indians "dwell together in a regular civil society," the school had grown in size, and "by the charity of well disposed persons, they had got spinning wheels, that Indian women may be trained up to Industry and diligence."[142]

Unfortunately, the Indians' hold on their land was about to be undermined by their old adversary Robert Hunter Morris, now the chief justice of New Jersey. Using the power of his position, along with what was probably a fraudulent will, Hunter was able to bring new pressure to bear on the Indians' title to the land. Despite representations from the SSPCK in Edinburgh and protests by the correspondents and by John Brainerd, Morris would not be denied this time. By late 1753, in the face of this pressure, plans were in place to move the Indian settlement, now known as Bethel, to the Susquehanna. John made several trips to western Pennsylvania to find a new place for the Cranberry Indians to settle. In the end, most of them relocated to villages in the Susquehanna Valley, although some stayed in New Jersey where William Tennent visited them once a week, catechized the children, and, on occasion, administered communion, activities for which the SSPCK provided some remuneration. John Brainerd, who had declined an offer to pastor at Newark in 1756 in order to stay with the Indians, accepted a renewed offer from that church in 1757. In addition to his work at Newark, he ministered to a number of other churches before moving in 1777 to Deerfield, Massachusetts, where he died four years later.[143]

Tatamy almost certainly worked for John Brainerd during his time at Cranberry and probably went with him on a trip to the Susquehanna in 1751. Although Tatamy was on good terms with the Moravians, there is no evidence that he ever joined them. William A. Hunter believes that Tatamy maintained his Presbyterianism throughout his life while continuing to act as an interpreter and negotiator in Pennsylvania and New Jersey. In September 1756, Tatamy was one of the negotiators who finalized the sale of the lands in New Jersey. He died sometime between late November 1760 and April 1761.[144] There is some evidence that other members of the Cranberry church joined the Moravian missions in western Pennsylvania and eastern Ohio in the 1750s and 1760s following their move to the Susquehanna.[145] But with the names of the Indians omitted from all of Brainerd's accounts, we know little of the subsequent impact of the work in New Jersey. One possible exception can be found in the "interesting account of a single family descended from David Brainerd's church," which was reported in the Methodist *Missionary Herald* in 1834.[146] Penned by a missionary then working with Indians in various parts of the west, it related a two-day meeting of Shawnee and Delaware Indians near the mouth of the Kansas River. During the meeting, this missionary spoke with two elderly sisters who had been converted at Brotherton, New York, under the preaching of Isaac Wabe, a disciple of Samuel Occum. The two women identified themselves as part of "David Brainerd's people." They traced their spiritual lineage to their grandmother, whom they identified as one of Brainerd's New Jersey converts. According to the two women, their grandmother remembered Brainerd as a "lovely young man" who "went about from house to house to talk about religion." Brainerd's behavior convinced the people that he was both humble and honest. It is a tantalizing hint, but no more than that, of the legacy of the work at Cranberry.[147]

David Brainerd remained in New Jersey until late April 1747, struggling with his steadily worsening illness. On April 7, he performed the wedding ceremony of his friend Jonathan Dickinson, who married a widow named Mary Crane, at Newark. Brainerd spent about two more weeks in New Jersey, attending to church business, including the examination of at least one minister, before leaving for New England. He traveled via New York and, by early May, had reached East Haddam. He proceeded north up the Connecticut River valley and stopped in various places until he arrived in Northampton, Massachusetts, on May 28.[148] Exactly why he ended up there at the home of Jonathan Edwards is unclear. There is no record that the two men had been in any direct contact since Brainerd's final appeal to Yale in 1743, although Edwards was certainly aware of Brainerd's work. While Brainerd must have been aware of Edwards's growing reputation and his publications, claims that Brainerd was Edwards's protégé are overstated. The only Edwards work Brainerd specifically mentioned was the *Treatise on Religious Affections* and that he did not read until he was in Boston just months before his death. There is no evidence that Brainerd and Edwards's daughter Jerusha were romantically involved—let alone engaged— prior to Brainerd's arrival in Northampton. The claims of the romance did not emerge until the middle of the nineteenth century. Since Brainerd was on his way to Boston, traveling along the Connecticut River was a logical path and Northampton was not far from the main route. The Edwards house was known for its hospitality and, since Brainerd had been in Longmeadow only a few days earlier, he may have learned there that his friend Eleazar Wheelock, desperately ill, was being taken care of there. If that is the case, he probably sought out Edwards as a sympathetic and hospitable fellow minister, rather than for any personal or romantic purposes.[149]

May 1747 was a particularly busy month even for the normally vibrant Edwards household: in addition to the two sick ministers, Sarah Edwards had just given birth to the couple's tenth child. Although Edwards remembered that Brainerd "appeared vastly better than, by his Account, he had been in the Winter," a doctor he consulted that first week in Northampton "could give him no encouragement that he should ever recover."[150] In early June, he set out for Boston, accompanied by Jerusha; it is possible that a romantic attraction developed between Brainerd and Jerusha either during his ten days at Northampton or on the trip but, again, there is no evidence. Like her sisters, Jerusha assisted Sarah in running the household and had already made several trips to Boston. On the way, the two stayed at the home of Ebenezer Parkman in Westborough, where Brainerd gave Parkman "an account of the origin of his mission and the success of it."[151] Brainerd arrived in Boston fatigued from the journey and suffered a further deterioration in his health the following week. He spent a total of about six weeks in Boston, where he stayed with Edward Bromfield, who had a reputation for hospitality and compassion. About a week after his arrival, he almost died, falling into a delirium for several days. During his recuperation, he experienced a tremendous assurance of his standing before God, declaring that "this feeling of the love of God in my heart, which I trust the spirit of God excited in me afresh, was sufficient to give me full satisfaction, and make me long, as I had many times before done, to be with Christ."[152]

He was also well enough to take up writing again. At the end of June, he wrote to Israel and exclaimed that he had "clear views of eternity." He expressed his anguish over those who died without Christ, challenged Israel with regard to his own salvation, and then urged him to stay committed to his training for the ministry. He finished by urging Israel not to be "discouraged because you see your elder brothers in the ministry die early," a reference not only to his own impending death but also to that of their brother Nehemiah, who had died in 1742.[153] Another letter was written to an unnamed "Candidate for the Work of Ministry," although this letter was not sent until he returned to Northampton. He encouraged this man—probably Nehemiah Greenman—to "live a life of great devotion and constant self-dedication" to God and "frequently to attend the great and precious duties of secret prayer and fasting."[154]

One final letter—undated although Edwards places it during Brainerd's Boston stay—was sent to his brother John at the renamed Indian settlement of Bethel. He urged John to "pursue after personal holiness, to be as much in fasting and prayer as your health will allow, and to live above the rate of common Christians." He also instructed John on the dangers of false religion and urged him to "crush all appearances of this nature among the Indians and never encourage any degrees of heat without light."[155] Finally, at the request of Thomas Prince, publicist of the awakenings, Brainerd made some editorial corrections to an upcoming publication of the writings of Thomas Shepard.[156]

During his time in Boston, he visited a number of ministers and then, when his health declined, entertained a constant stream of visitors at Bromfield's house. The guests included commissioners of the SPG—to whom he made the recommendation concerning Elihu Spencer and Job Strong—ministers from Boston and the surrounding area, and "many persons of considerable note and figure, and of the best character, and by some of the first rank." His minor celebrity status was, no doubt, in part a result of the publication of his journal the previous year. Some of those who visited him in Boston had read the journal and were inspired to give money for the ongoing work in New Jersey. He was also able to attend at least two services (on the same day) at the Old South Church.[157] He returned to Northampton, accompanied by Jerusha and Israel, on July 25, somewhat surprised at having survived the trip. He continued to discuss spiritual matters with Edwards and visitors. He also penned a preface to the Shepard publication wherein he noted that "true religion must be justly delineated," and he hoped that the "publication of the following small piece of the Rev. Mr. Shepard's will be made in some measure useful in that respect." "For," he went on, there was "something in these papers of the Rev. Mr. Shepard's that seems excellently calculated to be of service to those who are in the ministry in particular."[158]

By the end of August, he could no longer ride and was so weak that Edwards had his bed moved downstairs. On September 2, he attended public worship for the last time. During the following weeks, he received visitors (including John and Israel), wrote a number of letters, and edited his diary. After September 25, he was so ill that he no longer wrote in his diary but dictated the entries to Israel. His last entry came on October 2, when he said, "my soul was this day at turns, sweetly set on God: I longed to be 'with him' that I might 'behold his glory.'"[159] During these final days, he continued to look to the interests of the Cranberry settlement. In mid-September, he wrote to someone in Boston, seeking financial support for "another School-Master or some person to assist the School-Master." He also spoke often to Edwards about the "spiritual prosperity of his own Congregation of Christian Indians" and frequently had to interrupt himself as he was "drowned with Tears."[160]

By September 30, he was unable to leave his bed. Several days later, when Jerusha came into the room, he made the comment that has launched much speculation: "Dear Jerusha, are you willing to part with me? I am quite willing to part with you." But, to ruin this moment of romance, he went on to tell her that he was "willing to part with my dear Brother John; altho' I love him the best of any creature living."[161] Three days later, on October 7, John returned to David's side, and the two spent a great part of the next day discussing the future of the work at Bethel. His condition worsened that night and, in the words of Jonathan Edwards, David Brainerd "then expired, on Friday, October 9, 1747, when his soul, we may well conclude, was received by his dear Lord and Master, as an eminently faithful servant."[162]

Brainerd's funeral was held three days later. Edwards noted that among the attendees were "eight of the neighboring ministers, and seventeen other gentlemen of liberal education, and a great concourse of people." News of Brainerd's death, along with a lengthy eulogy, probably from the pen of Edwards, was published in the *Boston Gazette* on October 27, and his death was also noted in the *Pennsylvania Journal* the following week.[163] The young man who had lived a good number of months encumbered by the "disgrace" of his expulsion from Yale died with the respect of a great part of the evangelical world.

Ironically, perhaps, that respect had not been won by living the kind of life that normally brought the approbation of others. Brainerd had not been a

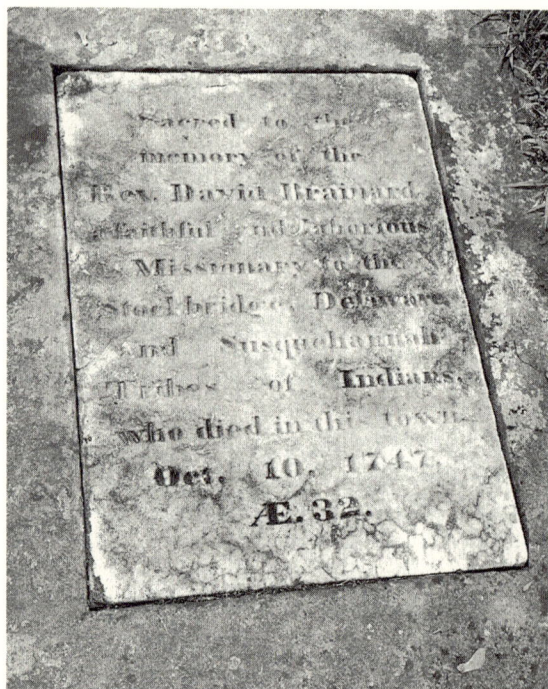

Brainerd's gravestone, Northampton, Massachusetts. Photo by Stan Sherer.

wealthy member of colonial society with strong political standing, such as his father and grandfather; he had not risen to the heights of the ministerial world through preaching and publishing as had men like Solomon Stoddard, Ebenezer Pemberton, or Jonathan Edwards. And, in his moment of confronting the conflict between established religion and the radicals of the awakening, he had not taken either of the paths that some of the protagonists had taken. Unlike James Davenport, he had not completely abandoned some of his more experiential moments (although, as we shall see, Edwards attempted to elide them from his life) and settled down to the obscurity of a pastorate. Nor had he confronted the establishment and waged war on it for decades as did Andrew Croswell.

Rather, he had taken a third way and blended both parts of his heritage. He had placed himself under the authority of other leaders, accepted their counsel, but had also refused opportunities to return completely to the ecclesiastical structure which he had challenged. In so doing, it became possible for him to gain the respect and admiration of much of that ecclesiastical structure while at the same time minimizing the amount of power its authority could exert over him. By working among Native Americans, he also virtually eliminated any possibility that his own congregation could work against him. Not long before he died, Brainerd made it clear to Edwards that he was in a position of spiritual contentment. "'Tis a great comfort to me," he told Edwards, "to think that I have done a little for God in the world." He also declared that he now had peace because he knew his heart was devoted to God.[164] David Brainerd reached the end of his life very much in control of the course that it had taken, which had allowed him to combine the two worlds that had been so much a part of forming who he was.

4

Jonathan Edwards's *Life of Brainerd*

"I have for the present," Jonathan Edwards wrote to his Scottish friend John Erskine, "been diverted from the design I hinted to you, of publishing something against some of the Arminian tenets, by something that divine providence unexpectedly laid in my way, and seemed to render unavoidable, viz. publishing Mr. Brainerd's Life."[1] At the time Edwards wrote to Erskine, in August 1748, he had been working on a comprehensive defense of Calvinism and refutation of Arminianism for a number of years. Only a subject of more immediate importance would have "diverted" him from this project.

Edwards's pressing concern in 1748 was his belief that the state of true religion in New England, in general, and in Northampton, in particular, had been declining since the gains of the revivals. Although Edwards saw some resurgence in visible sin, his greater concern was with what he believed was an overall loss of interest in religion. Many in the town, including some who had been awakened during the revival, were content with what Edwards saw as, at best, a mediocre Christianity and, at worst, an actual absence of saving grace. He believed that one of the reasons for this was that people who had undergone a truly experiential conversion were resting contentedly in that experience. For Edwards, true religion was not marked by a one-time experience but by an ongoing demonstration of a life conformed to the will of God.

During the summer and early fall of 1747, Edwards had recognized that David Brainerd embodied this ideal. Brainerd had enjoyed an experiential conversion but had gone on from there to live a life that conformed to the will of God not just in avoiding evil but in doing good. As Edwards would write to Eleazar Wheelock in September 1748, he believed that the *Life of Brainerd* would have a "very great tendency to promote the interest of true religion in general" and would also "open the eyes of the common people with regard [to] that wild sort of religion that has so much prevailed in your parts of the country."[2]

Ultimately, Edwards's determination to demand a life of true religion led him to propose new rules in his church, tightening admission to communion. This, in turn, would lead to a showdown with a majority of the church members, which would result in Edwards's dismissal from the church. Edwards worked on the *Life of Brainerd* through 1748 and 1749, in the midst of the struggle with his people over true religion and admission to communion. Published in 1749, the *Life* was not peripheral to Edwards's arguments over the proper Christian life, but intimately connected to it. By providing a real-life example, Edwards gave clarity to the more abstract concepts expressed in his other writings of the time.

"There Is a Great Decay of the Work of God amongst Us"

Edwards had come to Northampton in 1726 to serve as assistant to his maternal grandfather, Solomon Stoddard. When Stoddard died in 1728, Edwards stayed on as the town's only minister. In the winter of 1734–1735, Edwards preached a series of sermons on justification by faith which were clear and simple in their thrust. Salvation, according to Edwards, was the work of God, but it was the responsibility of the saint to live a life of obedience to God. These sermons ignited a fresh revival in Northampton, Edwards's account of which was later published as *A Faithful Narrative of the Surprizing Work of God*. Northampton had been visited again by the spirit of revival during the Great Awakening. George Whitefield had come to Northampton in October 1741—following a personal invitation from Edwards—and his preaching led to an awakening in the town. Both Edwards and the town embraced the revival to the fullest extent: participants in meetings were overwhelmed by the power of God; morals and manners were reformed; itinerant preachers came to town—although, of course, none denounced the local minister. Edwards himself often preached in other pulpits.[3]

However, by 1743, Edwards believed that the revivals were losing momentum. In May of that year, he wrote to James Robe in Scotland, informing him that, while "you have heard great things from New England of late," now "we have not such joyful news to send." Indeed, Edwards lamented, "there is a great decay of the work of God amongst us."[4] As historian Patricia J. Tracy has argued, in some ways, Edwards was viewing 1743 through the lens of 1735–1740 when, in his mind, the earlier revival had been followed by a loss of interest in religion and a resurgence of obvious sin.[5] Thus, much of Edwards's concern in 1743 focused on those who claimed to have experienced conversion but who were now not living lives that accorded with such a claim. While it was true that many in the town had been decisively changed, Edwards was concerned that, for others, "the temper that some of them show, and the behavior they have been of … make me much afraid lest there be a considerable number that have woefully deceived themselves."[6] Edwards was particularly distraught that many of those who claimed conversion did not even appear concerned about their sin. As he warned one earlier convert, "you have more cause, on some accounts a thousand times, to lament and humble yourself for sins that have been since conversion than before, because of the infinitely greater obligations that are upon you to live in God."[7]

For Edwards, a changed life was always the touchstone of a converting work of God. He firmly accepted the need for a transformative conversion experience in the Stoddardean fashion (although Edwards did not think that a single moment could always be identified). He allowed for a certain level of emotionalism as God worked in a person's heart, but the true evidence of conversion came from a changed life. He had addressed these two intertwined strands as early as 1735 in *A Faithful Narrative*. Some critics of that awakening had charged that what Northamptonites claimed to be God at work was really just overheated imaginations. While Edwards conceded that there had been events that were "something mysterious," he stressed that he had "used the utmost caution" to "teach persons the difference between what is spiritual and what is merely imaginary." And he defended the validity of the events of 1735 by noting that those who had experienced a conversion "generally seem to be persons who have had an abiding change wrought on them."[8] That is, while emotional experiences could be signs of a true converting work, only changed lives could validate such experiences.

Edwards repeated this line of reasoning during his initial defenses of the revivals of the 1740s, when emotional experiences were more common. In part, such experiences were more widespread because the awakening itself touched a larger number of churches and was longer lasting. But the increase in emotionalism also came about because many proponents of the revival were quite tolerant of emotional experiences. Edwards himself, as Douglas L. Winiarski has demonstrated, participated in some pretty raucous meetings, at least in the early days of the revival. His 1741 Yale commencement address, published as *The Distinguishing Marks of a Work of the Spirit of God*, defended the revivals against the charges of enthusiasm.[9] While Edwards conceded that he knew of a few instances when people had "for a short space been deprived, in some measure, of the use of reason," he also "never yet knew one lastingly deprived of their reason." Furthermore, Edwards believed it was not surprising that "a reformation, after a long continued and almost universal deadness, should at first, when the revival is new, be attended with such things."[10] Despite this defense, Edwards insisted that what marked the revivals as a true work of God was that they "lessen[ed] men's esteems of the pleasures, profits and honors of the world" and put them "upon earnest seeking the kingdom of God and his righteousness."[11]

Enthusiasm, of course, continued to be a target for those who opposed the revivals. Charles Chauncy, while conceding that there was "a great deal of real, substantial religion in the land," insisted that there was also "without dispute, a spirit of enthusiasm appearing in one place and another." This enthusiasm, declared Chauncy, was "a kind of religious Phrenzy," which caused those under its influence to believe they were the "special favourites of God." Those affected held a good opinion only of people who "are in their way of thinking and speaking," accusing those who oppose them of being "poor unconverted wretches."

And, where Edwards argued that good behavior usually validated a religious experience, Chauncy argued that the lack of discipline in the lives of many who claimed an experience invalidated those experiences.[12]

As such rhetorical assaults on the revival continued, Edwards sat down to write *Some Thoughts Concerning the Present Revival of Religion*, a longer, more systematic defense. Published in 1743, *Some Thoughts* was written in 1742 during the most divisive period of the revivals, when Yale was shut down and men like James Davenport were in full voice. *Some Thoughts* was an effort to defend the revivals against their detractors as well as to place them in the flow of redemption history.[13] The general thrust of *Some Thoughts* was to acknowledge that some excesses had occurred but then to defend them as a product of the extraordinary events taking place. Edwards conceded that "great numbers [had] run into many errors and mistakes with respect to their duty, and consequently into many acts and practices that are imprudent and irregular." But he argued that it would be impossible for any man to "behave himself in all respects prudently, if he were so strongly impressed with a sense of divine and eternal things…as had been frequent of late among the common people." Furthermore, Edwards argued, a "great deal of noise and tumult, confusion and uproar, and darkness mixed with light, and evil with good, is always to be expected in the beginning of something very extraordinary." Despite these excesses, in Edwards's mind the revivals were of God as demonstrated by the "great numbers" who "under this influence have been brought to a deep sense of their own sinfulness and vileness" and "have lately been brought to a new and great conviction of the truth and certainty of the things of the Gospel." In other cases, many "notoriously vicious persons have been reformed, and become externally quite new creatures."[14]

However, *Some Thoughts* also marks something of a shift in Edwards's thinking. Whereas *Faithful Narrative* and *Distinguishing Marks* had a tendency to minimize the errors of revivalists or to declare attacks on the awakenings to be inaccurate, *Some Thoughts* accepted that there had been severe errors on the part of "friends of the work of God." In some measure, Edwards still criticized opponents of the revivals, who had "eagerly catched at anything that has been wrong" and upon finding error had "made the most of it, and magnified it." Nonetheless, he conceded that the "errors of the friends of the work of God, and especially of the promoters of it, give vast advantage to the enemies of such a work." Edwards judged spiritual pride to be the "worst cause" of errors and the "chief inlet of smoke from the bottomless pit, to darken the mind, and mislead the judgment." Since spiritual pride was "apt to find fault with other saints" and to cause people to "stand at a distance from others, as better than they," Edwards held it to be a root cause of the public attacks on ministers, one of the most divisive practices of the radicals.[15]

Edwards echoed Chauncy when he accused some friends of the revivals of having practiced "wrong principles," among which were claims that they were guided by "immediate revelation," that success in their efforts was a sure sign of "God's approbation," and that some ministers had "assume[d] the same style and speak as with the same authority that the prophets of old did."[16] Edwards further noted that supporters of the revival apparently did not understand that some of the "passion which arises from natural principles" could mix with a true godly passion and become an "impure mixture that is prejudicial." This ignorance meant that "the Devil has special advantage" in undermining the work of God.[17] While not expressly condemning physical manifestations of the work of God, Edwards suggested that religious experiences "attended with the most violent affections and most vehement motions of the animal spirits" were "not always the best experiences."[18] As he had done in his earlier writings, Edwards argued that the way to "promote this work" was for Christians to live godly lives. Thus, while people should "abound in external duties of devotion," such as praying and going to meetings, there should also be a "proportionable care to abound in moral duties," which were "of much greater importance in the sight of God." External acts of worship which consisted of "bodily gestures, words, and sounds, are the cheapest part of religion," but obedience to God's moral commands of "self-denial, righteousness, meekness, and Christian love" were "of vastly the greatest importance in the Christian life."[19]

Some Thoughts cast a wide net in trying to explain the decline in the revival and, for the most part, was written in a diplomatic fashion. In private, however, Edwards was much more vociferous in placing the blame for the decline on the shoulders of the enthusiasts. He wrote a pair of letters to Scottish correspondents James Robe and William McCulloch in May 1743. In writing to Robe, he blamed "imprudent management in the friends of the work" for the wall that had arisen between supporters and opposers of the revival. To McCulloch, he lamented that the emphasis on experience had meant that "other duties that are of vastly greater importance, have been looked upon light in comparison."[20] By the following year, Edwards was even more discouraged by the behavior of many of those who had claimed conversion. In another letter to McCulloch, Edwards invoked images from the parable of the sower. He lamented that much of the seed of the revivals had fallen on stony ground or among the thorns. As a result, many "high professors are fallen, some into gross immoralities," while others now exhibited "spiritual pride, enthusiasm, and an incorrigible wildness of behavior." Because God had seen the "polluted flames that arose of intemperate, unhallowed zeal," he "in a great measure withdrew from us."[21] Enthusiasm, then, was more than just something that could be used as leverage by opponents of the revival: it was a distraction that emphasized experience over true religion and undermined the development of true Christian character.

In addition to his concerns over the declining spirituality of the people of Northampton, from 1743 onward, Edwards was also concerned with the spread of Arminianism. While Edwards and his fellow Calvinists argued that a true converting experience was evidenced by a life that conformed to biblical standards of behavior, the Arminians argued that a life that conformed to biblical standards of behavior could lead to a converting experience. The difference was crucial. One argued for the work of a sovereign God that was then sustained by an obedient saint, while the other argued for the work of an obedient saint that was then confirmed by an all-powerful God. For the Calvinist, a godly life did not lead to salvation, but the absence of a godly life was significant, albeit not conclusive, evidence that conversion had not yet occurred. In contrast to the issue of declining godliness and enthusiasm, Edwards did not see Arminianism to be a major problem in Northampton, but he recognized its pernicious influences on the wider religious community.[22]

By late 1745, believing that "Zion and the interest of religion are involved in innumerable and inextricable difficulties," Edwards was writing a much larger work designed to explain what he saw as genuine religion.[23] Developed from a series of sermons he delivered in Northampton, *A Treatise Concerning Religious Affections* marked a change in Edwards's approach to the waning of religious renewal. Rather than a simple defense of the revivals, *Religious Affections* was more a rebuke to the radical revivalists who had promoted experience over a disciplined Christian life. Edwards was at pains to stress that momentary enthusiasms, transcendent experiences, and brief periods of religious devotion did not, in and of themselves, prove that one had genuine religious affections. "Great effects on the body," declared Edwards, "certainly are no sure evidence that affections are spiritual; for we see that such effects oftentimes arise from great affections about temporal things." Nor, he insisted, did those who "spend much time in religion" and who were "zealously engaged in the external duties of worship" necessarily have true religion.[24]

Instead, as he had done in his earlier writings, Edwards insisted that evidence of genuine religion was found not in emotional experiences or feelings, but in the way one lived one's life. Truly religious people had their foundations "out of self, in God and Jesus Christ." Edwards insisted that "if there be no great and remarkable, abiding change in persons, that think they have experienced a work of conversion, vain are all their imaginations and pretenses." Desirable changes in one's nature included "evangelical humiliation," "the lamblike, dovelike spirit and temper of Jesus Christ," and a "spiritual appetite and longing of soul after spiritual attainments." Thus, in the first instance, the true Christian had a new character or, in biblical terms, was a new man. Following conversion, he was "not only restrained from sin, his very nature and heart [are] turned from it, unto holiness: so that thenceforward he becomes a holy person, and an enemy to sin."[25]

The culmination of all this, true affections "have their exercise and fruit in Christian practice." And the true Christian persevered in such a life "through all changes, and under all trials, as long as he lives." Edwards then explained that this "exercise and fruit" consisted of not only "universally avoiding wicked practices" but must also be "universal in the positives of religion." That is, he noted, "sins of omissions are as much breaches of God's commands, as sins of commission." This was something, it seems, that Edwards could not stress enough. Christians were to be "zealous of good works." As Patricia J. Tracy has pointed out, as Edwards sought to call his people to the proper Christian life, "his local enemy was apathy." Thus, the pages of *Religious Affections* are filled with descriptions of the true Christian life, which invoke terms such as perseverance, laboriousness, and diligence. For Edwards, true religion did not consist of a transcendent experience every five years or so with a life of materialism and apathy in between. Every true Christian "perseveres in [the] way of universal obedience, and diligent and earnest service of God, through all the various kinds of trials that he meets with, to the end of life."[26]

"The Right Way of Practicing Religion": *The Life of David Brainerd*

Despite the fact that *Religious Affections* was a tour de force of the true Christian life from an Edwardsian perspective, it was largely an irrelevancy in Northampton. By 1746, Edwards and the town were moving rapidly apart. The town was exhibiting increasing hostility to their minister's demands for religious purity, as well as finding fault with his salary requests. In one sense, Edwards, in *Religious Affections*, was trying to pull the town back to a partly mythical Puritan past while the townspeople were moving forward toward a more tolerant, easy-going world view.[27] In 1747, as David Brainerd lay dying by degrees in Edwards's house, he must have seemed the perfect spiritual counterpoint to the declension Edwards perceived in Northampton. Even before Brainerd's death, Edwards had contemplated publishing a version of the missionary's diaries. Although there were a number of lessons that could be inferred from or imputed to the diaries, it was David Brainerd as an example that was the central heartbeat of the work. As historian George Marsden has observed, the *Life of Brainerd* was "*Religious Affections* in the form of a spiritual biography."[28] Edwards saw Brainerd as living proof of what he had argued in *Religious Affections*.[29] Perhaps his parishioners could refute or ignore Edwards's theology but surely, he must have believed, they could not refute Brainerd's example.

Edwards's publication of the *Life of Brainerd* has led to the two men being inextricably linked in the minds of many. However, the relationship between them seems to have been largely based on the last four and a half months of Brainerd's life, about half of which he spent at Edwards's house in Northampton.[30] The two had enjoyed a "considerable Conversation and some Acquaintance" at Yale in 1743 at the time of Brainerd's final appeal. Following that, however, there seems to have been no direct contact between them, although Edwards claimed that he had had "much opportunity, before this, of particular information concerning him, from many that were well acquainted with him."[31] As early as 1745, he had heard of events at Crossweeksung (probably via Jonathan Dickinson) and had written to a friend that Brainerd was "remarkable for his piety, and eminent zeal for the good of souls, and his knowledge in divinity, and solidity of his judgment, and prudence of conduct."[32] Edwards seemed particularly intrigued by the possibility that the revival among the Indians was a sign that God's hand had not been completely withdrawn from the land. As he informed John MacLaurin the following year: "I know nothing of any remarkable revival in any part of New England. I have lately seen a journal of Mr. Brainerd's" which gave a "very remarkable and wonderful account of his success, among these, poor, ignorant people."[33]

However, Edwards knew little of Brainerd's life before the work at Crossweeksung brought him to the attention of others. Edwards was compelled to turn to others to obtain this information, in particular to John Brainerd. To John, he wrote, asking particularly for details on the Yale expulsion, David's family background, his childhood, how the SSPCK came to recruit him, his work at Kaunaumeek and the Forks of the Delaware, and whether there was anything more of his public journal other than that which was published in 1746. Edwards also asked John to see what information he could elicit from Jedidiah Mills, Gilbert Tennent, Ebenezer Pemberton, Aaron Burr, and Esther Sherman, one of David Brainerd's correspondents.[34] We know that Edwards also wrote at least twice to Joseph Bellamy seeking information, and he probably also solicited input from Samuel Buell and Samuel Hopkins.[35]

Thus, Edwards's impression of Brainerd's character was, in large part, formed by the young man's conduct while in his home. "His manner of praying," he recalled, was "very agreeable....He expressed himself with the strictest propriety." Brainerd's prayers "insisted much on the prosperity of Zion, the advancement of Christ's kingdom in the world, and the flourishing and propagation of religion among the Indians." His conversations "from first to last" were occupied with "the nature of the true religion of heart and practice." The night before he died, and "notwithstanding his bodily agonies," he spoke of the "interest of Zion," which "lay still with great weight on his mind."[36]

As the local pastor, to Edwards went the privilege of preaching the funeral sermon of this "eminently faithful Servant." Already, it seems, Edwards was planning some kind of publication of Brainerd's life, and the funeral sermon, published later that year as *True Saints, when Absent from the Body, Are Present with the Lord*, presented, in embryonic form, Brainerd as an example of the normal Christian life. Brainerd, said Edwards, "greatly abhorred the way of such, as live on their first work" of salvation and then "settled in a cold, lifeless, negligent, worldly frame." In contrast, while Brainerd had experienced the "holy influences of God's Spirit" at his conversion, he allowed these influences to work in a "continued course, from that time forward." Indeed, through his whole life, he "acted as one who had indeed sold all for Christ, and had entirely devoted himself to God, and made his glory his highest end." Even more than just living the right kind of life, Edwards noted, Brainerd "detested enthusiasm in all its forms and operations," and he "greatly abhorred" the "spiritual pride of such laymen, that are for setting themselves up as public teachers." In closing, Edwards called his audience to be "filled with the same spirit, animated with the like pure and fervent flame of love to God, and the like earnest concern to advance the kingdom and glory of our Lord and Master, and the prosperity of Zion."[37]

It is clear that Edwards's sermon contained the outline of the message he was intending to spread through the publication of Brainerd's diaries. However, as a number of authors have pointed out, because Edwards was determined to downplay the importance of esoteric experiences and harsh rhetoric, he did have to edit Brainerd's diaries in order to remove some of Brainerd's more enthusiastic or esoteric experiences.[38] This can be seen most readily in Edwards's treatment of Brainerd's conversion narrative. Gone, for example, was Brainerd's judgment that "Adam was a fool for being scared by that sword" which guarded the tree of life. Gone, too, was Brainerd's confession that he "longed to pull the eternal God out of his throne and stamp him under my feet." Edwards also removed Brainerd's declarations that he "quarreled with God for laying the guilt of Adam's sin to me" and that he thought God should "never make souls to damn 'em." These were removed because they hinted both at spiritual pride and at more enthusiastic experiences of which Edwards had been critical. Further, the latter comment could also be construed as a veiled criticism of the Calvinistic interpretation of salvation.[39]

Edwards also removed Brainerd's description of his vision of the mansion, one of the most vivid images in his conversion narrative.[40] Although Brainerd's conclusion regarding the futility of his prayers was orthodox, the vision was not. It was, in fact, exactly the kind of unorthodox behavior which had, in Edwards's mind, been responsible for the demise of the awakening and which had convinced unconverted people that they had really become Christians. Edwards rendered Brainerd's revelation that his prayers were useless thus:

> [T]hey were not performed from any love or regard to God. I saw that
> I had been heaping up my devotions before God, fasting, praying, etc.,
> and pretending, and indeed really thinking, at some times, that I was
> aiming at the glory of God; whereas I never once truly intended it, but
> only my own happiness.[41]

In so doing, Edwards deleted more than a page of Brainerd's manuscript, which described the mansion vision and which came after the first sentence in the above excerpt. Since it hinted at the things Edwards was critiquing, it could not be allowed to stand.

Apart from this (and other edits Edwards may have made, which we can no longer identify), much of the critique of radicals and separatists in the *Life of Brainerd* came in sections which Edwards openly added to the Brainerd diaries. Thus, in his lengthy appendix, Edwards asserted that Brainerd's religion "did apparently and greatly differ from that of many high pretenders to Religion." Edwards even went so far as to claim that Brainerd's conviction of sin, which preceded his conversion, "did not arise from any frightful impressions on his imaginations." This was true in the way Edwards rendered the account, but less than honest when one compares it to Brainerd's original narrative. Often, when Brainerd did critique separatists and enthusiasts, Edwards paraphrased him rather than letting Brainerd speak for himself, which raises the question of whether Brainerd was quite as vociferous in his critiques as Edwards portrayed him to be.[42]

But, while Edwards rounded off some of the sharper and less orthodox edges of Brainerd's life, the essential message he conveyed in the *Life of Brainerd* was true to its subject. Brainerd's whole diary bore testimony to his godliness, his living out those external signs of salvation upon which Edwards insisted. Brainerd's account of his conversion experience was, for the most part, exactly the kind of testimony for which Edwards was looking and also contained an implicit rejection of the Arminian position. Brainerd declared that he "proceeded a considerable length on a self-righteous foundation; and should have been entirely lost and undone, had not the mere mercy of God prevented." That is, the serious, sober religious works that Brainerd practiced had no value pertaining to salvation. Instead, God gave him "on a Sudden such a sense of my danger and the wrath of God, that I stood amazed and my former good frames, that I had pleased myself with, all presently vanished."[43] Here was no gradual, intellectual realization of sin. Instead, this was a man, content with his own progress, suddenly brought face-to-face with his inadequacy by a sovereign act of God. This prelude to salvation thus fitted precisely the Edwardsian model: a futile attempt to work out one's own salvation followed by God's sovereign intervention to bring one face-to-face with the need for salvation.

While Brainerd had a memorable, identifiable conversion experience, his Christian life did not stop there. There were no records of Brainerd wronging another or refusing to do God's will. Nor was there any mention of the sins Edwards was concerned about in Northampton, such as fornication or profane speech. At one point, Brainerd declared that "thirsting desires and insatiable longings possessed my soul after perfect holiness" and that he "felt that all my unhappiness arose from my being a sinner." This was the Edwardsian argument for godly living reflected in another's words. Brainerd's dedication to serve the Indians demonstrated that he had not sinned by omission. Indeed, Edwards wrote that, at one point, Brainerd "was so beat out by constant preaching to these Indians, yielding to their earnest and importunate desires, that he found it necessary to give himself some relaxation."[44] Here was the ultimate refusal to omit any good work: the Christian saint only relaxed once he had exhausted himself in the service of God.

In being obedient to God, Brainerd also epitomized his renunciation of the things of the world. "God's dealings towards me," Brainerd noted, had prepared him for "a life of solitariness and hardship; it appeared to me I had nothing to lose, nothing to do with earth, and consequently nothing to lose by a total renunciation of it." This lack of earthly pleasures meant that he had seen "so much of the excellency of Christ's kingdom, and the infinite desireableness of its advancement in the world."[45] Here was not only an encouragement to give up worldly pursuits but also a reminder that such a surrender brought eternal rewards, which were infinitely preferable to the material rewards sought by many in Edwards's Northampton congregation.

Brainerd also demonstrated a willingness to submit to leadership, something that was increasingly becoming an issue for Edwards in Northampton. Edwards utilized Brainerd's expulsion from Yale to emphasize the necessity for Christians to submit to their leadership. Brainerd's letter of apology was a masterful acknowledgment of the spiritual authority held by the leadership of Yale. And it was followed in the *Life* by Brainerd's declaration that he was "willing to do any thing" for the "sake of peace, and that I might not be a stumbling block and offence to others."[46]

In an editorial note to the event, Edwards underlined Brainerd's attitude even further, noting that Brainerd was "without the least Appearance of Rising of Spirit for any ill Treatment he supposed he had suffered." And in this note, Edwards revealed that, while the governors of Yale appeared willing to readmit Brainerd provided he enrolled for a final year, he had declined this opportunity because it was "contrary to what the Correspondents [of the SSPCK], to whom he was now engaged, had declared to be their mind."[47] So, in Edwards's reading, Brainerd turned down something he truly desired in order to obey those who were now in authority over him. And, of course, Edwards deleted the diary passages which demonstrated Brainerd's simmering anger against the authorities of Yale for their decisions regarding him.

It also seems likely that Edwards presented a somewhat stylized version of Brainerd's death. Erik Seeman has commented on the "model deathbed scene" of New England Puritanism. Surrounded by friends and family, dying people would be visited one last time by their minister. The minister would pray with them and discuss their beliefs with them to ensure they were going to heaven. In Edwards's portrayal of Brainerd's death, Brainerd did not need to be counseled. Rather, he spent his final hours discussing the future of the Indian mission with his brother John and discussing the work of ministers in general with a visiting preacher.[48] As with other examples, this is not to suggest that Edwards fabricated any of the details but rather that he included them in his account to emphasize that Brainerd had no doubts, no reservations about his salvation because he had lived in ongoing obedience to God.

Edwards, not content with letting the text speak for itself, had to be sure that the lessons of the *Life of Brainerd*, both positive and negative, were clearly understood. He thus added a forty-page appendix containing his own "Reflections and Observations on the Preceeding Memoirs of Mr. Brainerd." Edwards noted that, in Brainerd's life, there was an opportunity to "see the nature of true religion; and the manner of its operation." Indeed, Brainerd's religion "differed from that of some pretenders to the experience of a clear work of saving conversion," because it was not "the end of his work" but rather "the beginning of that work."[49]

In the details of this appendix, we can see most clearly the allusions to *Religious Affections*. Thus, Brainerd's religion was not "selfish and mercenary"; he appeared "to be of a meek and quiet Spirit, resembling the lamb-like, Dove-like spirit of Jesus Christ"; he was not like "a land-flood, which flows far and wide, with a rapid stream, bearing down all before it, and then dried up; but more like a stream fed by living Springs which . . . yet is a constant stream." Edwards stressed that Brainerd's life did not consist "only in experience, without practice." He lived the correct Christian life not just by being "negatively good, free from gross acts of Irreligion and Immorality" but also by having a "practice positively holy and Christian."[50]

Finally, although Arminians were not the principal target of the *Life of Brainerd*, Edwards did use Brainerd's story to fire a few shots in their direction. The story of Brainerd served to "confirm those doctrines usually called the doctrines of grace" and was "utterly inconsistent with the Arminian notion of conversion or repentance." Although Brainerd's mind was "full of the same cavils against the doctrines of God's sovereign grace, which are made by Arminians," as soon as he was "entirely convinced, that he was dead in sin," such thoughts ceased. Edwards declared, "Mr. Brainerd's religion was wholly correspondent to what is called the Calvinistical scheme."[51]

Edwards hoped that his account of Brainerd could "excite and encourage God's people to earnest prayers and endeavours for the advancement and enlargement of the kingdom of Christ in the world" and, in particular, "to pray for the conversion of the Indians on this continent." He also noted that there was a great deal in the memoirs to "excite to duty, us who are called to the work of the ministry." But he also declared that Brainerd's life "may afford instruction to Christians in general; as it shews in many respects the right way of practicing religion." It was this kind of allusion, that Brainerd was the model not for the extremely zealous, but for the average Christian, that would contribute to Edwards's dismissal from his pulpit barely a year after the publication of the *Life of Brainerd*.[52]

"With Respect to the Admission of Members": The Communion Controversy

Even while Edwards was preparing Brainerd's diaries for publication, the confrontation with the people of Northampton, precipitated by Edwards's concerns over their spiritual condition, had continued to brew. The antagonisms had begun as early as 1744, when Edwards penned the first in what would become a sequence of letters addressing what was, to his mind, his inadequate salary and the concomitant embarrassment of continually requesting an increase. That year was also the year of the "bad books" incident. A number of young men, who had somehow acquired a midwifery manual, had used their new knowledge to publicly humiliate some young girls in the town. In the subsequent disciplinary decisions, Edwards and a number of town leaders, including Colonel John Stoddard, an Edwards loyalist, were able to force some of the main perpetrators to publicly repent of their disrespect of church authority. But it was also clear that Edwards had lost the voluntary support of a large group of younger adults in the town, people who had been his most favored constituents in the awakenings of 1735 and 1742. For Edwards, the original conduct of the young men, as well as the disrespect they had shown during the investigation of the incident, was but one more sign that true religion had all but disappeared from Northampton.[53]

The growing hostility toward Edwards dissipated briefly in early 1748, probably because of sympathy toward him over the death of his daughter Jerusha. In March, he was voted a substantial salary, which was also hedged against inflation. But then, in June 1748, John Stoddard died unexpectedly, costing Edwards not only a friend but a valuable political ally. In his sermon at Stoddard's funeral, Edwards, in the New England tradition, cataloged Stoddard's many virtues. However, he concluded by interpreting Stoddard's death as part of God's judgment on the people of Northampton for their waning spirituality, a "testimony of the divine displeasure, added to all the other dark clouds God has lately brought over us."[54]

Not long after Stoddard's death, Edwards publicly proposed tightening the rules for acceptance into church membership. Under Solomon Stoddard's leadership, the Northampton church had accepted that most children would be baptized and become members. Since 1690, the church had allowed all adults who had "a knowledge of principles of religion" and who were "not scandalous by open sinful living" to participate in communion. Under this open communion policy, communicants did not have to provide a verbal narrative of their conversion as the pastor and the church accepted that not all those who took communion were, in fact, converted. Although Stoddard had initially advocated this position because of his belief in communion as a converting sacrament, that is, that God would use people's participation in communion as a means to bring them to conversion, most people favored open communion for the far more simple reason that they believed it to be impossible for anyone to make an accurate judgment as to the spiritual condition of anyone else. In practice, then, the vast majority of Northampton adults took communion and were full members of the church.[55]

Now, Edwards was proposing that applicants for full membership provide some kind of statement of their conversion, an indication that the applicant's faith was not just intellectual but was real and experiential and had resulted in a changed life. At the heart of this demand was not a simple change in theological interpretation, but a deep-seated belief that the church in Northampton, as presently construed, was failing to communicate the difference between true and false religion.[56] Edwards had hinted at this problem in *Religious Affections*. Although conceding in that publication that there would never be an entirely pure church, he argued that there would "come a time of much greater purity in the church of God, than has been in ages past." This would occur because "God will give much greater light to his people, to distinguish between true religion and its counterfeits." It was therefore incumbent upon the church to try to make this distinction since, in its absence, "God's people in general have their minds unhinged and unsettled, in things of religion."[57] It was right around this time that Edwards wrote to John Erskine of "divine providence unexpectedly" giving him the opportunity of "publishing Mr. Brainerd's Life."[58] Just as Edwards was looking to harden the requirements for membership, he was looking to publish a life that would demonstrate the "right way of practicing religion."

Then, in December 1748, Edwards lit the match that sparked the explosion. At that time, a young man, due to be married, applied for full membership, thus providing Edwards with a test case for his new standards. After meeting with Edwards, the man "hoped he could make such a profession" of faith as Edwards desired and left with a sample document which Edwards had drawn up, but he was also advised that he "might draw one himself in his own words." However, as word of Edwards's demands became public knowledge, the town was thrown into an uproar, and the young man returned the sample confession of faith, advising

Edwards that "he did not think that he was obliged to make it in order to [secure] admission into the church." Whether this was a heartfelt theological conviction or a decision driven by the attitude of the town is unclear.[59]

In February 1749, Edwards met with a church committee and laid out his new understanding of admission to communion. Although the committee denied his request to preach on the issue, there was a general consensus that he should publish something on the matter "with all speed." Not long after this, a young woman named Mary Hulbert came to Edwards seeking admission to full membership. After reading her profession of faith, Edwards was ready to admit her but insisted to the committee that the profession be read publicly. Refusing to allow this, the committee, in April, rejected the woman's application. In the meantime, Edwards had been writing on the subject and, shortly after this, sent the book to the printer. As Edwards advised William McCulloch, a "very great difficulty has arisen between me and my people," and he harbored some belief that it would "issue in a separation."[60]

Edwards's publication was entitled *An Humble Inquiry into the Rules of the Word of God Concerning Qualifications Requisite to a Compleat Standing and Full Communion in the Visible Christian Church*, his third publication that addressed the nature of and the rules surrounding conversion and the true religious life.[61] The *Humble Inquiry*, of course, was mainly concerned with defending Edwards's position with regard to admission to communion, and he asserted that it didn't "belong to the present question to consider and determine what the nature of Christian piety is." However, he rejected the idea that rote assent to church doctrines was sufficient proof of a person's spiritual position. To view actions such as "visibly joining in the public prayers and singing God's praises," "joining in the public confessions," and "keeping sabbaths and hearing the Word" as sure signs of true faith would be "a great mistake," since people had been taught to act in this way by the churches themselves. Thus, such actions were signs of acquiescence to church teachings rather than indisputable signs of salvation.[62]

Rather, Edwards argued, only those who "make a profession of real piety" should be admitted into full membership. Those who exhibited such religion, Edwards went on to write, were those who "comply with [the covenant of grace] internally and really," rather than those "who do so only externally." Edwards defended this position by reference to such texts as Psalms 51:6, "Behold thou desireth the truth in the inward parts," and 1 Samuel 16:7, "Man looketh upon the outward appearance, but the Lord looketh on the heart." Instead of lip service to tradition, Edwards wanted "an open solemn profession of being entirely for [Christ], and giving him the possession of our hearts, renouncing all competitors."[63] Because the purpose of the *Humble Inquiry* was to defend his general premise for restricting admission to communion, Edwards provided little detail on how to determine if someone were totally committed to Christ. And besides, he must have thought, he had already published a treatise, *Religious Affections*, that explained the difference between a simple display of piety and true religious affections. And if that weren't enough, he was in the process of providing his people with a literary example of the nature of true piety: *An Account of the Life of the Reverend Mr. David Brainerd.*

Denouement

By the summer of 1749, the slow-motion train wreck that was Edwards's relation with his church was moving toward its final stages. Both the *Life of Brainerd* and Edwards's book on communion were published in August.[64] The following month, Edwards seemed to hold out hope that the affair would be resolved in his favor. Writing to Ebenezer Parkman, minister at Westborough, Massachusetts, Edwards believed that his publication on the issue had been the means "by which the fermentation [in the town] seems to be much quelled for the present," although he remained "uncertain what the issue of the affair will be." However, he noted with a sense of gratitude that, even in the midst of the upheavals, there had appeared "some degrees of awakening in the minds of some of our young people, more than has been in five years before."[65]

In mid-October 1749, the Northampton church held its first formal meeting to address the controversy. By that time, Edwards had produced a trilogy of works which represented various aspects of his thinking on true and false Christians and how the church should determine and respond to each. *Religious Affections* provided the theological framework for Edwards's understanding of the nature of a true convert; the *Life of Brainerd* was an example, or a guide, for individuals seeking to live as true Christians; the *Humble Inquiry* was a specific application of Edwards's understanding of true Christianity.

In the *Humble Inquiry*, Edwards had not directly addressed the question of who would make the necessary judgments concerning an applicant's qualification for communion. However, it soon became clear that many of his Northampton opponents believed that Edwards himself, as the town's minister, would make that determination.[66] Certainly, although Edwards would later deny this charge, it is not hard to see why his opponents made it. In discussing communion itself, Edwards argued in the *Humble Inquiry* that the pastor acted in "the quality of Christ's minister, acts in his [Christ's] name, as representing him; and stands in the place where Christ himself stood at the first administration of this sacrament."[67] If the idea of Edwards as the sole judge of admission to the church was not bad enough, his members needed to look no further than the *Life of Brainerd* to see what standard the judge would use to measure the ideal Christian life. Despite Edwards's challenge in his appendix to the *Life*, it is likely that many in his church did not see in Brainerd's life the "right way of practicing religion," but rather an impossible ideal, an ideal that their pastor seemed hellbent on enforcing as a standard for admission to communion.

Whereas the *Humble Inquiry* was not widely read, the *Life of Brainerd* proved to be Edwards's most popular work: there are 1,953 subscribers listed on the work's opening pages.[68] The disparity in audience size is not surprising: by the middle of the eighteenth century, most theological writings were designed to bolster the status of the clergy.[69] Given this social context and what people in Northampton already knew about the main themes of the *Humble Inquiry*, the lack of circulation is not surprising. The *Life of Brainerd*, on the other hand, was different: it was the account of a person whose name was already reasonably well known to many people in New England. Dozens of members of Edwards's church subscribed to the volume, including two young men, Simeon Root and Oliver Warner, who had been disciplinary targets of the bad books case in 1744.[70]

In the meantime, the separation between Edwards and the church proceeded inexorably. On October 16, 1749, eleven church members signed a petition proposing either that Edwards renounce his new plans or that the church consider a separation from its pastor. Just over two weeks later, the precinct meeting formally rejected Edwards's new teachings, and a committee of nine men was formed to meet with Edwards. When no agreement could be reached, the town invited a number of local ministers to form an advisory council, which met on November 26, 1749. Even this council could not produce a resolution, so a final debate before a council of ministers and lay representatives from various churches took place in June 1750. Edwards was dismissed from the Northampton church by a vote of 10–9.[71]

Although Edwards and his family lived in Northampton for another year, and Edwards actually preached several times in the church, his term as the town's minister was finished. There can be no doubt that Edwards's demand to change the rules concerning admission to communion was the proximate reason for this dismissal. Equally, it is clear that the growing disagreement between pastor and people over the role of religion in everyday life had laid the foundation for this final battle. What role did the *Life of Brainerd* play in this drama? While there is no definitive paper trail linking the two, it is hard to believe that Edwards's decision to publish the *Life* just as the communion controversy was breaking out was a coincidence. Edwards must have believed that Brainerd's story would challenge the creeping worldliness in Northampton. And there are signs that others connected the events. In the remnants of Edwards's diary, he noted on three separate occasions between October and December 1749, as the debate reached its crescendo, that he had lent either the journals or the *Life* to parishioners.[72] And many of those involved in the key events between late 1749 and mid-1750 had subscribed to the *Life of Brainerd* and so probably read the book. These included Gad Lyman, who was one of the men who had signed the October 16 petition; Noah Cook, Jr., who was on the committee which formally rejected Edwards's new teachings at the November 2 precinct meeting; and Jonathan Judd and Chester Williams, who were among the ministers who formed the advisory council which met in late November. Finally, of the ministers who formed the council which voted on the disposition of the disagreement, Joseph Ashley, Chester Williams, and Oliver Partridge all voted for Edwards's dismissal and subscribed to the work, as did Samuel Bancroft, who voted against the dismissal.[73] While most of the votes may have been predictable, it seems plausible that the three men who voted in favor of Edwards's dismissal saw in the *Life of Brainerd* further confirmation of the strict new standards that Northampton's pastor wanted to apply to church membership.

While Edwards's concerns with enthusiasts, separatists, and Arminians were definitely part of the context within which he produced the *Life of Brainerd*, his main concern was to address what he saw as the declining religious sensibilities of his flock. By publishing the *Life* at the height of the communion controversy and informing readers that it could instruct "Christians in general" in "the right way of practicing religion," Edwards implied that this was the standard he would look for before admitting someone to communion. Edwards had crafted and created a brilliant moral biography with which he wanted to challenge and encourage his parishioners to a renewed commitment to Christ. And indeed, its lesson was not lost on the people of Northampton. Rather than responding by repentance, however, the townspeople decided to rid themselves of the messenger. In presenting David Brainerd's as the normative religious life, Edwards added one more nail to his ministerial coffin. Like many before him, Edwards had learned that one of the hardest sells was confronting lesser mortals with their own fallibility.

Epilogue: Edwards at Stockbridge

Edwards's immediate problem in the wake of this dismissal was to find employment in order to support his family. At first, he continued to preach in Northampton as a temporary measure while the town searched for a new minister, but this situation proved awkward enough that it was discontinued by November 1750. There was a small pro-Edwards contingent in Northampton who urged him to start a separate church in the town. Although it seems that he briefly considered the possibility, he eventually declined their offer. One of his Scottish friends, John Erskine, had been attempting to find a pulpit for him there, even before his dismissal. Despite his gratitude, Edwards discouraged this both because of the difficulties of moving his family and because he would have to be accepted without trial, making it possible that, if he did not live up to expectations, a church's "disappointment might possibly be so much the greater."[74] Instead, Edwards accepted appointment to the Indian mission at Stockbridge, where some of his flock knew him as a friend of David Brainerd, who had worked with them.[75] We cannot be certain why Edwards chose the Stockbridge post, although Rachel Wheeler has suggested that "perhaps it was his feeling of being unappreciated by a privileged people that predisposed Edwards to serve an underprivileged and disadvantaged congregation."[76] To this, we might add that Brainerd's portrayal of a unified Indian church which was loyal to its pastor may well have resonated with Edwards following the turmoil and divisions in Northampton.

Like most New England pastors, Edwards was aware of the failure of the Protestant churches to effectively evangelize the Indians. He must have read Solomon Stoddard's *Question: Whether God Is Not Angry with the Country for Doing So Little toward the Conversion of the Indians?* the 1723 sermon which attacked the people of New England for their failure to take the gospel to the

Indians.[77] Edwards had repeated some of Stoddard's themes in a 1738 sermon wherein he noted that the land had been free from Indian attacks for some time, and then launched into a stinging indictment of the failure of the people of New England to evangelize the Indians. He noted that part of the design of the original colonists had been "to instruct the Indians." However, not only had the church failed in this mission, it had "debauched 'em with strong drink; instead of communicating the glorious gospel that their souls might be saved, we have given 'em that which was poison to both their souls and bodies."[78]

Furthermore, Edwards included the conversion of Indians as proof that the events of the Great Awakening were, in fact, inspired by God. In *Some Thoughts*, he noted that some of the Indians who had "seemed to be next to a state of brutality" had now been "strangely opened to receive instruction, and have been deeply affected with concerns of their precious souls, and have reformed their lives." Many had abandoned drunkenness to become devout persons "brought truly and greatly to delight in the things of God."[79] Edwards also believed that the conversion of the Indians could be a sign of the imminent return of Christ. This idea was actually most clearly stated in his posthumous *A History of the Work of Redemption*, when he noted that the various Protestant missions among the Indians were "a preparation of providence for what God intends to bring to pass in the glorious times of the church." Indeed, Edwards thought it likely that God had ordered the invention of the compass in those times in order to provide for the salvation of the Indians.[80]

Edwards served a dual role as pastor of the English church at Stockbridge and missionary to the Indians, and his approach to this ministry has some parallels with the way Brainerd conducted his efforts in New Jersey. After feeling his way for the first year, Edwards's sermons to the Stockbridge Indians were primarily based on New Testament parables which offered practical illustrations and an emphasis on God's loving invitation to sinners.[81] It would be foolish to downplay Edwards's own ability to arrive at an effective means of preaching to an audience, but Brainerd's impact on the process seems clear. And, as had happened with Brainerd, Edwards's preaching was effective. He commented to Joseph Paice, a merchant in England and potential financial supporter of the work at Stockbridge, that "divine providence seems now in a remarkable manner to be opening a door in this place for the successful prosecution of this method of gaining the Indians," who now consisted "of above 200 souls."[82] Like Brainerd, Edwards fully believed that the Indian converts were part of God's kingdom. His world, like Brainerd's, was redivided into the friends of God and the enemies of God with both Indians and whites in each division. Also like Brainerd, Edwards took to condemning colonists for their failure to demonstrate the love of God to the Indians, and he spent a great deal of time attempting to protect the interests of the Indians, especially when it came to the issue of land ownership.[83]

Edwards's literary example of the right way of practicing religion had done little to convince the majority of people in Northampton that much was lacking from their spiritual life. But for men like Gideon Hawley, who joined Edwards at Stockbridge in 1752, it was an inspiration. In 1753, he wrote, "I read my Bible and Mr. Brainerd's Life, the only books I brought with me, and from them have a little support."[84] Hawley was only one of many who found inspiration in the *Life of Brainerd*. And inspiration was found not only in America. The *Life* would have a wide-reaching impact through a version published on the other side of the Atlantic in 1768. Had Jonathan Edwards lived to read this version, the resultant shock might have put him in the grave. True, the David Brainerd who emerged from this new version of his *Life* was still a dedicated servant of God. He still avoided the excesses of enthusiasm, embraced the things of God, and served as an example to other Christians. However, this David Brainerd no longer rejected the "loose notions" of Arminianism.[85] Indeed, in some ways, he almost endorsed them.

5

John Wesley's *Life of Brainerd*

On August 8, 1767, John Wesley preached in Newcastle and, at the conclusion of the sermon, took up a collection for Indian schools in America. "A large sum of money is now collected," he noted but "will money convert Heathens?" Better, he wrote, to "[f]ind preachers of David Brainerd's spirit, and nothing can stand before them."[1] Nor were preachers the only ones who could learn from Brainerd, according to Wesley. The following year, he wrote to a Miss March and encouraged her to read Brainerd's story as it provided a "pattern of self-devotion and deadness to the world!"[2] That same year, 1768, Wesley introduced Brainerd to a wider audience with the publication of *An Extract of the Life of the Late Rev. David Brainerd, Missionary to the Indians.*[3] Like Jonathan Edwards, John Wesley saw Brainerd as an example of the Christian life lived right, someone who could speak to all believers.

But Wesley also saw in Brainerd an answer to a number of specific issues he was confronting among his followers. First, Wesley was concerned about the increasing failure, both in conduct and effectiveness, of the men commissioned as itinerant ministers for the burgeoning Methodist movement. Second, Wesley was concerned about the growing materialism that he discerned in the Methodist ranks. Finally, in the late 1760s, Wesley had decided to provide formal support to the embryonic Methodist movement in America. Brainerd, as an effective American minister whose personal life was beyond reproach, was the perfect example for Wesley to bring forward to support his teachings and policies. However, just as Edwards had to edit Brainerd's manuscript writings before using him as an example, so Wesley had to edit Edwards's *Life of Brainerd* to render Brainerd acceptable for use within Methodism.

John Wesley's England and the Rise of Methodism

It may be a truism to identify any era as one of change, but it is an accurate description of eighteenth-century England. And John Wesley witnessed most of it: born June 15, 1703—the same year as Edwards—he died in 1791. John was the fifteenth of nineteen children born to Samuel and Susanna Wesley in the village of Epworth, Lincolnshire. Since Samuel Wesley was the rector of Epworth, John grew up in the world of the established church and was subject to Samuel's theological instruction. Equally important to John's spiritual development was the role of his mother. She believed that parents had first to break the will of their children but could then teach them by emphasizing the dual roles of piety and reason. Thus, John Wesley's spiritual character was shaped by ideas of spiritual discipline and experiential faith, as well as more formal theological teaching. On a more prosaic note, his childhood was also marked by persistent financial struggles, the product of both Samuel's inadequate income and his almost non-existent monetary skills.[4]

Despite the Wesleys' financial constraints, John was sent to Oxford to train for the ministry. He graduated in 1724, then received a fellowship to Lincoln College in 1726. While at Oxford, John developed a number of habits that, although often revised, would serve him for most of his life. One was the use of systematic Christian disciplines to strengthen his Christian experience. At Oxford, he practiced this as part of a group of young people that became known as the Holy Club; its members included his younger brother Charles and a young George Whitefield. During his Oxford years, Wesley also developed a love of reading the stories of Christian saints whose personal piety he particularly valued. Some of the people about whom he read were more mystical in their expressions of faith and so expanded Wesley's theological boundaries.[5]

In 1735, the Wesley brothers traveled to the new British colony of Georgia to serve as minister-missionaries. Although John Wesley was frustrated in his efforts to instill in the colonists the kind of spiritual discipline he had practiced at Oxford, by the time he returned to England in 1737, he was more concerned about his own spiritual condition. His doubts had apparently begun before he left England and were magnified by his encounters with a group of Moravians onboard ship during the Atlantic crossing. These men and women seemed, to Wesley, to possess a deep-rooted, simple assurance that they were truly converted and exhibited a spiritual peace regardless of their circumstances. By the time he returned to England in 1737, he believed that he had not yet truly found God's salvation. As he recorded in his journal on his return to England, "I left my native country in order to teach the Georgian Indians the nature of Christianity. But what have I learned myself in the meantime? Why (what I the least of all suspected), that I who went to America to convert others was never myself converted."[6]

For several months following his return from Georgia, Wesley went through a period of intense soul searching. Then, on May 24, 1738, in the evening, he "went very unwillingly to a [Moravian] society at Aldersgate Street, where one was reading from Luther's Preface to the Epistle to the Romans." As Wesley later recalled, as the minister described the change which God works in the heart through faith in Christ, his heart was "strangely warmed. I felt I did trust in Christ, Christ alone for salvation, and an assurance was given me that he had taken away *my* sins, even *mine*, and saved *me* from the law of sin and death."[7] Regardless of exactly what happened at Aldersgate—and there is a debate among scholars—it became the pivotal event in Methodist development. From that moment on, Wesley's theological emphasis was altered and brought with it an abrupt change in the content and nature of his preaching. While he never surrendered his call for believers to live a disciplined, holy life, he now understood this lifestyle to be the consequence of a discernable conversion experience.[8]

Shortly after his conversion experience, John Wesley set off to visit the Moravian headquarters at Herrnhut. While he was gone, Charles—who had undergone his own conversion three days before John—preached, witnessed, and wrote the first of his hymns. John returned to London in September and joined Charles in preaching salvation by faith. In December, George Whitefield, just returned from America, also came to London, and large numbers of people were converted under the ministry of the three men. By the early 1740s, John had begun the itinerant ministry which became the hallmark of Methodism. To assist in these efforts, he recruited a handful of Anglican ministers and a larger number of lay preachers to take the message of salvation to the people of England.[9]

Happily for Wesley, the foundational period of Methodism coincided with favorable conditions and developments in English society. Itinerancy, a key factor in Methodism's growth, was facilitated by improvements in national transportation. Changes which had begun prior to 1750 accelerated over the next twenty years. Turnpike authorities were allowed to requisition local labor, collect tolls, and carry out repairs to roads and to construct bridges. The increased attention paid to the roads also raised the level of safety of those who traveled them. Methodism also benefited from the rapid population growth in the second half of the eighteenth century. Much of this demographic increase took place in the new urban centers, and Methodist preachers consistently found some of their most responsive audiences among artisans, tradespeople, and urban industrial workers.[10]

Methodism also benefited from a substantially religious society which exhibited high levels of personal religious devotion and piety, facilitated in part through a massive increase in the availability of reading material. The demand for all kinds of printed material had exploded when the Licensing Act lapsed in 1695, and more than half of all publications were religious in nature. They circulated far beyond academic and ministerial circles, becoming available to the average Briton. Wesley proved to be extraordinarily adept at plugging into the demand for this literature. Furthermore, the Toleration Act of 1689 had led to an increase in and acceptance of dissenting groups such as the Quakers and Baptists as well as schismatics within Anglicanism, such as the Methodists.[11]

Methodism did have a few early hiccups. The British religious spirit was exclusively Protestant in nature, and Protestantism was an increasingly important component of English or British national identity. The Glorious Revolution had guaranteed a Protestant monarch and, in passing the Act of Settlement, Parliament passed over fifty persons who had closer genetic ties to Anne in order to settle the succession on George of Hanover.[12] Wesley had the misfortune to begin his public preaching at the time of the initial French success in the War of the Austrian Succession (1740–1748), which was coupled with fears of a new Jacobite rebellion in Scotland, and many of the attacks against early Methodist gatherings were often galvanized by a belief that the movement was papist in nature. So aware was Wesley of the accusations that he held Jacobite sympathies that, in February 1744, he delayed a trip out of London lest he be thought to be complying with an order for all papists to leave town.[13] As late as 1745 in Tolcarn, a local informed Wesley that "[a]ll the gentlemen of these parts say that you have been a long time in France and Spain and are now sent hither by the Pretender, and that these [Methodist] societies are to join him."[14]

Wesley's unorthodox measures, especially his outdoor preaching, also fostered other suspicions in various parts of English society: Anglican clergy saw Wesley as a threat to the church; dissenters saw him as competition; the gentry feared the Methodists as levelers. Large crowds, especially of laborers and poorer people, gathering outdoors were a potential threat to the social order. Wesley's methods were interpreted as "enthusiasm," which was as much a term of derision in England as in America. All of this criticism was ironic given Wesley's own belief in and commitment to the British nation, its Protestant values, and its hierarchical nature. Grudging acceptance of Wesley's work with the poorer people was won by his introduction of education and spiritual discipline to many of his rough early converts. With the demise of the Jacobite threat, the survival of the Hanoverian dynasty was assured, and accusations against Methodists of Catholic sympathies virtually disappeared. Indeed, from the 1750s on, there seemed little suspicion of Wesley and the Methodists at the national level, and future attacks on them were mostly sparked by local animosities.[15]

Wesley, Brainerd, and Edwards

Wesley first encountered information about Brainerd more than two years after the latter's death, and his response was decidedly mixed. In his journal entry of December 9, 1749, Wesley recorded that he "read the surprising 'Extract of Mr. Brainerd's Journal.' Surely then God hath once more 'given to the Gentiles repentance unto life!'" Yet Wesley was also grieved:

> [Brainerd condemned] what the Scripture nowhere condemns; in prescribing to God the way wherein He should work; and (in effect) applauding himself, and magnifying his own work, above that which God wrought in Scotland or among the English in New-England: Whereas, in truth, the work among the Indians, great as it was, was not to be compared to that at Cambuslang, Kilsyth or Northampton.[16]

Wesley wrote no more of the journal at the time, so one is left to wonder exactly how he thought Brainerd was "applauding himself" and "magnifying his own work." Certainly, Wesley's own experience in Georgia should have reminded him that preaching to Native Americans was a different proposition than preaching to British citizens who were biblically literate.

Brainerd does not appear in any more of Wesley's surviving writings prior to the 1767 quote which opened this chapter. It seems likely that Wesley's renewed admiration for Brainerd stemmed from reading the 1765 Edinburgh edition of Edwards's *Life of Brainerd*, which, in addition to Edwards's account, contained the *Mirabilia*, Ebenezer Pemberton's ordination sermon, and Brainerd's account of his first year working at Kaunaumeek and the Forks of the Delaware. This was not the first time Wesley had encountered an Edwards publication. As with many other British evangelicals, Wesley's first introduction to Northampton's minister was Edwards's *Faithful Narrative of the Surprizing Work of God*. In fact, the *Faithful Narrative*, which Wesley first read in late 1738, was almost as pivotal to him as the Aldersgate experience. Edwards's work both helped Wesley to understand his own conversion experience more fully and offered him a model of local church-based revival that enabled him to preach the gospel within the constraints of Anglicanism.[17]

So impressed was Wesley with the *Faithful Narrative* that he published an edited version in 1744. It was the first of five Edwardsian works that Wesley published in edited form. The other four were *The Distinguishing Marks of a Work of the Spirit* (1744), *Some Thoughts Concerning the Revival* (1745), *Treatise Concerning Religious Affections* (1773), and *The Life of David Brainerd* (1768). Wesley edited all of these works to bring them into line with his own goals. In some cases, changes were cosmetic: he removed purely American references that had little meaning in England, and he pruned Edwards's style to make it easier to read and understand for an audience perhaps less educated than many of the theologians to whom the original works were addressed. In other cases, Wesley's motivation was clearly theological: in particular, he removed references to Calvinism from the New Englander's works. In *Some Thoughts*, Wesley understandably deleted an entire section where Edwards had parenthetically observed that the belief that one could be perfectly free from sin was "agreeable to the notion of the Wesleys and their followers, and some other high pretenders to spirituality in these days."[18]

When it came to David Brainerd, there is no doubt that Wesley was drawn to him both by his success with the Indians and by his personal spirituality. And Wesley saw in Brainerd's life an example he could use to address pressing problems within Methodism. But it is also possible that Wesley identified with Brainerd on a personal level. Like Wesley, Brainerd traveled in order to preach the gospel and, while Wesley's accommodations were usually more refined than Brainerd's self-built houses in the field, Wesley would surely have identified with the lack of a permanent home. There was also a similarity between Wesley's rejection by the established church of his day and Brainerd's expulsion by the administration at Yale. Curiously, the two men also shared the dubious honor of having been accused of harboring Jacobite sympathies.

And it could well be that Wesley was both envious of and challenged by Brainerd's bachelor status. Wesley's interactions with women in general were often rocky. His family had expressed concern over his relationships with women, some of whom were married, during his time at Oxford; his involvement with Sophey Hopkey in Georgia had been one of the factors leading to his decision to leave the colony; Wesley's own marriage to Mary Vazeille, never happy, was punctuated by numerous separations (in addition to those caused by his travels) and came to an end in 1777. Indeed, Wesley had noted in his journal a month *after* his marriage that no "Methodist preacher can answer it to God to preach one sermon or travel one day less in a married than in a single state. In this respect surely 'it remaineth that they who have wives should be as though they had none.'" Perhaps even more poignantly, only weeks before he had first read of Brainerd's solo efforts in the field, Wesley had lost the chance to marry Grace Murray the woman who was perhaps his one true love. It is not unreasonable to think that Wesley saw in Brainerd what might have been.[19]

Despite whatever personal attraction Wesley may have felt for Brainerd and, in addition to Brainerd as a general example of the ideal Christian life, the 1765 publication of Edwards's *Life of Brainerd* proved to be serendipitous for Wesley. By the 1760s, Methodism was experiencing a number of growing pains that presented both opportunities and problems to the Wesleyan movement. Wesley's *Extract of the Life of Brainerd* was one of several tools that he used to embrace the opportunities and address the problems.

"Want of Life and Diligence in the Preachers": Methodist Ministers

One of the problems that beset Wesley from the early days of the movement was an inconsistency among his preachers.[20] In part, this may have stemmed from the recruitment of lay preachers, men who had not trained for the ministry with the goal of making it a lifetime calling. Whatever the reasons, the attrition rate was substantial. Of the sixty-two Methodist ministers counted in 1745, thirty-six of them either left the movement or were expelled in subsequent years. Thomas Williams, one of Wesley's earliest recruits, incurred the Wesleys' indignation for preaching anticlericalism and then seeking ordination. When he resorted to spreading gossip about the brothers, this led to upheavals in various societies, and John Wesley expelled him. Williams then repented of his transgressions and established the Methodist work in Ireland, but then abandoned both the Ireland work and his new wife. He disappeared from the Methodist records after 1755. Methodism was also afflicted by the publicized moral failings of a number of preachers, including James Wheatley and Wesley's brother-in-law Westley Hall. Both men were guilty of serial sexual misconduct with female members of Methodist societies. In addition to the disruption this caused within the movement, it also added ammunition to the weapons of the anti-Methodists.[21]

What had been an unwelcome backdrop to Methodist success threatened to become a full-scale disaster in the 1760s, as wayward and discontented preachers embraced new extremes of enthusiasm. Wesley himself had never been definitive about his attitude toward supernatural expressions of the power of God. For a brief period at the beginning of his public ministry, he embraced the French Prophets, openly endorsing a prophetic word one of their number had uttered that endorsed his work. Although he later denounced them, he never really absolutely rejected them, as Hillel Schwartz has observed: "Wesley condemned the French Prophets but often accepted their tenets."[22] Some charismatic manifestations—demon possession, divine healing, speaking in tongues—had occurred among Wesley's followers in the early days of the Methodist revival. Although Wesley dismissed some occurrences as enthusiasm, he was reluctant to condemn such manifestations out of hand. Ultimately, he tended to fall back on the assumption that, if such events issued in conversion, then they were genuine. In fact, at the 1745 conference, it was asserted that "saving faith is often given in dreams or visions of the night."[23]

In the late 1750s and early 1760s, enthusiasm within the Methodist movement began to combine with claims of perfectionism. To this day, scholars and other interpreters of Wesley's theology have been unable to reach a consensus as to Wesley's concept of perfectionism. In particular, they disagree as to whether Wesley, at any time in his life, believed it possible for Christians to achieve a sinless life. In 1759, his *Thoughts on Christian Perfection* defined perfection as the condition whereby one did not willingly break a known law, a concept that was repeated at the 1759 conference. However, at the same conference, Wesley also asserted that perfection, that is, the complete abandonment of voluntary transgression of God's law, could happen instantaneously, a teaching with which not all Methodist ministers agreed.[24]

While scholars—and Wesley—may be unable to define perfectionism, in the early 1760s, some Methodist preachers could. The most notorious of these were two who were active in London, George Bell and Thomas Maxfield. Both men appear to have encouraged some of the wildest expressions of enthusiasm yet seen in the Methodist ranks, while Bell, in addition, had been incessantly preaching Christian perfection. Bell finally concluded that he had attained full sinless perfection and was not only without any sin at all but was now possessed of a perfect intellect, incapable of producing an erroneous thought or vision. Bell also claimed that there was no longer any need for the sacraments. Some of those who sat under his preaching also came to believe that they were no longer capable of sin and would never die. In early 1763, Bell announced that he had come to understand that Jesus would return to the earth on February 28, 1763, bringing with him the destruction of the world. Numbers of people fled London, fearing an earthquake. Bell was imprisoned and, when the predicted apocalypse resolutely refused to arrive, was disowned by Wesley. In response, Maxfield severed ties with Wesley and began to publicly denounce him. The London societies lost more than 20 percent of their number, although losses elsewhere were minimal. Far worse, for Wesley, was the damage this incident did to the reputation of Methodism.[25]

In the wake of the London catastrophe, it is little wonder that the 1766 conference declared that the reason that Methodists were not wholly devoted to God was because "we are enthusiasts; looking for the end without using the means."[26] However, the London catastrophe was only the more visible tip of an increasingly troublesome iceberg as the actions of wayward preachers often led to followers abandoning Methodism. Thus, by the mid-1760s, concern over the character and conduct of preachers was a central issue for Wesley. At the Methodist conference in 1765, one minister had been restrained from preaching due to doubts about his moral character. In June 1767, Wesley instructed itinerant preacher Christopher Hopper to direct a number of harsh rebukes to several ministers for not following Wesley's instructions. In 1768, he wrote to Hopper and merchant and Methodist supporter George Merryweather on the problems caused by the fornication of a preacher named John Heslop.[27]

In addition to frustrations over the public failings of preachers, Wesley was also concerned that many preachers simply lacked the ability or the commitment—or both—to succeed in their work. At the 1765 conference, it was noted that many preachers could not arrest the decline of members because the preachers "have not light or not weight enough." In 1766, on being admitted as a preacher, William Ellis was asked whether he was "determined to apply all [his] time in the work of God," and if he would "recommend fasting both by precept and example." The following year, Wesley wrote to his brother Charles, declaring that one of the hindrances to the work of God was "the littleness of grace (rather than of gifts) in a considerable part of our preachers[.] They have not the whole mind of Christ." Finally, in 1768, the year Wesley published *Extract of the Life of Brainerd*, the Methodist conference asked, "what can be done to revive and enlarge" the work of God? Among the long list of answers was the directive: "Let every preacher read carefully over the Life of Mr. Brainerd. Let us be followers of him as he was of Christ, in absolute self-devotion, in total deadness to the world, and in fervent love to God and man."[28]

In the eyes of John Wesley, then, David Brainerd was the ideal counterexample to the conduct of a number of his preachers. Confronted with both the failings of many of the Methodist preachers and the fallout from those failings, Wesley turned to Brainerd as an example of the life he expected from Methodist ministers. Brainerd preached the gospel with great success. He fasted and prayed regularly, he was generous with the small amount of money at his disposal, he lived in simple accommodations in the American forests and never claimed a better lot in life. A great deal of Brainerd's diary entries noted the time he spent in prayer and fasting, activities which Wesley encouraged in all Methodists but particularly in his preachers. Thus, Brainerd comments such as "I set apart this day for fasting and prayer to bow my soul before God"; "I was enabled in secret prayer to raise my soul to God, with desire and delight"; "I spent this day in fasting and prayer"; and "I spent this day alone in fasting and prayer" echoed Wesley's expectations.[29] Moreover, Brainerd practiced these activities throughout his life and so allowed Wesley to demonstrate that it was possible to continue these disciplines on a long-term basis and in the most adverse of circumstances.

Brainerd's life among the Indians also conformed to the kind of commitment Wesley expected from his followers, particularly his preachers. For example, Brainerd's description of his early days at Kaunaumeek were the epitome of a simple lifestyle. Brainerd lived "poorly with regard to the comforts of life: most of my diet consists of boiled corn, and hasty-pudding. I lodge on a bundle of straw."[30] For Wesley, this was a demonstration that Christians could live and minister in difficult conditions. Moreover, Brainerd lived in such conditions not because he had to but because he had chosen to. This was borne out by Jonathan Edwards's footnote appended to Brainerd's decision to forgo pastoring a local church in favor of the mission to the Indians. Edwards noted, "[I]t was not from necessity, or for want of opportunity to settle in the ministry among the English, that he was determined to forsake all outward comforts, and to go and spend his life among the brutish savages."[31] For Wesley, this emphasized that Brainerd had chosen to live a simpler lifestyle in order to further the work of God.

But, and this was of equal or greater importance to Wesley, Brainerd also lived a life without scandal. There were no hints of sexual impropriety, no wild prophecies to bring shame upon his work. The one hint of scandal, Brainerd's expulsion from Yale, was restored by the Edwards footnote noting Brainerd's "very Christian spirit" and "the least appearance of rising of spirit for any ill-treatment he had suffered." Wesley reinforced Brainerd's godly responses to this trial by adding one of the very few of his own comments found in the book. "What manner of spirit were these governors of," asked Wesley, "and do these dare to call themselves Christians[?]" Wesley thus emphasized Edwards's interpretation of Brainerd as the victim of college authorities who were opposing the work of God.[32]

In the coming years, Wesley occasionally pointed even faithful preachers to Brainerd's example. He reminded Christopher Hopper in 1771, "Methodist preachers cannot have always accommodations fit for gentlemen. But let us look upon David Brainerd, and praise God for what we have." Wesley challenged one of his American preachers in 1773 to "read Brainerd again and see your pattern! He was a good soldier of Jesus. Ah! But he first suffered, and then he saw the fruit of his labour. Go and do likewise!"[33] For Wesley, while Brainerd was an example for all Christians, in 1768 he first provided a model for the Methodist ministers, the men on whom Wesley's organization depended for future success. By the time of the 1780 conference, Brainerd was an even more emphatic role model than he had been in 1768. Once again, the question was asked: "What can be done in order to revive the work of God where it is decayed?" The first part of the response repeated that of 1768, insisting that "every preacher read carefully over the 'Life of David Brainerd.' Let us be followers of him, as he was of Christ, in absolute self-devotion, in total deadness to the world, and in fervent love to God and man." But to this was added the assertion: "let us but secure this point, and the world and the devil must fall under our feet."[34]

"What Will Gold or Silver Do?": The Problem of Wealth

Running through much of John Wesley's writings was a kind of Protestant ascet-icism. While Wesley did not suggest that Christians should abandon the world in the manner of medieval mystics, he did insist that Christians, and in particular Methodists, should commit their time and their funds to the extension of God's kingdom. The specifics of this were probably most clearly captured in the *Rules of the Band Societies* (1738) and the *General Rules* (1743), which were repub-lished, with only minor changes, throughout Wesley's lifetime.[35] The *General Rules* carried expected demands, such as keeping the Sabbath holy, abstaining from "spirituous liquors," and avoiding blasphemy. However, Wesley also insisted that Methodists avoid wearing expensive or ostentatious clothing, "borrowing without a probability of paying," and "laying up treasures upon earth." In 1744, in the supplementary *Directions Given to the Band Societies*, Wesley insisted that Methodists should not wear "needless ornaments, such as rings, ear-rings, neck-laces, lace, ruffles."[36]

Wesley was convinced that material goods and wealth itself carried both profound risk and profound opportunity for the true Christian. Wealth could corrupt one's spirit and prevent one from doing the work of God. In *Earnest Appeal*, Wesley noted that he feared money would "cleave to me, and I should not be able to shake it off before my spirit returns to God."[37] In *A Farther Appeal*, he was even more vociferous, arguing that "the sinfulness of fine apparel lies chiefly in its expensiveness. In that it is robbing God and the poor."[38] Rather than indulg-ing oneself in the pursuit of things, Wesley asserted in *The Use of Money* (1760), it was "of the highest concern that all who fear God know how to employ" wealth since "in the present state of mankind it is an excellent gift of God, answering the noblest end."[39] If Christians understood wealth, they could use it as a means to serve God. This approach was summed up in one of the more famous Wesley aphorisms: "having first gained all you can, and secondly, saved all you can, then give all you can."[40] Wesley wanted his followers to stay engaged with the world, pursue their employment, but recognize that the money that was generated was ultimately provided by God and should be used for God's purposes. A simple lifestyle also kept more time free to engage in prayer, fasting, and other activities that were appropriate for a Christian.

In this insistence on a simple lifestyle, Wesley was less than successful. At the 1765 conference, the same year in which the Edinburgh version of Edwards's *Life of Brainerd* appeared, the participants agreed on some of the causes of a decline in Methodist zeal. They concluded, in part, that after initial success, "many Methodists grew rich, and thereby lovers of the present world." This led them to marry unconverted persons and to indulge in "worldly prudence, maxims, customs."[41] For John Wesley, concerned over the softening of Methodists, David Brainerd provided the perfect counterpoint.

In addition to the simple lifestyle and commitment to disciplines such as prayer and fasting, which Wesley believed laypersons needed as much as ministers, he saw in Brainerd someone who retained a generous nature in the midst of difficult conditions. In January 1744, Brainerd had noted:

> [God had] provided for me bountifully, so that I have been enabled in about fifteen months past, to bestow to charitable uses, about an hundred pounds. Blessed be the Lord, that he has so far used me as his steward to distribute a portion of his goods. May I always remember that all I have comes from God. Blessed be the Lord that has carried me through all the toils, fatigues and hardships of the year past.[42]

Not only was Brainerd living a simple life, his excess funds were used to further the work of God, exactly as Wesley taught his followers. Wesley must have enjoyed Brainerd's efforts to raise money for the Christian school at Crossweeksung. In November 1745, Brainerd had "left the Indians, and spent the remaining part of this week in travelling to various parts of New-Jersey, in order to get a collection for the use of the Indians, and to obtain a school-master to instruct them."[43] Even when Brainerd lay dying, his thoughts turned to the financial support of the work of God. In Edwards's narrative of the last days of Brainerd's life, he had noted that, about three weeks before his death, Brainerd had written a letter to a "gentleman in Boston" regarding support for the Indian school. At a meeting of like-minded men convened in response to the letter, a sum of £275 was committed for the work of God's kingdom, thus reinforcing the Wesleyan view of wealth.[44]

Wesley did not have to wield his editing pen on the *Life* when it came to the questions of generosity and of a simple lifestyle. Instead, the entire work was a testimony of one who had practiced what Wesley preached. Brainerd chose a life of relative poverty in order to further God's kingdom, he spent much of his time in prayer and fasting, he gave away most of the little money he possessed, and he spent part of his final days seeking financial support to continue God's work among the Indians.

"Respecting the Dear Americans": American Methodism

The later 1760s also brought a new opportunity that surely acted as a catalyst for Wesley's *Extract*: the initial institutional decision to promote Methodism in the American colonies.[45] There is no evidence to suggest that Wesley envisaged overseas work as part of the Methodist mandate in the early years of his ministry. Nonetheless, Wesley was nothing if not adaptable, and, as the world changed over the course of his life, he changed with it in regard to this subject. In this, he was not the leader, but he endorsed, at least in part, the work of others. In January 1758, Wesley met Nathaniel Gilbert of Antigua and three of his servants and noted that the servants "appear to be much awakened." Toward the end of that year, he baptized two of these servants, observing that one was "the first African Christian I have known" and noting that "shall not our Lord in due time have these heathens also 'for his inheritance'?" However, Wesley's reluctance to relinquish control of his preachers meant that the Methodist work in Antigua was initiated by the Gilberts with no official endorsement from the conference.[46]

The origin of Methodist work in the regions which would become the United States came at the hands of Methodists who had immigrated and then became lay preachers without any official endorsement from Wesley or the conference. In April 1768 (again, the year that Wesley published the *Extract*), Thomas Taylor, an English Methodist, living in self-enforced exile in New York, wrote directly to Wesley, requesting his—and the conference's—assistance in supporting the new work. Wesley, while not sanctioning any work in America, had kept himself abreast of religious developments in the colonies. He had followed reports of the Great Awakening, republished Edwards's works, met with Gilbert Tennent and fellow Presbyterian clergyman Samuel Davies when they had come to England to solicit funds for the new College of New Jersey, and subsequently maintained a regular correspondence with Davies.[47]

Taylor's letter recounted the growth of American Methodism, described the problems that were being experienced in purchasing and repairing an appropriate building in New York, requested financial assistance, and then, in the final paragraph, asked Wesley to send a qualified preacher who was both wise and a disciplinarian. The original letter was written in April 1768. It is not known when Wesley received it, but we do know it was printed and distributed in England in the later part of 1768, perhaps shortly after the conference in August of that year, where Wesley had read the letter to his preachers. At the conference of 1769, Wesley issued an official call for preachers to go to America to aid the Methodists there. From 1769 through 1774, eight men answered Wesley's challenge and emigrated to America.[48] While Wesley published his version of the *Life of Brainerd* primarily to challenge his English preachers, the fact that it told of the success of an American minister made it particularly apropos at a time when the Methodists were looking for their first recruits to cross the Atlantic.

Thus, the publication of the *Extract of the Life of Brainerd* in 1768 was not simply random timing. The availability of Brainerd's entire story in 1765 had coincided with the problems Wesley was having with many of his preachers, the increasing laxity in practice of many Methodists, and the emergence of America as a place of opportunity for Methodism. The story of David Brainerd was thus a model of the Christian lifestyle for Wesley's preachers in particular and for Methodists in general and took place in the new arena then being opened for their work.

Extracting a *Life of Brainerd*

Just as Edwards had seen Brainerd's diaries as diamonds in the rough, having intrinsic value but needing to be refined, Wesley saw the Edinburgh edition of the *Life of Brainerd* and, in particular, the Edwardsian commentary in the same way. Before it could be published as a tool for instruction, Wesley had to render it theologically acceptable. There was, of course, a great deal of common ground between Wesley's theology and that found in Edwards's *Life*.[49] Wesley was unequivocal in his acceptance of the doctrine of original sin and the concomitant need for a conversion experience. Man's heart, Wesley declared, was "always the same, that it 'was only evil *continually*'—every year, every day, every hour, every moment. He never deviated into good."[50] This was the first great distinction between Christianity and other religions. Whereas Christianity argued that "there is in every man a 'carnal mind which is enmity against God,'" other religions instead supposed that, in some people at least, "the natural good much overbalances the evil."[51] In large part, Wesley's emphatic statements on original sin were a stand against the growing number of people in England who believed that humans possessed a natural moral virtue which had been buried under religion and superstition. For people who held to such a belief, the way to eradicate moral failure was to eradicate superstition.[52]

Given the existence of original sin, people clearly needed salvation. And, like Edwards, Whitefield, and other Calvinists, Wesley believed that salvation was only available through a true conversion experience. Although Wesley taught on the need for conversion in the years following Aldersgate, it was not until 1760 that he published his first sermon on the topic.[53] In *The New Birth*, Wesley wrote that conversion "is that great change which God works in the soul when he brings it into life: when he raises it from the death of sin to the life of righteousness."[54] To counter the suggestion that merely living a good life and fulfilling church requirements was sufficient, Wesley declared that those who trusted in attending church and partaking of the sacraments would do "as well as your unholy neighbours; as well as your neighbours that die in their sins. For you will all drop into the pit together, into the nethermost hell."[55]

Obviously, in Brainerd's story, Wesley had multiple instances of a person under the effects of sin entering into a new life through conversion. Brainerd had written of his own experience when "the way of salvation opened to me with such wisdom, suitableness and excellency, that I wondered I should ever think of any other way of salvation; was amazed that I had not dropped my own contrivances, and complied with this blessed and excellent way before." Moreover, Brainerd made entries that proved his salvation was not a false moment of conviction, remembering that "the Lord by his grace so shined into my heart, that I enjoyed full assurance of his favour; and my soul was unspeakably refreshed."[56]

In a similar vein was the story of the conversion of Tatamy, Brainerd's interpreter. For Wesley, the account of Tatamy's conversion was a classic tale of new birth: Tatamy started with no knowledge of Christ or the salvation available to him; he gradually awoke to the gift that was available, struggled to accept this salvation, and eventually experienced the "new birth."[57] Brainerd's testimony that, prior to conversion, Tatamy "was not guilty of some wicked actions as others were guilty of. He had not been used to steal, quarrel and murder" was also useful to Wesley, as it reinforced Wesley's teaching that living a good life was not sufficient in itself to lead to salvation.[58]

However, whereas Edwards was a thoroughgoing Calvinist, Wesley, although eclectic in his theology (which was subject to change throughout his life), was heavily influenced by his Anglican roots. Like most Anglicans, Wesley's theology accepted some of the teachings of Luther and Calvin but maintained a commitment to sacraments, prayer books, and many of the outward forms of religion.[59] One important product of Wesley's theological background was that he rejected the idea of predestination, not only on theological grounds but because he viscerally detested the teaching that only a certain elect could be saved. As early as 1739, in the published sermon *Free Grace*, Wesley declared that predestination represented "God as worse than the devil—more false, more cruel, more unjust." Those who held to predestination believed that "the greater part of mankind God hath ordained to death." Because of this, Wesley wrote, he came to "abhor the doctrine of predestination." Instead, Wesley taught, "the grace or love of God," from "whence cometh our salvation, is free in all, and free for all."[60]

Wesley did not argue that all people had experienced salvation or would experience salvation. But, in contrast to the limited atonement preached by men such as Edwards and Whitefield, Wesley argued that all people *could* experience salvation. To make this argument, Wesley introduced the concept of prevenient (or preventing) grace. Put succinctly, he held that the presence of God in the world, manifested conclusively by the work of Christ on the cross, had fundamentally altered the spiritual condition of all humanity. The cross had made salvation *possible* to all because it had restored to people a measure of free will that enabled them to choose God. As he expressed in a sermon entitled *On Working Out Our Own Salvation*, even if it was allowed that "all the souls of men are dead in sin by *nature*; this excuses none, seeing there is no man that is in a state of mere nature." All people were surrounded by the grace of God, which enabled them to overcome their inherent sinfulness and choose salvation.[61]

Wesley also argued that prevenient grace meant that it was possible that works done prior to conversion held some value, that they were fruits of repentance. While Wesley was certain that good works could not bring about salvation, he believed that they were not entirely without spiritual value. The conference of 1745 had affirmed that works performed preconversion were "not done as God hath 'willed and commanded them to be done,'" yet went on to declare that "we know not how to say that they are an abomination to the Lord in him who feareth God, and from that principle, does the best he can."[62] In *The Scripture Way of Salvation*, Wesley wrote, "God does undoubtedly command us both to repent and to bring forth fruits meet for repentance; which if we willingly neglect we cannot reasonably expect to be justified at all. Therefore both repentance and fruits meet for repentance are in some sense necessary to justification." In assigning even this modicum of value to preconversion works, Wesley marked off another distinction between his views and Calvinist doctrine.[63]

Because of his theological differences with the Calvinism of Edwards and of Brainerd, Wesley had to use his editing pen when it came to preparing his version of Brainerd's life.[64] The most obvious target was the fourth point in Edwards's appendix, where Edwards explained how Brainerd's life confirmed "those Doctrines usually called the Doctrines of Grace."[65] While Edwards had dealt with the framework of salvation in general, he spent substantial space defending

Calvinism against Arminianism. Thus, Edwards argued that Brainerd's mind was "full of the same Cavils against the Doctrines of God's Sovereign Grace, which are made by the Arminians," but God so dealt with Brainerd that a "full end had been put to this Cavilling and Opposition." Edwards also asserted that Brainerd's conversion was founded on the doctrines which "Arminians most object against" and that it was "entirely a supernatural work" and "in no regard produced by his strength of labor." He concluded the section by claiming, "Mr. Brainerd's religion was wholly correspondent to what is called the Calvinistical Scheme."[66] Edwards probably did not have Wesley and his teachings in mind when he wrote the appendix, but the section clearly contradicted much of what Wesley taught about salvation. Although there were sections that Wesley could have used to bolster his argument, he obviously felt that it was easier to delete the entire section, and he renumbered the subsequent sections of the appendix to leave his readers none the wiser.[67]

In addition to Edwards's longer Calvinist conclusions, there were also smaller, more implicit endorsements of Calvinism that needed to be removed. At one point in the account of his own conversion, Brainerd noted that, before his conversion, he had a "great inward Opposition to [the] Sovereignty of God. I could not bear, that it should be wholly at God's pleasure to save or damn me, just as he would." However, after grappling with these issues for a period of time, Brainerd came to see "no safety in owning my self in the hands of a Sovereign God, and that I could lay no Claim to any Thing better than Damnation."[68] While Wesley did not expunge this entire section as he did with part of Edwards's appendix, he did undertake some extraordinarily judicious editing. As might be expected, Wesley removed references to explicit and implicit appeals to the sovereignty of God. However, he also deleted Brainerd's opening paragraph of this section (quoted in part above) and so connected Brainerd's conclusion to his third point about his difficulties in finding out how to come to Christ and to believe in the doctrine of faith alone. Thus, Wesley rendered the section so that it read as if Brainerd struggled with, but then understood, salvation by faith alone.[69]

Wesley also turned his attention to passages that smacked of rejecting all preconversion works as without merit. In some cases, Wesley's editing was particularly egregious, as can be seen in the following comparison:

Edwards's *Life*

Sometime in February 1738–9, I set apart a day for fasting and prayer, and spent the day in almost incessant cries to God for mercy, that he would open up my eyes to see the evil of sin, and the way of life by Jesus Christ. And God was pleased that day to make considerable discoveries of my heart to me: But still I trusted in all the duties I performed; though there was no manner of goodness in the duties I then performed, there being no manner of respect to the glory of God in them, nor any such principle in my heart: yet God was pleased to make my endeavors that day a means to show my helplessness in some measure.[70]

Wesley's *Extract*

Sometime in February 1738–9, I set apart a day for secret fasting and prayer, and spent the same in almost incessant cries to God for mercy, that he would open up my eyes to see the evil of sin, and the way of life by Jesus Christ. God was pleased that day to make considerable discoveries of my heart to me: and to make my endeavors a means to show my helplessness in some measure.[71]

In making these changes, Wesley essentially changed the entire thrust of Brainerd's argument. Brainerd had made it clear that all of the duties he performed were worthless. God used the uselessness of these actions to show Brainerd how helpless he was to bring about his own salvation. Under Wesley's editorial hand, Brainerd's efforts were rewarded by God with a revelation of Brainerd's own helplessness. Thus, for Brainerd, truth was given in spite of his actions whereas, for Wesley, truth was given *because* of Brainerd's actions.

In a similar fashion, Wesley altered the meaning of part of the story of Tatamy's conversion:

Mirabilia

After [Tatamy] had been for some time in this condition, sensible of the impossibility of helping himself by anything he could do, or of being delivered by any created arm, so that he "had given up all for lost" as to his own attempts, and was become more calm and composed; then he says it was borne in upon his mind as if it had been audibly spoken to him, "There is hope, there is hope."[72]

Wesley's *Extract*

After [Tatamy] had been for some time in this condition, sensible of the impossibility of helping himself, then he says it was borne in upon his mind as if it had been audibly spoken to him, "There is hope, there is hope."[73]

While Wesley was in agreement with the idea that one's own works could not bring about salvation, he did not want his readers to think that their good works prior to salvation were a waste of time.

On other occasions, Wesley limited himself to footnotes to correct what he believed were errors in Brainerd's story. For example, when Brainerd concluded that his commitment to religious duties prior to his conversion meant that he had "proceeded on a self-righteous foundation," a clear declaration of the standard Calvinist contempt for any attempt at self-righteousness,[74] Wesley felt compelled to add a footnote, commenting, "I doubt that. I believe this was True Religion as far as it went."[75] In so doing, Wesley affirmed his own theological view that good works performed as part of the process of repentance did indeed assist one on the road to salvation.

In a similar vein, Brainerd had recounted how Tatamy was not "guilty of some wicked actions as others were guilty of. He had not been used to steal, quarrel and murder." But when Brainerd noted that Tatamy had declared that he had "never done one good thing" prior to his conversion, Wesley was compelled to add the parenthetical comment "meaning he had never done any thing from a right principle, and with a right view, though he had done many things that were materially good." In so doing, Wesley reasserted his argument for the value of works performed as acts of repentance.[76]

John Wesley's *Extract of the Life of David Brainerd* does not occupy the same place of significance in his corpus as Jonathan Edwards's *Life of Brainerd* does in his. In part, this is because, despite the vast quantity of Edwards's publications, Wesley probably outdid him. However, the difference is more than simply numbers because, while Edwards's *Life* was a virtually unique publication for him, Wesley's *Extract* was one of a number of spiritual biographies that Wesley reissued under his own name.[77] Wesley also had the biographies of many Methodists published when he thought they could be helpful to others. For Wesley, spiritual biographies were meant to help the reader's own spiritual development. In most cases, they followed a standard pattern: religious background but deadness in sin, beginning of conviction, attempts at self-justification, conversion, postconversion struggles culminating in a life of obedience.[78] Clearly, David Brainerd's story fit in this general pattern. In addition, he exemplified another Methodist virtue: he died with his focus on the things of God. As Henry Rack has expressed it, "almost as important for the early Methodists as a life well lived was a death well died."[79]

There is no doubt that David Brainerd fit the general pattern for a Wesley-endorsed life. Wesley's *Extract* proved to be as popular in England as its colonial antecedent had been in America, going through a total of eight more printings and four editions. In part, this was directly related to Wesley's editing technique, which left his versions shorter than the originals and thus more accessible and economical to the average person.[80] Whereas Edwards had been primarily concerned with presenting a model of the "right way of practicing religion" for all Christians, Wesley was concerned with making Brainerd an example to Methodist leaders more than to the rank and file, challenging his preachers to "look upon David Brainerd." But Wesley had merely scratched the surface of Brainerd's posthumous abilities. For, in the hands of a new generation of British evangelists, David Brainerd would not only be an ideal Christian and an example to preachers, he would become the prototypical missionary.

6

From Wesley to Woodstock

The story of David Brainerd lost none of its popularity in the years after Wesley's 1768 publication. In addition to the four Wesley editions, the Edwards version was published in several editions in Britain following the 1765 Edinburgh edition. The British editions increasingly offered variations to the text, reducing it in length, adding prefaces, and appending accounts of new missionary endeavors in America. Then, in the early nineteenth century, the first of what can be described as biographies of Brainerd began to appear. These works were composed of narratives written by editors or publishers interspersed with extracts from the words of Brainerd and/or Edwards.

In addition to the increasing varieties of the Brainerd story, there came the development of new applications of the life lessons which Brainerd exemplified. In the late eighteenth and early nineteenth centuries, the primary example was Brainerd as missionary. This was obviously something that was part of Brainerd's life but was not the primary lesson which Edwards and Wesley had hoped would be learned. By the later nineteenth century and into the early twentieth, Brainerd, while still a missionary, became specifically a vigorous, masculine, college-age missionary. And, in post–World War II America, Brainerd would enter his most adventurous phase, becoming, by turns, civil rights campaigner, student radical, and hippie.

"Read David Brainerd": The Birth of British Protestant Missions

On May 12, 1806, Henry Martyn, a new chaplain for the East India Company, arrived in Calcutta, India. On surveying the scene before him, he noted in his diary that he was "most abundantly encouraged by reading D. Brainerd's account of the difficulties attending a mission to the heathen. Oh, blessed be the memory of that beloved saint! No uninspired writer ever did me so much good."[1] In his attitude toward Brainerd, Martyn was typical of many of the British Protestant missionaries and ministers who left their homeland for outposts of the empire beginning in the late eighteenth century. Brainerd was more than a literary example; he became both a real, personal inspiration and a subject worthy of study in missionary training schools.

Although John Wesley had expurgated the Calvinism of Brainerd and Edwards from his *Extract of the Life of Brainerd*, many leading ministers and theologians had read versions of Edwards's works—including the *Life of Brainerd*—that were faithful to the original text. At least one well-known British Calvinist was irate over Wesley's assault on Edwards's Calvinism. John Collett Ryland (1723–1792), on comparing the Edwards version of the *Life of Brainerd* with Wesley's, made the marginal note: "shamefully omitted of Wesley all these pages which spake much against his principles." However, many British Calvinists were struck by the way in which both Edwards and Brainerd, in spite of their commitment to the sovereign role of God in conversion, were able to embrace evangelical preaching. Edwards's theology and Brainerd's example became important components in the development of a more moderate form of Calvinism, which was able to embrace both predestination and evangelical preaching. This moderate Calvinism, in turn, was key in the formation of the modern Protestant mission movement.[2]

One of those inspired by Edwards's thinking was Andrew Fuller (1745–1815), who in 1785 published *The Gospel Worthy of All Acceptation*, a work critical to the development of evangelical Calvinism within the Baptist denomination. Fuller introduced his work by explaining that he had been challenged by the lives of men such as John Eliot and David Brainerd, who had "preached Christ with so much success to the American Indians." Since these men "appeared to have none of the [theological] difficulties" by which Fuller "felt himself encumbered," he went to the "throne of grace, to implore instruction and resolution." He also recalled that Edwards's *Inquiry into the Freedom of the Will* was "calculated to disburden the Calvinistic system of a number of calumnies." Although the *Gospel Worthy* led to the development of a Calvinism which promoted evangelism, it was not a call to missions per se. That call came from the pen of another Baptist minister, a man who was a close friend of Fuller.[3]

William Carey (1761–1834) grew up an Anglican, converted to nonconformism while still a teenager, and aligned himself with the Baptist confession in 1783. In 1789, Carey accepted a call to the Baptist church in Leicester, a move which brought him into closer contact with Fuller's circle. Carey, who had been fascinated by travel accounts, such as those of Captain James Cook, as a child, prodded other ministers to form a mission society, but they declined to take what was seen to be a radical step. They did, however, encourage Carey to write on the need for a concerted missionary effort. In May 1792, Carey published *An Enquiry into the Obligations of Christians, to Use Means for the Conversion of the Heathens*, a work inspired by a number of missionaries, including David Brainerd.[4]

In order to convince Christians of their obligations to preach the gospel, Carey had to overcome their objections to mission work, including those which were theological in nature. *An Enquiry* ran only ninety-two pages and was divided into five sections, including a refutation of theological arguments against missions, a refutation of practical objections to missions, and a discourse on the duty of Christians and the means they should use to carry out Christ's command. Carey opened his work by declaring that it was the responsibility of the church to "use every lawful method to spread the knowledge" of Christ. Noting that, on Christ's resurrection, he had "sent forth his disciples to preach the good tidings," Carey proposed to examine "whether the commission given by our Lord to his disciples be not still binding on us." This was a key break with the older Calvinist thinking, which held that the apostles were the only ones commissioned to go out and preach the gospel.[5]

The second objection which Carey claimed prevented people from promoting mission work was the "uncivilized, and barbarous way of living" of those who would be the target audience of missions. Such a consideration, he declared, "was no objection to an Elliot [*sic*] or a Brainerd." In fact, argued Carey, the "uncivilized state of the heathen" should "furnish an argument *for*" sending out missionaries, since it was the "most effectual means of their civilization." Indeed, he noted, "such effects did in a measure follow the afore-mentioned efforts of Elliot [*sic*], Brainerd, and others amongst the American Indians."[6]

Carey also invoked Eliot and Brainerd when considering the third objection to missions: the fear of death on the mission field at the hands of those to whom one was preaching. With an insight uncommon to an Englishman of the time, Carey suggested that most acts of brutality reported against Europeans may have originated in "some real or supposed affront [to local peoples], and were therefore, more properly, acts of self-defence, than proofs of ferocious dispositions." To support this argument, Carey noted that "Elliot [*sic*], Brainerd, and the Moravian missionaries, have been very seldom molested," insisting that most native peoples had "principally expressed their hatred of Christianity on account of the vices of nominal Christians." In concluding his *Enquiry*, Carey reminded his readers that they were "exhorted to lay up treasure in heaven," and a great reward must await Paul, Eliot, Brainerd, and others who "have given themselves wholly to the work of the Lord."[7]

An Enquiry, which became the first great mandate of this renewed mission effort, did not focus on presenting Brainerd's as a model Christian life for others to follow. Instead, Carey reimaged Brainerd as an exemplification of the missionary life. Increasingly, British missionaries attempted to model not only their life, but their work, on Brainerd. One of those was William Carey himself who, in November 1793, arrived in India as the second missionary of the newly formed Baptist Missionary Society (BMS). Portions of a diary Carey kept, apparently in conscious emulation of Brainerd, have survived, and his respect for the American can be found there. On one occasion, he acknowledged being "much humbled by

Brainerd—O what a disparity betwixt me and him; he always constant, I uncon-
stant as the wind." Of course, Carey also had to deal with problems unknown to
Brainerd, lamenting on another occasion that he could not pray in the woods
as Brainerd had done "for fear of tygers." Carey gave his whole life to missions
in India, settling in the Danish enclave of Serampore because of opposition to
his plans from the East India Company. He and his family lived and worked in
India for more than forty years; Carey died at Serampore, aged seventy-three,
in 1834.[8]

The nascent English missionary spirit which Carey sparked led to the formation of a number of missionary societies. The BMS had been formed in October
1792, just five months after the publication of Carey's *Enquiry*. It began sending
missionaries to India in January 1793, to Africa in 1795, and in 1814 expanded
to Jamaica. In 1795, the ecumenical London Missionary Society (LMS) was officially formed. The roots of the LMS are complex and disparate, but at least two
of those who contributed to its foundation urged people to look to Brainerd's
example. One was Melville Horne, whose 1794 *Letters on Missions* declared that
the "labours of a Brainerd and an Elliot [sic] deserve to be had in everlasting
remembrance." David Bogue, addressing the LMS founding meeting in 1795, also
invoked the spirit of Brainerd. In refuting the claim that it was not yet time for
the conversion of the heathen, Bogue pointed to what had "already been effected
by the preaching of the gospel among the heathen" by men such as "Brainard
[sic], [Azariah] Horton and others." He went on to remind his audience that the
Indians were "converted by the power of the gospel: and the same glorious truths
confirmed by the holy lives of our missionaries, and accompanied by the energy
of the Spirit, will, I trust, still produce the same effects."[9]

In order to raise mission awareness, new publications appeared, such as
the quarterly *Evangelical Magazine*, sponsored by Andrew Fuller, David Bogue,
and others, which began publication in 1793. Although intended to promote
evangelical Protestantism in general, part of every issue was set aside to document the "progress of the Gospel throughout the kingdom." The publication
quickly became a voice for mission promoters. Bogue published a preliminary
appeal regarding missions in the September 1794 issue, and reports on the LMS
made frequent appearances. The fourth volume, published in 1796, featured
an excerpted version of the life of David Brainerd, totaling about twenty-five
pages across three issues. The editors noted that "few lives are more interesting
than that of Mr. Brainerd." They hoped that their readers would "perceive how
easily God can provide instruments for his work" and that his success, "in circumstances most discouraging," would provide "the clearest demonstration that
those difficulties which, to us, appear insuperable, instantly vanish at the presence of the Almighty."[10] In similar fashion, the Anglican periodical *Missionary
Register* serialized the *Life of Brainerd* in 1816.[11]

As the mission spirit grew, some of its proponents recognized a need for
more specific and formal instruction for those determined to preach the gospel
beyond the shores of Britain. Such training usually took place either outside of or
in addition to training at more recognized educational institutions. Supporters of

missions most frequently turned to two sources for instructional inspiration: the writings of the Moravians and the *Life of Brainerd*. Thus, at David Bogue's academy at Gosport, which turned out 40 percent of all LMS missionaries through 1825 and 70 percent of those who went to India, missionary lectures given by Bogue were mainly based on his reflections on the lives of past missionaries, including Brainerd. Although the Anglican Church Missionary Society (CMS) did not, apparently, invoke Brainerd during its founding period, when it set up its first library in 1799, there were only eight books, one of which was the *Life of Brainerd*. Student-led mission societies at Scottish universities encouraged their members to read the *Life of Brainerd* (along with those of other missionaries) and even to present papers on their readings.[12]

Unsurprisingly, as Andrew Walls has noted, "David Brainerd became the principal model of early British missionary spirituality."[13] Brainerd was frequently cited and referred to by the mission boards. The CMS candidates expected to be asked if they had read Brainerd's *Life*, and, by the 1820s, the LMS Committee of Examination required candidates to read the *Life of Brainerd* along with several other biographies. William Crow was judged to be a good candidate after his initial examination and was subsequently given a copy of the *Life* and a month to read it and write an essay on his perspective on the "character, difficulties, and privations of a Christian Missionary."[14] There are also frequent references to Brainerd in the writings of missionaries and mission candidates. In some cases, these men seemed to be challenged by Brainerd's example of the ideal Christian. Samuel Pearce (1766–1799), a friend of William Carey, spent several days in prayer in 1793 in order to devote himself to missions. During this time, he read Brainerd's *Life* and noted that the "exalted devotion of that dear man" made him question his own devotion. Nonetheless, he felt that Brainerd's "feelings, prayers, desires, comforts, hopes and sorrows" were his. Pearce himself was held in high esteem by his contemporaries and, when he died in 1799, having never left England, it seemed simple to connect him to David Brainerd. Andrew Fuller noted that "memoirs of his life must be published: he is another Brainerd."[15]

Aspiring missionaries either wanted to or quickly learned that they were expected to incorporate lessons from Brainerd in their applications. William Miller, in his written application to the LMS, declared that he desired the "ardent love and compassion which [Brainerd] manifested toward those who were ignorant and far from God," as well as Brainerd's "exquisite tenderness of conscience and deep abhorrence of sin."[16] Similarly, BMS missionary John Chamberlain declared, "I long to be like [Brainerd]. Surely, if ever I arrive at the heavenly world, I shall be eagerly desirous of seeing him."[17] The widely respected Scottish minister Robert Murray McCheyne (1813–1843), after reading the *Life of Brainerd*, declared that he could not "express what I think when I think of [Brainerd]. To-night, more set upon missionary enterprize than ever."[18]

Perhaps the person who most identified with Brainerd was Englishman Henry Martyn (1781–1812). Martyn was not a missionary in the purest sense of the word but, rather, made his way to India as a chaplain for the East India Company. In Brainerd, Martyn found a model of both personal piety and commitment to missions. Martyn's diary, in many ways, echoes Brainerd's desire for personal purity, noting, for example, that he "thought of David Brainerd, and ardently desired his devotedness to God and holy breathings of soul." Brainerd also inspired Martyn in his goal of mission work. Shortly before his departure for India, he noted that a reading of Brainerd had led him to a time of prayer "for the advancement of Christ's kingdom, and that I might be sent to the poor heathen."[19]

Martyn turned to Brainerd as he struggled with romantic feelings for Lydia Grenfell. In June 1805, about a month before sailing for India and a year after first meeting Grenfell, Martyn confided to his journal, "I clearly perceived that my own inclination upon the whole was not to marriage." For, he went on, when he thought of Brainerd, "how he lived among the Indians, travelling freely from place to place, can I conceive that he would have been so useful had he been married?" Martyn also found practical instruction and personal inspiration in Brainerd's life. While en route to India, he read the book of Acts "to see how the apostles addressed ignorant heathens and afterwards Brainerd's descriptions of the difficulties which attended his mission." Martyn found that Brainerd helped him to be "more divested of these romantic notions, which have sometimes inflated me with false spirits." Martyn, like Brainerd, died young, aged just thirty-one. Before his death, he forwarded all of his papers to his executors in England. Martyn's story was quickly rushed into print, first appearing in 1816, and soon took its place alongside Brainerd's and others as necessary reading for those contemplating a life of mission work.[20]

Another to find practical help in Brainerd's example was the second CMS chaplain to New South Wales, Samuel Marsden. Marsden was a Cambridge-educated evangelical Anglican, a correspondent of the politician William Wilberforce, and was influenced by both Wesleyans and Moravians. In 1793, Marsden and his wife, Elizabeth, set sail, and Marsden received his first experience with a captive audience, the ship's crew and its convict passengers, who refused to respond to his preaching. During the voyage, he noted that he had been "reading of Mr. Brainerd's success among the Indians," and he determined that the "same power can also effect a change upon those hardened ungodly sinners to whom I am about to carry the words of eternal life."[21]

Various versions of the *Life of Brainerd* were regularly republished in the early decades of the nineteenth century. But in 1808, they were joined by a work which took a different approach. That year, John Styles, a popular Methodist minister in Brighton, published *The Life of David Brainerd, Missionary to the Indians*, which went through two British and two American editions. Although Styles took even greater liberties with the original texts than had Wesley, this was not what set it apart. Styles presented a narrative story of Brainerd's life in Styles's words with Brainerd's own words, when used, enclosed in quotation marks. This was the opposite of the method used by Edwards and Wesley, who had kept their interpolations to a minimum and set them apart using brackets. In a sense, then, Styles's version was a rhetorical device which used Brainerd's words to support Styles's arguments.[22]

Styles laid heavy stress on Brainerd the missionary, describing him in the opening paragraph as "the missionary of the cross." Brainerd's introspective passages were pared down while his zeal for missions was played up. Thus, when Brainerd decided to refuse the calls from Millington and Easthampton, Styles declared that this was because he "preferred a 'Wigwam' among brutish savages; an exile from his native land; the loneliness of a dreary solitude: the difficulties and intense labors of an Indian mission." Styles offered his own retrospective of Brainerd's life, which he placed before a reduced portion of Edwards's "Reflections and Observations." "Twenty such men," declared Styles, "laboring for ten years, what would they not accomplish."[23]

But perhaps more important to Styles, Brainerd taught men "the value and honor which we ought to put upon the missionaries of Christ." Since ministers who "labor in civilized places" are esteemed, then missionaries, argued Styles, "have an infinitely higher claim upon our regard." Missionaries needed the prayers and deserved the financial support of other Christians. And, in Styles's eyes, Brainerd was the forerunner of the movement which was beginning to spread throughout the world. "He was," wrote Styles, "the morning-star of a missionary day," and Styles imagined that Brainerd now felt his "heaven enriched while he contemplates the enlargement of Emmanuel's empire."[24] Thus, at the hands of an Englishman, John Styles, and in the minds and hearts of other Englishmen, like Henry Martyn and William Carey, David Brainerd was morphed from being a model of the right way to live a Christian life to being a preeminent example of mission work. And in the first decades of the nineteenth century, the British missionary zeal motivated young Americans, and they, too, discovered the missionary example of David Brainerd.

"Conduct Worthy of the Closest Imitation": American Antebellum Missions

The growing mission spirit in Britain filtered across the Atlantic and inspired two generations of American Protestants to take up its cause. And, just as Brainerd had inspired Carey and others, so he would inspire the new American missionaries. The movement was largely catalyzed at Andover Theological Seminary (ATS), which had been founded by orthodox Protestant ministers in response to liberal Protestant and Unitarian currents in New England. The development of a coordinated American mission effort can be traced to 1808 when Samuel J. Mills, Jr., a new student at ATS, created the Society of Inquiry on the Subject of Missions. Operating in secrecy and carefully screening its members, the society grew slowly but, in 1810, four of its members—Mills, Adoniram Judson, Samuel Nott, and Samuel Newell—petitioned church leaders in Massachusetts to form an organization for promoting mission efforts. The petitioners made it clear that they believed they had been called to missions and were prepared to come under the direction of the London Missionary Society if their local leaders were not willing to assist them. Such transatlantic patronage was not necessary as the petition resulted in the establishment of the American Board of Commissioners for Foreign Missions (ABCFM) in 1810. While the ABCFM was the first American mission agency—and the most active over the next fifty years—it was followed by a plethora of other groups which, among them, sent American Protestants to every inhabited continent except Australia. Mission promoters emphasized the commands of Christ, the inadequacies of other religions, and the reality that all peoples had the same value in the sight of God.[25]

In 1812, three of the original four petitioners from ATS—Newell, Judson, and Nott—along with Gordon Hall and Luther Rice were ordained as the first ABCFM missionaries to Asia. The commissioning sermon was delivered by Leonard Woods, a professor of theology at Andover, who reminded the ordainees and his audience that there was no need to despair over the magnitude of the task, since God was well able to bring about the conversion of the heathen. All that was required was faith in God, a faith that had been demonstrated by, among others, David Brainerd.[26] The sermon was published by Samuel T. Armstrong of Boston. Those who purchased a copy would find, on the first page, an Armstrong promotion for another recently published work: the first American edition of John Styles's *Life of David Brainerd*, which became the most common American version for at least the next ten years. Appropriately, given the role of Brainerd in inspiring the new missionaries, the advertisement noted that Brainerd exhibited "conduct worthy of the closest imitation."[27]

The salient points of Styles's edition were discussed in the previous section, but one other feature was especially important to the leaders of the mission movement. By 1812, these men were increasingly concerned about the growing number of uneducated, rough-and-ready men who insisted on preaching in an enthusiastic manner wherever they chose (shades of the eighteenth-century fear of unordained itinerants). In contrast, promoters of missions emphasized the need for a solid theological education.[28] Here, Brainerd presented a problem since his expulsion from Yale meant that he had preached without the full education that New England leaders now demanded. Fortunately, Styles had mounted a frontal literary assault on Yale regarding the expulsion. While conceding that Brainerd's zeal "sometimes carried him beyond the bounds of prudence," Styles judged that the "circumstances of this expulsion are peculiarly disgraceful to the college." The men who decided to expel Brainerd were, in Styles's view, "deadly in their hate, and so marvellously wise, that they can decide on a man's character from one or two words and actions."[29] Thus, Brainerd did not lack credentials because of his own unwillingness to learn, but because of the harsh judgment of others.

In 1822, a new version of the Brainerd story issued from the pen of Sereno Edwards Dwight, a great-grandson of Jonathan Edwards. Dwight included most of Edwards's *Life*, most of the *Mirabilia*, Brainerd's narrative letter to Pemberton, Pemberton's sermon at Brainerd's ordination, and most of Brainerd's additional writings (such as his letters) which had been included in Edwards's *Life* but removed by Wesley and Styles. Dwight described Styles's edition as a "cheap...volume; made at a time, when the feelings of the British nation had not been roused to a deep interest in Missions and Missionaries." Of course, the feelings of the British nation *had* been roused toward missions, and Styles's version had been produced with an eye toward cost. Dwight explicitly connected his version to the growing mission movement, declaring that the "friends of Missions are now numerous, and are rapidly increasing. With their interest in Missions, is associated, of course, an interest in faithful Missionaries." While the *Life* would be "altogether useful to the private christian," Brainerd's account of the work at Crossweeksung would be "peculiarly useful to the Missionary." For this person, the account would provide an "example of self-denial, of patience under privations and sufferings."[30] Dwight's version gained further popularity when the American Sunday School Union published it in an abridged version, which went through multiple printings.[31]

Many American mission promoters were haunted by the failure of Indian missions. They frequently blamed white Christians for that failure rather than, as had happened in the colonial era, the Indians themselves. As Gordon Hall, part of the first group of Americans to go to Asia, expressed it, Native Americans had been "so fatally corrupted by their intercourse with the whites, and so inveterately prejudiced against the Christian name, that for the present it seems almost in vain to attempt to evangelize them." Six years after this observation, Hall and Samuel Newell included American Christians among those responsible for the failure of Indian missions, declaring, "had but a small portion of the spirit of Elliot [sic], of the Mayhews, and of Brainerd dwelt in the American churches," those churches would have responded better to the "ignorance and wretchedness" of the Indians.[32]

Some attempts were made to reach the Indians, and the promotion of these attempts often invoked a hyperbolic view of Brainerd and other colonial missionaries. "K.C.," writing in the ABCFM's *Panoplist and Missionary Magazine*, asked rhetorically, what should motivate the American church to evangelize the Indians? In answer, he appealed to the "success, which has attended the exertions of former missionaries." He pointed out that, despite lacking "efficient [mission] societies," Brainerd, John Eliot, and the Mayhews were so successful that "thousands are now rejoicing in heaven, and praising God." Indeed, the ABCFM held Brainerd in such high regard that its first domestic mission station, established among the Cherokee Indians in 1817, was named after him. And in an 1824 article in the *Missionary Herald*, the successor publication to the *Panoplist*, the editors excerpted large portions of Brainerd's *Mirabilia Dei Inter Indios* as an example of successful "Methods of Preaching to the Indians."[33]

Despite the initial hopes for a new round of Indian missions, by the 1830s, pessimism had set in, caused by both an absence of results and the removal policies of the U.S. government, in particular the brutalities of the Jackson administration. As the *Missionary Herald* noted in 1834, the Indians had been "almost constantly the objects of the white man's fraud and oppression," and the American church had neglected and abandoned the work among the Indians. This, argued the *Herald*, was why there had been "so little fruit from the labors" of men such as "Elliot [sic], the Mayhews, Brainerd, and other eminently holy" workers.[34]

By this time, American mission efforts increasingly looked to overseas fields, and Brainerd was linked to such efforts. In 1818, preaching at the annual meeting of the ABCFM, Samuel Spring reminded his audience that, since the Reformation, "there has been impressive evidence of the utility of missionary exertions. I refer to the Elliots [sic], the Mayhews, and the Brainerds of our own land, and to [Christian Frederick] Swartz, [John Theodore] Vanderkemp, and [Claudius] Buchanan and others who have made such inroads upon Satan's territory in Asia and Africa."[35] Writing in the Congregationalist Quarterly Christian Spectator, William Swan reminded his readers that the mission fields of the world still lacked workers. He imagined the workers crying out to American Christians and asking, "[D]o none of you pant to tread in the footsteps of Brainerd, and [Henry] Martyn, and [Gordon] Hall?"[36] Ashbel Green told students at Princeton Theological Seminary who were uncertain as to whether they should embrace a missionary call that they "scarcely need to be advised to read the lives of Brainerd, or Martyn" and to "imbibe and cherish their spirit."[37]

Others wanted to draw more pointed lessons from the examples of past missionaries. The Christian Review was concerned that it was natural for people, after their initial enthusiasm for a project, to "relax in their ardor, and presently sink into a state of comparative indifference in neglect." The mission effort was no exception to this, so the Review reminded its readers that the "achievements of such men as Eliot, and Brainerd, and Carey" meant that others were "bound to do the more, when a few have done so much." The Quarterly Christian Spectator ominously warned its readers that Brainerd and John Eliot were "noble hearted missionaries, but they were alone. When they died, none followed up their exertions."[38]

With the Brainerd thread running through the mission tapestry, it is hardly surprising that numbers of young American ministers found personal inspiration in his story. Cyrus Kingsbury, missionary to the Choctaw Indians, argued that the most effective way to end the "moral darkness and cruel superstition" which surrounded the Indians was to set up schools where "children and youth" could receive "correct religious and moral instruction, and where they would be gradually formed to habits of sober industry." In setting up such schools, noted Kingsbury, the "observations of Mr. Brainerd…are worthy of particular notice."[39]

But for most missionaries, Brainerd spoke to them on a more personal level. Levi Parsons, part of the first ABCFM contingent to Palestine, seemed to literally follow in Brainerd's footsteps. Just as Brainerd, while at Yale, had once noted that he walked in the "fields alone at noon, and in prayer found such unspeakable sweetness and delight in God," so Parsons remembered that, while at Middlebury College, "after prayers in the chapel, I took my Bible, and retired to a grove west of the college." Later, as he wrestled with the idea of becoming a missionary, Parsons noted that he was "much refreshed by perusing the life of Brainerd. How completely devoted to God, how ardent his affections!" He believed that many "perishing Indians will remember his earnest desire for their good, with gratitude and love." After deciding to go to Palestine, he recalled that it was the "lives of the most distinguished missionaries, such as Brainerd, Buchanan, and the Moravians, and the fortitude, piety and faithfulness which they uniformly maintained" which had significantly influenced his decision.[40]

Parsons's companion on his journey to Palestine, Pliny Fisk, also found inspiration in Brainerd. Writing to friends at Andover, Fisk closed by rejoicing that ATS "exhibits more and more of the spirit of [Richard] Baxter, and [Philip] Doddridge, and Brainerd, and Martyn." When he and Parsons were tempted to lament their living conditions, they remembered what "Brainerd must have suffered when sick among the Indians." When Parsons died, virtually in Fisk's arms in Palestine in 1822, Fisk remembered that, in their last conversation, the two had speculated on being welcomed into heaven by "some ministering spirit, and for ought we know, by Abraham, or Moses, or Brainerd, or Martyn." Granted, these were the musings of two young men at a time of great stress, but the statement is still extraordinary. When thinking of who might welcome Parsons at the gates of heaven, they bypassed Paul, Peter, and all the other New Testament luminaries and postulated instead David Brainerd.[41]

Parsons was not the only missionary to die on the field, perhaps from pushing himself too hard. And indeed, some promoters seemed to connect Brainerd's example with these fatalities and were critical of Brainerd's overexertion, which they saw as a cause of his early death. William Swan noted that he could not count it "among the virtues of David Brainerd or Henry Martyn, though their memory is as sweet to us as the dew of heaven, that they subjected themselves to trials which so soon exhausted all their strength, and snatched them so prematurely away." Joseph Tracy also sounded a note of caution that Brainerd had been less careful with his life than God required. In issuing this caution, Tracy emphasized that this was of "additional interest, [because of] the failures of health of foreign missionaries." Tracy was also one of the few, if not the only person, to criticize Brainerd over his expulsion from Yale. While Tracy judged Clap's demand for a public apology to be too harsh, he also noted that Brainerd's later destruction of his own diaries demonstrated that he was "guilty of improprieties of which we have no account."[42]

Although not strictly part of the missionary wave which was exposed to Brainerd's example, a testimony to the impact of Brainerd was found in the autobiography of the Indian minister William Apess. Born in 1798, Apess, who claimed Pequot ancestry, was a Methodist who spent at least seven years as a minister and missionary in New England. Apess's autobiography, *A Son of the Forest*, was published in 1829, then republished in a rewritten form in 1831. Apess declared that he was "indebted, in a great measure" to a number of past Christians, including Brainerd, whom he described as "a man of remarkable piety and a missionary with the Crosweek [*sic*] Indians to his death."[43]

Brainerd also became an example to women missionaries during the antebellum years, particularly through the ministry of Mary Lyon at Mount Holyoke College. Founded in 1837 as a female complement to nearby Amherst College, Mount Holyoke was extraordinarily popular and always received more applicants than there were places. Lyon's vision was strongly endorsed by a number of clergy from the neo-Edwardsian New Divinity movement, and she deliberately cultivated an atmosphere of revival and promoted the works of Edwards to her students.[44]

Although women were precluded from serving as missionaries since no Protestant church allowed women to be ordained, Lyon sought other paths whereby her students could serve in the mission field. By training women with missionary zeal as teachers, then encouraging them to marry men who were planning on traveling overseas, Lyon was able to open a conduit for women on the foreign mission field. In this way, David Brainerd became an important model for Lyon and the missionary women who emerged from Mount Holyoke. The ABCFM heavily favored married couples for its overseas postings, believing they were better equipped to face the trials of life in the field. The ABCFM also believed that marriage would reduce the likelihood that male missionaries would succumb to immorality. Mount Holyoke graduates easily fit the type of wife for which the ABCFM was looking: dedicated to missions and trained to teach women and children. Brainerd thus served as an example to the women at Holyoke as much as he served as an example to men at other institutions.[45]

It was the emphasis on women as godly missionary wives which promoted belief in the Brainerd–Jerusha Edwards betrothal. While, as noted earlier, the precise origins of this myth cannot be pinned down, the burst of antebellum missions imprinted it on American evangelicalism. The earliest written statement about the betrothal comes from an inheritor of the New Divinity, Edwards A. Park, a professor of theology at Andover. Park traced his doctrinal lineage from Jonathan Edwards through Samuel Hopkins and Nathanael Emmons. In 1854, Park published *Memoir of the Life and Character of Samuel Hopkins, D.D.* and made the claim that Brainerd and Jerusha Edwards were betrothed, although he did not develop this observation into any lengthy discussion. Since American promoters wanted their missionaries to marry, Jerusha Edwards was elevated from Brainerd's nurse to his fiancée, who herself had a zeal for the mission field: she was reinvented as an eighteenth-century Mount Holyoke woman.[46]

One of the women inspired by Brainerd, although not a Holyoke graduate, was Ann "Nancy" Judson, wife of Adoniram Judson, who had been one of the founders of the Mission Society at Andover. Reading Brainerd's life was one of the things that led Ann Judson to Burma, where she served alongside her husband. Adoniram was imprisoned by Burmese forces during the British-Burma War in the 1820s, and Ann lived with him in prison for six months, caring for him and their sick daughter. Ann was desperately ill when Adoniram was released and, although she lived long enough to write an account of her ordeal, she died in 1826, shortly after completing her story. Following her death, her diaries were published, and she became a model for Holyoke women as well as a posthumous endorser of the growing Brainerd legend.[47]

In one sense, Brainerd's antebellum career added nothing new to his resume. He had previously been the ideal Christian, an example to preachers, and a model missionary. But it was in the nineteenth-century United States that he first combined all three of these activities. And so it was that Brainerd was recruited to inspire and motivate the few—foreign missionaries—and the many: the Protestants who never left America. Also important, by appropriating Brainerd's example, they kept him alive for a new generation of Christians. And after the bloodshed of the Civil War and the trials of Reconstruction, a new wave of American missionaries would set forth, once again accompanied by David Brainerd.

"The Fountain Head of Nineteenth-Century Missions": The Student Mission Movement, 1886–1920

Homer W. Hodge, who would later publish and edit his own version of the life of David Brainerd, recalled a trip to Northampton in the company of pastor/ author E. M. Bounds. Bounds had once declared to Hodge that he would "rather see the grave of David Brainerd at Northampton, Massachusetts, than anything on earth." So, in 1912, the two men traveled to Massachusetts and found what Hodge described as a "sacred plot of ground and the slab that marked his resting place." There, they "wept and prayed and thanked God" and "also partook of the blessed communion while there, and placed an emblem of immortality upon his tomb before departing."[48]

Beginning with Laurel Hill Cemetery in Pennsylvania in the 1830s, many Protestants turned graves, tombs, and cemeteries into locations that, as Colleen McDannell has explained it, had the "ability physically to articulate the Christian promise of eternal life."[49] While this particular expression of admiration was unusual, the two men were not the only evangelicals who made this pilgrimage: Adoniram Judson Gordon wrote wistfully of wandering through the Northampton graveyard in the snow, and when the General Association of Massachusetts met in Northampton, the attendees went as a group to pay their respects to Brainerd's memory.[50] However, men like Hodge and Bounds did not simply celebrate Brainerd's life, they also used it to inspire a new wave of Protestant missions, which exploded from the Western world in the late nineteenth and early twentieth centuries.

The number of U.S. Protestant mission agencies grew in the latter half of the nineteenth century as did the level of commitment to reaching the world for Christ. The goals of these organizations were inexorably intertwined with the view of secular adventurers who believed that the vigorous, egalitarian United States was destined to spread ideas of tolerance and democracy to the world. While Protestant missionary views of this vision ranged from fully embracing it to completely rejecting it, the vast majority of mission advocates accepted it as inevitable and concentrated on ameliorating its more detrimental consequences. Just as secular Americans dreamed of the triumph of American culture, so Protestant Americans dreamed of the triumph of Protestant Christianity. As Congregational theologian Lewis French Stearns declared, there was "no question that Christianity has been from the first certain of its universal conquest. No other religion can vie with it. There is no likelihood that any religion will ever appear to enter into rivalry with it."[51]

The most vigorous proponents of a renewed mission drive came from the ranks of American and European college students. The origins of the student mission movement lie in two connected events which took place in 1886. The first of these was a summer conference for YMCA leaders held at the Northfield, Massachusetts, home of evangelist D. L. Moody (1837–1899). Although Moody's reputation and charismatic personality enabled him to hold the interest of the student leaders, he felt uneasy around intellectuals and asked his friend A. T. Pierson (1837–1911) to come to Northfield to make some addresses to those assembled. Pierson, who had been working on a book regarding the mission issue, readily agreed. Pierson presented his audience with a detailed plan for the evangelization of the world. Later in the conference, the students organized a second meeting at which the sons of missionaries and attendees from other countries spoke of the need of those nations to hear the gospel. Further inspired by this, at the end of the conference, a hundred students pledged to go abroad as missionaries.[52]

The second event which catalyzed this new mission thrust was the publication of Pierson's 1886 *The Crisis of Missions*. Probably the most influential mission-promotion publication of the period, *Crisis of Missions* was a whirlwind global tour demonstrating to its readers how barriers to world evangelization had been removed in recent years. Pierson argued that the non-Christian world was more open than ever before to the gospel message. The crisis, as Pierson saw it, was the refusal or inability of Western and, in particular, American churches to respond to these opportunities. Without immediate enthusiastic action on the part of Christians, there was a danger that many "open" nations would close up again.[53]

While Pierson and others believed that leadership of this new mission thrust should be the responsibility of college-educated people, this presented certain recruitment problems. White, middle-class American college students were part of a culture that emphasized family responsibility, material success, and the idea of individual triumph over difficulties and challenges—a life full of character and achievement. Alongside this was the idea that civilized U.S. society had a responsibility to improve the lot of the rest of humanity. Mission promoters had to interpret the call for evangelization within this cultural milieu and repackage it in a way that appealed to college-educated Americans. Promoters highlighted the hardships and challenges waiting on the foreign mission field and emphasized that only those Christians with deep-rooted character could hope to succeed. Potential recruits who were afraid of falling into obscurity if they served overseas were reminded that eternal glories, including everlasting recognition, awaited faithful servants of God. And finally, bringing the gospel to a people who did not know it would automatically mean an improvement in the life of those people.[54]

Thus, promoters created a paradigm wherein men and women who chose to serve abroad would be people of character, embarking on the highest call known to humanity and changing the lives of thousands both in the here and now and for eternity. As A. T. Pierson put it, "a special seal and sanction" along with a "peculiar consecration of character" were to be found in missionaries. Sherwood Eddy declared that "men of character and leadership were never more needed than at this hour of the world's history." The approach was clearly effective: by 1926, about 48,000 American students had filled out volunteer forms. Of these, about a quarter actually went to the mission field, in roughly equal numbers of men and women. Two-thirds of them were between eighteen and twenty-five.[55]

In December 1888, the YMCA organized the Student Volunteer Movement (SVM) as its mission arm and named John R. Mott (1865–1955) as the SVM's first chair. The new structure facilitated continued growth, and the SVM's first quadrennial convention, held in Cleveland, Ohio, in 1891, drew 558 student delegates, 31 current missionaries, and 32 members of mission boards.[56] With its slogan of "The Evangelization of the World in This Generation," the SVM, working with affiliated organizations around the globe, was the mainstay of U.S. Protestant missions until World War I; the war's aftermath first dampened, then shattered, the movement's optimism.

Mott became the man most able to inspire service in others and the mainstay of the organization. He emphasized that the whole church needed to be involved in the work of missions. Home churches needed to be self-sacrificing, generous, and mission-minded, prayerfully supporting workers in the field. The field workers themselves needed to be of the appropriate spiritual nature. As Mott asserted, "[O]n the spirituality of the missionary more than upon any other one factor on the mission field depends the evangelization of the world." While Mott and other leaders suggested many ways in which pastors could develop the correct attitude in churches and potential recruits, one of those frequently mentioned was reading missionary biographies. Such works, he pointed out, could aid in the "preparation of missionary sermons and addresses" and would "help young men and young women determine their missionary responsibility." Echoing such thinking, Robert Speer declared, "there is power in these life stories. See it in the unmeasured and continuing influence of the life of David Brainerd."[57]

Leaders of the student mission movement had no hesitation in turning to David Brainerd as one of those missionaries who should be read and emulated. Another leader in the movement, Adoniram Judson Gordon (1836–1895), who had wandered through the Northampton cemetery, told a student mission convention in 1894 of his recent visit to the town "in order that I might visit what to me is a most sacred grave." There, he had "sought out an old churchyard and brushed away the snow, and read the simple inscription, 'David Brainerd, Missionary to the American Indians.' As I stood there I said to myself, 'I do not hesitate to declare that I am now standing at the fountain head of nineteenth century missions.'" Potential missionaries had ample opportunity to peruse Brainerd's life. Between 1884 and 1925, two new versions of Edwards's *Life of Brainerd* appeared, as well as a new biography, ten compilations of missionary lives containing the Brainerd story, and frequent references to him in promotional literature, pamphlets, magazines, and published missionary sermons and lectures.[58]

What drew the student leaders to Brainerd? First and foremost, it seems, was his commitment to prayer, which was considered essential in the missionary endeavor. However, whereas Edwards (and Brainerd) saw prayer as primarily a means of communion between the Christian and God, an indication of true

spirituality, mission promoters looked to prayer primarily as a means of bringing about the conversion of the lost. It was a component of mission work, in
addition to being a sign of Christian character, both of which were required for
success. References to Brainerd's prayer life in the literature of the movement,
therefore, were almost always connected to the success of his work.

Gordon noted that the "key to Brainerd's wonderful success" was due to him
"praying whole days for the anointing of the Holy Ghost to come upon him." In
the introduction to his *Memoirs of Rev. David Brainerd*, J. M. Sherwood declared
that the "secret of [Brainerd's] remarkable success" was the "large measure of
the spirit of Prayer which characterized his life." E. M. Bounds characterized
Brainerd's prayer life with the aphorism that Brainerd was "with God mightily
in prayer and God was with him mightily." Don O. Shelton argued that the constant goal of Brainerd's prayers was "the turning of the Indians from the power
of Satan unto God." R. F. Horton, speaking at the 1900 London conference on
world missions, asserted that it was "an absolutely unfailing fact that the great
missionaries have been great athletes in prayer." Brainerd was proof of this as he
had "taken care that he should be with God from first to last."[59]

Other promoters offered more prosaic and challenging pictures of what a
commitment to prayer had meant for Brainerd. Robert E. Speer asked an audience to think of "David Brainerd kneeling down under the trees by the banks of
the Delaware, damp with the perspiration of his prayers, while the chill winter
winds whistled through the forest above him." P. S. Hyde took readers to the
Indian religious ceremony which Brainerd had tried to prevent. Hyde began the
account by quoting Brainerd's description of his all-night prayer session. Hyde
described how, as the feast started, Brainerd entered the circle of dancing Indians
and "commanded them to cease the wild dance. Like tigers cowed by a lamb, they
submitted docilely to the man of God." Thus, concluded Hyde, the "fervent effectual prayer of the righteous man availed much." In case any missed the lesson,
Hyde declared: "fellow toilers in India, we want to make preachers and teachers
here for the church of God! Do we keep in mind that there is a work far more
fundamental than that for us in our efforts to hasten the conquest of India, and
that is to teach men to pray?"[60]

Not surprisingly, Brainerd's self-denial was also an important example
to those who promoted his story, a key component of the Christian character
which was seen as so important to a successful life in missions. Thus, John Mott
believed that Brainerd had so successfully practiced self-denial that "his life [was]
hid with Christ in God." Donald Fraser, speaking at the 1906 SVM convention,
opined, "the supreme lessons of the lives of such men as Brainerd, of Moody, of
Hudson Taylor, and others is just the unmeasured possibilities for evangelization that lie in a single life wholly yielded to God." W. J. Lhamon marveled that
Brainerd "rejoiced in tribulation for Christ's sake, and having put his hand to the
plow, he never looked back, but his double desire was only that God might be
glorified and the neglected red men redeemed."[61]

Other authors chose to demonstrate Brainerd's self-denial by referring to
the physical hardships of his work. In so doing, they simultaneously reminded

readers of the real trials that still existed in the mission field while rebuking them for preferring the comforts of modern American society. Charles Galloway waxed poetic when he described Brainerd roaming "through the forests, destitute of all creature comforts, with not a human being who could speak a word of English, living on the coarsest fare." Archibald McLean (1849–1920), the foreign mission secretary for the Disciples of Christ, declared that Brainerd was "willing to spend his life, even to the latest moment, in dens and caves of the earth, if the kingdom of God might thereby be advanced." The authoritative *Encyclopedia of Missions* also supported this view. "It is hard to realize," the editors wrote, the "brave self-denial involved at that time in this young man's going alone in a dense and track-less forest to live among savages."[62]

In order to remind readers that a life of service to God was not simply the lot of those unable to succeed in U.S. society, some authors emphasized another aspect of Brainerd's self-denial, focusing on his decision to reject the calls from Easthampton and Millington. McLean asserted that these "rich and prosperous churches sought his services, but he declined their tempting offers." Jessie Brown Pounds told the same story, calling them "some of the best churches in New England." Don Shelton declared that, although Brainerd was "urged to become a pastor in New England and on Long Island, he deliberately chose the harder task of ministering to the savages."[63]

In order to reassure ambitious Americans that service in the mission field might bring temporal obscurity but eternal approbation, some authors eschewed such specific examples and instead pointed out the way Brainerd was remembered by posterity. Thus, Shelton also declared that "no American of the century in which he lived, has exerted a more far-reaching influence than he." Brainerd, indeed, "stands as one of the bravest, truest, greatest missionaries by whom the world has been enriched." W. J. Lhamon noted that Brainerd's memoirs had been "read and wept over for a hundred and fifty years by Christians of all lands and creeds and conditions." Perhaps J. M. Sherwood put it best: "As the lives of men are written down in human History and estimated by the world, the life of David Brainerd was singularly uneventful and insignificant—an infinitesimal factor in human existence." But Sherwood was sure that Brainerd's name would "travel down the centuries, hallowed in the memory of the good, and regarded as one of the brightest stars in the constellations of Christian worthies."[64]

Finally, some promoters made every effort to emphasize that the Cross-weeksung revival had also brought improvements for the Indians in the here and now, thus pointing out to their audience that mission work was a legitimate and viable way to improve the world. Adoniram Judson Gordon noted the reduction in alcohol consumption, Charlotte Yonge reminded readers that the Delawares had renounced "their heathen customs and their acquired vice of drunken-ness, and practic[ed] some amount of industry," while P. S. Hyde observed that Brainerd was "never satisfied with any mere emotional manifestations in his converts. Their profession [of faith] was brought to the test of practical life. And it is because of the moral reformations wrought in these wild men that these revivals have their outstanding significance for all times."[65]

Others who wanted to remind their audiences of the material improvements of the Indians to whom Brainerd ministered bordered on the hysterical in their claims. Lhamon insisted that missions improved the societies wherein they operated. When churches are built, "schools spring up; intelligence transplaces ignorance; reason conquers superstition; and notions of popular education win their way. Commerce and civilization follow as inevitably as education in the wake of Christian missions." In keeping with these grand goals, Brainerd's contribution to civilization was truly remarkable. "He solved for us," declared Lhamon, "the perplexing Indian problem, had we as a nation been wise enough to see it. We have yet to learn that the best of missionaries are the greatest of statesmen, and that the keys of the kingdom of peace are in their hands."[66]

J. M. Sherwood made the same outlandish claims. "Brainerd and his co-workers on the same field," declared Sherwood, "really solved for us the Indian problem and we have been almost a century and a half finding it out!" Brainerd, according to Sherwood, had a clearly marked-out policy of "honest dealing, evangelization, education, teaching the industrial arts." Had the United States but followed this pattern, he lamented, the "long dark record of injustice, cruelty, perfidy, treaty-breaking" might not have happened.[67] While the claims of Lhamon and Sherwood and, to a lesser extent, others regarding secular improvements are at best exaggerations and at worst lies, they do underline what these people saw as one of the goals of foreign missions. Rooted in a sense of cultural superiority, these men and women were offering a sort of evangelized imperialism. Change would not come from gunboats, diplomats, and treaties, but from the gospel of Christ preached by highly committed men and women imbued with a deeply spiritual character.

David Brainerd, then, at the turn of the nineteenth century had once more evolved. He was now a rugged young man who, for no reason other than his commitment to God, had turned his back on the material rewards of a colonial pastorate and plunged into a howling wilderness to bring the gospel to heathens. He had seen remarkable success, not because of the sovereignty of God (Edwards) or his dedication to obedient service (Wesley) but because he had been committed to prayer and self-denial. As a result of this, not only were Indians won to the kingdom, but their everyday lives were improved and their society changed. But, if some of the claims made on behalf of Brainerd during the heyday of the Student Volunteer Movement seem outlandish, they are tame compared to some of those advanced in the later decades of the twentieth century.

"The Long Enduring Chain of Influence": Postwar Protestants

In looking at the years following World War II, the posthumous career of David Brainerd becomes more difficult to define. This is not because of any loss of interest in his story, which grew almost exponentially, but because changes in American Protestantism meant that it was no longer possible to identify a single clear thread to which Brainerd's story could be connected. In the postwar years, church attendance and seminary enrollment skyrocketed and an economic boom led to the construction of hundreds of new churches across the country. Religion, broadly defined, received the imprimatur of civil authorities, which was perhaps best exemplified by Dwight Eisenhower's oft-quoted assertion that "our form of government makes no sense unless it is founded in a deeply felt religious faith and I don't care what it is." The generalization inherent within this comment meant that Protestants increasingly shared the spiritual marketplace with other faiths.[68]

Faced with this competition for souls, Protestant churches sought methods to both gain new and keep old adherents. The most successful in achieving this was a new incarnation of evangelicalism. Evangelicals created their own sub-culture fueled by institutions which were committed to the evangelical world view. Evangelical leaders established the National Association of Evangelicals and *Christianity Today*, the flagship periodical of the movement; established or expanded a number of seminaries; and gained increasing access to radio and television outlets. In addition to regular churches, parachurch organizations—groups which operated outside denominational structures—exploded in popularity. As early as 1945, a Youth for Christ rally in Chicago was attended by 70,000 people. Not apparent in the immediate postwar period, this evangelical subculture would be the vehicle through which its participants would reengage the wider culture in subsequent years.[69]

The Protestant mission burden after the war was also largely assumed by evangelicals. Mainline churches, afflicted by self-doubt over the appropriateness of missions and cognizant of the imperialist and racist overtones of a great deal of previous mission efforts, moved away from the idea of converting non-Christians. Evangelicals, on the other hand, believed that their emphasis on converting individuals rather than redeeming cultures would help them to avoid the imperialist cant of earlier missionaries. This renewed emphasis on individual conversion brought two important changes to U.S. Protestantism. First, since every Christian had been converted, then every Christian could tell someone else how to become a Christian. No longer was there a need for ordained ministers, professors of theology, or even college-educated people to be recruited to the mission field. Instead, any Christian, with some brief training, could become an evangelist (shades of those lay ministers of the Great Awakening). To facilitate this, mission-oriented parachurch groups sprang up to carry the gospel to the world.

Second, since conversion was individual rather than cultural, there was a mission field right outside one's front door. If you couldn't go to India, you could certainly make it to the local shopping center to share the gospel with others. These two assumptions meant an explosion in the number of people involved in ministry. Although it is difficult to be definitive, some estimates suggest that the number of Americans serving as long-term (or career) missionaries may have been as high as 35,000 in 1980. In addition to this were the tens of thousands of predominantly young people who embarked upon short-term commitments which lasted anywhere from several weeks to several years. For example, Youth with a Mission, one of the largest of the parachurch mission groups, claimed 1,000 participants in its three-week mission at the 1972 Munich Olympics.[70]

In this new world of American Protestantism, David Brainerd came to occupy a wide variety of roles, although his roles as an example of the proper Christian life and of a model missionary continued to be important. Brainerd was first reintroduced to postwar Americans in 1949 with the publication of Philip E. Howard's edited *The Life and Diary of David Brainerd*.[71] Howard integrated both Edwards's *Life* and Brainerd's journal, greatly reduced the length of the volume (he was especially merciless on Edwards's editorial comments), included a brief sketch of the life of Edwards, but refrained from adding his own editorial comments. As Howard noted, his goal was to make "available again a fairly complete record of the self-denying life and strenuous labors of David Brainerd as he preached the gospel to the American Indians."[72] Judging by the publication history, he was successful in this goal, as the work went through a number of printings, as well as several condensed versions. In 1989, rights to the volume were acquired by Baker Books, which issued its seventeenth printing of the volume in October 2007.[73]

One can assume, then, that many thousands of Christians drew inspiration from Brainerd's story. Of these, one story is especially poignant. Jim Elliot was a twenty-one-year-old college student who had read numerous missionary biographies when he was introduced to Brainerd sometime around the middle of 1949.[74] For Elliot, Brainerd was both a challenge to holy living and an inspiration to missions. In August 1949, Elliot recorded that he had had a "spiritual stir over reading David Brainerd's diary. If I were honest, my writing would be more in anguish as his is. But how cold I have grown, and how careless about it all." Several months later, he wrote that he desired that he might "receive the apostle's passion, caught from vision of Thyself, Lord Jesus. David Brainerd's diary stirs me on to such in prayer."[75]

Elliot's tribute to Brainerd becomes more compelling, given his own life story. Elliot's last mention of Brainerd in his diaries was dated October 27, 1949. At that time, Elliot noted that in reading of the final months of Brainerd's life, he was "much encouraged to think of a life of godliness in the light of an early death."[76] Less than seven years later, Elliot and four other men were dead, killed by Huaroni Indians in eastern Ecuador. Elliot was only twenty-eight when he died, a year younger than Brainerd was when he passed away in Jonathan Edwards's parsonage. The deaths of Elliot and his coworkers were reported on radio stations and in major newspapers such as the *New York Times* and the *Chicago Tribune*. Their work was described in feature articles in both *Time* and *Life*. As had happened with Henry Martyn and Ann Judson, Jim Elliot's life itself became an inspiration to others. When Elliot's widow, Elisabeth, published *Through Gates of Splendor*, the story of her late husband's life, it became an instant bestseller. In her preface to the 1978 edited version of Jim Elliot's *Journal*, she noted that she had "never counted the pile of letters I have received from the readers of Jim's biography, *Shadow of the Almighty*, many of whom said it had been the greatest influence in their lives of any book except the bible [*sic*]."[77]

While Elliot was inspired both personally and as a missionary by Brainerd, beginning in the 1950s, Protestant writers co-opted Brainerd to demonstrate that evangelicalism was relevant to modern society and could address the hot issues confronting the church. In 1954, the year of the *Brown v. Board of Education* decision, William Thomson Hanzsche, a Presbyterian minister in New Jersey, enrolled Brainerd posthumously in the civil rights movement. Much of Hanzsche's account was conventional enough, noting that Brainerd was a man completely devoted to God and an example for Christians in the 1950s. However, Hanzsche was also willing to embroider Brainerd's story: Jerusha Edwards, like Brainerd, "wanted to be a missionary to the Indians"; the settlement at Cranbury apparently included an industrial school, a carpenter shop, and an infirmary complete with a nurse; while ill in Boston, Brainerd was carried into the pulpit of the Old South Church and proceeded to "preach to a breathless crowd."[78]

While such additions may be amusing, and are essentially harmless, the underlying theme truly distorted the Brainerd story. In Hanzsche's world, not only did Brainerd address racism, he actually "solved the problem which distresses the modern world—the problem of race and class prejudice—the problem of the relationship of the white race towards those whose skin is of another color." Amazingly, Hanzsche claimed that no one, even in Hanzsche's day, had done more in so short a time to "turn the Christian people from race prejudice than did David Brainerd." Brainerd's work had "made the Christian colonist see the Indian in a new light." But it was attitudes toward not just the Indians that were affected: Brainerd's work, Hanzsche insisted, "precipitated a new understanding of the Negro. Totally uncivilized savages from the heart of Africa were brought over as field slaves; but a new sympathy to other races began to be practiced by the Churches. Agitations against slavery arose." He concluded his essay with the absurd declaration that, from the time of Brainerd through the rest of the eighteenth century, "there never was any race distinction in Church membership in the American colonial church."[79] Bizarre as Hanzsche's claims were, they were an effort to connect evangelicalism to one of the pressing concerns of his own day.

More than ten years later, Clyde S. Kilby, a long-time professor at Wheaton College, one of the epicenters of evangelicalism, made his own efforts to connect Brainerd to contemporary concerns. Writing on Brainerd as part of an edited collection, *Heroic Colonial Christians*, and using the Yale manuscripts, Kilby portrayed Brainerd as a campus radical. In the twenty-nine pages of biography, Kilby used the word "young" on eight occasions and made three other references to Brainerd's age. Even more pointed was the way in which Kilby described Brainerd's life. Kilby argued that Brainerd was caught between the past, represented by men like Thomas Clap, and "the wave of the future," represented by men like George Whitefield. In Kilby's narrative, Brainerd was restored to the role that had been elided by Edwards: the undisciplined zealot, someone so fired up by the rightness of his cause that he occasionally acted inappropriately. But, Kilby noted, this behavior was fueled by Brainerd's "deep and impelling motive to serve God with all his strength." Brainerd thus became a youthful

"ringleader" of the campus radicals, a man opposed to the "conservative faction" then running the campus.[80] However, while Brainerd never wavered in his
commitment to his beliefs, he later acknowledged that his methods were not
always appropriate. Kilby thus acknowledged the legitimacy of the grievances of
the campus protestors of his own day while implying that their methods were
unacceptable.

Lest anyone miss Kilby's point, he reinforced it in the analytical section of
his essay. Kilby lamented the fact that Brainerd seemed indifferent to the finer
things in life, as he "denied himself, unscripturally...many of the legitimate joys
of life." However, he was also bemused that Brainerd could live in a time "seeth-
ing with political and national upheavals" but have nothing to say about such
events. Kilby also criticized Brainerd for not attempting to understand more
fully the culture of the Delawares. Had he taken the time to "understand and
capitalize on the favorable aspects of the Indian's culture, rather than to assume
the Indian simply and hopelessly savage," he might have been "a more effectual
missionary."[81] Here, Kilby seemed to be sympathizing with the campus radicals
of the day, hinting that the church, unlike Brainerd, must have something to say
about the "political and national upheavals." There could also be an allusion to
Vietnam, possibly suggesting that Christians should not assume the Vietnamese
to be "simply and hopelessly savage." While such specifics may not have been
Kilby's aim he, too, was trying to make Brainerd relevant to the people of his time
by pointing out both his failures and successes.

A more specific attempt to make Brainerd approachable to youth movements was Richard A. Hasler's 1975 *Journey with David Brainerd*, published by
one of the foremost campus evangelical groups: InterVarsity.[82] Hasler directed
his work to people who had been caught up in the Protestant revival of the early
1970s known as the Jesus Movement, which several observers had likened to
the Great Awakening. Growing out of a series of street rallies and meetings in
southern California, the Jesus Movement tended to focus on hippies and other
counterculture groups. Like the awakenings of the eighteenth century, the Jesus
Movement had its share of detractors, and there were undoubtedly unorthodox positions taken by a number of its leaders. Hasler believed that the life of
Brainerd could provide guidance for people "searching passionately for a direct,
immediate and personal experience of God" and argued that Brainerd had four
lessons for his readers. Brainerd, wrote Hasler, was "an extraordinary example
of absolute devotion to God"; he distinguished "between superficial piety and
authentic Christian experience"; he inspired readers to "engage in missionary
service"; and he modeled a "compassionate empathy for the forgotten and dis-
possessed peoples of the world." Hasler's work was not a biography but rather a
collection of forty short chapters designed to be used as a devotional guide. As
Hasler noted, the book was to be read "creatively, in the same devotional spirit in
which [it was] first written."[83]

The forty chapters themselves were not complicated. Usually no more than
a page or two, they comprised a number of selections from Brainerd's writings which spoke to the theme of the chapter followed by a suggested prayer

composed by Hasler. In the prayers, Hasler's determination to connect the eighteenth century to the twentieth was demonstrated. In chapter 3, entitled "Piety and Knowledge," Hasler included several passages from Brainerd where the missionary had struggled to balance college life with piety. Hasler's prayer was aimed at the college students caught up in the Jesus Movement. "How do I balance," it read, "the warm piety of my new life with the rational inquiry of my intellectual senses?"[84] In chapter 14, Hasler focused on the divisions that the Jesus Movement had caused when converts had criticized older church members who refused to adopt their new ways of worship. "May I pray for coworkers whose styles are different from my own," wrote Hasler. "[M]ay I pray for those who personally attack me. Draw me close in fellowship to all who claim allegiance to Christ." In chapter 38, "Distinguishing True and False Religion," Hasler spoke to the concerns some observers had expressed regarding the authenticity of the Jesus Movement. The prayer for this chapter asked God for wisdom in the midst of "pseudo-religious enthusiasm," to enable one to "distinguish between the real and the counterfeit." Furthermore, the reader was asked to pray in order to "not absolutize my own spiritual adventure nor ostracize all who do not fit into the same pattern."[85]

Hasler also spoke directly to the concerns of the seventies generation in chapters which addressed social justice. In "Intercession: Empathy for the Indians," Hasler's prayer addressed the issue of race relations. His prayer asked that God help people to "identify with the red, black, brown and yellow peoples of the world and see things as they see them." He returned to this in chapter 23, where his prayer asked that the "church will increasingly represent the rich diversity of red, black, brown, yellow and white people in the world." In "A Social Conscience," Hasler included a selection from Brainerd's writings which featured the missionary's criticism of the abusive actions of whites. Hasler's prayer left no doubt as to his perspective. "God of justice," it began, "what really happened at the massacre at Wounded Knee in 1890? What really happened at the confrontation in Wounded Knee in 1973?" He continued:

> [T]he more I reflect upon our national treatment of the Indians—
> broken treaties, personal indignities and the plunder of their lands—
> the more I realize that apathy like my own has contributed to such
> shame. Raise up in our generation, O God, advocates who will plead
> the cause of the Indians and of all dispossessed peoples of the world.

Hasler encouraged his readers to pray that their faith would have muscle as the prayer went on to ask, "does my personal faith impel me to move out in benevolent social action on behalf of those who suffer from demeaning poverty, racial discrimination, the arrogance of political power and the ravages of war?"[86]

When we look at writers like Hanzsche, Kilby, and Hasler, there is a temptation to simply dismiss the obvious anachronisms and strained connections between Brainerd and their own day. However, their work also points to something less obvious. Modern American evangelicalism has, often fairly, been perceived to be

Town welcome sign, present-day Cranbury, New Jersey.

isolationist, determined to separate itself from the wider community. What this narrow selection of authors demonstrates, however, is another, albeit smaller, trend: the desire to continually reinvent evangelical Protestantism in order to increase its appeal to the wider community. Co-opted into these efforts, David Brainerd has come a long way from the orderly, homogeneous world of colonial New England into which he was born.

Conclusion

David Brainerd, like most people, was a complex individual who can only be understood within his own formative cultural and historical context. Without this context, Brainerd arrives on the mission field as little more than a religious desperado grasping at a final straw after having his original goals torn away by a too-powerful establishment. In contrast to this cameo role, Brainerd in reality had fairly extensive control over his route to the Indians of New Jersey. He may not have planned on it when he entered Yale in 1739, but he certainly made a very conscious decision to pursue such work in 1743 and again in 1744. In so doing, he created another way to circumvent the ecclesiastical and civil authorities who were, in his mind, opposing the work of God. This, in turn, led him to a very individualistic expression of his commitment to his faith. While he may not have had the complete autonomy of an itinerant preacher, in pastoring a church of Indians, he came very close.

With an understanding of Brainerd's cultural context, it is also possible to reevaluate his work among the Indians. Granted, on the question of race and culture, despite Brainerd's efforts to understand the Indians, it never occurred to him that they could truly become Christian disciples without abandoning their traditional way of life and adopting the European mode. Christianity was a religion of civilization, and civilization required ordered fields, schoolhouses, and workshops, not hunting expeditions and random conversations about truth and God.

But, to simply dismiss Brainerd as another failed, culturally insensitive colonial missionary is to gloss over a multitude of comments and incidents that enable us to build a more multidimensional understanding of his work. While it is true that Brainerd continued to hold to the standard model of preaching to a passive audience, he did not begin his work in either Pennsylvania or New Jersey by simply preaching and hoping for an audience. Rather, just as he had done in New Haven, he went to where the people were, often meeting with individuals or families, before beginning to preach to a larger group. His efforts to move "his" Indians into a settled, colonial-style town did not commence until after he had seen conversions and, as such, can be seen as an effort to facilitate instruction for the purpose of their growth, rather than being rooted solely in a belief that Native Americans needed to be civilized before they could be converted.

Furthermore, Brainerd demonstrated no qualms about accepting that God could work among a non-European people. When the spirit fell on Indian meetings and brought conviction of sin, Brainerd saw this as irrefutable proof that the work was of God, just as he and other revivalists had judged events in New England. Again, without arguing that Brainerd had lost all of his cultural blinders, his experiences during the revivals enabled him, at times, to separate people less on the basis of race and more on how they responded to God. Just as some of his fellow students were his brethren in the Lord because God was working in them and through them, so the Indians who responded to God became his people.

The other side of this coin was his willingness, on occasion, to challenge authorities based on their attitude toward the work of God. In New England, he had refused Clap's demands for an apology and disobeyed legal directives in order to lead separatist meetings at New Haven, because those authorities were opposing what God was doing. So, in New Jersey, he confronted both rum merchants and land usurpers because their actions were in opposition to the work of God among the Indians.

However, Brainerd's responses were also limited by his upbringing as part of the Connecticut establishment. Thus, although he was willing to confront others when it was necessary to do the work of God, he was far less willing to bring permanent division to the church or to raise a standard of open rebellion. While he challenged anti-revivalists and rum sellers, he did not publicly stand up for the New Haven separatists nor join in the New Jersey riots. He adopted a more moderate opposition to authority in large part because of his desire to create a unique space for himself. Brainerd, as a product of a Connecticut society which emphasized community values and of the revivals which promoted individual conversion, constructed for himself a distinctly personal space which was also connected to the society which surrounded him.

David Brainerd emerges from this book as one who was willing to abandon much, but not all, of his cultural baggage. While it is easy to see in him the continuation of colonial ethnocentrism, one can also see just how transformative the Great Awakening was for some individuals. It challenged not only the religious aspects of their lives but also their preconceptions regarding structure, culture, and authority. We would also do well to keep in mind that Brainerd was among the Indians for a little more than three and a half years before his illness forced him off the field. We are left to consider how much more he might have changed had he lived another twenty years or more. Grasping the nuances of David Brainerd's life in turn suggests that historians have more avenues to explore in order to understand completely the ramifications of the religious and social upheavals that began in the 1740s.

Examination of Brainerd's biographers, hagiographers, and others also tells us much about American religious culture. Brainerd inspired and continues to inspire, not because of all that he gained in his life but because of all he gave up. In contrast to many of those around him, Brainerd often sought not to be accepted by political and ecclesiastical powers and the promise of material gain but to oppose them. Whether the establishment at Yale, the divided church at Easthampton, or the proprietary power in New Jersey, he consistently made decisions that placed him at odds with many of those at the center of power. Given this, it is curious to see that many of those who reinterpreted Brainerd did so in a way that was designed to restore him to the mainstream. Jonathan Edwards removed his enthusiasm, John Wesley removed his Calvinism, the student mission movement removed his physical weakness. Others added to his legacy: he became, among other things, a crusader for civil rights and a student spokesperson. Certainly, we can see in this the American tendency to use exemplary lives to promote specific agendas, often by presenting a combination of truth and myth.

While we should recognize the myths and their purposes, we should also recall the strands of truth running through myth and why the two were blended. One of the classic legends of American history is George Washington and his cherry tree. The famous (or infamous) "I cannot tell a lie" never took place, but the myth itself emphasizes an essential truth regarding Washington's integrity and honesty. In the same way, accounts of David Brainerd that are more folklore than reality contain threads of truth beneath the surface. While many legends about Brainerd are corruptions or inventions of a later time, simply dismissing them misses the point. An account of Brainerd from the 1940s illustrates this well. Mrs. Walter Person, writing for the Women's Missionary Federation of the Evangelical Lutheran Church, assured her readers that Brainerd's "prayers were heard and answered." One example she cited occurred during a journey to a "particularly savage tribe of Indians." Two Indian scouts, who had secretly followed Brainerd for hours, returned to their village when he made camp for the night. They then made their way back to Brainerd's campsite with others from their tribe to kill Brainerd (Person offered no explanation as to why two armed Indians would need reinforcements). When they reached it, they found him in prayer. Before they could attack, "a rattlesnake slipped up to [Brainerd], lifted its head, flicked its poisonous tongue near his face, and then for no apparent reason slithered away into the darkness." Needless to say, the Indians stole away and welcomed Brainerd when he came to preach to them.[1]

If we simply dismiss Person's account (and its original, uncited source) as naiveté or foolishness, we miss the important lesson that it conveyed. Whether or not Person and her audience believed the story, no evangelical familiar with the Bible who heard or read it would miss its parallel to an account in the book of Acts. There, the author, probably Luke, described the apostle Paul's shipwreck on the island of Malta. While gathering wood to make a fire, Paul was bitten by a viper. The local residents assumed that this was the judgment of the gods on a murderer. But Paul shook the snake off and continued about his business with no ill effects, convincing the locals he was a god. Brainerd's encounter with the rattlesnake, thus, represents his own holiness and dedication to God.[2] In a similar fashion, authors who, in the words of historian Joseph A. Conforti, created a "frontier saint who subsisted on bear meat and Indian corn meal" were inviting parallels with biblical figures such as John the Baptist and Elijah.[3]

Looking through this prism, we can see powerful truths represented in some of the accounts of Brainerd described in previous chapters. Within the context of his times, Brainerd did consistently stand up for people who existed outside the centers of power, he did leave many of the comforts of colonial society in order to take the gospel to a despised people, and he was a dedicated servant of God as Edwards portrayed him as well as being the steady, irreproachable preacher of Wesley's account. And, while the contentions of authors such as Hanzsche and Shelton are overblown, Brainerd did challenge some of the racial preconceptions of his day and was a key figure in a student rebellion against the authority of his college masters. As such, Brainerd's legacy, while often demonstrating the excesses of American mythology, should also remind us of the truth that lies at the heart of many of those myths.

There seems little doubt that the popularity of David Brainerd among Protestants will continue as will the telling and retelling of his life, with most accounts probably leaning heavily on Edwards's interpretation. Ranelda Hunsicker's *David Brainerd*, published in 1999 as part of Bethany House Publishing's Men of Faith series, is a good example.[4] Brainerd, clean-cut, handsome, and healthy, gazes directly at the reader from the cover of the book. There are, however, no extant portraits of Brainerd, and it is unlikely that his tuberculosis-wracked body would have looked as good as this idealized portrait. Excluding this publisher's sop to modern marketing, Hunsicker's biography is an accurate, albeit brief work. She refrained from including any of the more esoteric stories and argued that there was no definitive proof of a Brainerd–Jerusha Edwards romantic entanglement. Returning to the Edwardsian approach, Hunsicker's work was designed to be an inspiration to a new generation of Christians. She listed Wesley, Carey, Martyn, and Elliot among those inspired by Brainerd. She also declared that Brainerd's life was "gilded by God's grace, reminding readers that He delights to make himself known in the midst of human weakness."[5] Hunsicker did not indulge in blatant presentist attempts to make Brainerd relevant to the political issues of the day. In many ways, her account reflects that of Jonathan Edwards: the man of God who retains an even disposition; pursues not secular recognition but selfless devotion to God; and has an unwillingness to challenge religious authorities.

However, while Edwards may have furnished us with the picture of Brainerd that dominates our understanding of him today, beyond the Edwards construct other facets of Brainerd's true character and nature emerge. More multifaceted than either his detractors or admirers imagine(d), he was ethnocentric, culturally aware, orthodox, mystical, accommodating, confrontational, inspirational, and forgettable, a complex character to go along with the complex times in which he lived. As such, he speaks to human nature not only in eighteenth-century America, but also in our own day.

Appendix I

Brainerd Manuscript Diaries

As noted in the text, Brainerd was required to keep public journals and to periodically send them to the SSPCK. Only three copies of these are known to have survived. Although there are a large number of differences between these copies and what was published as *Mirabilia Dei Inter Indios* and *Divine Grace,* none of these differences are substantial. For that reason, I have not referred to them in the text. They are listed here for informational purposes.

The Connecticut Historical Society in Hartford holds a manuscript copy of Brainerd's public journal for the period June 19, 1745, to June 19, 1746. Norman Pettit has noted that only a small portion of the work is in Brainerd's hand and has identified this manuscript as being sent to Eleazar Wheelock, but the date of Brainerd's letter to Wheelock (December 1745) seems to mitigate against this (see Pettit, "Editor's Introduction," *JEY* 7).

A second copy is held in the Special Collections of the Edinburgh University Library (Dc.7.68). Again, Pettit has noted that the writing is not Brainerd's. The entries run from November 24, 1745, to May 10, 1746. Although the provenance of this copy is not clear, it is most likely one of those sent to the SSPCK.

The third copy is held in the library of the American Philosophical Society in Philadelphia (B B74j). The writing does not appear to be Brainerd's, and the provenance of the document is unknown. The entries run from July 14, 1745, to November 20, 1745, making it equivalent to the first half of the public journal. It is possible that this copy was intended to be sent to Boston or New York for publication.

Appendix II

Life of Brainerd *and* Mirabilia *Publications*

As noted in the text, Brainerd's public journal, Edwards's *Life,* and Wesley's *Extract* have all been regularly republished. This list, which is not exhaustive, is an attempt to provide a sense of just how widespread such republishing has been. In most cases, only the city of publication has been noted. The two exceptions to this are editions published by the American Tract Society and Baker Books since these were so ubiquitous. Information has been obtained from Norman Pettit, "Editor's Introduction," *JEY* 7; Thomas H. Johnson, *The Printed Writings of Jonathan Edwards* (Princeton, N.J.: Princeton University Press, 1940); and WorldCat.

1746 Brainerd, *Mirabilia* and *Divine Grace Displayed,* Philadelphia.

1749 Edwards, *Life of Brainerd.* Boston.
Doddridge, *Abridgement of Mr. David Brainerd's Journal.* Edinburgh.

1756 *Historiesch verhaal…Brainerd* (*Life*). Utrecht, Netherlands. Dutch.

1765 *Life* with *Mirabilia* and Pemberton sermon. Edinburgh.

Mirabilia. Edinburgh.

1768 Wesley, *Extract of Life.* Bristol.

1771 Wesley, *Extract of Life.* Bristol.

1793 *Life of Brainerd.* Worcester, Mass.
Life. London.

1798 *Life of Brainerd. With Journal of Charles Beatty.* London.
Life, with Beatty's Journal, Pemberton's Sermon. Edinburgh.
Wesley, *Extract of the Life.* London and Bristol.

Brainerd, *Mirabilia*.
Edinburgh.
Brainerd, *Divine Grace*.
Edinburgh.

1800 Wesley, *Extract*. London.
1808 Styles, *Life*. London.
1811 *Life*. Newark, N.J.:.
Divine Grace. Newark, N.J.:.
1812 Styles, *Life of Brainerd*.
Boston.
Wesley, *Extract*. Dublin.
1815 Wesley, *Extract*. Penryn.
1818 *Life*. London.
1820 *Life*. New York: American
Tract Society.
Styles, *Life of Brainerd*.
London.
1821 *Life*. Boston.
Styles, *Life of Brainerd*.
London.
Styles, *Life of Brainerd*.
Boston.
1822 Dwight, *Memoirs*. New Haven,
Conn.
1824 *Life*. Edinburgh.
1825 Wesley, *Extract*. London.
1826 *Life and Journal*. Edinburgh:
H. S. Baynes.
Life and Labours of Brainerd.
Edinburgh.
1829 *Life* (James Montgomery).
Glasgow.
1830 Dwight, *Memoirs*.
New York.
Life. New York: American
Tract Society.
1833 *Life*. New York: American
Tract Society.
1834 *Life* (Josiah Pratt). London.
1835 *Life*. London: Religious Tract
Society.
1837 William Peabody, *Life* with
Life of Edwards. Boston.
William Peabody, *Life* with
Life of Edwards. London.

1838 *Quelques Réflexions…*
Missionnaire Brainerd.
Lausanne.
1840 William Peabody, *Life* with
Life of Edwards. Boston.
Life of Brainerd. New York:
American Tract Society.
1843 *The Missionary in the*
Wilderness. Philadelphia.
1845 *Life* (Josiah Pratt). London.
1847 William Peabody, *Life*.
New York.
1851 *Das Leben des*
Indianermissionars David
Brainerd. Zürich.
Life (Horatius Bonar).
Edinburgh.
Life. Edinburgh.
1852 William Peabody, *Life* with
Life of Edwards. Boston.
1854 William Peabody, *Life*
of Brainerd, with Life of
Edwards. New York.
1856 *Life* (William Peabody).
New York.
Life (Josiah Pratt). London.
1858 *Life*. London.
1860 *Das Leben von David Brainerd*
(*Life*). New York: American
Tract Society. German.
1862 *Indian-missionären David*
Brainerds lefwerne (*Life*).
Stockholm. Swedish.
1884 Dwight, *Memoirs*. New York.
Life (including Dwight,
Memoirs. J. M. Sherwood).
New York.
1885 Dwight, *Memoirs*
(J. M. Sherwood).
New York.
1891 *Life* (including Dwight,
Memoirs. J. M. Sherwood).
New York.
1900 *Life*, with *Journal*. New York:
American Tract Society.

1902   *Diary of Brainerd*. London.
1920   *Hero of the Forest*.
1925   *Life* (Homer Hodge).
       New York.
1941   Smith, *David Brainerd:*
       The Man of Prayer.
1949   Smith, *David Brainerd:*
       His Message for Today.
       Life & Diary of David
       Brainerd. Chicago.
1950   *Life and Diary*. Newark, Del.
       Day, *Flagellant on Horseback*.
1953   Pearce, *David Brainerd*.
1955   *Life and Diary*. Chicago.
1958   *Vida y diario de David*
       Brainerd. Buenos Aires.
1961   Wynbeek, *Beloved Yankee*.
1970   Dwight, *Memoirs of Brainerd*.
       St. Clair Shores, Mich.
1971   *Life* and *Diary*. Grand Rapids,
       Mich.
1972   *David Brainerd's Personal*
       Testimony.
1975   Hasler, *Journey with David*
       Brainerd.
1978   *Life and Diary of Brainerd*.
       Grand Rapids, Mich.: Baker.
       Life. Grand Rapids, Mich.:
       Baker (reprint of Moody?).

       Med livet…Brainerd (based
       on *Life?*). Oslo. Norwegian/
       juvenile.
1980   *Life and Diary of Brainerd*.
       Chicago: Moody.
1981   *Life and Diary of Brainerd*.
       Grand Rapids, Mich.: Baker.
1984   *Teibidu Pureinodu ui ilgi*
       (*Life*). Seoul: South Korea.
1985   *Life* (Norman Pettit).
       New Haven, Conn.
1988   *Life and Diary*. Grand Rapids,
       Mich.: Baker.
1989   *Life and Diary of Brainerd*.
       Grand Rapids, Mich.: Baker.
1996   Thornbury, *David Brainerd:*
       Pioneer Missionary.
1997   Stubbs, *Burning and Shining*
       Light.
1999   Hunsicker, *David Brainerd*.
       Minneapolis.
       Historiesch verhaal…Brainerd
       (*Life*). Rumpt. Dutch.
2005   *Dawei Bulaina zhuan* (*Life*).
       Xianggang, China.
2006   *Life and Diary of Brainerd*.
       Peabody, Mass.
2007   *Life and Diary*. New York.
       Life and Diary. (New York?).

Abbreviations

Annals: William B. Sprague, *Annals of the American Pulpit,* 9 vols. New York: Robert Carter, 1857–1869.

Dexter, *Biographical Sketches:* Franklin Bowditch Dexter, *Biographical Sketches of the Graduates of Yale College, with Annals of the College History,* 6 vols. New York: Holt, 1885–1912.

Edwards, *Life of Brainerd:* Jonathan Edwards, *An Account of the Life of the Reverend Mr. David Brainerd.* Boston: D. Henchman, 1749.

Haddam Town Records: manuscript records of the town of Haddam. Held in the town clerk's office, Haddam, Connecticut.

JAH: Journal of American History.

JEY: The Works of Jonathan Edwards, 26 vols., edited by Perry Miller, John E. Smith, and Harry S. Stout. New Haven, Conn.: Yale University Press, 1957–2008.

MAB–IND. REC. MIC: Records of the Moravian mission among the Indians of North America, a microfilm, publication of Research Publications of New Haven, Connecticut; photographed from original materials at the Archives of the Moravian Church, Bethlehem, Pennsylvania.

NEQ: New England Quarterly.

New Jersey Archives: New Jersey Colonial Documents, 33 vols. Trenton: New Jersey Historical Society, 1880–1928.

PaCR: Samuel Hazard, ed., *Pennsylvania Colonial Records,* 16 vols. Harrisburg, 1838–1853.

PRCC: J. H. Trumbull and C. J. Hoadly, eds., *The Public Records of the Colony of Connecticut,* 15 vols.

Hartford, Conn.: Case, Lockwood, & Brainard, 1850–1890.

SSPCK Records: Records of the Society in Scotland for Propagating Christian Knowledge. RG GD95, National Archives of Scotland, Edinburgh. Specific volumes of the SSPCK records are abbreviated thus: GMM: General Meeting Minutes RG GD95/1/x; DMM: Directors Meeting Minutes (aka Committee Minutes) RG GD95/2/x.

WJWO/A: Oxford/Abingdon edition of *The Works of John Wesley,* 36 vols. to date, edited by Frank Baker. Nashville, Tenn.: Abingdon Press and New York: Oxford University Press, 1975–.

WMQ: William and Mary Quarterly, 3rd ser.

Notes

Introduction

1. The number of works which reference portions of Brainerd's life truly are legion. A representative sample: Jane T. Merritt, *At the Crossroads: Indians & Empires on a Mid-Atlantic Frontier, 1700–1763* (Chapel Hill: University of North Carolina Press for the Omohundro Institute of Early American History and Culture, 2003), 94, 95, 124; James Merrell, *Into the American Woods: Negotiators on the Pennsylvania Frontier* (New York: Norton, 1999), 83–90; Colin G. Calloway, *New Worlds for All: Indians, Europeans, and the Remaking of Early America* (Baltimore, Md.: Johns Hopkins University Press, 1997), 89; Timothy D. Hall, *Contested Boundaries: Itinerancy and the Reshaping of the Colonial American Religious World* (Durham, N.C.: Duke University Press, 1994), 80; Richard L. Bushman, *From Puritan to Yankee: Character and the Social Order in Connecticut, 1690–1765* (Cambridge, Mass.: Harvard University Press, 1967), 195–198, 242; Sandra M. Gustafson, *Eloquence Is Power: Oratory and Performance in Early America* (Chapel Hill: University of North Carolina Press for the Omohundro Institute of Early American History and Culture, 2000), 78–90.

2. The three principal sources are Brainerd's introduction to his conversion narrative, Gen. Mss. 214, Beinecke Library, Yale University; Brainerd, *Mirabilia Dei Inter Indios; or, The Rise and Progress of a Remarkable Work of Grace among a Number of the Indians in the Provinces of New-Jersey and Pennsylvania* (Philadelphia: William Bradford, 1746); Jonathan Edwards, *An Account of the Life of the Reverend Mr. David Brainerd* (Boston: D. Henchman, 1749) (hereafter, *Life of Brainerd*). Their limitations and constructed natures are discussed in the chapters which follow.

3. The scholarship on the revivals is, of course, voluminous and cannot even be summarized here. Most of the relevant sources will be cited in the chapters which follow. Much of the recent scholarship is discussed in Thomas S. Kidd, *The Great Awakening: The Roots of Evangelical Christianity in Colonial America* (New Haven, Conn.: Yale University Press, 2007), see esp. the introduction, xiii–xix.

4. Milton Coalter, *Gilbert Tennent, Son of Thunder: A Case Study of Continental Pietism's Impact on the First Great Awakening in the Middle Colonies* (New York: Greenwood, 1986); Douglas L. Winiarski, "Jonathan Edwards, Enthusiast? Radical Revivalism and the Great Awakening in the Connecticut Valley," *Church History* 74, no. 4 (December 2005), 683–739.

5. Christopher M. Jedrey, *The World of John Cleaveland: Family and Community in Eighteenth-Century New England* (New York: Norton, 1979); Thomas S. Kidd, "Daniel Rogers' Egalitarian Great Awakening," *Journal of the Historical Society* 7, no. 1 (March 2007), 111–135. Examples of lay responses can be found in Kidd, "The Healing of Mercy Wheeler," *WMQ* 63, no. 1 (2006): 149–170; and Douglas L. Winiarski, "Souls Filled with Ravishing Transport: Heavenly Visions and the Radical Awakening in New England," *WMQ* 61, no. 1 (January 2004), 3–46.

6. David Silverman, *Faith and Boundaries: Colonists, Christianity, and Community among the Wampanoag Indians of Martha's Vineyard, 1600–1871* (New York: Cambridge University Press, 2005); Merritt, *At the Crossroads;* Rachel Wheeler, *To Live upon Hope: Mohicans and Missionaries in the Eighteenth-Century Northeast* (Ithaca, N.Y.: Cornell University Press, 2008).

7. Richard W. Pointer, "'Poor Indians' and the 'Poor in Spirit': The Indian Impact on David Brainerd," *NEQ* 67, no. 3 (September 1994): 403–426; and Pointer, *Encounters of the Spirit: Native Americans and European Colonial Religion* (Bloomington: Indiana University Press, 2007), 103–121.

8. For various analyses of Brainerd and melancholy, see Gail Thain Parker, "Jonathan Edwards and Melancholy," *NEQ* 41, no. 2 (June 1968), 193–212; David Weddle, "The Melancholy Saint: Jonathan Edwards' Interpretation of David Brainerd as a Model of Evangelical Spirituality," *Harvard Theological Review* 81, no. 3 (1988), 297–318; John A. Grigg, "The Lives of David Brainerd" (Ph.D. diss., University of Kansas, 2002), 211–230.

9. Norman Pettit, "Editor's Introduction," *JEY* 7:71–75; Richard Steele, *"Gracious Affection" and "True Virtue" According to Jonathan Edwards and John Wesley* (Metuchen, N.J.: Scarecrow, 1994), 230–241; Grigg, "Lives of David Brainerd," 259–365.

Chapter 1

1. Daniel Wadsworth, *The Diary of Rev. Daniel Wadsworth, Seventh Pastor of the First Church of Christ in Hartford,* ed. George Leon Walker (Hartford, Conn.: Case, Lockwood, and Brainard, 1894), 71; Matthew 10:34. All biblical quotations are taken from the Authorized King James Version.

2. "The Decline of Piety: Samuel Willard, *The Peril of the Times Displayed,* 1700," 5–10, quotes on 5; "A Plea for Fervent Preaching: Solomon Stoddard, *Defects of Preachers Reproved,* 1723," 11–16, quote on 15; "Revival Preaching before the Awakening: Gilbert Tennent, *Solemn Warning,* 1735," 16–18, quote on 16, all in *The Great Awakening: Documents on the Revival of Religion,* ed. Richard L. Bushman (New York: Atheneum for the Institute of Early American History and Culture at Williamsburg, Virginia, 1970); Frank Lambert, *Inventing the "Great Awakening"* (Princeton, N.J.: Princeton University Press, 1999), 21–53; George Marsden, *Jonathan Edwards: A Life* (New Haven, Conn.: Yale University Press, 2003), 201; Michael J. Crawford, *Seasons of Grace: Colonial New England's Revival Tradition in Its British Context* (New York: Oxford University Press, 1991), 19–80, quote on 49; Solomon Stoddard, *The Duty of Gospel-Ministers to Preserve a People from*

Corruption. Set Forth in a Sermon Preached at Brookfield, October 16, 1717...(Boston: Samuel Phillips, 1718; Evans No. 1998), 22–24; William Williams, *A Painful Ministry: The Peculiar Gift of the Lord of the Harvest to Be Sought by Prayer and Acknowledged with Thankfulness* (Boston: B. Green, 1717; Evans No. 1940), 10.

3. W. R. Ward, *The Protestant Evangelical Awakening* (Cambridge: Cambridge University Press, 1992), 43, 70–77, 103–106; Crawford, *Seasons of Grace*, 81, 82; Gordon Rupp, *Religion in England, 1688–1791* (Oxford: Clarendon, 1986), 325; Kenneth Silverman, *The Life and Times of Cotton Mather* (New York: Harper & Row, 1984), 230–236; F. Ernest Stoeffler, *The Rise of Evangelical Pietism* (Leiden: Brill, 1965), 14, 20, 228–243; Susan O'Brien, "Eighteenth-Century Publishing Networks in the First Years of Transatlantic Evangelicalism," in *Evangelicalism: Comparative Studies of Popular Protestantism in North America, the British Isles, and Beyond, 1700–1990,* ed. Mark A. Noll, David W. Bebbington, and George A. Rawlyk (New York: Oxford University Press, 1994), 38–57; O'Brien, "A Transatlantic Community of Saints: The Great Awakening and the First Evangelical Network, 1735–1755," *American Historical Review* 91 (December 1986), 811–832; Marsden, *Jonathan Edwards,* 194, 200, 201.

4. Lambert, *Inventing,* 54–81; Ward, *Protestant Evangelical Awakening,* 229, 230, 244–246, 275; Thomas S. Kidd, *The Great Awakening: The Roots of Evangelical Christianity in Colonial America* (New Haven, Conn.: Yale University Press, 2007), 13–34; Marsden, *Jonathan Edwards,* 150–173.

5. Ward, *Protestant Evangelical Awakening,* 169, 170, 182; Marsden, *Jonathan Edwards,* 201–204; Rupp, *Religion in England,* 340–342; Lambert, *Inventing,* 92–110; Kidd, *Great Awakening,* 43–45, 83, 84.

6. David Brainerd, Diary Introduction, Gen. Mss. 214, Beinecke Library, Yale University, 19; Solomon Stoddard, *A Guide to Christ; or, The Way of Directing Souls That Are under the Work of Conversion. Compiled for the Help of Young Ministers: And May Be Serviceable to Private Christians Who Are Enquiring the Way to Zion* (Boston: J. Allen, 1714; Evans No. 1716).

7. A more detailed discussion of the constructed nature of other parts of Brainerd's narrative is presented later in this chapter.

8. On the development of Stoddard's theology of conversion, see N. Ray Hiner, "Preparing for the Harvest: The Concept of New Birth and the Theory of Religious Education on the Eve of the First Great Awakening," *Fides et Historia* 9, no. 1 (Fall 1976), 8–25; Paul R. Lucas, "Solomon Stoddard and the Origin of the Great Awakening in New England," *Historian* 59, no. 4 (Summer 1997): 741–758; Michael Schuldiner, "Solomon Stoddard and the Process of Conversion," *Early American Literature* 17, no. 3 (Winter 1982–1983), 215–226; Philip F. Gura, "Solomon Stoddard's Irreverent Way," *Early American Literature* 21, no. 1 (Spring 1986), 29–43; Ralph J. Coffman, *Solomon Stoddard* (Boston: Twayne, 1978), 141–175; Crawford, *Seasons of Grace,* 72–75. Not all New England ministers welcomed Stoddard's approach. For detailed discussions of Stoddard's literary battles, see Gura, "Irreverent Way"; and Paul R. Lucas, *Valley of Discord: Church and Society along the Connecticut Rover, 1636–1725* (Hanover, N.H.: University Press of New England, 1976), 146–202.

9. Stoddard, *Guide to Christ,* 2, 12, 80; Solomon Stoddard, *A Treatise Concerning Conversion Shewing the Nature of Saving Conversion to God and the Way Wherein It Is Wrought* (Boston: D. Henchman, 1719; Evans No. 2072), 55.

10. Brainerd, Diary Introduction, 5, 10.

11. Brainerd, Diary Introduction, 7–9, 26.

12. Brainerd, Diary Introduction, 12, 13, 19. Another convert of the period, Nathan Cole, who was frustrated when he could not find salvation, also remembered that his "heart rose against God exceedingly." See Michael J. Crawford, "The Spiritual Travels of Nathan Cole," *WMQ* 33, no. 1 (January 1976), 89–126, quote on 94.

13. Brainerd, Diary Introduction, 26, 28, and unnumbered insert.

14. Brainerd, Diary Introduction, 28, 29, and unnumbered page.

15. Brainerd, Diary Introduction, 30; Richard Warch, *School of the Prophets: Yale College, 1701–1740* (New Haven, Conn.: Yale University Press, 1973), 126; Marsden, *Jonathan Edwards,* 38, 39; William T. Youngs, Jr., *God's Messengers: Religious Leadership in Colonial New England, 1700–1750* (Baltimore, Md.: Johns Hopkins University Press, 1976), 15–17.

16. Warch, *School of the Prophets,* 251–255; Joseph Conforti, *Samuel Hopkins and the New Divinity Movement: Calvinism, the Congregational Ministry, and Reform in New England between the Great Awakenings* (Grand Rapids, Mich.: Christian University Press, 1981), 21, 22; Louis Leonard Tucker, *Puritan Protagonist: President Thomas Clap of Yale* (Chapel Hill: University of North Carolina Press, 1962), 69, 70; Marsden, *Jonathan Edwards,* 34, 35; Mark Valeri, *Law and Providence in Joseph Bellamy's New England: The Origins of the New Divinity in Revolutionary America* (New York: Oxford University Press, 1994), 11; Brainerd, Diary Introduction, 31.

17. Warch, *School of the Prophets,* 191.

18. Brainerd, Diary Introduction, 31, 32.

19. Brainerd, Diary Introduction, 31–33.

20. *George Whitefield's Journals* (1905; reprint, Gainesville, Fla.: Scholars, 1969), 482; Tucker, *Puritan Protagonist,* 15–17, 117; Warch, *School of the Prophets,* 313, 314; *Sketches of the Life of the Late Rev. Samuel Hopkins, D.D.,* ed. Stephen West (Hartford, Conn.: Hudson and Gordon, 1805), 30, 31; Kidd, *Great Awakening,* 84–90.

21. Brainerd, Diary Introduction, 34.

22. Brainerd, Diary Introduction, 34; Christopher M. Jedrey, *The World of John Cleaveland: Family and Community in Eighteenth-Century New England* (New York: Norton, 1979), 23; Bruce C. Daniels, *The Fragmentation of New England: Comparative Perspectives on Economic, Political, and Social Divisions in the Eighteenth Century* (New York: Greenwood, 1988), 81; Conforti, *Samuel Hopkins,* 22; David W. Stowe, "'The Opposers Are Very Much Enraged': Religious Conflict and Separation in New Haven during the Great Awakening, 1741–1760," *Connecticut Historical Society Bulletin* 56 (1991), 211–235. My thanks to Doug Winiarski for bringing this article to my attention.

23. Brainerd, Diary Introduction, 35; Haddam Town Records, Land Records III: Part 2, folio 229, 230. Brainerd also had received land almost two years earlier from his brothers Hezekiah and Nehemiah, which made up part of the parcel he sold to Camp. See folio 196.

24. *Life of Hopkins,* 31.

25. Brainerd, Diary Introduction, 35, 36.

26. *Life of Hopkins,* 31, 32; Stephen Nissenbaum, ed., *The Great Awakening at Yale College* (Belmont, Calif.: Wadsworth, 1972), 12; "Gilbert Tennent to George Whitefield, New York, April 25, 1741," in *Great Awakening at Yale,* ed. Nissenbaum, 26, 27; Coalter, *Gilbert Tennent,* 72–75; Kidd, *Great Awakening,* 96–99; Warch, *School of the Prophets,* 314.

27. Gilbert Tennent, *The Danger of an Unconverted Ministry* (Boston: Rogers & Fowle, 1742; Evans No. 5070), 13; Harry S. Stout, *The New England Soul: Preaching and Religious Culture in Colonial New England* (New York: Oxford University Press, 1986), 198, 199; Brainerd, Diary Introduction, 32.

28. Tennent, *Danger of an Unconverted Ministry,* 16; Elizabeth Nybakken, "In the Irish Tradition: Pre-Revolutionary Academies in America," *History of Education Quarterly* 37, no. 2 (Summer 1997), 163–183; David Lovejoy, *Religious Enthusiasm in the New World: Heresy to Revolution* (Cambridge, Mass.: Harvard University Press, 1985), 184; Stout, *New England Soul,* 200.

29. *Life of Hopkins,* 32; Dexter, *Biographical Sketches,* I:664, 696.

30. *Life of Hopkins,* 32–35.

31. Coalter, *Gilbert Tennent,* 63; Ebenezer Pemberton, *The Knowlege* [*sic*] *of Christ Recommended, in a Sermon Preach'd in the Public Hall at Yale College in New-Haven, April 19th, 1741* (New London: T. Green, 1741; Evans No. 4779), 4, 6, 16, 17, 20.

32. Pemberton, *Knowlege of Christ Recommended,* 20, 21, 23, 26, end papers.

33. Marsden, *Jonathan Edwards,* 214–219; Kidd, *Great Awakening,* 106–112; Bushman, *From Puritan to Yankee,* 184; C. C. Goen, *Revivalism and Separatism in New England, 1740–1800: Strict Congregationalists and Separate Baptists in the Great Awakening* (New Haven, Conn.: Yale University Press, 1962), 18–22.

34. *The Querists: A Short Reply to Mr. Whitefield's Letter,* in *The Great Awakening: Documents Illustrating the Crisis and Its Consequences,* ed. Alan Heimert and Perry Miller (Indianapolis, Ind.: Bobbs-Merrill, 1967), 134–146, quotes on 138. Originally published in Philadelphia, the pamphlet also circulated in New England.

35. *The Wonderful Wandering Spirit,* in *The Great Awakening,* ed. Heimert and Miller, 147–151, quote on 148.

36. Charles Chauncy, *Enthusiasm Described and Caution'd Against,* in *The Great Awakening,* ed. Heimert and Miller, 228–256, quote on 231, 232.

37. Lovejoy, *Religious Enthusiasm,* 87–110; Phyllis Mack, "Women as Prophets during the English Civil War," in *The Origins of Anglo-American Radicalism,* ed. Margaret Jacob and James Jacob (Boston: Allen & Unwin, 1984), 214–230.

38. Lovejoy, *Religious Enthusiasm,* 25–29; T. Wilson Hayes, "John Everard and the Familist Tradition," in *Origins of Anglo-American Radicalism,* ed. Jacob and Jacob, 60–69.

39. Hillel Schwartz, *The French Prophets: The History of a Millenarian Group in Eighteenth-Century England* (Berkeley: University of California Press, 1980), 14–36, 43–45, 78–98; Schwartz, *Knaves, Fools, Madmen, and That Subtile Effluvium: A Study of the Opposition to the French Prophets in England, 1706–1710* (Gainesville: University Press of Florida, 1978), 21, 25.

40. Timothy D. Hall, *Contested Boundaries: Itinerancy and the Reshaping of the Colonial American Religious World* (Durham, N.C.: Duke University Press, 1994), 41–70; John Walsh, "'Methodism' and the Origins of English-Speaking Evangelicalism," in *Evangelicalism: Comparative Studies,* ed. Noll et al., 19–37, esp. 32; Stout, *New England Soul,* 192–201, quotes on 197 and 201.

41. *The Querists,* 144.

42. Charles Chauncy, *Seasonable Thoughts on the State of Religion in New-England* (Boston: Samuel Eliot, 1743; Evans No. 5151), 171; Chauncy, *Enthusiasm Described and Caution'd Against,* in *The Great Awakening,* ed. Heimert and Miller, 228–256, quote on 232; Stout, *New England Soul,* 202–204.

43. *Wonderful Wandering Spirit,* 148.

44. Chauncy, *Enthusiasm Described and Caution'd Against,* 240.

45. Gilbert Tennent to Stephen Williams, n.d., Gratz Collection, case 8, box 25, Historical Society of Pennsylvania. Though the letter is undated, a later note postulates "c. 1740." Internal evidence would suggest 1741 to be a more likely date; Coalter, *Gilbert Tennent,* 93, 94. Tennent was also concerned because he was being cited as the proximate

cause for the rise in lay preachers. He sent the same letter to Benjamin Lord and Jonathan Edwards. See Coalter, *Gilbert Tennent*, 188n8.

46. Lovejoy, *Religious Enthusiasm*, 195–197; Stout, *New England Soul*, 198, 199, 202, 208, 209; Hall, *Contested Boundaries*, 91–97; Erik R. Seeman, *Pious Persuasions: Laity and Clergy in Eighteenth-Century New England* (Baltimore, Md.: Johns Hopkins University Press, 1999), 158–173.

47. Anonymous to the *Boston Weekly Post-Boy*, September 28, 1741; Goen, *Revivalism and Separatism*, 20–22.

48. On the general interaction between students and revivalists, see Stephen Nissenbaum "Introduction," in Nissenbaum, ed., *Great Awakening at Yale*, 4, 5; Tucker, *Puritan Protagonist*, 121–123; Stout, *New England Soul*, 200.

49. Dexter, *Biographical Sketches*, I:632–637, quote on 636; Tucker, *Puritan Protagonist*, 40–45.

50. Tucker, *Puritan Protagonist*, 127, 128.

51. Tucker, *Puritan Protagonist*, 67.

52. Franklin Bowditch Dexter, *Documentary History of Yale University, 1701–1745* (New York: Arno and the New York Times, 1969), 351. Dexter suggested that this rule was put into place for the specific purpose of disciplining Brainerd (350). Since Brainerd was not expelled until November and, by all accounts, his offense occurred during the semester, this can not have been the case.

53. Marsden, *Jonathan Edwards*, 233.

54. Douglas L. Winiarski, "Jonathan Edwards, Enthusiast? Radical Revivalism and the Great Awakening in the Connecticut Valley," *Church History* 74, no. 4 (December 2005), 683–739. The quotes are from 738 and 739.

55. Jonathan Edwards, *The Distinguishing Marks of a Work of the Spirit of God*, JEY 4:213–288.

56. Edwards, *Distinguishing Marks*, 226–248. The quotes are found at 226 and 241; Marsden, *Jonathan Edwards*, 233–238.

57. Edwards, *Distinguishing Marks*, 260, 269, 270. This interpretation is also found in Conforti, *Samuel Hopkins*, 28, 29. Winiarski has argued that *Distinguishing Marks* was the beginning of Edwards's move away from the radicals; see Winiarski, "Jonathan Edwards, Enthusiast?" 730. In a sense, both positions are correct, given different perspectives. *Distinguishing Marks* provided neither the blanket condemnation of the revival that Clap wanted nor the outright endorsement that men like James Davenport and Andrew Croswell would have recognized.

58. *Boston Weekly Post-Boy*, September 28, 1741; Goen, *Revivalism and Separatism*, 22.

59. Although he does not deal with this meeting specifically, my description is drawn from Peter Charles Hoffer, *Sensory Worlds in Early America* (Baltimore, Md.: Johns Hopkins University Press, 2003), 166–186.

60. "Samuel Johnson to George Berkeley, 3 October, 1741," in *Great Awakening at Yale*, ed. Nissenbaum, 57.

61. Thomas Clap to Solomon Williams, June 8, 1742, Gratz Collection, case 7, box 12, Historical Society of Pennsylvania.

62. The response of Clap and other members of the First Church can be found in the *Boston Weekly Post-Boy*, October 5, 1741. For the connection between the confrontations and the separate meetings in New Haven, see *Boston Weekly Post-Boy*, September 28, 1741; Goen, *Revivalism and Separatism*, 22, 86, 87.

63. As will be seen in chapter 4, Edwards also had a self-interest in playing down any rebellion on the part of Brainerd.

64. Edwards, *Life of Brainerd,* 18; Records of the Yale Corporation, 1716–1760, and Papers of President Thomas Clap, YRG 2-A-5, folders 1–3, both in the Yale University Archives, Manuscripts and Archives Division, Sterling Memorial Library; Thomas Clap, *The Annals or History of Yale-College, in New-Haven, in the Colony of Connecticut* (New Haven, Conn.: John Hotchkiss and B. Mecom, 1766; Evans No. 10262). Apparently, Brainerd later reconstructed the expulsion and recorded it in his private diary during his time at Kaunaumeek. This diary was in the possession of Thomas Brainerd, who was a minister in Philadelphia, as late as 1860. See Thomas Brainerd, *The Life of John Brainerd* (Philadelphia: Presbyterian Publication Committee, 1861), 130n.

65. Edwards, *Life of Brainerd,* 18, 19; "Edwards to John Brainerd, 14 December, 1747," *JEY* 16:242.

66. Edwards, *Life of Brainerd,* 20, 21; Dexter, *Biographical Sketches,* I:698.

67. Jared Ingersoll, "An Historical Account of Some Affairs Relating to the Church, Especially in Connecticut, Together with a Notation of Some Other Things of a Different Nature," Jared Ingersoll Papers 1740–1779, Peter Force series 7E, mss. 19,061, reel 16, Library of Congress; Edwards, *Life of Brainerd,* 81–83; Bushman, *From Puritan to Yankee,* 254.

68. John Cleaveland Diary, Papers of John Cleaveland, box 1 folder 5, Phillips Peabody Library, used by permission; quote from January 15, 1742. Cleaveland leaped to Brainerd's defense over a different charge ten days later; see diary entry for January 26, 1742; Edwards, *Life of Brainerd,* 82.

69. Rhys Isaac, *The Transformation of Virginia, 1740–1790* (Chapel Hill: University of North Carolina Press for the Omohundro Institute of Early American History and Culture, 1999), 172–177; Isaac, "Evangelical Revolt: The Nature of the Baptists' Challenge to the Traditional Order in Virginia, 1765–1775," *WMQ* 32, no. 3 (July 1974), 346–368; Isaac, "Religion and Authority: Problems of the Anglican Establishment in Virginia in the Era of the Great Awakening and the Parsons' Cause," *WMQ* 30, no. 1 (January 1973), 4–36; Stowe, "The Opposers Are Very Much Enraged."

70. "New Haven Church Members: Memorial to the Congregation, December 28, 1741," in *Great Awakening at Yale,* ed. Nissenbaum, 116, 117.

71. "Covenant of the New Haven Separate Church, May 7, 1742," in *Great Awakening at Yale,* ed. Nissenbaum, 119, 120.

72. John Cleaveland Diary, January 26, February 20, 23, March 2, 9, 1742.

73. John Cleaveland Diary, March 19, 20, 21, 22, April 18, May 9, 1742; "Benjamin Colman to George Whitefield, June 3, 1742," in *Glasgow Weekly History,* no. 45, 3, 4.

74. *Boston Weekly Post-Boy,* March 1, 1742.

75. Tucker, *Puritan Protagonist,* 134, 135; Leonard Bacon, *Thirteen Historical Discourses on the Completion of Two Hundred Years, from the Beginning of the First Church in New Haven* (New Haven, Conn.: Durrie and Peck, 1839), 220–222 and 222n. Bacon argues that the call to Burr came after the separation and that Burr accepted but for reasons unknown never took up his role.

76. "Colman to Whitefield, June 3, 1742"; "Report of a Committee of the Connecticut General Assembly, on a Passage Relating to the College in Governor Law's Speech," in Dexter, *Documentary History of Yale,* 356–358; Clap to Jonathan Dickinson, May 3, 1742, in *Great Awakening at Yale,* ed. Nissenbaum, 117, 118; "*Boston Evening Post:* Account of the Troubles at Yale, April 26, 1742," in *Great Awakening at Yale,* ed. Nissenbaum, 145, 146; Jedrey, *World of John Cleaveland,* 28; Richard Warch, "The Shepherd's Tent: Education and Enthusiasm in the Great Awakening," *American Quarterly* 20, no. 2 (Summer 1978), 177–198, esp. 184.

77. Record Book of the Fairfield East Consociation, Property of the Connecticut Conference of the United Church of Christ, Hartford, Connecticut; Daniels, *Fragmentation of New England,* 123; Edwards, *Life of Brainerd,* 22; Dexter, *Biographical Sketches,* I:29–33, 262, 263, 523–529, 648, 649.

78. Conforti, *Samuel Hopkins,* 9–22; Valeri, *Law and Providence,* 9–24; Dexter, *Biographical Sketches,* I:664; Harry S. Stout, "The Great Awakening in New England Reconsidered: The New England Clergy," *Journal of Social History* 8, no. 1 (Autumn 1974), 21–47.

79. Lucy Abigail Brainard, *The Genealogy of the Brainerd-Brainard Family in America, 1649–1908* (Hartford, Conn.: Hartford Press, 1908), I: part 1:5–27; Brainerd, *Life of John Brainerd,* 21, 22. Any record of Daniel's arrival from England seems to have been lost. For example, although his name appears in Virkus's works on immigrants, Virkus cites Lucy Brainard's *Genealogy.* See Frederick Adams Virkus, ed., *Immigrant Ancestors: A List of 2,500 Immigrants to America before 1750* (Baltimore, Md.: Genealogical Publishing, 1980), 15. One variation on the story is that Daniel was kidnapped or "decoyed" in England and was subsequently sold to the Wadsworth family. Another account says that Daniel lived with the Wylys family. See Brainard, *Genealogy,* I: part 1:15 and 15n; and Brainerd, *Life of John Brainerd,* 21 and 22n.

80. Bruce C. Daniels, *The Connecticut Town: Growth and Development, 1635–1790* (Middletown, Conn.: Wesleyan University Press, 1979), 9, 13–17; Philip J. Greven, Jr., *Four Generations: Population, Land and Family in Colonial Andover, Massachusetts* (Ithaca, N.Y.: Cornell University Press, 1970), 41–47; Anthony N. B. Garvan, *Architecture and Town Planning in Colonial Connecticut* (New Haven, Conn.: Yale University Press, 1951), 51–77; Bushman, *From Puritan to Yankee,* 54.

81. Haddam Town Records I. The town records are silent on the activities of merchants or private builders during this period. Brainerd, *Life of John Brainerd,* 24–28; Brainard, *Genealogy,* I: part 1:27–29, 39, 40; part 2:41; part 4:44; Greven, *Four Generations,* 45–48; John F. Martin, *Profits in the Wilderness: Entrepreneurship and the Founding of New England Towns in the Seventeenth Century* (Chapel Hill: University of North Carolina Press for the Omohundro Institute of Early American History and Culture, 1991), 149–161.

82. Brainard, *Genealogy,* I: part 1:40, 43; part 7:41–44; Brainerd, *Life of John Brainerd,* 28–31.

83. The description and analysis of Haddam in the first half of the eighteenth century which follow draw on a number of studies of Connecticut and New England towns: Bushman, *From Puritan to Yankee;* Greven, *Four Generations;* Daniels, *Connecticut Town;* Daniels, *Fragmentation of New England;* Jackson Turner Main, *Society and Economy in Colonial Connecticut* (Princeton, N.J.: Princeton University Press, 1985); Michael Zuckerman, *Peaceable Kingdoms: New England Towns in the Eighteenth Century* (New York: Knopf, 1970); Edward M. Cook, Jr., *The Fathers of the Towns: Leadership and Community Structure in Eighteenth-Century New England* (Baltimore, Md.: Johns Hopkins University Press, 1976); Kenneth A. Lockridge, *A New England Town, the First Hundred Years: Dedham, Massachusetts, 1636–1736* (New York: Norton, 1970); Charles S. Grant, *Democracy in the Connecticut Frontier Town of Kent* (New York: Columbia University Press, 1961).

84. "Estate of Daniel Brainerd," 1715, Hartford Probate District, Town of Haddam, No. 736, microfilm held at Connecticut State Library.

85. T. H. Breen, "An Empire of Goods: The Anglicization of Colonial America, 1690–1776," *Journal of British Studies* 25, no. 4 (October 1986), 467–499; "Estate of Hezekiah Brainerd," 1727, Town of Haddam, Hartford Probate District, No. 740, microfilm copy at Connecticut State Library.

86. "Estate of Hezekiah Brainerd."

87. Ian K. Steele, *The English Atlantic, 1675–1740: An Exploration of Commerce and Communication* (New York: Oxford University Press, 1986), 121, 122, 154–158; Alan Taylor, *American Colonies: The Settling of North America* (New York: Penguin, 2001), 303–306, 310–314; Jack P. Greene, *Pursuits of Happiness: The Social Development of Early Modern British Colonies and the Formation of American Culture* (Chapel Hill: University of North Carolina Press, 1988), 65–71, 76–80; Alison Gilbert Olson, *Making the Empire Work: London and American Interest Groups* (Cambridge, Mass.: Harvard University Press, 1992), 110.

88. *PRCC,* 5:363, 561 (ferry license); 6:207, 225, 233, 240, 270, 281, 304, 329, 407–409; 7:58 (land grant); Cook, *Fathers of the Towns,* 1–3, 85, 86, 154–156; Main, *Society and Economy,* 323; Daniels, *Fragmentation of New England,* 18, 77–93, quote on 82. For further information on Hezekiah's service to the colony, see John A. Grigg, "The Lives of David Brainerd" (Ph.D. diss., University of Kansas, 2001), 69–71.

89. Colin G. Calloway, *The Western Abenakis of Vermont, 1600–1800: War, Migration, and the Survival of an Indian People* (Norman: University of Oklahoma Press, 1990), 108–132; Daniel K. Richter, *Facing East from Indian Country: A Native History of Early America* (Cambridge, Mass.: Harvard University Press, 2001), 151–184.

90. Zuckerman, *Peaceable Kingdoms.*

91. *PRCC,* 4:229.

92. Rev. Jeremiah Hobart to Rev. Timothy Woodbridge, January 3, 1698–9, "The Wyllys Papers: Correspondence and Documents Chiefly of Descendants of Governor George Wyllys of Connecticut, 1590–1796," *Collections of the Connecticut Historical Society* 21 (1924), 354.

93. *PRCC,* 4:341; Zuckerman, *Peaceable Kingdoms,* 123–153.

94. Marsden, *Jonathan Edwards,* 150–169; Lambert, *"Pedlar in Divinity": George Whitefield and the Transatlantic Revivals, 1737–1770* (Princeton, N.J.: Princeton University Press, 1994), 62–69; Cedric B. Cowing, *The Saving Remnant: Religion and the Settling of New England* (Urbana: University of Illinois Press, 1995), 275, 276. Goen, *Revivalism and Separatism,* makes no mention of any separate activities in Haddam.

95. Brainerd, *Life of John Brainerd,* 28–31, quote on 30; Brainard, *Genealogy,* part 1:42–44, quote on 42; Norman Pettit, "Introduction," in *JEY* 7:33–35.

96. "Diary of Joshua Hempstead, 1711–1758," *Collections of the New London Historical Society* 1 (1901), 184; *PRCC,* 7:90, 109, 113, 114, 116.

97. *PRCC,* 7:371; Brainerd, Diary Introduction, 2.

98. The manuscript version of the Diary Introduction is held by the Beinecke Library at Yale. At the top of p. 30, Brainerd noted, "I have corrected no further DB," while at the bottom of the page and carrying over to the top of p. 31, there is the notation, "The authors [*sic*] own corrections by another pen." We know that Brainerd was correcting it in the last months of his life, but we do not know when he first compiled this account. It is impossible to know if Brainerd had written a rough draft in Northampton after agreeing to allow Jonathan Edwards to publish his diaries, or if he had written months, or years, earlier for another reason. The first date is July 12, 1739, but this seems to have been arrived at by extrapolating backward from the time of his entry to Yale in August 1739. See Edwards, *Life of Brainerd,* 244.

99. Daniel B. Shea, Jr., *Spiritual Autobiography in Early America* (Princeton, N.J.: Princeton University Press, 1968), 182–233, quotes on 187. My thanks to Doug Winiarski for emphasizing the importance of this aspect of Brainerd's introduction.

100. Brainerd, Diary Introduction, 1. Other published accounts which include this structure: Kenneth P. Minkema, "A Great Awakening Conversion: The Relation of Samuel Belcher," *WMQ* 44, no. 1 (January 1987), 121–126; Crawford, "Nathan Cole."

101. James Janeway, *A Token for Children. Being an Exact Account of the Conversion, Holy and Exemplary Lives and Joyful Deaths of Several Young Children. To Which Is Added a Token for the Children of New England* (Boston: Nicholas Boone, 1700; Evans No. 914). See also Seeman, *Pious Persuasions,* 46; Zuckerman, *Peaceable Kingdoms,* 78, 79, n. 63, 297, 298.

102. Janeway, *Token,* 32.

103. Brainerd, Diary Introduction, 1; Janeway, *Token,* 34.

104. Brainerd, Diary Introduction, 2; Thomas Brainerd, *Life of John Brainerd,* 31; E. Emory Johnson and Hosford B. Niles, "East Haddam," in *History of Middlesex County, Connecticut, with Biographical Sketches of Its Prominent Men* (New York: Beers, 1884), 323; David D. Field, *The Genealogy of the Brainerd Family in the United States, with Numerous Sketches of Individuals* (New York: n.p., 1857), 252, 253; Charles William Manwaring, ed., *A Digest of the Early Connecticut Probate Records* (1904–1906; reprint, Baltimore, Md.: Genealogical Publishing, 1995), I:364.

105. "Estate of Hezekiah Brainerd"; Main, *Society and Economy,* 34, 54, 55.

106. Daniels, *Connecticut Town,* 25; Haddam Town Records II.

107. Brainerd, Diary Introduction, 3.

108. James W. Schmotter, "Ministerial Careers in Eighteenth-Century New England: The Social Context, 1700–1760," *Journal of Social History* 9, no. 2 (Winter 1975), 249–267, esp. 250, 251. A hint of the family's tendencies as it pertained to education can be found in Hezekiah's will wherein he directed that Nehemiah—the second son—be "bred up in learning befitted to be serviceable thereby," without specifying that Nehemiah enter the ministry. See Hezekiah Brainerd's will.

109. Bushman, *From Puritan to Yankee,* 73–83, 122–131, 164–182; Conforti, *Samuel Hopkins,* 18, 19; Grant, *Democracy in Kent,* 3–11; Daniels, *Connecticut Town,* 45–63; Main, *Society and Economy,* 115; Kidd, *Great Awakening,* 13–24.

110. Durham Town Meeting, December 2, 1736, Durham Town Records 2, 1730–1769, Town Clerk's Office, Durham, Connecticut. See similar instructions for December 2, 1737, December 12, 1738, and December 11, 1739.

111. Brainerd, Diary Introduction, 2; Marsden, *Jonathan Edwards,* 122, 126, 150–152.

112. Main, *Society and Economy,* 132–135, 201–205, quote on 205; Daniels, *Connecticut Town,* 17. James W. Schmotter has also noted that a career in the ministry and/or a college degree made it possible for a young man to "escape the dull, difficult life of a farmer or small artisan." Schmotter, "Ministerial Careers," 249–267, quote on 253.

113. Samuel Hopkins went through the same preparation. See *Life of Hopkins,* 26, 27.

114. Haddam Town Records II; Dexter, *Biographical Sketches,* I:9–21.

115. "Memoirs of the Life of the Rev. Dr. Johnson, and Several Things Relating to the State Both of Religion and Learning in His Times. Written 1768–1770," in *Samuel Johnson, President of King's College, His Career and Writing,* ed. Herbert Schneider and Carol Schneider (New York: Columbia University Press, 1929), I:6.

116. David D. Field, *A History of the Towns of Haddam and East Haddam* (Middletown, Conn.: Loomis, 1814; Evans, 2nd ser., No. 31473), 28.

117. Quoted in Leonard Bacon, *Thirteen Historical Discourses on the Completion of Two Hundred Years, from the Beginning of the First Church in New Haven* (New Haven, Conn.: Durrie and Peck, 1839), 201n; Trumbull is quoted in Dexter, *Biographical Sketches,* I:21.

118. Dexter, *Biographical Sketches,* I:21, 441; Thomas Brainerd, *The Life of John Brainerd* (Philadelphia: Presbyterian Publication Committee, 1861), 32, 35, 36, 51.

119. Brainerd, Diary Introduction, 3.

120. Brainerd, Diary Introduction, 3, 4.

121. Brainerd, Diary Introduction, 3, 4; Nehemiah's movements following graduation are not known. He had interviewed at East Haddam in 1735 but had not been retained. He finally accepted the pulpit at Eastbury in 1739. Since his father's will had left him land, he may have supported his family by farming until moving to Eastbury. Alternatively, since he was Fiske's son-in-law, he may have been living in Fiske's house and serving as an assistant at Haddam. Dexter, *Biographical Sketches,* I:441; Records of the Congregational Church of Buckingham/Eastbury/East Glastonbury I:33, microfilm copy at Connecticut State Library; Second Congregational Church, East Haddam, Record Book, 1736–1895, transcription, Connecticut Historical Society, Hartford, Ms77690c, used by permission. On ministerial apprenticeships, see Youngs, *God's Messengers,* 17–24.

122. Records of the Fairfield East Consociation.

123. "Colman to Whitefield, June 3, 1742"; Jonathan Dickinson to Thomas Foxcroft, July 27, 1742, Thomas Foxcroft Selected Correspondence, Manuscripts Division, Department of Rare Books and Special Collections, Princeton University Library, used by permission; Valeri, *Law and Providence,* 40–44; Edwards, "Keeping the Presence of God," *JEY* 22:519–535, quote on 533; Edwards, *Some Thoughts Concerning the Present Revival of Religion, JEY* 4:290–530, quote on 411; Hall, *Contested Boundaries,* 91–97.

124. "Resolves of the General Consociation," in *Great Awakening at Yale,* ed. Nissenbaum, 129–132.

125. Edwards, *Life of Brainerd,* 32.

126. Record Book of the Fairfield East Association, July 29, 1742.

127. Edwards, *Life of Brainerd,* 32.

128. "Governor Law's Address to the General Assembly, May, 1742," in *Great Awakening at Yale,* ed. Nissenbaum, 132–135, quote on 134; "Report of a Committee of the Connecticut General Assembly, on a Passage Relating to the College in Governor Law's Speech," in Dexter, *Documentary History of Yale,* 356–358. See also Tucker, *Puritan Protagonist,* 130, 131.

129. "Report of a Committee," 357, 358.

130. *PRCC,* 7:454–457. The best treatment of itinerancy and why it was seen as subversive is Hall, *Contested Boundaries.*

131. *PRCC,* 7:456.

132. *PRCC,* 7:483, 484; Goen, *Revivalism and Separatism,* 59–62; Wadsworth, *Diary of Wadsworth,* 83, 87.

133. Brainerd's account of his time from moving to Ripton until his licensing examination can be found in Edwards, *Life of Brainerd,* 22–38. Most of the entries contain some mention of his spiritual exercises with the two quotes being found on 25 and 24, respectively. Specific mention of work with the Indians is at 23, 24, 27, and 37, and preparation for examination at 26, 30.

134. Edwards, *Life of Brainerd,* 25, 28, 37.

135. Edwards, *Life of Brainerd,* 38.

136. Fairfield East Association, July 29, 1742.

137. Fairfield East Association, June 17 and 18, 1735.

138. Fairfield East Association, June 17 and 18, 1735.

139. Manuscript sermon of the Reverend David Brainerd, missionary to the Indians, Personal Papers RG30, Yale Divinity School Library (hereafter, Brainerd Sermon).

140. That the sermon is Brainerd's seems to be in little doubt. It was presented to Yale by a collateral descendant of Brainerd's, and the handwriting is consistent with other fragments attributed to Brainerd in various locations. The date of 1740 in the

library's title is unlikely, however. That would place the sermon in either his freshman or sophomore years at Yale. Unless it is a sermon prepared for a class he was taking, it seems more appropriate to date the manuscript from 1742 or later. The discussion of the sermon which follows was originally published, in a longer form, in John Grigg, "'A Principle of Spiritual Life': David Brainerd's Surviving Sermon," *NEQ* 77, no. 2 (June 2004), 273–282. I gratefully acknowledge the *Quarterly*'s permission to reproduce the argument here.

141. Brainerd Sermon.

142. Fairfield East Association, July 29, 1742.

143. Edwards, *Life of Brainerd,* 39, 40, 43, 48, 49; Valeri, *Law and Providence,* 19, 22, 23. In addition to those occasions when Brainerd noted that he preached, there are numerous cases where he spent Sundays in other towns without specifically noting that he preached, although it seems likely he did so.

144. Edwards, *Life of Brainerd,* 31, 33; Bacon, *Thirteen Historical Discourses,* 220, 222n.

145. Edwards, *Life of Brainerd,* 41, 42; Goen, *Revivalism and Separatism,* 86, 87; Bacon, *Thirteen Historical Discourses,* 222n.

146. Edwards, *Life of Brainerd,* 41, 42, 44, 45.

147. Edwards, *Life of Brainerd,* 51; "John Maltby to Eleazar and Mrs. Wheelock, New Haven, November 18, 1742," in *Great Awakening at Yale,* ed. Nissenbaum, 176–178; Dexter, *Biographical Sketches,* I: 493; Goen, *Revivalism and Separatism,* 87.

148. Edwards, *Life of Brainerd,* 51.

149. Edwards, *Life of Brainerd,* 52n.

150. Henry Hunter, *A Brief History of the Society in Scotland for Propagating Christian Knowledge…*(London: n.p., 1795), 32; Donald E. Meek, "Scottish Highlanders, North American Indians and the SSPCK: Some Cultural Perspectives," *Records of the Scottish Church History Society* 23 (1989), 378–396, esp. 383.

151. SSPCK Records, GMM 4:86, 96, 123–125, 156, 157; DMM 5:408, 417.

152. Edwards, *Life of Brainerd,* 52.

153. "Ebenezer Pemberton, to the Marquis of Lothian, President of the Society, December 8, 1742," *Christian Monthly History* 5 (March–August 1744), 20, 21.

154. SSPCK Records, GMM 4:307.

155. Edwards, *Life of Brainerd,* 53–59 and 54n; *JEY* 7:190n.

156. Edwards, *Life of Brainerd,* 58, 59; Records of the First Congregational Church of Branford, microfilm of copy held at Connecticut State Library, supplied by the Family History Research Library, Salt Lake City. My thanks to Doug Winiarski for information on this source. The church records do not specify when Brainerd and Buell were in Branford; the meeting which references their visit was held in early 1747. November 1742 is the only mention of Branford in Brainerd's surviving writings, and his description of the meeting seems to suggest that anti-revivalists may have taken exception to its conduct.

157. Edwards, *Life of Brainerd,* 59; *Annals* I:321.

158. Edwards, *Life of Brainerd,* 46, 55–59.

159. Pettit, "Editor's Introduction," *JEY* 7:57, 58; Goen, *Revivalism and Separatism,* 46, 47, 78, 79; William Haynes, *The Stonington Chronology, 1649–1976, Being a Year-by-Year Record of the American Way of Life in a Connecticut Town* (Chester, Conn.: Pequot Press for the Stonington Historical Society, 1976), 35; see also William S. Simmons and Cheryl L. Simmons, eds., "Preface," in their *Old Light on Separate Ways: The Narragansett Diary of Joseph Fish, 1765–1776* (Hanover, N.H.: University Press of New England, 1982).

160. Edwards, *Life of Brainerd,* 60.

161. "David Brainerd to Joseph Bellamy, February 4, 1743," Papers of Jonathan Edwards, series V, box 28, folder 1530, Beinecke Library, Yale University.

162. *Great Awakening at Yale,* ed. Nissenbaum, 179; "The General Assembly Condemns the Shepard's Tent," in *Great Awakening at Yale,* ed. Nissenbaum, 183–185; Warch, "Shepherd's Tent," 177–198; Leigh Eric Schmidt, "'A Second and Glorious Reformation': The New Light Extremism of Andrew Croswell," *WMQ* 43, no. 2 (April, 1986): 214–244; Harry S. Stout and Peter Onuf, "James Davenport and the Great Awakening in New London," *JAH* 71, no. 3 (December 1983), 556–578; Rupp, *Religion in England,* 172–179.

163. Edwards, *Life of Brainerd,* 60.

164. "Timothy Allen to Eleazar Wheelock, New London, February 27, 1743," in *Great Awakening at Yale,* ed. Nissenbaum, 185–187; Stout and Onuf, "James Davenport and the Great Awakening"; Warch, "Shepherd's Tent," 190–195; Goen, *Revivalism and Separatism,* 62, 63, 69, 70; *Annals* I:398.

165. Brainerd to Bellamy, February 4, 1743.

166. Brainerd to Bellamy, February 4, 1743.

167. David Brainerd to Joseph Bellamy, March 26, 1743, in Letters to Joseph Bellamy from Various Correspondents, vault folio BX 9225.B515A4a, Presbyterian Historical Society, Philadelphia.

168. Brainerd to Bellamy, February 4, 1743.

169. Edwards, *Life of Brainerd,* 48, 49.

170. Brainerd to Bellamy, February 4, 1743; Schmidt, "Second and Glorious Reformation," 225.

171. Brainerd to Bellamy, March 26, 1743.

Chapter 2

1. Edwards, *Life of Brainerd,* 52.

2. Edwards, *Life of Brainerd,* 60–64; Nathaniel S. Prime, *A History of Long Island, from Its First Settlement by Europeans to the Year 1845* (New York: Robert Carter, 1845), 176; William S. Pelletreau, "East Hampton," in *History of Suffolk County, New York, with Illustrations, Portraits, and Sketches of Prominent Families and Individuals* (New York: Munsell, 1882), 15; Robert Cray, Jr., "More Light on a New Light: James Davenport's Religious Legacy, Eastern Long Island, 1740–1840," *New York History* 73, no. 1 (1992), 13–16. Azariah Horton acknowledged the work of both Davenport and Mills in preaching to the Montauk Indians. It seems likely that Mills would have stopped in Easthampton while on the island. See Horton's journals originally published in *Christian Monthly History* and reprinted as part of John Strong, "Azariah Horton's Mission to the Montauk 1741–44," in *The History and Archaeology of the Montauk,* ed. Gaynell Stone (Stony Brook, N.Y.: Suffolk County Archaeological Association and Nassau County Archaeological Committee, 1993), 195.

3. Henry Hunter, *A Brief History of the Society in Scotland for Propagating Christian Knowledge…*(London: n.p., 1795), 32; Dexter, *Biographical Sketches,* I:536, 537; SSPCK Records, GMM 4:279, 280. Although there was some effort on the part of the correspondents in New York to persuade Horton to move to the Delaware Valley, in April 1742 he had made it clear he wanted to stay on Long Island. In 1752, Horton became the minister at Hanover, now Madison, New Jersey, where he retired in 1776 and died the following year at the age of sixty-two. See Strong, "Azariah Horton's Mission"; and John A. Strong and Zsuzsanna Török, "Taking the Middle Way: Algonquian Responses to the Reverend

Azariah Horton's Mission on Long Island (1741–1744)," *Long Island Historical Journal* 12, no. 2: (1999) 145–158.

4. Strong, "Azariah Horton's Mission," 213.

5. Edwards, *Life of Brainerd,* 63.

6. Edwards, *Life of Brainerd,* 64, 65; David Brainerd to Joseph Bellamy, March 26, 1743, Letters to Joseph Bellamy from Various Correspondents, vault folio BX 9225.B515A4a, Presbyterian Historical Society, Philadelphia; "Ebenezer Pemberton to the SSPCK, June 22, 1743," *Christian Monthly History* 5 March–August, 1744: 27–29. The nature of the Delawares' "contention with the English" will be discussed below.

7. A history of the praying Indians is Richard W. Cogley, *John Eliot's Mission to the Indians before King Philip's War* (Cambridge, Mass.: Harvard University Press, 1999). See also Dane Morrison, *A Praying People: Massachusett Acculturation and the Failure of the Puritan Mission, 1600–1690* (New York: Lang, 1998). For the impact of the war on the praying towns, see Morrison, *Praying People,* 166–177; and James D. Drake, *King Philip's War: Civil War in New England, 1675–1676* (Amherst: University of Massachusetts Press, 1999), 177. On Martha's Vineyard, see David Silverman, *Faith and Boundaries: Colonists, Christianity, and Community among the Wampanoag Indians of Martha's Vineyard, 1600–1871* (New York: Cambridge University Press, 2005). The impact of King Philip's War is discussed at 78–120.

8. Richard F. Lovelace, *The American Pietism of Cotton Mather: Origins of American Evangelicalism* (Grand Rapids, Mich.: Christian University Press, 1979), 274–280; Kenneth Silverman, *The Life and Times of Cotton Mather* (New York: Harper & Row, 1984), 237–243; Douglas L. Winiarski, "Native American Popular Religion in New England's Old Colony, 1670–1770," *Religion and American Culture* 15, no. 2 (2005), 147–186; William Kellaway, *The New England Company 1649–1776: Missionary Society to the American Indians* (New York: Barnes and Noble, 1962), 249–251; James Axtell, *The Invasion Within: The Contest of Cultures in Colonial North America* (New York: Oxford University Press, 1985), 242–245, 247–263; John Frederick Woolverton, *Colonial Anglicanism in North America* (Detroit, Mich.: Wayne State University Press, 1984), 99–104; Daniel O'Connor, ed., *Three Centuries of Missions: The United Society for the Propagation of the Gospel, 1701–2000* (New York: Continuum, 2000), 32, 33; Owanah Anderson, "Anglican Mission among the Mohawk," in *Three Centuries of Missions,* ed. O'Connor, 235–248.

9. Christopher Hill, "Propagating the Gospel," in *Historical Essays, 1600–1750, Presented to David Ogg,* ed. H. E. Bell and Richard Lawrence Ollard (New York: Barnes and Noble, 1963), 35–59; Thomas S. Kidd, *The Protestant Interest: New England after Puritanism* (New Haven, Conn.: Yale University Press, 2004); Gregory J. Goodwin, "Christianity, Civilization, and the Savage: The Anglican Mission to the American Indian," *Historical Magazine of the Protestant Episcopal Church* 42, no. 2 (1973), 93–110, esp. 96. A broader discussion of the role of Protestantism in British identity is in Linda Colley, *Britons: Forging the Nation, 1707–1837* (New Haven, Conn.: Yale University Press, 1992), 11–54.

10. Solomon Stoddard, *Question: Whether God Is Not Angry with the Country for Doing So Little toward the Conversion of the Indians?* (Boston: B. Green, 1723), esp. 6–12, quotes on 6, 10, 11, 12; Kidd, *Protestant Interest,* 104–106; George M. Marsden, *Jonathan Edwards: A Life* (New Haven, Conn.: Yale University Press, 2003), 117, 118.

11. Hunter, *Brief History,* 5–21, quote on 8; Callum G. Brown, *Religion and Society in Scotland since 1707* (Edinburgh: Edinburgh University Press, 1997), 85, 86; Margaret Connell Szasz, *Scottish Highlanders and Native Americans: Indigenous Education in the Eighteenth-Century Atlantic World* (Norman: University of Oklahoma Press, 2007), 73–77.

12. Hunter, *Brief History*, policy on schools, 20, 21; number of schools, 16; quotes on 6, 14, 20, 21; T. M. Devine, *The Scottish Nation: A History, 1700–2000* (New York: Viking, 1999), 94–95; Szasz, *Highlanders and Native Americans*, 72.

13. Hunter, *Brief History*, 30–32; Kidd, *Protestant Interest*, 29–50; Szasz, *Highlanders and Native Americans*, 115–119; SSPCK Records, GMM 4:66. On the SSPCK's first efforts in northeastern America and its change in policy toward colonial governments, see John A. Grigg, "How This Shall Be Brought About": The Development of the SSPCK's American Policy," *Itinerario*, 32, no. 3 (2008), 43–60.

14. Shirley W. Dunn, *The Mohicans and Their Land, 1609–1730* (New York: Purple Mountain Press and Fleischmanns, 1994), 162, 220, 221, 231, 232, 251–259; Patrick Frazier, *The Mohicans of Stockbridge* (Lincoln: University of Nebraska Press, 1992), 1–15; Rachel Wheeler, *To Live upon Hope: Mohicans and Missionaries in the Eighteenth-Century Northeast* (Ithaca, N.Y.: Cornell University Press, 2008), 33, 34.

15. Samuel Hopkins, *Historical Memoirs Relating to the Housatunnuk Indians* (Boston: S. Kneeland, 1753), 1–7; Sergeant Diary in Hopkins, *Historical Memoirs*, 6, 7, quotes on 6; Frazier, *Mohicans of Stockbridge*, 16–20; Wheeler, *To Live upon Hope*, 34–40.

16. Hopkins, *Historical Memoirs*, 13–34, quotes from Sergeant to Adam Winthrop of the New England Company, 19; and Sergeant Diary, 33; Frazier, *Mohicans of Stockbridge*, 20–36; Kellaway, *New England Company*, 270, 271; Wheeler, *To Live upon Hope*, 40–48; Michael C. Batinski, *Jonathan Belcher, Colonial Governor* (Lexington: University Press of Kentucky, 1996), 70, 71.

17. Sergeant Diary in Hopkins, *Historical Memoirs*, 61–63, 74; Frazier, *Mohicans of Stockbridge*, 45, 46.

18. Williams's will did not make this statement explicitly, but the trustees of his estate interpreted the will in this fashion. See *A True Copy of the Last Will and Testament of the Late Reverend Daniel Williams, D.D.* (London: R. Burleigh, 1717), 16–19; and cf. SSPCK Records, GMM 3:212.

19. Edwards, *Life of Brainerd*, 65, 66; "Ebenezer Pemberton to the SSPCK, June 22, 1743," *Christian Monthly History* 5: March–August, 1744, 27–29, quote on 28; Frazier, *Mohicans of Stockbridge*, 58.

20. Sergeant Diary in Hopkins, *Historical Memoirs*, 8; Edwards, *Life of Brainerd*, 66; David Brainerd to John Brainerd, April 30, 1743, in Edwards, *Life of Brainerd*, 261, 262, quote on 261; David Brainerd to Ebenezer Pemberton, November 5, 1744, in "Appendix: Containing a Short Account of the Endeavours, That Have Been Used by the Missionaries of the Society in Scotland for Propagating Christian Knowledge, to Introduce the Gospel among the Indians upon the Borders of New York, etc.," published as part of E. Pemberton, *A Sermon Preached in New-ark, June 12, 1744, at the Ordination of Mr. David Brainerd, a Missionary among the Indians* (Boston: Rogers & Fowle, 1744), 25, 26. Kaunaumeek, also referred to as Cannoomeek, is near the site of present-day Brainard, New York (formerly known as Brainard's Bridge), and not far from New Lebanon, New York. The present-day name comes not from David but from a Brainard who settled there in the nineteenth century. See Thomas Brainerd, *Life of John Brainerd* (Philadelphia: Presbyterian Publication Committee, 1861), 59n; and Frazier, *Mohicans of Stockbridge*, 45.

21. David Brainerd to John Brainerd, in Edwards, *Life of Brainerd*, 261, 262. His first two months at Kaunaumeek are in Edwards, *Life of Brainerd*, 65–73, quote on 71; Frazier, *Mohicans of Stockbridge*, 23, 24, 37, 38.

22. David Brainerd to John Brainerd, in Edwards, *Life of Brainerd*, 262.

23. Edwards, *Life of Brainerd*, 66.

24. Edwards, *Life of Brainerd,* 67. Edwards notes that, in the summer, Brainerd was reflecting on his "past Errors and misguided Zeal at *College*"; *Life of Brainerd,* 74.

25. *An Abridgement of the Statutes and Rules of the Society in Scotland for Propagating Christian Knowledge* (Edinburgh: Robert Fleming, 1732), 46.

26. Brainerd to Pemberton, 27, 28; Edwards, *Life of Brainerd,* 67–71; Frazier, *Mohicans of Stockbridge,* 58, 59.

27. Brainerd to Pemberton, 27.

28. Sergeant Diary in Hopkins, *Historical Memoirs,* 15.

29. Edwards, *Life of Brainerd,* 71; Brainerd to Pemberton, 27; Dunn, *Mohicans and Their Land,* 220.

30. Joseph Bellamy to David Brainerd, March 7, 1743, Letters to Joseph Bellamy from Various Correspondents, Presbyterian Historical Society; Wheeler, *To Live upon Hope,* 69–79; George Henry Loskiel, *History of the Mission of the United Brethren among the Indians in North America,* trans. Christian Ignatius La Trobe (London: John Stockdale, 1794), 38.

31. MAB–IND. Heinrich Joachim Senseman to Brother Anton, Shekomeko, June 5, 1743, box 111, folder 8, item 4, trans. Elizabeth Price. My thanks to the Moravian Archives for a copy of the original and to Cindy Jungenberg, Arvid E. Miller Memorial Library-Museum, Mohican Nation, Bowler, Wisconsin, and to Dr. Patrick Frazier for making the Price translation available. See also Frazier, *Mohicans of Stockbridge,* 64. The only thing that mitigates against the visitor being Brainerd was his claim about Indians being converted under his ministry. Since Brainerd had been at Kaunaumeek for less than three months at this time, this claim seems somewhat questionable. However, since a number of Indians had been converted under Sergeant's ministry, which included Kaunaumeek, there may once again be a translation issue, or a case of mistaken identity, or even as Senseman suspected, Brainerd was really visiting to obtain information about the Moravian work.

32. Brainerd Diary Leaf, Mission House, Stockbridge, Massachusetts, property of the Trustees of Reservations; Edwards, *Life of Brainerd,* 40, 65; Wheeler, *To Live upon Hope,* 135, 140–144; "Christian Indians Buried at Bethlehem, PA.," in William C. Reichel, ed., *Memorials of the Moravian Church* (Philadelphia: Lippincott, 1870), 148.

33. Edwards, *Life of Brainerd,* 72n; *Abridgement of the Statutes and Rules,* 46–48, quote on 46; Szasz, *Highlanders and Native Americans,* 79–95.

34. On Indian education, see Margaret Connell Szasz, *Indian Education in the American Colonies, 1607–1783* (1988; Reprint, Lincoln, Neb.: Bison, 2007); and Axtell, *The Invasion Within,* 179–217.

35. *A Letter from the Revd Mr. Sergeant of Stockbridge, to Dr. Colman of Boston* (Boston: D. Henchman, 1743), 3.

36. "Pemberton to the SSPCK, June 22, 1743," 28, 29; Brainerd to Pemberton, 29, 30; Edwards, *Life of Brainerd,* 71n, 72, 72n; SSPCK Records, GMM 4:314; SSPCK Records, General Ledger (GD95/8/3), 236. That the interpreter ran the school is inferred from Brainerd's reference to his "visits" and the complete absence of any record of Brainerd conducting regular activities there.

37. Brainerd to Pemberton, 26, 28; Brainerd Diary Leaf, Mission House, Stockbridge; Edwards, *Life of Brainerd,* 74; Crawford, *Seasons of Grace,* 90–97.

38. Edwards, *Life of Brainerd,* 76–79, quotes on 76, 77; Brainerd to Pemberton, 28, 29; Brainerd Diary Fragment, August 15, 1743, Gen. Mss. 214, David Brainerd Miscellaneous Diaries and Papers, Beinecke Library, Yale University.

39. Edwards, *Life of Brainerd,* 79, 80, quotes on 80.

40. Edwards, *Life of Brainerd,* 80–84. For a more detailed analysis of his appeal to Yale, see below.

41. David Brainerd to John Brainerd, in Edwards, *Life of Brainerd,* 263; see Edwards, *Life of Brainerd,* 84–103, for the October to March period with illness specifically mentioned at 87, 88, 89, 95.

42. Edwards, *Life of Brainerd,* 87(2). Pages 87 and 88 are repeated; this particular journey to Kinderhook is recorded on the second 87.

43. Edwards, *Life of Brainerd,* 91 (ordination), 95; Frazier, *Mohicans of Stockbridge,* 58, 59; Axtell, *Invasion Within,* 198.

44. Edwards, *Life of Brainerd,* 95, 96. On the church at Salisbury, see Goen, *Revivalism and Separatism,* 61 and 307; for that at Canaan, 110, 256, 322.

45. Edwards, *Life of Brainerd,* 105n.

46. Frazier, *Mohicans of Stockbridge,* 23, 24, 37, 38.

47. Unknown author, quoted in Edwards, *Life of Brainerd,* 85; Sergeant to [Isaac] Hollis in Hopkins, *Historical Memoirs,* 115; Frazier, *Mohicans of Stockbridge,* 70, 71. Hollis was a London clergyman who committed to paying full tuition and board for twelve Indian scholars.

48. Brainerd to Pemberton, 31; Edwards, *Life of Brainerd,* 105n; "Ebenezer Pemberton to the Society, June, 1744," *Christian Monthly History* 6 (August–December 1744), 17–19.

49. Aaron Burr to David Brainerd, May 16, 1743, Letters to Joseph Bellamy from Various Correspondents.

50. Burr to Brainerd, May 16, 1743.

51. Edwards, *Life of Brainerd,* 72.

52. Edwards, *Life of Brainerd,* 74; Brainerd Diary, in Brainerd, *Life of John Brainerd,* 54, 55.

53. Edwards, *Life of Brainerd,* 81–83.

54. Edwards, *Life of Brainerd,* 83.

55. Brainerd, Diary Introduction, 34.

56. This does not necessarily mean that Edwards was being dishonest in the reason that he recorded in *Life of Brainerd,* for that may have been the reason that Brainerd offered to his supporters at the time.

57. Edwards, *Life of Brainerd,* 104 (East Hampton), 104n (Millington); Christopher M. Jedrey, *The World of John Cleaveland: Family and Community in Eighteenth-Century New England* (New York: Norton, 1979), 35–53, 136–172.

58. Edwards, *Life of Brainerd,* 104, 105, 166. Neither Nathaniel Huntting's records nor those of the town of Easthampton have any record of this issue. This does not necessarily mean anything since there is no record in either place of the successful call to Samuel Buell in 1746; see *Records of the Town of East-Hampton, Long Island, Suffolk County, N.Y.* (Sag Harbor, N.Y.: J. H. Hunt, 1937–1957; UMI PS0337); and Records of the First Church of Easthampton, Long Island Collection, East Hampton Library, Easthampton, New York. There are a number of nineteenth-century sources which describe the affair, but none cite authoritative evidence. See, for example, Richard Webster, *A History of the Presbyterian Church in America, from Its Origin until the Year 1760* (Philadelphia: Joseph M. Wilson, 1857), 595; *Annals* III:104; Prime, *History of Long Island,* 176; Pelletreau, "East Hampton," 15. Also see Goen, *Revivalism and Separatism,* 184, 185; and Samuel Buell, *A Faithful Narrative of the Remarkable Revival of Religion in the Congregation of East-Hampton on Long Island in the Year of Our Lord 1764* (New York: Samuel Brown, 1766), 4, 5. Although he does not specifically mention this event, Robert Cray, Jr., demonstrates the

divisions and upheavals that continued for years after Davenport's ministry in eastern Long Island in "More Light on a New Light."

59. There was a Daniel Brainerd (1715–c. 1800) who was part of the third generation (as was David) and who lived in East Haddam until 1767. There was also a Daniel Brainerd (1721–1777) who was part of the fourth generation and held a number of town and assembly positions; see Lucy Abigail Brainard, *The Genealogy of the Brainerd-Brainard Family in America, 1649–1908* (Hartford, Conn.: Hartford Press, 1908), I: part 1:41–43; part 3:42–44, 47.

60. Records of the 2nd Congregational Church of East Haddam, Parish of Millington, 4:30–32, 34, Connecticut State Library, microfilm reel 178.

61. Edwards, *Life of Brainerd,* 104. It should also be noted that Clap clearly did not torpedo the Millington call.

62. Edwards, *Life of Brainerd,* 105–107, quote on 105.

63. Edwards, *Life of Brainerd,* 105n, 106n.

64. Edwards, *Life of Brainerd,* 23, 24, 42. See also 27, 30, 37 for other references to "heathen."

65. Edwards, *Faithful Narrative, JEY* 4:104.

66. Edwards, *Life of Brainerd,* 40, 65 (Pachgagotch), 63 (Montauk).

67. John Van Engen, "Conversion and Conformity in the Early Fifteenth Century," in *Conversion: Old Worlds and New,* ed. Kenneth Mills and Anthony Grafton (Rochester, N.Y.: University of Rochester Press, 2003), 30–65.

68. Van Engen, "Conversion and Conformity," 34–39, 50, 51, quotes on 35, 39, 50, 51.

69. On Brainerd's growing alienation from wealth, see Richard W. Pointer, *Encounters of the Spirit: Native Americans and European Colonial Religion* (Bloomington: Indiana University Press, 2007), 108, 109; and chapter 5, below.

70. Edwards, *Life of Brainerd,* 105–107.

71. Brainerd Diary Fragment, April 27, 1744, Beinecke Library.

72. Brainerd to Pemberton, 30.

73. Brainerd Diary Fragment, April 29 and May 1, 1744, Beinecke Library.

74. Brainerd to Ebenezer Pemberton, 32, 33; Edwards, *Life of Brainerd,* 109. The name of the settlement is uncertain but may have been Hunter's Settlement.

75. Amy Schutt, *Peoples of the River Valleys: The Odyssey of the Delaware Indians* (Philadelphia: University of Pennsylvania Press, 2007), 3; Ives Goddard, "Delaware," in *Northeast,* ed. Bruce G. Trigger, vol. 15 of *Handbook of North American Indians,* ed. William C. Sturtevant (Washington, D.C.: Smithsonian Institution Press, 1978), 213–239; C. A. Weslager, *The Delaware Indians: A History* (New Brunswick, N.J.: Rutgers University Press, 1972), 31–38.

76. Reverend John Heckewelder, *History, Manners and Customs of the Indian Nations Who Once Inhabited Pennsylvania and the Neighbouring States* (1876; reprint, Bowie, Md.: Heritage, 1990), 49–51.

77. Herbert C. Kraft, *The Lenape: Archaeology, History, and Ethnography* (Newark: New Jersey Historical Society, 1986), 26, 41, 45, 52–62, 84, 92–96, 99, 110–114, 117; David J. Werner, "The Zimmerman Site, 36-Pi-14," 126; Patricia Marchiando, "Bell-Browning Site, 28-Sx-19," 147, 154, 155; Herbert C. Kraft, "The Miller Field Site, Warren County, New Jersey," 42, 43, all in *Archeology in the Upper Delaware Valley: A Study of the Cultural Chronology of the Tocks Island Reservoir,* ed. W. Fred Kinsey (Harrisburg: Pennsylvania Historical and Museum Commission, 1972); Weslager, *Delaware Indians,* 56–61; Jay F. Custer, *Prehistoric Cultures of the Delmarva Peninsula: An Archeological Study* (Newark: University of Delaware Press, 1989), 93–103; Schutt, *Peoples of the River Valleys,* 12–21.

78. Schutt, *Peoples of the River Valleys,* 21–27; Weslager, *Delaware Indians,* 61–63.

79. Heckewelder, *History,* 236–238, 254; Weslager, *Delaware Indians,* 66, 67; Kraft, *Lenape,* 161–169, 191, 192; David Zeisberger, "History of the Northern American Indians," translated by Archer Butler Hulbert and William Nathaniel Schwarze, *Ohio Archaeological and Historical Quarterly* 19, nos. 1–2 (January and April 1910), 131; Schutt, *Peoples of the River Valleys,* 27, 28; Axtell, *Invasion Within,* 16, 17.

80. Peter Lindestrom, *Geographia Americae with an Account of the Delaware Indians,* trans. Amandus Johnson (Philadelphia: Swedish Colonial Society, 1925), 207, 208; Zeisberger, "History," 132, 133; Kraft, *Lenape,* 176, 177; Schutt, *Peoples of the River Valleys,* 29, 30; Jane T. Merritt, *At the Crossroads: Indians & Empires on a Mid-Atlantic Frontier, 1700–1763* (Chapel Hill: University of North Carolina Press for the Omohundro Institute of Early American History and Culture, 2003), 105–112; Heckewelder, *History,* 245–248; M. R. Harrington, *Religion and Ceremonies of the Lenape* (New York: Museum of the American Indian, 1921), 61–66.

81. David Brainerd, *Divine Grace Displayed; or, The Continuance and Progress of a Remarkable Work of Grace among Some of the Indians Belonging to the Provinces of New-Jersey and Pennsylvania* (Philadelphia: William Bradford, 1746), 213.

82. Elisabeth Tooker, ed., *Native North American Spirituality of the Eastern Woodlands* (New York: Paulist, 1979), 104–124; Weslager, *Delaware Indians,* 69–71; Kraft, *Lenape,* 169–176; Schutt, *Peoples of the River Valleys,* 29, 30.

83. The following discussion of Delaware-European relations is drawn from Schutt, *Peoples of the River Valleys,* 31–167; Weslager, *Delaware Indians,* 98–172; Francis Jennings, *The Ambiguous Iroquois Empire: The Covenant Chain Confederation of Indian Tribes with English Colonies from Its Beginnings to the Lancaster Treaty of 1744* (New York: Norton, 1984), 116–119, 159–162; Jennings, "'Pennsylvania Indians' and the Iroquois," in *Beyond the Covenant Chain: The Iroquois and Their Neighbors in Indian North America, 1600–1800,* ed. Daniel K. Richter and James H. Merrell (Syracuse, N.Y.: Syracuse University Press, 1987), 75–91; Albright G. Zimmerman, "European Trade Relations in the 17th and 18th Centuries," in *A Delaware Indian Symposium,* ed. Herbert C. Kraft (Harrisburg: Pennsylvania Historical and Museum Commission, 1972), 57–70; Peter C. Mancall, *Deadly Medicine: Indians and Alcohol in Early America* (Ithaca, N.Y.: Cornell University Press, 1995), 42–44; Jay Miller, "The Delaware as Women: A Symbolic Solution," *American Ethnologist* 1, no. 3 (August 1974), 507–514.

84. Gabriel Thomas, "An Historical Account of the Province and Country of Pennsilvania; and of West-New-Jersey in America," in *Narratives of Early Pennsylvania, West New Jersey and Delaware 1630–1707,* ed. Albert Cook Myers (New York: Barnes and Noble, 1967), 309–352, quote on 341.

85. Jennings, *Ambiguous Iroquois Empire,* 271–273, 293, 294, 309–314; Weslager, *Delaware Indians,* 173–178, 184–187; Schutt, *Peoples of the River Valleys,* 74–81.

86. The following discussion of the struggle for the Forks of the Delaware through the period of the Walking Purchase is drawn from Weslager, *Delaware Indians,* 187–190; Jennings, *Ambiguous Iroquois Empire,* 318–342; Schutt, *Peoples of the River Valleys,* 81–89; Jennings, "The Scandalous Indian Policy of William Penn's Sons: Deeds and Documents of the Walking Purchase," *Pennsylvania History* 37 (January–October 1970), 19–39; Steven Craig Harper, *Promised Land: Penn's Holy Experiment, the Walking Purchase, and the Dispossession of the Delawares, 1600–1763* (Bethlehem, Pa.: Lehigh University Press, 2006), 46–86. Dissenting from some of the more broadly accepted interpretations of the events is Marshall Joseph Becker. See, for example, Becker, "The Moravian Mission in the Forks of the Delaware: Reconstructing the Migration and

Settlement Patterns of the Jersey Lenape during the Eighteenth Century through Documents in the Moravian Archives," *Unitas Fratrum* 21 and 22 (1987), 83–168; and Becker, "Native Settlements in the Forks of the Delaware, Pennsylvania, in the 18th Century: Archaeological Implications," *Pennsylvania Archaeologist* 58, no. 1 (1988), 43–60.

87. *PaCR,* 4:575, 576; Schutt, *Peoples of the River Valleys,* 89–93; Weslager, *Delaware Indians,* 190–194; Jennings, *Ambiguous Iroquois Empire,* 342–345; Francis Jennings, "The Delaware Interregnum," *Pennsylvania Magazine of History and Biography* 89, no. 2 (April 1965): 174–198; Miller, "Delaware as Women"; Harper, *Promised Land,* 86–102.

88. *PaCR,* 4:624, 625; Schutt, *Peoples of the River Valleys,* 96–103; William A. Hunter, "Moses (Tunda) Tatamy, Delaware Indian Diplomat," in *A Delaware Indian Symposium,* ed. Herbert C. Kraft (Harrisburg: Pennsylvania Historical and Museum Commission, 1972), 71–88, esp. 73, 74; Anthony F. C. Wallace, *King of the Delawares: Teedyuscung 1700–1763* (Philadelphia: University of Pennsylvania Press, 1949), 38, 39.

89. Harper, *Promised Land,* 71–89, quote on 71; Jennings, *Ambiguous Iroquois Empire,* 345.

90. "The Twelve Little Women," in *The White Deer and Other Stories Told by the Lenape,* ed. John Bierhorst (New York: Morrow, 1995), 99–104.

91. Sally Schwartz, *"A Mixed Multitude": The Struggle for Toleration in Colonial Pennsylvania* (New York: New York University Press, 1987), 81–103, quotes on 93; Thomas J. Sugrue, "The Peopling and Depeopling of Early Pennsylvania: Indians and Colonists, 1680–1720," *Pennsylvania Magazine of History and Biography* 116, no. 1 (January 1992), 3–31; Patrick Griffin, *The People with No Name: Ireland's Ulster Scots, America's Scots Irish, and the Creation of a British Atlantic World, 1689–1764* (Princeton, N.J.: Princeton University Press, 2001), 99–143, 150; Jack P. Greene, *Pursuits of Happiness: The Social Development of Early Modern British Colonies and the Formation of American Culture* (Chapel Hill: University of North Carolina Press, 1988), 137–141; Alan Taylor, *American Colonies: The Settling of North America* (New York: Penguin, 2001), 262, 263; Brendan McConville, *These Daring Disturbers of the Public Peace: The Struggle for Property and Power in Early New Jersey* (Ithaca, N.Y.: Cornell University Press, 1999), 47–66; Ned C. Landsman, *Scotland and Its First American Colony, 1683–1765* (Princeton, N.J.: Princeton University Press, 1985), 99–162.

92. Schwartz, *"Mixed Multitude,"* 103–119; James G. Leyburn, *The Scotch-Irish: A Social History* (Chapel Hill: University of North Carolina Press, 1962), 169–172; Landsman, *Scotland and Its First American Colony,* 169–191; Taylor, *American Colonies,* 262, 263.

93. Joseph Mortimer Levering, *A History of Bethlehem, Pennsylvania, 1741–1892* (1903; reprint, New York: AMS, 1971), 51–83, 107–118, 127–177; Earl P. Olmstead, *David Zeisberger: A Life among the Indians* (Kent, Ohio: Kent State University Press, 1997), 23–33; Elma E. Gray, *Wilderness Christians: The Moravian Mission to the Delaware Indians* (Ithaca, N.Y.: Cornell University Press, 1956), 24–37; Schwartz, *"Mixed Multitude,"* 127–135; Craig Atwood, *Community of the Cross: Moravian Piety in Colonial Bethlehem* (University Park: Pennsylvania State University Press, 2004), 118, 119; Bryan F. Le Beau, *Jonathan Dickinson and the Formative Years of American Presbyterianism* (Lexington: University Press of Kentucky, 1997), 134; Milton Coalter, *Gilbert Tennent, Son of Thunder: A Case Study of Continental Pietism's Impact on the First Great Awakening in the Middle Colonies* (New York: Greenwood, 1986), 96–112.

94. Leyburn, *Scotch-Irish,* 273–277; Schwartz, *"Mixed Multitude,"* 103–112; Griffin, *People with No Name,* 113–115.

95. Marilyn Westerkamp, *Triumph of the Laity: Scots-Irish Piety and the Great Awakening, 1625–1760* (New York: Oxford University Press, 1988), 165–213; Webster, *History of the Presbyterian Church*, 141–143, 162–177, 182–185; Landsman, *Scotland and Its First American Colony*, 175–191, 227–255; Coalter, *Gilbert Tennent*, 55–96, 113–125; Le Beau, *Jonathan Dickinson*, 107–130.

96. Le Beau, *Jonathan Dickinson*, 131–149; Coalter, *Gilbert Tennent*, 113–129; Westerkamp, *Triumph of the Laity*, 208–213; Webster, *History of the Presbyterian Church*, 192–198, 206–217.

97. *PaCR*, 4:675.

98. *PaCR*, 4:677–679, 686, 739.

99. *PaCR*, 4:742–748; James H. Merrell, *Into the American Woods: Negotiators on the Pennsylvania Frontier* (New York: Norton, 1999), 42–53; Jennings, *Ambiguous Iroquois Empire*, 356–363; Schwartz, *"Mixed Multitude,"* 176–178.

100. Brainerd to Pemberton, 33.

101. See, for example, Francis Daniel Pastorius, "Circumstantial and Geographical Description of Pennsylvania," in *Narratives*, ed. Myers, 384, 437.

102. Edwards, *Life of Brainerd*, 109.

103. "SSPCK to Ebenezer Pemberton, September 8, 1743," *Christian Monthly History* 5 March–August, 1744: 29–31, quote on 31; "Correspondents Minutes, April 5, 1744," *Christian Monthly History* 6 (August–December 1744), 20, 21; Edwards, *Life of Brainerd*, 111; Dexter, *Biographical Sketches*, I:45, 46.

104. Edwards, *Life of Brainerd*, 111, 112; "Ebenezer Pemberton to the SSPCK, June, 1744," *Christian Monthly History* 6:August–December, 1744 17–19, quote on 18, 19.

105. Ebenezer Pemberton, *A Sermon Preached in New-ark, June 12, 1744, at the Ordination of Mr. David Brainerd* (Boston: Rogers & Fowle, 1744), quotes on 11, 12, 13, 15.

106. Pemberton, *Sermon Preached*, 17, 18; Edwards, *Life of Brainerd*, 112.

107. Edwards, *Life of Brainerd*, 109–111, 114–120; Brainerd Diary Leaf, Morgan Library, New York, MA unacc. RV Auto. Misc American.

108. Edwards, *Life of Brainerd*, 121.

109. Schutt, *Peoples of the River Valleys*, 27–30.

110. Edwards, *Life of Brainerd*, 121, 122.

111. Edwards, *Life of Brainerd*, 122.

112. Carole Blackburn, *Harvest of Souls: The Jesuit Missions and Colonialism in North America, 1632–1650* (Montreal: McGill-Queen's University Press, 2000), 33–35.

113. Edwards, *Life of Brainerd*, 121, 122.

114. Edwards, *Life of Brainerd*, 125.

115. Brainerd to Pemberton, 34.

116. Edwards, *Life of Brainerd*, 125, 126.

117. SSPCK Records, GMM 4:123–125, 156, 157; Sergeant Diary, in Hopkins, *Historical Memoirs*, 88–92, quote on 91.

118. In a footnote commenting on Brainerd's initial decision to work among the Indians, Edwards described the scope of Brainerd's mission as "the Indians living near the Forks of Delaware River in Pennsylvania and the Indians on the Susquehanneh [sic] River."

119. David Brainerd Diary, Gratz Collection, Historical Society of Pennsylvania.

120. Brainerd to Pemberton, 34, 35.

121. Peter C. Mancall, *Valley of Opportunity: Economic Culture along the Upper Susquehanna, 1700–1800* (Ithaca, N.Y.: Cornell University Press, 1991), 27–43; Schutt, *Peoples of the River Valleys*, 64–74; Weslager, *Delaware Indians*, 197, 198; Jennings, *Ambiguous Iroquois Empire*, 289–304.

122. Edwards, *Life of Brainerd,* 126, 127; Brainerd to Pemberton, 35. On the name of the village, see Becker, "Native Settlements in the Forks of the Delaware," 55.

123. Brainerd to Pemberton, 35; Edwards, *Life of Brainerd,* 127, 128.

124. Brainerd Diary Fragment, October 6 and 7, in Brainard, *Genealogy,* unnumbered pages.

125. Brainerd to Pemberton, 35, 36; Edwards, *Life of Brainerd,* 126–128; Brainerd Diary Fragment, October 6 and 7, in Brainard, *Genealogy,* unnumbered pages.

126. Edwards, *Life of Brainerd,* 134, 143.

127. Brainerd to Pemberton, 33, 37, 38; David Brainerd, Diary Fragment, July 20 and 26, Gratz Collection, Historical Society of Pennsylvania.

128. Merrell, *Into the American Woods,* 19–27, 129–136, quote on 130; Brainerd to John Sergeant, March 25, 1745, Historical Society of Pennsylvania, Ferdinand J. Dreer Collection, 125:1, American Clergy, vol. II.

129. Edwards, *Life of Brainerd,* 109, 123. Further notations regarding preaching at this settlement can be found on 140, 151, and (probably) 153. On the specific location, see John Cunningham Clyde, "The Scotch-Irish of the Forks of the Delaware," in his *The Scotch-Irish of Northampton County* (Northampton, Pa.: Northampton County Historical and Genealogical Society, 1926), I:424–517. See also Clyde, *History of the Allen Township Presbyterian Church* (Philadelphia: Presbyterian Historical Society, 1876), 9–21.

130. Edwards, *Life of Brainerd,* 129. Although Edwards did not name the settlement, it was probably not the same place as the one near where Brainerd lived, as Edwards was usually specific about that location; Edwards, *Life of Brainerd,* 135, 136, 144; Webster, *History of the Presbyterian Church,* 184, 185.

131. Edwards, *Life of Brainerd,* 146, 147.

132. Westerkamp, *Triumph of the Laity,* 212, 213; Theodore G. Tappert, "The Influence of Pietism in Colonial American Lutheranism," in *Continental Pietism and Early American Christianity,* ed. F. Ernest Stoeffler (Grand Rapids, Mich.: Eerdmans, 1976), 13–33; James Tanis, "Reformed Pietism in Colonial America," in *Continental Pietism and Early American Christianity,* ed. Stoeffler, 34–73.

133. Edwards, *Life of Brainerd,* 148.

134. Brainerd to Sergeant, March 25, 1745, Historical Society of Pennsylvania.

135. Edwards, *Life of Brainerd,* 149; on the importance of written communications, see Merrell, *Into the American Woods,* 193–197.

136. Exactly when Tatamy underwent his conversion experience is not clear. Brainerd's account of the process was entered in his public diary in July 1745 on the day he baptized Tatamy and his wife. In February, Brainerd had noted the absence of his translator, who was definitely with him when he went to the Susquehanna in May. Brainerd was in New England for most of March and the first part of April. So it seems likely that the February–May window corresponds to the time during which Tatamy suffered through his preconversion agonies. See Edwards, *Life of Brainerd,* 147–149.

137. On Tatamy, see Hunter, "Moses (Tunda) Tatamy."

138. Brainerd, *Mirabilia Dei Inter Indios; or, The Rise and Progress of a Remarkable Work of Grace among a Number of Indians in the Provinces of New-Jersey and Pennsylvania* (Philadelphia: William Bradford, 1746), 9, 10. The full description of Tatamy's conversion is at 7–15.

139. Edwards, *Life of Brainerd,* 136, 138.

140. Brainerd, *Mirabilia,* 10, 11.

141. Brainerd, *Mirabilia,* 11.

142. Brainerd, *Mirabilia,* 8, 13.

143. Brainerd, *Mirabilia,* 66.

144. Brainerd, *Mirabilia,* 70.

145. Brainerd, *Mirabilia,* 71, 72.

146. Silverman, *Faith and Boundaries,* 33–38, quotes on 33. Silverman makes a similar point about the differences between English mission efforts and those of the Spanish and French on p. 34.

147. Brainerd, *Mirabilia,* 71. See also Richard Pointer, *Encounters of the Spirit: Native Americans and European Colonial Religion* (Bloomington: Indiana University Press, 2007), 114–116.

148. James H. Merrell, "Shamokin, 'the Very Seat of the Prince of Darkness': Unsettling the Early American Frontier," in *Contact Points: American Frontiers from the Mohawk Valley to the Mississippi, 1750–1830,* ed. Andrew R. L. Cayton and Fredrika J. Teute (Chapel Hill: University of North Carolina Press, 1998), 16–59, esp. 22–25.

149. Merrell, "Shamokin," 24–29; Mancall, *Valley of Opportunity,* 27–70; and Mancall, *Deadly Medicine,* 51, 52, 60, 87, 114.

150. Merrell, "Shamokin," 18; Mancall, *Valley of Opportunity,* 36, 37; Brainerd, *Mirabilia,* 43.

151. Edwards, *Life of Brainerd,* 152, 153; "Bishop A. G. Spangenberg's Journal of a Journey to Onondaga in 1745," in *Moravian Journals Relating to Central New York, 1745–1766,* ed. William M. Beauchamp (1916; reprint, New York: AMS, 1976), 7.

152. Merritt, *At the Crossroads,* 72, 73.

153. Brainerd, *Mirabilia,* 53–56, quotes on 53. On various aspects of the rise and practices of the Indian, particularly Delaware, prophets, see Merritt, *At the Crossroads,* 123, 124; and Gregory Evans Dowd, *A Spirited Resistance: The North American Indian Struggle for Unity, 1745–1815* (Baltimore, Md.: Johns Hopkins University Press, 1992), 23–33, esp. 27–29 for the Otseningo seer and Brainerd's encounter.

154. Brainerd, *Mirabilia,* 54–56.

155. Pointer, *Encounters of the Spirit,* 117, 118, quote on 117.

156. Edwards, *Life of Brainerd,* 152, 153, quotes on 153.

157. Edwards, *Life of Brainerd,* 149, 150.

158. Edwards, *Life of Brainerd,* 154, 155.

159. Edwards, *Life of Brainerd,* 155.

160. Brainerd, *Mirabilia,* 1.

Chapter 3

1. SSPCK Records, GMM 4:387; "Edwards to the Reverend John MacLaurin," *JEY* 16:203–207, quote on 206; Jonathan Dickinson to Thomas Foxcroft, April 9, 1746, Thomas Foxcroft Selected Correspondence, Manuscripts Division, Department of Rare Books and Special Collections, Princeton University Library, used by permission.

2. The public journal was originally published in two parts. The first part was entitled *Mirabilia Dei Inter Indios; or, The Rise and Progress of a Remarkable Work of Grace among a Number of the Indians in the Provinces of New-Jersey and Pennsylvania* (Philadelphia: William Bradford, 1746). The second part, published later the same year, was entitled *Divine Grace Displayed; or, The Continuance and Progress of a Remarkable Work of Grace among Some of the Indians Belonging to the Provinces of New-Jersey and Pennsylvania* (Philadelphia: William Bradford, 1746). The two volumes have continuous pagination and came to be published as one volume usually referred to as *Mr. Brainerd's Journal among*

the Indians. Here, I will refer to the two separately as Brainerd, *Mirabilia,* and Brainerd, *Divine Grace.* For the publication history of Brainerd's public journal, see Norman Pettit, "Editor's Introduction," in *JEY* 7:74. Edwards, *Life of Brainerd,* does cover this period but mostly focuses on Brainerd's personal life.

3. "Letters of Instructions to Missionaries," in *An Abridgement of the Statutes and Rules of the Society in Scotland for Propagating Christian Knowledge* (Edinburgh: Robert Fleming, 1732), 47.

4. SSPCK Records, GMM 4:335 and 367. The SSPCK reviewed a journal in November 1744, although that has not survived. A second journal, which corresponds to most of the second half of the public journal which was published in 1746, is held in the Edinburgh University Library's Special Collections (Dc.7.68). See appendix I.

5. Horton's journal survived since it was published in *Christian Monthly History.* It was republished in 1993 as part of John Strong, "Azariah Horton's Mission to the Montauk, 1741–44," in *The History and Archaeology of the Montauk,* ed. Gaynell Stone (Stony Brook, N.Y.: Suffolk County Archaeological Association and Nassau County Archaeological Committee, 1993), 191–220.

6. Frank Lambert, *Inventing the "Great Awakening"* (Princeton, N.J.: Princeton University Press, 1999), 143–150. Prince's letter is reproduced on 146, and the quotations are taken from that reproduction.

7. Michael Crawford, *Seasons of Grace: Colonial New England's Revival Tradition in Its British Context* (New York: Oxford University Press, 1991), 183–195; Lambert, *Inventing,* 148, 149; Samuel Blair, *Short and Faithful Narrative, of the Late Remarakable* [*sic*] *Revival of Religion in the Congregation of New-Londonderry and Other Parts of Pennsylvania: As the Same Was Sent in a Letter to the Rev. Mr. Prince of Boston* (Philadelphia: William Bradford, 1744).

8. Richard W. Pointer, *Encounters of the Spirit: Native Americans and European Colonial Religion* (Bloomington: Indiana University Press, 2007), 115, 235n59.

9. Edwards, *Life of Brainerd,* 155.

10. Brainerd, *Mirabilia,* 1.

11. C. A. Weslager, *The Delaware Indians: A History* (New Brunswick, N.J.: Rutgers University Press, 1972), 261; Jane T. Merritt, *At the Crossroads: Indians & Empires on a Mid-Atlantic Frontier, 1700–1763* (Chapel Hill: University of North Carolina Press for the Omohundro Institute of Early American History and Culture, 2003), 154.

12. James Axtell, *The Invasion Within: The Contest of Cultures in Colonial North America* (New York: Oxford University Press, 1985), 280; James H. Merrell, "'The Customes of Our Country': Indians and Colonists in Early America," in *Strangers within the Realm: Cultural Margins of the First British Empire,* ed. Bernard Bailyn and Philip D. Morgan (Chapel Hill: University of North Carolina Press for the Omohundro Institute of Early American History and Culture, 1991), 117–156, esp. 148–152, quote on 148.

13. Edwards, *Life of Brainerd,* 157 (quote); Brainerd, *Mirabilia,* 1, 2.

14. Brainerd, *Mirabilia,* 2.

15. Merritt, *At the Crossroads,* 103, 104; Gunlög Fur, "Reading Margins: Colonial Encounters in Sápmi and Lenapehoking in the Seventeenth and Eighteenth Centuries," *Feminist Studies* 32, no. 3 (Fall 2006), 491–521, esp. 506–508 and 515–517; Fur, "'Some Women Are Wiser than Some Men': Gender and Native American History," in *Clearing a Path: Theorizing the Past in Native American Studies,* ed. Nancy Shoemaker (New York: Routledge, 2002), 75–103, esp. 88–91.

16. Brainerd, *Mirabilia,* 2, 3.

17. Brainerd, *Mirabilia,* 3, 4.

18. Kenneth M. Morrison, *The Solidarity of Kin: Ethnohistory, Religious Studies, and the Algonkian-French Religious Encounter* (Albany: State University of New York Press, 2002), 91. For a similar account among the Montagnais, see Axtell, *Invasion Within,* 100.

19. Merritt, *At the Crossroads,* 96, 97.

20. Brainerd, *Mirabilia,* 5–7, 16; Edwards, *Life of Brainerd,* 158, 159.

21. Ned C. Landsman, *Scotland and Its First American Colony, 1683–1765* (Princeton, N.J.: Princeton University Press, 1985), 177–191, 227–255.

22. Brainerd, *Mirabilia,* 7–16, quotes on 7, 8, 15; Edwards, *Life of Brainerd,* 159, 160, quote on 160.

23. Brainerd, *Mirabilia,* 16, 17.

24. Brainerd, *Mirabilia,* 17–20, quote on 19.

25. Brainerd, *Mirabilia,* 20, 21.

26. Brainerd, *Mirabilia,* 21.

27. Douglas L. Winiarski, "Jonathan Edwards, Enthusiast? Radical Revivalism and the Great Awakening in the Connecticut Valley," *Church History* 74, no. 4 (December 2005), 683–739. In particular, see the eyewitness account of these events on 736–739.

28. Brainerd, *Mirabilia,* 25–27, quotes on 25, 26.

29. Brainerd, *Mirabilia,* 27–30, quotes on 8, 29, 33.

30. Brainerd, *Mirabilia,* 27–34, quotes on 29, 33, 34, 73.

31. Brainerd, *Mirabilia,* 29, 34, 35.

32. Brainerd, *Mirabilia,* 35; Edwards, *Life of Brainerd,* 161.

33. Brainerd, *Mirabilia,* 34–36.

34. Brainerd, *Mirabilia,* 37, 38.

35. Brainerd, *Mirabilia,* 39, 40.

36. Brainerd, *Mirabilia,* 41–44, quotes on 42, 44; Edwards, *Life of Brainerd,* 162, 163, quotes on 163.

37. Brainerd, *Mirabilia,* 44, 45; MAB–IND, Martin Mack, "Shamokin Diary," September 25, 1745, reel 28, box 217, folder 12b.

38. Brainerd, *Mirabilia,* 45, 46; Edwards, *Life of Brainerd,* 164.

39. Brainerd, *Mirabilia,* 46–49.

40. Brainerd, *Mirabilia,* 49–57, quotes on 50, 54.

41. Edwards, *Life of Brainerd,* 165.

42. Brainerd, *Mirabilia,* 55.

43. Brainerd, *Mirabilia,* 57–59; Richard W. Pointer, "'Poor Indians' and the 'Poor in Spirit': The Indian Impact on David Brainerd," *NEQ* 67, no. 3 (September 1994), 403, 421.

44. He probably finished the journal during a three-week trip through New Jersey to raise money to support a schoolteacher at Crossweeksung. During this time, he spent several days at Elizabeth-town and Freehold. See Edwards, *Life of Brainerd,* 167, 168.

45. Brainerd, *Mirabilia,* 65–67.

46. Brainerd, *Mirabilia,* 67–72, quotes on 67, 68.

47. Brainerd, *Mirabilia,* 72–74.

48. Brainerd, *Mirabilia,* 72, 73.

49. Pemberton, *Sermon Preached,* 3, 13; Brainerd, *Mirabilia,* 70–72, 76. On the issue of Brainerd's shift in the emphasis of his sermons, both Paul Harris and Richard Pointer have posited that Tatamy suggested to Brainerd that he change his focus; they argue that Tatamy would have heard this kind of message from the Moravians. See Paul Harris, "David Brainerd and the Indians: Cultural Interaction and Protestant Missionary Ideology," *American Presbyterians* 72, no. 1 (Spring 1994), 1–9; and Pointer, "'Poor Indians' and

the 'Poor in Spirit.'" While attractive, this thesis raises several questions. First, Brainerd began to emphasize the compassion of God in sermons he delivered while Tatamy was absent undergoing his own spiritual travail. And, although these sermons were preached to colonists, it would have been logical for him to use a successful model with the Indians. Second, if we accept that Tatamy underwent some kind of conversion due to his time with Brainerd, then it follows that he did not believe he had been converted or come to true religion owing to his experiences with the Moravians. It does not seem to follow that he would then come to Brainerd and suggest he follow the Moravian model, one which Tatamy's own actions seemed to invalidate. However, I should stress that there is simply not enough evidence to provide a definitive answer. My own reading of Brainerd persuades me of the argument I have put forth, but both Harris and Pointer make strong cases for their analyses. For the record, Brainerd only commented that it was God who "enabled me in a Manner somewhat *uncommon* to set before them the *Lord Jesus Christ* as a kind and compassionate Saviour." See *Mirabilia*, 16, 17.

The claims of earlier Moravian historians that their missionaries were responsible for Brainerd's shift are questionable for two reasons. First, at the time that many of the Moravians were writing these accounts, they were seeking to rebuild an image in England that had been tarnished, and linking themselves with Brainerd may have been an attempt to help in this effort. See J. C. S. Mason, *The Moravian Church and the Missionary Awakening in England, 1760–1800* (Rochester, N.Y.: Boydell Press and the Royal Historical Society, 2001), 9–44, 151, 152. Apparently, the earliest claim of a Moravian influence on Brainerd came in 1767 in David Cranz's *The History of Greenland*. Cranz declared, without documentation, that "[w]e are credibly informed":

> [A]s long as [Brainerd] continued the usual method of preaching, and endeavoured to convince the Indians by arguments, he could effect nothing; but...as soon as he benefited by the example of his neighbours [i.e., the Moravians], of whose success he was an eye-witness, and ventured without any preface, to preach the Saviour and his love, to the benighted natives such an extensive awakening ensued, that both he and all the ministers of his persuasion who witnessed it, were astonished, and led to ascribe glory to God.

See Cranz, *The History of Greenland*...(London: Longman, Hurst, Rees, Orme, and Brown, 1820), 216, 217. Other Moravian claims are less credible since the authors seem confused as to which Brainerd they are discussing. George Loskiel, writing in 1794, told of three Moravian leaders who, in early 1749

> went to a town in the Jerseys where Mr. Brainard had preached the gospel to the Indians, baptized about fifty, and made some good regulations among them. They wished him all possible success. The Brethren in Bethlehem were also of opinion, that they ought not in the least to interfere with the labors of this good man among the Indians, but rather to support him with their prayers.

See Loskiel, *History of the Mission of the United Brethren*, 114. Even more confused was John Heckewelder, who asserted that Moravians had visited the "Rev. David Brainerd" in July 1747 at his mission in New Jersey and that "some time after this," Brainerd visited the Moravians in Bethlehem. Since Brainerd was sick in bed in Boston and Northampton in July 1747 and was deceased by October, Heckewelder, too, must be referring to John. See Heckewelder, *A Narrative of the Mission of the United Brethren among the Delaware and Mohegan Indians, from Its Commencement, in the Year 1740, to the Close of the Year 1808* (Philadelphia: McCarty and Davis, 1820), 38.

50. Brainerd, *Mirabilia,* 68–70.

51. Brainerd, *Mirabilia,* 77–79; David Brainerd to Eleazar Wheelock, December 30, 1745, in Papers of Eleazar Wheelock, No. 745680, courtesy of Dartmouth College Library. For those wont to see the shadow of Jerusha Edwards and matrimony in these words, Brainerd noted to Bradford that he had been encouraged to find a "man who might be my companion."

52. Brainerd, *Mirabilia,* 78, 79.

53. Brainerd, *Divine Grace,* 83–91, quotes on 90, 91.

54. Brainerd, *Divine Grace,* 90; "The Shorter Catechism," had been in common use since 1647, is in *The Constitution of the Presbyterian Church in the United States of America* (Philadelphia: Presbyterian Board of Publication, 1839), 381–404; Norman Pettit, *JEY* 7:345n.

55. Nicholas P. Cushner, *Why Have You Come Here? The Jesuits and the First Evangelization of Native America* (New York: Oxford University Press, 2006), 87–93.

56. Silverman, *Faith and Boundaries,* 49–63; Hopkins, *Historical Memoirs,* 59.

57. Brainerd, *Divine Grace,* 84, 90, 129–131, 141, 142, 184, 185, 228. The questions and the expected answers are on 202–207. See also Silverman, *Faith and Boundaries,* 56–60.

58. Brainerd, *Divine Grace,* 99.

59. Brainerd, *Divine Grace,* 100–103.

60. "David Brainerd to John Brainerd," in Edwards, *Life of Brainerd,* 268.

61. Brainerd, *Divine Grace,* 105–107.

62. *A Letter from the Revd Mr. Sergeant of Stockbridge, to Dr. Colman of Boston* (Boston: D. Henchman, 1743), 3; Brainerd, *Divine Grace,* 105–107, 112. Brainerd's surviving records do not identify the schoolmaster. Norman Pettit suggested his name may have been Ebenezer Hayward. See *JEY* 7:359n3. The Axtell quote is from *Invasion Within,* 188; and see also Axtell, "The Power of Print in the Eastern Woodlands," in his *After Columbus: Essays in the Ethnohistory of Colonial North America* (New York: Oxford University Press, 1988), 86–99.

63. Brainerd, *Divine Grace,* 143.

64. "Shorter Catechism," 399.

65. Leigh Eric Schmidt, *Holy Fairs: Scottish Communions and American Revivals in the Early Modern Period,* 2nd ed. (Grand Rapids, Mich.: Eerdmans, 2001), 11–55; Arthur Fawcett, *The Cambuslang Revival* (London: Banner of Truth Trust, 1971), 115, 118–123; Crawford, *Seasons of Grace,* 218, 219; Landsman, *Scotland and Its First American Colony,* 227–255; Erik R. Seeman, *Pious Persuasions: Laity and Clergy in Eighteenth-Century New England* (Baltimore, Md.: Johns Hopkins University Press, 1999), 96–106.

66. Brainerd, *Divine Grace,* 143–153, quotes on 147, 148, 149, 151; Schmidt, *Holy Fairs,* 55.

67. Edwards, *Life of Brainerd,* 161.

68. Brainerd, *Divine Grace,* 112, 113.

69. Cushner, *Why Have You Come Here?* 71–75 (Sinaloa), 152, 153 (New France). On the praying towns, among a large number of works, see Jean M. O'Brien, *Dispossession by Degrees: Indian Land and Identity in Natick, Massachusetts, 1650–1790* (New York: Cambridge University Press, 1997); and Richard W. Cogley, *John Eliot's Mission to the Indians before King Philip's War* (Cambridge, Mass.: Harvard University Press, 1999). Quote on Stockbridge from Hopkins, *Historical Memoirs,* 43; Brainerd scouted lands for the Delawares at the Forks within six weeks of his arrival there, Edwards, *Life of Brainerd,* 115.

70. Sergeant, *Letter,* 6; Axtell, *Invasion Within,* 148–167; Cushner, *Why Have You Come Here?* 152, 153; Francis G. Hutchins, *Mashpee: The Story of Cape Cod's Indian Town* (West Franklin, N.H.: Amarta, 1979), 66–69, 88, 89.

71. Brainerd, *Divine Grace,* 135, 136, 139; Edwards, *Life of Brainerd,* 177; Pointer, *Encounters of the Spirit,* 114.

72. Brainerd, *Mirabilia,* 64; Brainerd, *Divine Grace,* 103, 132, 135.

73. Richard White, *The Middle Ground: Indians, Empires, and Republics in the Great Lakes Region, 1650–1815* (Cambridge: Cambridge University Press, 1991), 14–18.

74. Brainerd, *Divine Grace,* 110, 111; Edwards, *Life of Brainerd,* 174.

75. Edwards, *Life of Brainerd,* 173, 174.

76. Michael C. Batinski, *The New Jersey Assembly, 1738–1775: The Making of a Legislative Community* (Lanham, Md.: University Press of America, 1987), 121–125, 147; Thomas L. Purvis, *Proprietors, Patronage, and Paper Money: Legislative Politics in New Jersey, 1703–1776* (New Brunswick, N.J.: Rutgers University Press, 1986), 200–216; Brendan McConville, *These Daring Disturbers of the Public Peace: The Struggle for Property and Power in Early New Jersey* (Ithaca, N.Y.: Cornell University Press, 1999), 116–145. The process was, of course, much more complex than this. Both Purvis and McConville offer excellent studies of the causes, events, and consequences.

77. McConville, *These Daring Disturbers,* 69–76, 85–87.

78. James Alexander and Robert Hunter Morris, "State of the Facts, Concerning the Late Riots at Newark in the County of Essex, & in Other Parts of New Jersey; December 24, 1746," *New Jersey Archives* VI:397–418, quotes on 397, 398.

79. Alexander and Morris, "State of the Facts," 406, 407.

80. Alexander and Morris, "State of the Facts," 398, 406; Schwartz, *"Mixed Multitude,"* 177, 178.

81. Edwards, *Life of Brainerd,* 178, 179; Brainerd, *Divine Grace,* 143, 144.

82. Brainerd, *Divine Grace,* 144n; Edwards, *Life of Brainerd,* 180.

83. Le Beau, *Jonathan Dickinson,* 175, 176; McConville, *These Daring Disturbers,* 145, 146. For a different perspective on Brainerd's role in the land dispute, see Harris, "Brainerd and the Indians," 7, 8.

84. See, for example, Schutt, *Peoples of the River Valleys,* 74–93; Alan Taylor, *The Divided Ground: Indians, Settlers, and the Northern Borderlands of the American Revolution* (New York: Knopf, 2006), 34–45; Daniel Mandell, *Behind the Frontier: Indians in Eighteenth-Century Massachusetts* (Lincoln: University of Nebraska Press, 1996), 66–71.

85. Schwartz, *"Mixed Multitude,"* 92–99; Maldwyn A. Jones, "The Scotch-Irish in British America," in *Strangers within the Realm: Cultural Margins of the First British Empire,* ed. Bernard Bailyn and Philip D. Morgan (Chapel Hill: University of North Carolina Press for the Institute of Early American History and Culture, 1991), 296; Merrell, *Into the American Woods,* 158–167; Griffin, *People with No Name,* 113–114, 136–143.

86. John Wood Sweet, *Bodies Politic: Negotiating Race in the American North, 1730–1830* (Baltimore, Md.: Johns Hopkins University Press, 2003), 105, 106.

87. McConville, *These Daring Disturbers,* 167–174.

88. Merritt, *At the Crossroads,* 36.

89. Brainerd, *Divine Grace,* 129, 131–135.

90. SSPCK Records, GMM 4:374, 375, 379, 388.

91. Brainerd, *Mirabilia,* 40.

92. Brainerd, *Divine Grace,* 116–118.

93. Peggy Brock, "New Christians as Evangelists," in *Missions and Empire,* ed. Norman Etherington (New York: Oxford University Press, 2005), 132–152, esp. 132–134 and 150–152, quote on 133.

94. Silverman, *Faith and Boundaries,* 60–63; Douglas L. Winiarski, "Native American Popular Culture," *Religion and American Culture* 15, no. 2 (2005), 147–186, esp. 156, 157;

Sergeant Diary in Hopkins, *Historical Memoirs,* 61; Axtell, *Invasion Within,* 225–227; Mandell, *Behind the Frontier,* 56. See also Brock, "New Christians as Evangelists," for similar results in Africa.

95. Edwards, *Life of Brainerd,* 194, 198–200, quotes on 194 and 200.

96. Edwards, *Life of Brainerd,* 200–205.

97. Ian K. Steele, *The English Atlantic, 1675–1740: An Exploration of Commerce and Communication* (New York: Oxford University Press, 1986), 265–268; Michael Warner, *The Letters of the Republic: Publication and the Public Sphere in Eighteenth-Century America* (Cambridge, Mass.: Harvard University Press, 1990), 19–26; David Brainerd to William Bradford, September 20, 1746, Gen. Mss. 214, David Brainerd Miscellaneous Diaries and Papers, folder 5, Beinecke Library; David Brainerd to William Bradford, April 20, 1747, Gratz Collection, case 8, box 21, Historical Society of Pennsylvania; Frank Lambert, "'Pedlar in Divinity': George Whitefield and the Great Awakening, 1737–1745," *JAH* 77, no. 3 (December 1990), 812–837; Susan O'Brien, "Eighteenth-Century Publishing Networks in the First Years of Transatlantic Evangelicalism," in *Evangelicalism: Comparative Studies of Popular Protestantism in North America, the British Isles, and Beyond, 1700–1990,* ed. Mark A. Noll, David W. Bebbington, and George A. Rawlyk (New York: Oxford University Press, 1994), 38–57, esp. 41–43.

98. Brainerd, *Divine Grace,* 169.

99. Brainerd, *Divine Grace,* 174–181, quote on 177.

100. Brainerd, *Divine Grace,* 89, 91, 92, 104.

101. Quoted in Lambert, *Inventing,* 146.

102. This account of the conversion is from Brainerd, *Divine Grace,* 154–160, although the man was previously mentioned in *Mirabilia,* 22, and *Divine Grace,* 113.

103. Brainerd, *Divine Grace,* 187, 188. He made a similar disclaimer at the end of the first part of the public journal; see *Mirabilia,* 75.

104. Brainerd, *Divine Grace,* 160, 161.

105. Brainerd, *Divine Grace,* 220–226, quotes on 224, 226; Carole Blackburn, *Harvest of Souls: The Jesuit Missions and Colonialism in North America, 1632–1650* (Montreal: McGill-Queen's University Press, 2000), 31–34.

106. Brainerd, *Divine Grace,* 218–220. See also Merritt, *At the Crossroads,* 108–112, on Delawares and dreams.

107. Brainerd, *Divine Grace,* 94–98.

108. Brainerd, *Divine Grace,* 191.

109. Brainerd, *Divine Grace,* 191.

110. Brainerd, *Divine Grace,* 169, 183, 249–253. One of Tennent's elders who signed the attestation was Walter Ker, a well-respected and -connected farmer and landowner. See Landsman, *Scotland and Its First American Colony,* 3, 180–182, 188–190, 221, 244–246, 249.

111. Axtell, *Invasion Within,* 280.

112. Kenneth M. Morrison, *The Solidarity of Kin: Ethnohistory, Religious Studies, and the Algonkian-French Religious Encounter* (Albany: State University of New York Press, 2002), in particular the chapter "The Solidarity of Kin: The Intersection of Eastern Algonkian and French-Catholic Cosmologies," 147–172, quotes on 147, 161, 172. In attempting to explain the work of both scholars (see the following note for the citation for Salisbury) in such a short space, I realize I run the risk of mischaracterizing their arguments, but I trust I have not done so. I also recognize that much of the discussion which follows implicitly rejects a great deal of Morrison's argument. Regardless, those interested in the scholarly analysis of conversion can do worse than to start with these two books and with the broader scholarship of both men.

113. Neal Salisbury, "'I Loved the Place of My Dwelling': Puritan Missionaries and Native Americans in Seventeenth-Century Southern New England," in *Inequality in Early America,* ed. Carla Gardina Pestana and Sharon V. Salinger (Hanover, N.H.: University Press of New England, 1999), 111–133, quote on 113.

114. William S. Simmons, "Red Yankees: Narragansett Conversion in the Great Awakening," *American Ethnologist* 10, no. 2 (May 1983), 253–271, esp. point 5 on 266, 267.

115. Silverman, *Faith and Boundaries,* 33–38, 52, 53; Cushner, *Why Have You Come Here?* 87–93; Viviana Díaz Balsera, *The Pyramid under the Cross: Franciscan Discourses of Evangelization and the Nahua Christian Subject in Sixteenth-Century Mexico* (Tucson: University of Arizona Press, 2005), 27–29, quote on 29; Ramón A. Gutiérrez, *When Jesus Came, the Corn Mothers Went Away* (Stanford, Calif.: Stanford University Press, 1991), 58–64.

116. Elisabeth Tooker, ed., *Native North American Spirituality of the Eastern Woodlands* (New York: Paulist, 1979), 69, 70.

117. Christopher P. Gavaler, "The Empty Lot: Spiritual Contact in Lenape and Moravian Religious Beliefs," *American Indian Quarterly* 18, no. 2 (Spring 1994), 215–228. Gavaler was addressing the contrast between Moravians and Delawares, but his points are relevant to my argument here.

118. My discussion of this issue owes much to Richard Pointer's analysis of Brainerd, although we disagree on some issues. See Pointer, "'Poor Indians' and the 'Poor in Spirit'"; and Pointer, *Encounters of the Spirit,* 103–121.

119. Edwards, *Life of Brainerd,* 67, 68.

120. Brainerd, *Divine Grace,* 147.

121. Pointer, *Encounters of the Spirit,* 115.

122. Edwards, *Life of Brainerd,* 178; Pointer, *Encounters of the Spirit,* 114.

123. Brainerd to Pemberton, 36, 37; Brainerd, *Divine Grace,* 208, 209.

124. Brainerd, *Divine Grace,* 209–211.

125. Brainerd, *Mirabilia,* 29, 37.

126. Brainerd, *Mirabilia,* 69.

127. Brainerd, *Mirabilia,* 60, 61.

128. Nancy Shoemaker, *A Strange Likeness: Becoming Red and White in Eighteenth-Century North America* (New York: Oxford University Press, 2004), 129, 130, 134–137.

129. Brainerd to Pemberton, 37; Brainerd, *Mirabilia,* 56, 57.

130. Brainerd, *Divine Grace,* 208.

131. Brainerd, *Divine Grace,* 242, 243. It is also almost certain that this was a last-minute addition that Brainerd was forced to add to satisfy a procedural rule of the SSPCK. In doing so, it is probable that Brainerd recycled and expanded the appendix he had added to his November 1744 report to Pemberton. Although the evidence, in my mind, is persuasive, the explanation itself is far too lengthy and tedious to go into here.

132. Edwards, *Life of Brainerd,* 204–213.

133. Edwards, *Life of Brainerd,* 213–217, quotes on 214, 215.

134. "David Brainerd to Israel Brainerd," in Edwards, *Life of Brainerd,* 268, 269.

135. Edwards, *Life of Brainerd,* 217.

136. Edwards, *Life of Brainerd,* 218.

137. Richard Webster, *A History of the Presbyterian Church in America, from Its Origin until the Year 1760* (Philadelphia: Joseph M. Wilson, 1857), 563–568; SSPCK Records, GMM 4:397; Edwards, *Life of Brainerd,* 220.

138. John Brainerd to Ebenezer Pemberton, quoted in Thomas Brainerd, *The Life of John Brainerd* (Philadelphia: Presbyterian Publication Committee, 1861), 116–118.

139. John Brainerd Journal, in Brainerd, *Life of John Brainerd,* 119.

140. Brainerd, *Life of John Brainerd,* 142, 143; Edwards, *Life of Brainerd,* 230.

141. "Job Strong to His Parents," quoted in Brainerd, *Life of John Brainerd,* 144, 145.

142. SSPCK Records, GMM 4:426.

143. SSPCK Records, GMM 4:436, 447, 448, 450, 451, 516, 570; 5:38; Weslager, *Delaware Indians,* 261–281; Pettit, "Editor's Introduction," *JEY* 7:65–67; Webster, *History of the Presbyterian Church,* 563–568; Burr, *The Journal of Esther Edwards Burr,* ed. Carol F. Karlsen and Laurie Crumpacker (New Haven, Conn.: Yale University Press, 1984), 208, 209.

144. William A. Hunter, "Moses (Tunda) Tatamy, Delaware Indian Diplomat," in *A Delaware Indian Symposium,* ed. Herbert C. Kraft (Harrisburg: Pennsylvania Historical and Museum Commission, 1974), 71–88.

145. Richard C. Hasler, "David Zeisberger's 'Jersey Connection,'" *Transactions of the Moravian Historical Society* 30 (1998): 37–53; Goshen Diary, box 171, folder 12, item 1; and box 171, folder 11, item 1, MAB–IND.

146. "Indians West of Missouri: Extracts from a Letter of Mr. Byington: Early Missionary Labors among the Indians," *Missionary Herald* 30, no. 12 (December 1834), 453–455; William R. Hutchison, *Errand to the World: American Protestant Thought and Foreign Missions* (Chicago, Ill.: University of Chicago Press, 1987), 63–69.

147. "Relics of Early Indian Churches," *Missionary Herald* 30, no. 12(December, 1834): 454, 455.

148. Edwards, *Life of Brainerd,* 218–223; Yale Annals 48 volume 1701–1745

149. Edwards, *Life of Brainerd,* 223; "Brainerd to John Brainerd," in Edwards, *Life of Brainerd,* 273–275; Steele, *English Atlantic,* 121, 122. Edwards made the point about the proximity of Northampton to the Boston–New York route when he invited George Whitefield to preach in 1740; see "Edwards to Whitefield," *JEY* 16:79–81. The Edwards-Brainerd relation is discussed in chapter 4. Among the authors who describe Brainerd as Edwards's protégé are Pettit, "Editor's Introduction," *JEY* 7:10; Szasz, *Indian Education in the American Colonies,* 211; Patricia Tracy, "The Romance of David Brainerd and Jerusha Edwards," in *Three Essays in Honor of the Publication of the "Life of David Brainerd,"* ed. Wilson H. Kimnach (New Haven, Conn.: Privately published, 1985). Despite Tracy's claim about the Brainerd-Edwards mentorship, her essay is an excellent summary of the development of the Brainerd-Jerusha romance/engagement. See also chapter 6, below. On the hospitality of the Edwards household, see Marsden, *Jonathan Edwards,* 323.

150. Edwards, *Life of Brainerd,* 223, 224.

151. Edwards, *Life of Brainerd,* 225; Francis G. Walett, ed., *The Diary of Ebenezer Parkman, 1703–1782* (Worcester, Mass.: American Antiquarian Society, 1974), 156.

152. Edwards, *Life of Brainerd,* 225–231; Walett, ed., *Diary of Ebenezer Parkman,* 157; Hamilton Andrews Hill, *History of the Old South Church (Third Church) Boston, 1669–1884* (Boston: Houghton & Mifflin, 1890), I:581; Thomas Prince, *The Case of Heman Considered* (Boston: S. Kneeland, 1756), 28–33 and unnumbered excerpt from the *Boston Gazette.*

153. "David Brainerd to Israel Brainerd," in Edwards, *Life of Brainerd,* 269–271; Dexter, *Biographical Sketches,* I:441.

154. "David Brainerd to a Young Gentleman, a Candidate for the Work of Ministry," in Edwards, *Life of Brainerd,* 271–273; cf. Edwards, *Life of Brainerd,* 54 and 54n. Pettit identifies the man as Greenman in *JEY* 7:190n and 494n.

155. "David Brainerd to John Brainerd," in Edwards, *Life of Brainerd,* 273–275.

156. Edwards, *Life of Brainerd,* 229.

157. Hill, *History of the Old South Church,* I:581; Edwards, *Life of Brainerd,* 226, 229, 230, 232, 233.

158. Brainerd, preface to Thomas Shepard, *Meditations and Spiritual Experiences of Mr. Thomas Shepard* (Boston: Rogers & Fowle, 1747), i–vi; Edwards, *Life of Brainerd,* 237.

159. Edwards, *Life of Brainerd,* 238–253, quote on 250.

160. Edwards, *Life of Brainerd,* 240, 248.

161. Edwards, *Life of Brainerd,* 251.

162. Edwards, *Life of Brainerd,* 253.

163. Edwards, *Life of Brainerd,* 253; *Boston Gazette, or Weekly Journal,* October 27, 1747; *Pennsylvania Journal, or Weekly Advertiser,* November 5, 1747.

164. Jonathan Edwards, "True Saints, when Absent from the Body, Are Present with the Lord," *JEY* 25:225–256, quote on 252.

Chapter 4

1. "Edwards to the Reverend John Erskine, August 31, 1748," *JEY* 16:247–250, quote on 249.

2. "Edwards to Eleazar Wheelock, September 14, 1748," *JEY* 16:251.

3. Patricia J. Tracy, *Jonathan Edwards, Pastor: Religion and Society in Eighteenth-Century Northampton* (New York: Hill and Wang, 1979), 51–137; George M. Marsden, *Jonathan Edwards: A Life* (New Haven, Conn.: Yale University Press, 2003), 115–267.

4. "Edwards to James Robe," *JEY* 16:108–110, quote on 108.

5. Tracy, *Jonathan Edwards, Pastor,* 118–122, 168–172.

6. "Edwards to the Reverend Thomas Prince," *JEY* 16:115–127, quote on 126–127.

7. "Edwards to Deborah Hatheway," *JEY* 16:91–95, quote on 92.

8. *A Faithful Narrative of the Surprising Work of God, JEY* 4:189, 208.

9. Douglas L. Winiarski, "Jonathan Edwards, Enthusiast? Radical Revivalism and the Great Awakening in the Connecticut Valley," *Church History* 74, no. 4 (December 2005), 683–739; Tracy, *Jonathan Edwards, Pastor,* 132–134, 138, 139; Marsden, *Jonathan Edwards,* 233–238.

10. *The Distinguishing Marks of a Work of the Spirit of God, JEY* 4:264, 268.

11. *Distinguishing Marks, JEY* 4:251.

12. Charles Chauncy, "Enthusiasm Described and Caution'd Against," in *The Great Awakening: Documents Illustrating the Crisis and Its Consequences,* ed. Alan Heimert and Perry Miller (Indianapolis, Ind.: Bobbs-Merrill, 1967), 232–234, 237, 255; Edward M. Griffin, *Old Brick: Charles Chauncy of Boston, 1705–1787* (Minneapolis: University of Minnesota Press, 1980), 60–70.

13. C. C. Goen, "Editor's Introduction," *JEY* 4:65–78; Marsden, *Jonathan Edwards,* 263–267; Tracy, *Jonathan Edwards, Pastor,* 139–141.

14. *Some Thoughts Concerning the Present Revival of Religion in New England, JEY* 4:317, 318, 326–328.

15. *Some Thoughts, JEY* 4:409, 411, 414, 418, 422.

16. *Some Thoughts, JEY* 4:432, 451, 457.

17. *Some Thoughts, JEY* 4:458, 459, 461.

18. *Some Thoughts, JEY* 4:465.

19. *Some Thoughts, JEY* 4:496, 522–524.

20. "Edwards to McCulloch, May 12, 1743," *JEY* 16:107; "Edwards to Robe, May 12, 1743," *JEY* 16:109.

21. "Edwards to McCulloch," *JEY* 16:134, 135.

22. David D. Hall, "Editorial Introduction," *JEY* 12:83, 84; Tracy, *Jonathan Edwards, Pastor*, 185, 186.

23. "Edwards to a Correspondent in Scotland, November, 1745," *JEY* 16:181.

24. *Religious Affections, JEY* 2:131, 132, 163; Marsden, *Jonathan Edwards*, 284–290; Tracy, *Jonathan Edwards, Pastor*, 141–145.

25. *Religious Affections, JEY* 2:253, 311, 340, 341, 357, 376.

26. *Religious Affections, JEY* 2:383–386, 388; Tracy, *Jonathan Edwards, Pastor*, 186.

27. Marsden, *Jonathan Edwards*, 291–305; Tracy, *Jonathan Edwards, Pastor*, 147–170.

28. Marsden, *Jonathan Edwards*, 331.

29. Brainerd read *Religious Affections* while he was in Boston. See "Brainerd to John Brainerd," in Edwards, *Life of Brainerd*, 273, 274.

30. Brainerd first arrived at Northampton in late May 1747. After twelve days, he set off for Boston. He did not return to Northampton until late July and died in early October. Edwards, *Life of Brainerd*, 223–253.

31. Edwards, *Life of Brainerd*, 223.

32. "Jonathan Edwards to a Correspondent in Scotland," *JEY* 16:185.

33. "Jonathan Edwards to John MacLaurin," *JEY* 16:206.

34. "Jonathan Edwards to John Brainerd," *JEY* 16:241–244.

35. "Edwards to Joseph Bellamy," *JEY* 16:246.

36. Edwards, *Life of Brainerd*, 224, 235, 253.

37. Edwards, *Life of Brainerd*, 253; Jonathan Edwards, *True Saints, when Absent from the Body, Are Present with the Lord*, *JEY* 25:246, 247, 250, 255.

38. Since my focus in this chapter is primarily on how Edwards used Brainerd as a model for other Christians, I am not devoting time to explanations of Edwards's editing process. For a more detailed analysis, see Norman Pettit, "Editor's Introduction," *JEY* 7:71–84; John A. Grigg, "The Lives of David Brainerd" (Ph.D. diss., University of Kansas, 2002), 259–315. A side-by-side comparison of the first thirty-six pages of the manuscript diary and Edwards's *Life* are provided in *JEY* 7:100–153. Also see Marsden, *Jonathan Edwards*, 321–333.

39. David Brainerd Diary, Gen. Mss. 214, Beinecke Library, Yale University, 11, 12, 13.

40. Brainerd Diary, 26 and unnumbered insert.

41. Edwards, *Life of Brainerd*, 12, 13.

42. Edwards, "Appendix," in *Life of Brainerd*, 278. Again, more information on the editing process can be found in Pettit, "Editor's Introduction"; and Grigg, "Lives of David Brainerd." For examples of Edwards paraphrasing Brainerd, see *Life of Brainerd*, 229–236.

43. Edwards, *Life of Brainerd*, 4, 5.

44. Edwards, *Life of Brainerd*, 29, 30, 159.

45. Edwards, *Life of Brainerd*, 185.

46. Edwards, *Life of Brainerd*, 81, 82.

47. Edwards, *Life of Brainerd*, 83n.

48. Edwards, *Life of Brainerd*, 253; Erik R. Seeman, *Pious Persuasions: Laity and Clergy in Eighteenth-Century New England* (Baltimore, Md.: Johns Hopkins University Press, 1999), 61–67.

49. Edwards, "Appendix," in *Life of Brainerd*, 276, 277.

50. Edwards, "Appendix," 281, 283, 285, 286.

51. Edwards, "Appendix," 297–300.

52. Edwards, "Appendix," 305–308.

53. Tracy, *Jonathan Edwards, Pastor,* 157–165; Marsden, *Jonathan Edwards,* 291–305.

54. "A Strong Rod Withered and Broken," *JEY* 25: 329; Marsden, *Jonathan Edwards,* 343–345.

55. Lucas, *Valley of Discord,* 156–159, 195, 196, 199; Marsden, *Jonathan Edwards,* 351; Tracy, *Jonathan Edwards, Pastor,* 22–50. Quotation is from the notebook of church member Edward Taylor, quoted in Tracy, *Jonathan Edwards, Pastor,* 23.

56. Marsden, *Jonathan Edwards,* 341–352; Tracy, *Jonathan Edwards, Pastor,* 166.

57. *Religious Affections, JEY* 2:86, 89; David D. Hall, "Editor's Introduction," *JEY* 12:53, 57, 58.

58. "Edwards to the Reverend John Erskine," *JEY* 16:249.

59. "Narrative of the Communion Controversy," *JEY* 12:508; Marsden, *Jonathan Edwards,* 347; Tracy, *Jonathan Edwards, Pastor,* 172.

60. "Narrative of the Communion Controversy," *JEY* 12:508–511, quote on 509; "Edwards to McCulloch," *JEY* 16:271; Marsden, *Jonathan Edwards,* 347; Tracy, *Jonathan Edwards, Pastor,* 172. Although denied the opportunity to preach on Sundays on his new approach, Edwards did give a series of midweek lectures in February and March 1750 on the subject. See "Lectures on the Qualifications for Full Communion in the Church of Christ," *JEY* 25:349–440.

61. For analysis of the *Humble Inquiry,* see Hall, "Editor's Introduction," in *JEY* 12:62–68, although the entire introduction addresses the controversy. See also Tracy, *Jonathan Edwards, Pastor,* 169–181; and Marsden, *Jonathan Edwards,* 352–356.

62. *Humble Inquiry, JEY* 12:181, 190.

63. *Humble Inquiry, JEY* 12:205, 206, 208, 221.

64. The exact publication dates of the two books are not clear. Although the *Life of Brainerd* was originally expected in May, in two separate letters written on May 23, 1749, Jonathan Edwards alludes to the fact that he does not know if it has yet appeared. See "Edwards to William McCulloch," and "Edwards to James Robe," *JEY* 16:274 and 281. In fact, the first public notice that the book was ready appeared in the *Boston Weekly Newsletter* on August 10, 1749. *Humble Inquiry* also appeared in August; see "Narrative of the Communion Controversy," *JEY* 12:511.

65. "Edwards to Ebenezer Parkman," *JEY* 16:293.

66. Hall, "Editorial Introduction," *JEY* 12:61, 62; Tracy, *Jonathan Edwards, Pastor,* 176.

67. *Humble Inquiry, JEY* 12:256.

68. On the limited exposure of *Humble Inquiry,* see James Russell Trumbull, *History of Northampton, Massachusetts from Its Settlement in 1654* (Northampton, Mass.: Northampton Press of Gazette, 1902), II:205; Tracy, *Jonathan Edwards, Pastor,* 177; and Wilson H. Kimnach, editorial comments, *JEY* 25:351. On the popularity of the *Life of Brainerd,* see Marsden, *Jonathan Edwards,* 333; and George S. Claghorn, editorial comment, *JEY* 16:250. The count of subscribers comes from Claghorn.

69. Michael Warner has noted that such books were "accumulated to form the libraries essential to the status and collective identity of the clergy." See Warner, *The Letters of the Republic: Publication and the Public Sphere in Eighteenth-Century America* (Cambridge, Mass.: Harvard University Press, 1990), 19–26, quote on 21.

70. Tracy, *Jonathan Edwards, Pastor,* 161; all references to subscribers come from Edwards, *Life of Brainerd,* subscription list.

71. Trumbull, *History of Northampton,* II:205–207, 214, 223. For full descriptions of all of the events surrounding Edwards's dismissal, see "Narrative of the Communion Controversy," *JEY* 12:507–619; Tracy, *Jonathan Edwards, Pastor,* 171–181; Marsden, *Jonathan Edwards,* 357–361.

72. Jonathan Edwards, Diary and Memorandum Book, 1733–1757, 47, 48, Jonathan Edwards Collection, Gen Mss. 151, series I, Writings of Jonathan Edwards, box 21, folder 1267, Beinecke Library, Yale University.

73. Trumbull, *History of Northampton,* II:223.

74. Marsden, *Jonathan Edwards,* 363–365; "Edwards to Erskine," *JEY* 16:356. It is not completely clear how many other calls Edwards may have received. In November 1750, he indicated to John Erskine that there was "some prospect of my having invitations to one or two places"; see *JEY* 16:363. One of these, as Edwards noted in a later letter to Erskine, was to Virginia, but the call came after he accepted the position at Stockbridge. See *JEY* 16:492. Patricia Tracy identified the location as Lunenberg, Virginia, and noted that Edwards was also under consideration at Canaan, Connecticut, although her source was limited to Perry Miller's 1949 biography. See Tracy, *Jonathan Edwards, Pastor,* 261n27. In his introduction to the sermon "The Peace Which Christ Gives His True Followers," Wilson H. Kimnach also noted the possibility of a call to Canaan (*JEY* 25:536); see also Marsden, *Jonathan Edwards,* 575n22; and Rachel Wheeler, "'Friends to Your Souls': Jonathan Edwards' Indian Pastorate and the Doctrine of Original Sin," *Church History* 72, no. 4 (2003), 736–765, esp. 743n26.

75. Marsden, *Jonathan Edwards,* 364, 385.

76. Wheeler, "Friends to Your Souls," 743.

77. Solomon Stoddard, *Question: Whether God Is Not Angry with the Country for Doing So Little toward the Conversion of the Indians?* (Boston: B. Green, 1723; Evans No. 2479).

78. "Indicting God," *JEY* 19:763.

79. *Some Thoughts, JEY* 4:329, 330.

80. *A History of the Work of Redemption, JEY* 9:45.

81. Wheeler, "Friends to Your Souls," 748–760.

82. "To Joseph Paice," *JEY* 16:442; Marsden *Jonathan Edwards,* 387.

83. See, for example, "To Sec. Andrew Oliver," *JEY* 16:534–537. For various perspectives on Edwards's work at Stockbridge: Marsden, *Jonathan Edwards,* 380–431; Wheeler, "Friends to Your Souls"; and Gerald R. McDermott, "Jonathan Edwards and the American Indians: The Devil Sucks Their Blood," *NEQ* 72, no. 4 (December 1999), 539–557.

84. Quoted in Pettit, "Editor's Introduction," *JEY* 7:3.

85. "To the First Church of Christ, Northampton," *JEY* 16:484.

Chapter 5

1. "Wesley Journal," *WJWO/A* 22:98.

2. "John Wesley to Miss March, July 5, 1768," in *The Letters of the Reverend John Wesley, A.M.,* ed. John Telford (London: Epworth, 1931), 5:95, 96.

3. John Wesley, *An Extract of the Life of the Late Rev. David Brainerd, Missionary to the Indians* (Bristol, England: W. Pine, 1768). All references are to the 1812 Dublin printing by R. Napper of the fourth edition.

4. Henry D. Rack, *Reasonable Enthusiast: John Wesley and the Rise of Methodism,* 3rd ed. (London: Epworth, 2002), 45–60; Stanley Ayling, *John Wesley* (London: Collins, 1979), 15–27; Michael Reed, *The Georgian Triumph* (Boston: Kegan Paul, 1983), 20–23; W. Stephen Gunter, *The Limits of "Love Divine": John Wesley's Response to Antinomianism and Enthusiasm* (Nashville, Tenn.: Kingswood, 1989), 70, 71; John C. English, "The Heart Renewed: John Wesley's Doctrine of Christian Initiation," *Wesleyan Quarterly Review* 4, nos. 2–3 (May–August 1967), 118.

5. Rack, *Reasonable Enthusiast*, 98–106; Ayling, *Wesley*, 28–59; Jeremy Black, *Eighteenth-Century Britain, 1688–1783* (New York: Palgrave, 2001), 95.

6. "Wesley Journal," *WJWO/A* 18:214; Rack, *Reasonable Enthusiast*, 107–132; Ayling, *Wesley*, 60–85. Interestingly, the Moravian leader Augustus Spangenberg, who met Wesley during this time, believed that "grace really dwells and reigns in [him]." See Rack, *Reasonable Enthusiast*, 115.

7. "Wesley Journal," *WJWO/A* 18:249, 250.

8. Rack, *Reasonable Enthusiast*, 145–157; Ayling, *Wesley*, 86–97; Richard Steele, *"Gracious Affection" and "True Virtue" According to Jonathan Edwards and John Wesley* (Metuchen, N.J.: Scarecrow, 1994), 129, 130.

9. Mark A. Noll, *The Rise of Evangelicalism: The Age of Edwards, Whitefield, and the Wesleys* (Downers Grove, Ill.: InterVarsity, 2003), 95–99, 125; Ayling, *Wesley*, 104–127.

10. Black, *Eighteenth-Century Britain*, 14, 15, 29, 35–39, 45–52, 61–63, 115; Reed, *Georgian Triumph*, 156–160; Anthony Armstrong, *The Church of England, the Methodists and Society, 1700–1850* (Totowa, N.J.: Rowman and Littlefield, 1973), 90, 91.

11. Black, *Eighteenth-Century Britain*, 125–134; Linda Colley, *Britons: Forging the Nation 1707–1837* (New Haven, Conn.: Yale University Press, 1992), 40–43.

12. Colley, *Britons*, 46.

13. Colley, *Britons*, 77, 79–85; Black, *Eighteenth-Century Britain*, 245–247; David Hempton, *Methodism and Politics in British Society, 1750–1850* (Stanford, Calif.: Stanford University Press, 1984), 31–33; Armstrong, *Church of England*, 103.

14. "Wesley Journal," *WJWO/A* 20:78.

15. Reed, *Georgian Triumph*, 24; Hempton, *Methodism and Politics*, 32, 33; Black, *Eighteenth-Century Britain*, 138, 139, 245–247; Armstrong, *Church of England*, 92–95.

16. "Wesley Journal," *WJWO/A* 20:315. Wesley was probably reading Philip Doddridge's 1748 condensed version of the 1746 Philadelphia edition of Brainerd's public journal. See Steele, *"Gracious Affection,"* 235.

17. "Wesley Journal," *WJWO/A* 19:16; Steele, *"Gracious Affection,"* 132–134, 234.

18. *JEY* 4:341; Steele, *"Gracious Affection,"* 182–267.

19. Rack, *Reasonable Enthusiast*, 70–81, 123–132, 257–269; *WJWO/A* 20:380.

20. The quote in the section heading is from appendix II, "The 'Form of Discipline,' or the 'Code of Laws,' Issued by the Conference of 1797," in *Handbook and Index to the Minutes of the Conference: Showing the Growth and Development of the Wesleyan Methodist Constitution from the First Conference, 1744, to 1890*, ed. Charles Wansbrough (London: Wesleyan Methodist Book Room, 1890), 251. Although the words are not Wesley's, as will be demonstrated, they are reflective of his thinking.

21. Rack, *Reasonable Enthusiast*, 333, 334; Gunter, *Limits of "Love Divine,"* 30–33, 181–201.

22. Hillel Schwartz, *The French Prophets: The History of a Millenarian Group in Eighteenth-Century England* (Berkeley: University of California Press, 1980), 202–207, quote on 207.

23. *Minutes of the Methodist Conferences from the First Held in London, by the Late Rev. John Wesley, A.M., in the Year 1744* (London: John Mason, 1862), I:9; Rack, *Reasonable Enthusiast*, 186–188, 195–197.

24. Rack, *Reasonable Enthusiast*, 334–337, 395–399; Gunter, *Limits of "Love Divine,"* 210, 211. Space does not allow for a full discussion of Wesley's teachings on perfectionism and the resulting controversies. For different perspectives, see Gunter, *Limits of "Love Divine,"* 202–214; Kenneth J. Collins, *The Scripture Way of Salvation: The Heart of John Wesley's Theology* (Nashville, Tenn.: Abingdon, 1997), 171–181; Thomas C. Oden, *John Wesley's Scriptural Christianity* (Grand Rapids, Mich.: Zondervan, 1994), 311–327.

25. Gunter, *Limits of "Love Divine,"* 215–226; Rack, *Reasonable Enthusiast,* 334–341.

26. *Minutes of the Methodist Conferences,* I:69.

27. *Minutes of the Methodist Conferences,* I:51; *Letters of John Wesley,* 5:64, 65, 107, 108.

28. *Minutes of the Methodist Conferences,* I:52, 54, 79, 82; *Letters of John Wesley,* V:51–53.

29. Wesley, *Extract,* 46, 51, 59, 61.

30. Wesley, *Extract,* 48.

31. Edwards footnote, Wesley, *Extract,* 69.

32. Wesley, *Extract,* 55, 56.

33. *Letters of John Wesley,* 5:282 and 6:57.

34. *Minutes of the Methodist Conferences,* I:579.

35. *The Nature, Design, and General Rules of the United Societies* and *Rules of the Band Societies* in *WJWO/A* 9. The quote in the section head is from "Wesley's Journal," *WJWO/A* 22:98.

36. *WJWO/A* 9:70–72, 79.

37. *An Earnest Appeal to Men of Reason and Religion, WJWO/A* 11:87.

38. *A Farther Appeal to Men of Reason and Religion, Part II, WJWO/A* 11:256.

39. *The Use of Money, WJWO/A* 2:268.

40. *The Use of Money, WJWO/A* 2:277; Rack, *Reasonable Enthusiast,* 367; Samuel J. Rogal, "John Wesley and the Attack on Luxury in England," *Eighteenth-Century Life* 3, no. 3 (March 1977): 91–94.

41. *Minutes of the Methodist Conferences,* I:52. By the 1780s, Wesley was so frustrated over the materialism of many Methodists that *The Danger of Riches* directly attacked Methodists who were ignoring God's commands about money. See *WJWO/A* 3:227–246. For a discussion on why Wesley's message on wealth may have fallen on deaf ears, see Outler, "Introductory Note," *WJWO/A* 3:227.

42. Wesley, *Extract,* 61, 62.

43. Wesley, *Extract,* 143.

44. Edwards note, Wesley, *Extract,* 236.

45. The quote in the section header is from Joseph Pilmore's journal, quoted in Frank Baker, *From Wesley to Asbury: Studies in Early American Methodism* (Durham, N.C.: Duke University Press, 1976), 81.

46. "Wesley Journal," *WJWO/A* 21:134, 172; Christi-An C. Bennett, "John Wesley: Founder of a Missionary Church?" *Proceedings of the Wesley Historical Society* 50 (May 1996), 160, 161. Wesley identified the two as servants, as did Henry D. Rack; see Rack, *Reasonable Enthusiast,* 476, 477. Bennett identified them as "servants" (quotation marks in the original), suggesting she had some question over their status. Norman W. Taggart identified them as "converted slaves"; see Taggart, "Methodist Foreign Missions: The First Half-Century," *Proceedings of the Wesley Historical Society* 45 (October 1986): 167.

47. Rack, *Reasonable Enthusiast,* 484–488; Baker, *From Wesley to Asbury,* 33–59, 70–73.

48. Baker, *From Wesley to Asbury,* 73–85.

49. Wesley blended together three separate and partially overlapping accounts of Brainerd's life in order to compile his *Extract:* the 1765 Edinburgh edition of Edwards's *Life of Brainerd,* a version of *Mirabilia* (either the 1748 Doddridge *Abridgement* or the two-volume Philadelphia version), and Brainerd's narrative letter to Pemberton, which had been included as an appendix to the published version of Pemberton's ordination sermon. See Steele, *"Gracious Affection,"* 234, 235.

50. *Original Sin, WJWO/A* 2:176.

51. *Original Sin, WJWO/A* 2:183.

52. Albert C. Outler, "Introductory Comment," *WJWO/A* 2:170, 171.

53. Outler, "Introductory Comment," *WJWO/A* 2:186, 187.

54. *The New Birth, WJWO/A* 2:193, 194.

55. *The New Birth, WJWO/A* 2:195.

56. Wesley, *Extract,* 14.

57. Brainerd, *Mirabilia,* 8–15; Wesley, *Extract,* 107–110.

58. Wesley, *Extract,* 109.

59. English, "Heart Renewed," 114–192, esp. 119, 120.

60. *Free Grace, WJWO/A* 3:544, 545, 555, 556; William R. Cannon, "Salvation in the Theology of John Wesley," *Methodist History* 9 (1970), 42–54, esp. 44, 45; Gunter, *Limits of "Love Divine,"* 227–243; Rack, *Reasonable Enthusiast,* 451–455.

61. *On Working Out Our Own Salvation, WJWO/A* 3:207; Cannon, "Salvation," 44, 45; English, "Heart Renewed," 154–159; Collins, *Scripture Way,* 38–45.

62. Collins, *Scripture Way,* 59–68, quote on 63; English, "Heart Renewed," 141, 142, 164, 169–171; Gunter, *Limits of "Love Divine,"* 104–117, 261–266.

63. *The Scripture Way of Salvation, WJWO/A* 2:162.

64. The analysis which follows considers only a small portion of Wesley's editing. For more details, see Steele, *"Gracious Affection,"* 230–241; and John A. Grigg, "The Lives of David Brainerd" (Ph.D. diss., University of Kansas, 2002), 331–336, 339–345, 350–353.

65. Edwards, *Life of Brainerd,* 297.

66. Edwards, *Life of Brainerd,* 298, 300.

67. Edwards, *Life of Brainerd,* 297–305; cf. Wesley, *Extract,* 270.

68. Edwards, *Life of Brainerd,* 10, 11; cf. Wesley, *Extract,* 11, 12. I realize the difficulties of making comparisons in this fashion. Unfortunately, short of quoting large chunks of text from both works, there is no way around this.

69. Wesley, *Extract,* 11.

70. Edwards, *Life of Brainerd,* 6.

71. Wesley, *Extract,* 8.

72. Brainerd, *Mirabilia,* 13.

73. Wesley, *Extract,* 109.

74. Wesley, *Extract,* 8.

75. Wesley, *Extract,* 8n.

76. Wesley, *Extract,* 107–110; Brainerd, *Mirabilia,* 11, 12.

77. See Zondervan edition of *The Works of John Wesley* (Grand Rapids, Mich.: Zondervan, 1872), 14:199–318, for a complete list of all works, including biographies, which Wesley "revised and abridged from various authors."

78. Rack, *Reasonable Enthusiast,* 421–428.

79. Rack, *Reasonable Enthusiast,* 429.

80. Steele, *"Gracious Affection,"* 236; M. X. Lesser, "An Honor Too Great: Jonathan Edwards in Print Abroad," in *Jonathan Edwards at Home and Abroad: Historical Memories, Cultural Movements, Global Horizons,* ed. David W. Kling and Douglas A. Sweeney (Columbia: University of South Carolina Press, 2003), 297–319.

Chapter 6

1. Martyn, *Journal and Letters of Henry Martyn,* ed. Samuel Wilberforce (1851; reprint, New York: Protestant Episcopal Society for the Promotion of Evangelical Knowledge, 1861), 327.

2. D. Bruce Hindmarsh, "The Reception of Jonathan Edwards by Early Evangelicals in England," in *Jonathan Edwards at Home and Abroad: Historical Memories, Cultural Movements, Global Horizons,* ed. David W. Kling and Douglas A. Sweeney (Columbia: University of South Carolina Press, 2003), 201–221, esp. 207–212, Ryland quote on 202; David W. Bebbington, "Remembered around the World: The International Scope of Edwards's Legacy," in *Jonathan Edwards at Home and Abroad,* ed. Kling and Sweeney, 177–200, esp. 180, 183, 184; Stuart Piggin, *Making Evangelical Missionaries 1789–1858: The Social Background, Motives, and Training of British Protestant Missionaries to India* (Abingdon, Oxfordshire: Sutton Courtenay, 1984), 79–93; Richard Carwardine, *Transatlantic Revivalism: Popular Evangelicalism in Britain and America, 1790–1865* (Westport, Conn.: Greenwood, 1978), 59–66; J. A. De Jong, *As the Waters Cover the Sea: Millennial Expectations in the Rise of Anglo-American Missions, 1640–1810* (Kampen: Kok, 1970), 175, 176.

3. Andrew Fuller, *The Gospel Worthy of All Acceptation; or, The Duty of Sinners to Believe in Jesus Christ,* 3rd ed. (New York: Isaac Collins, 1801), vi, ix; Hindmarsh, "Reception of Jonathan Edwards," 207–209; Brian Stanley, *The Bible and the Flag: Protestant Missions and British Imperialism in the Nineteenth and Twentieth Centuries* (Leicester: Apollos, 1990), 59–61; Bebbington, "Remembered around the World," 184; De Jong, *As the Waters Cover the Sea,* 175–177.

4. William Carey, *An Enquiry into the Obligations of Christians, to Use Means for the Conversion of the Heathens. In Which the Religious State of the Different Nations of the World, the Success of Former Undertakings, and the Practicability of Further Undertakings, Are Considered* (1792; reprint, London: Baptist Missionary Society, 1934); Stanley, *Bible and Flag,* 56–58; Stuart Piggin, "The Expanding Knowledge of God: Jonathan Edwards's Influence on Missionary Thinking and Promotion," in *Jonathan Edwards at Home and Abroad,* ed. Kling and Sweeney, 266–296, esp. 272–275. For more on Carey himself, see H. Leon McBeth, "The Legacy of the Baptist Missionary Society," *Baptist History and Heritage* 27, no. 3 (1992): 3–13; Mary Drewey, *William Carey, Shoemaker and Missionary* (London: Hodder and Stoughton, 1978), 7–36; E. Daniel Potts, *British Baptist Missionaries in India, 1793–1837: The History of Serampore and Its Missions* (Cambridge: Cambridge University Press, 1967), 7–9.

5. Carey, *Enquiry,* 3, 5, 6.

6. Carey, *Enquiry,* 36, 37, 68, 69, 70.

7. Carey, *Enquiry,* 71, 86, 87.

8. Drewey, *William Carey,* 41–61, 200; B. G. Worrall, *The Making of the Modern Church: Christianity in England since 1800* (London: Society for the Propagation of the Gospel, 1993), 189–191; Carey, *The Journal and Selected Letters of William Carey,* ed. Terry G. Carter (Macon, Ga.: Smyth and Helwys, 2000), unpaginated. On the connections between the diaries of Carey and Brainerd, see A. de M. Chesterman, "The Journals of David Brainerd and of William Carey," *Baptist Quarterly* 19, no. 4 (1961), 147–156. For a more detailed discussion of the content and impact of *An Enquiry,* see De Jong, *As the Waters Cover the Sea,* 178, 179.

9. Stanley, *Bible and Flag,* 56, 57; Raymond Brown, *The English Baptists of the Eighteenth Century* (London: Baptist Historical Society, 1986), 122; *A Collection of Letters Relative to Foreign Missions: Containing Several of Melville Horne's "Letters on Missions," and Other Interesting Communications from Foreign Missionaries. Interspersed with Other Extracts* (Andover, Mass.: Galen War, 1810), 78; David Bogue, "Objections against a Mission to the Heathen, Stated and Considered. Sermon VI. Preached at Tottenham Court Chapel, before the Founders of the Missionary Society, on Thursday

the 24th September, 1795," in *Sermons Preached in London, at the Formation of the Missionary Society, September 22, 23, 24, 1795. To Which Are Prefixed Memorials, Respecting the Establishment and First Attempts of That Society* (London: Barrett and March, 1797; Evans No. 32384), 178, 191; Piggin, *Making Evangelical Missionaries,* 107–110. For a more detailed examination of the formation of the LMS, see De Jong, *As the Waters Cover the Sea,* 182–189.

10. Editorial comments in the *Evangelical Magazine for 1793,* 4, and *Evangelical Magazine* 4 (November 1796), 441. "Life of the Late Rev. David Brainerd of New-England, Missionary to the American Indians" was excerpted in *Evangelical Magazine* 4 (November 1796), 441–449; 4 (December 1796), 485–492; and 4 (Supplement for 1796), 529–538. *Evangelical Magazine* can be found in the *Missionary Periodicals* database (http://research.yale.edu:8084/missionperiodicals) maintained by Yale University Divinity School Library (accessed April 11, 2006). Also see J. C. S. Mason, *The Moravian Church and the Missionary Awakening* (Rochester, N.Y.: Boydell, 2001), 73–75; De Jong, *As the Waters Cover the Sea,* 185.

11. Andrew F. Walls, "The Evangelical Revival, the Missionary Movement, and Africa," in *Evangelicalism: Comparative Studies of Popular Protestantism in North America, the British Isles, and Beyond, 1700–1990,* ed. Mark A. Noll, David W. Bebbington, and George A. Rawlyk (New York: Oxford University Press, 1994), 327n2.

12. Piggin, "Expanding Knowledge of God," 275; Andrew F. Walls, "Missions and Historical Memory: Jonathan Edwards and David Brainerd," in *Jonathan Edwards at Home and Abroad,* ed. Kling and Sweeney, 255; Piggin, *Making Evangelical Missionaries,* 156–158, 175–181, 229, 231; Stuart Piggin and John Roxborogh, *The St. Andrews Seven: The Finest Flowering of Missionary Zeal in Scottish History* (Carlisle, Pa.: Banner of Truth Trust, 1985), 43, 49, 50; Stanley, *Bible and Flag,* 57; Brown, *English Baptists,* 122. For a more detailed examination of the formation of the CMS, see De Jong, *As the Waters Cover the Sea,* 189–193.

13. Walls, "Evangelical Revival," 310.

14. Piggin, "Expanding Knowledge of God," 278, 279.

15. Mason, *Moravian Church and the Missionary Awakening,* 167, 168; S. Pearce Carey, *Samuel Pearce, M.A., the Baptist Brainerd* (London: Carey, n.d.), 167, 168, 212, 213; and "Andrew Fuller to Mrs. Pearce," in Carey, *Samuel Pearce,* 214.

16. Quoted in Piggin, "Expanding Knowledge of God," 275.

17. Quoted in Piggin, "Expanding Knowledge of God," 277.

18. McCheyne, *The Works of the Late Rev. Robert Murray McCheyne* (New York: Robert Carter, 1847), II:20.

19. Piggin, *Making Evangelical Missionaries,* 19; John R. C. Martyn, *Henry Martyn (1781–1812): Scholar and Missionary to India and Persia: A Biography* (Lewiston, N.Y.: Mellen, 1999), 20–26; Martyn, *Journal and Letters of Henry Martyn,* 38, 141.

20. Piggin and Roxborogh, *St. Andrews Seven,* 27, 49, 50, 69; Walls, "Missions and Historical Memory," 253; Piggin, "Expanding Knowledge of God," 274–279; Martyn, *Henry Martyn,* 42, 125, 126; Martyn, *Journal and Letters of Henry Martyn,* 233, 327; George Smith, *Henry Martyn: Saint and Scholar* (New York: Revell, 1892), 60. For details on the relationship between Martyn and Grenfell, see Martyn, *Henry Martyn,* 29–42. Despite his statements regarding the benefits of staying single, it seems Martyn never ceased to court Grenfell.

21. Samuel Marsden, *Memoirs of the Life and Labours of the Rev. Samuel Marsden,* ed. J. B. Marsden (London: Religious Tract Society, 1858), 4, 8; Mason, *Moravian Church and the Missionary Awakening,* 186; Samuel Marsden, *The Letters and Journals of Samuel*

Marsden, 1765–1838, ed. John Rawson Elder (London: Kierk, 1932), 17–56; A. T. Yarwood, *Samuel Marsden: The Great Survivor* (Melbourne, Australia: Melbourne University Press, 1977), 1–30.

22. John Styles, *The Life of David Brainerd, Missionary to the Indians, with an Abridgement of Diary and Journal* (Boston: Samuel T. Armstrong, 1812; Evans, 2nd ser., No. 26824); Richard Steele, *"Gracious Affection" and "True Virtue" According to Jonathan Edwards and John Wesley* (Metuchen, N.J.: Scarecrow, 1994), 236, 237; Norman Pettit, "Editor's Introduction," *JEY* 7:75, 76.

23. Styles, *Life of Brainerd,* 13, 83, 290.

24. Styles, *Life of Brainerd,* 291, 292.

25. John A. Andrew, *Rebuilding the Christian Commonwealth: New England Congregationalists and Foreign Missions, 1800–1830* (Lexington: University Press of Kentucky, 1976), 20–24; Joseph R. Tracy, "History of the American Board of Commissioners of [*sic*] Foreign Missions," in his *History of American Missions to the Heathens, from Their Commencement to the Present Time* (1840; reprint, New York: Johnson Reprint, 1970), 33–43, 55, 72, 73, 225; Joseph A. Conforti, *Jonathan Edwards, Religious Tradition, and American Culture* (Chapel Hill: University of North Carolina Press, 1995), 74–76; William R. Hutchison, *Errand to the World: American Protestant Thought and Foreign Missions* (Chicago, Ill.: University of Chicago Press, 1987), 45, 46. My focus here is on the way in which Brainerd was both an inspiration to and a model for American missionaries. The mission impulse in the antebellum United States was, of course, much more complex than the outline I have presented.

26. Leonard Woods, *A Sermon Delivered at the Tabernacle in Salem, February 6, 1812, on Occasion of the Ordination of the Rev. Messrs. Samuel Newell, Adoniram Judson, Samuel Nott, Gordon Hall, and Luther Rice, Missionaries to the Heathen in Asia* (Boston: Samuel T. Armstrong, 1812); Hutchison, *Errand to the World,* 48, 49.

27. Extract from John Styles's *Life of David Brainerd* was part of an advertisement for the first American publication; located on the opening leaf of Woods, *A Sermon Delivered at the Tabernacle;* see also Conforti, *Jonathan Edwards,* 69.

28. Nathan O. Hatch, *The Democratization of American Christianity* (New Haven, Conn.: Yale University Press, 1989), 18–20.

29. Styles, *Life of Brainerd,* 31–35, quotes on 31, 33, 34.

30. Sereno Edwards Dwight, ed., *Memoirs of the Rev. David Brainerd: Missionary to the Indians...by Rev. Jonathan Edwards, of Northampton* (New Haven, Conn.: S. Converse, 1822), 8–10; Pettit, "Editor's Introduction," *JEY* 7:76.

31. Pettit, "Editor's Introduction," *JEY* 7:77.

32. Gordon Hall, *The Duty of the Christian Churches in Respect to Foreign Missions: A Sermon Preached in the Tabernacle, Philadelphia, on Sabbath Morning, February 16, 1812* (Philadelphia: Thomas and William Bradford, 1812), 13; Hutchison, *Errand to the World,* 63, 64; Gordon Hall and Samuel Newell, *The Conversion of the World; or, The Claims of Six Hundred Millions and the Ability and Duty of the Churches Respecting Them* (Andover, Mass.: Flagg and Gould for the ABCFM, 1818), 55; Andrew, *Rebuilding the Christian Commonwealth,* 93–95.

33. K.C., "What Are the Motives Which Should Induce the Churches in the United States to Attempt the Conversion and Civilization of the Indians?" *Panoplist and Missionary Magazine* 12, no. 1 (January 1816), 122; "Letter from the Treasurer of the American Board," *Panoplist and Missionary Herald* 14, no. 7 (1818), 339; Tracy, "History of the American Board," 334; "Methods of Preaching to the Indians," *Missionary Herald* 20, no. 4 (April 1824), 134.

34. "Indians West of Missouri. Extracts from a Letter of Mr. Byington: Early Missionary Labors among the Indians," *Missionary Herald* 30, no. 12 (December 1834), 453–455; Hutchison, *Errand to the World*, 63–69.

35. Samuel Spring, *A Sermon Preached at New Haven, Connecticut, before the American Board of Commissioners for Foreign Missions, at Their Ninth Annual Meeting, September 10, 1818* (Boston: Samuel T. Armstrong, 1818), 11.

36. William Swan, "Review of Letters on Missions," *Quarterly Christian Spectator* 2, no. 4 (December 1830), 646; Conforti, *Jonathan Edwards*, 50; Lawrence Buell, *New England Literary Culture, from Revolution through Renaissance* (New York: Cambridge University Press, 1986), 31.

37. Ashbel Green, "An Address Delivered to the Students of the Theological Seminary at Princeton, May 16, 1831," *Biblical Repertory and Theological Review*, n.s., 3, no. 3 (July 1831), 350–360, quote on 358.

38. "Causes Which Have Impeded the Spread of Christianity," *Quarterly Christian Spectator* 4, no. 3 (September 1832), 404; "The Missionary Cause: The Obligations of Christians to Spread the Gospel Accumulative," *Christian Review* 1, no. 3 (September 1836), 325–337.

39. Cyrus Kingsbury, "The Establishment of Mission Schools among the Indians within the Territory of the United States," in *Memoirs of American Missionaries, Formerly Connected with the Society of Inquiry Respecting Missions in the Andover Theological Seminary* (Boston: Pierce and Parker, 1833), 265.

40. Dwight, *Memoirs of Brainerd*, 49; Parsons, *Memoir of the Rev. Levi Parsons, Late Missionary to Palestine*, comp. Daniel O. Morton (1824; reprint, New York: Arno, 1977), 18, 52, 94.

41. Alvan Bond, *Memoir of the Rev. Pliny Fisk*, A.M., *Late Missionary to Palestine* (Boston: Crocker and Brewster, 1828), 170, 182, 259.

42. Swan, "Review of Letters on Missions," 635; Joseph Tracy, *The Great Awakening: A History of the Revival of Religion in the Time of Edwards and Whitefield* (1845; reprint, New York: Arno, 1969), 237, 238; Conforti, *Jonathan Edwards*, 76, 77.

43. For a fuller description of Apess's life as well as some discussion of the limitations of the sources, see Apess, *On Our Own Ground: The Complete Writings of William Apess, a Pequot*, ed. Barry O'Connell (Amherst: University of Massachusetts Press, 1992); William Apess, *A Son of the Forest*, in O'Connell, ed., *On Our Own Ground*, 52, 82.

44. Conforti, *Jonathan Edwards*, 89–95; Amanda Porterfield, *Feminine Spirituality in America: From Sarah Edwards to Martha Graham* (Philadelphia: Temple University Press, 1980), 11–15, 16–19.

45. Conforti, *Jonathan Edwards*, 102–105; Amanda Porterfield, *Mary Lyon and the Mount Holyoke Missionaries* (New York: Oxford University Press, 1997), 60, 61. The ABCFM did express concern that the prevalence of married missionaries "renders our missions expensive, compared with the papal missions"; *Missionary Herald* 38, no. 11 (1842), 423.

46. Conforti, *Jonathan Edwards*, 103–106; Edwards A. Park, *Memoir of the Life and Character of Samuel Hopkins, D.D.* (Boston: Doctrinal Tract and Book Company, 1854), 21.

47. Porterfield, *Mary Lyon*, 54–61; Dana L. Robert, *American Women in Mission: A Social History of Their Thought and Practice* (Macon, Ga.: Mercer University Press, 1997), 7, 8, 11, 15, 18, 19, 36–38, 43–46; Joan J. Brumberg, *Mission for Life: The Story of the Family of Adoniram Judson* (New York: Free Press, 1980), 102–107.

48. Homer W. Hodge, "Foreword," in *The Life of David Brainerd, Missionary to the Indians*, ed. Homer W. Hodge (New York: Christian Alliance Publishing, 1925), 5, 6.

49. Colleen McDannell, *Material Christianity: Religion and Popular Culture in America* (New Haven, Conn.: Yale University Press, 1995), 107–119.

50. Conforti, *Jonathan Edwards*, 62, 63.

51. Robert H. Wiebe, *The Search for Order, 1877–1920* (New York: Hill and Wang, 1967), 224–239; Robert T. Handy, *A Christian America: Protestant Hopes and Historical Realities* (New York: Oxford University Press, 1971), 117–128, Stearns quote on 122; Hutchison, *Errand to the World*, 91–95.

52. Handy, *Christian America*, 129, 130; Michael Parker, *The Kingdom of Character: The Student Volunteer Movement for Foreign Missions (1886–1926)* (Lanham, Md.: American Society of Missiology and University Press of America, 1998), 1–3; Dana L. Robert, *Occupy until I Come: A. T. Pierson and the Evangelization of the World* (Grand Rapids, Mich.: Eerdmans, 2003), 145–150.

53. Arthur T. Pierson, *The Crisis of Missions; or, The Voice Out of the Cloud* (New York: Baker and Taylor, 1886), esp. 273–310; Parker, *Kingdom of Character*, 1–9, 67–70; Hutchison, *Errand to the World*, 117; Robert, *Occupy until I Come*, 140–144.

54. Parker, *Kingdom of Character*, 19–29.

55. Pierson, *Crisis of Missions*, 252, 256; Sherwood Eddy quoted in Parker, *Kingdom of Character*, 23; statistics from Parker, *Kingdom of Character*, 18–20.

56. Parker, *Kingdom of Character*, 12–16; C. Howard Hopkins, *John R. Mott, 1865–1955: A Biography* (Grand Rapids, Mich.: Eerdmans, 1979), 60, 61, 88.

57. John R. Mott, *The Evangelization of the World in This Generation* (New York: Student Volunteer Movement for Foreign Missions, 1900), 165, 166, 182–190; Mott, *The Pastor and Modern Missions: A Plea for Leadership in World Evangelization* (New York: Student Volunteer Movement for Foreign Missions, 1904), 188, 189, 215; Robert E. Speer, *Missionary Principles and Practices: A Discussion of Christian Missions and of Some Criticisms upon Them* (New York: Revell, 1902), 393, 394; Hutchison, *Errand to the World*, 118–124.

58. A. J. Gordon, "The Spirit in His Work and Preparation for the Missionary Enterprise," in *The Student Missionary Enterprise; or, The World's Conquest: Addresses and Discussions of the Second International Convention of the Student Volunteer Movement for Foreign Missions, Held at Detroit, Michigan, February 28 and March, 1, 2, 3, 4*, ed. Max Wood Moorhead (Boston: T. O. Metcalf, 1894), 123.

59. A. J. Gordon, *The Holy Spirit in Missions: Six Lectures* (New York: Revell, 1893), 208, 209; J. M. Sherwood, "Life and Character of Brainerd," in *Memoirs of Rev. David Brainerd, Missionary to the Indians of North America*, ed. Sherwood (New York: Funk and Wagnalls, 1884), xxxviii; E. M. Bounds, *Power through Prayer*, 11th ed. (New York: Marshall Brothers, n.d.), 72, 73; Don O. Shelton, *Heroes of the Cross in America* (Philadelphia: Westminster, 1905), 74; R. F. Horton, "The Spiritual Preparation of the Missionary," in *Students and the Missionary Problem: Addresses Delivered at the International Student Missionary Conference, London, January 2–6, 1900* (London: Student Volunteer Missionary Union, 1900), 181.

60. Speer, *Missionary Principles and Practices*, 488; P. S. Hyde, "David Brainerd: The Man of Prayer," in *God's Heroes: Our Examples* (Mysore City, India: Epworth League of the Methodist Episcopal Church, [1910]), 68, 75.

61. John R. Mott, "Losing Ourselves in the Cause," in *Addresses and Papers of John R. Mott* (New York: Association Press, 1946), II:579; Donald Fraser, "Spiritual Prerequisites for the Persuasive Presentation of Christ," in *Students and the Modern Missionary Movement: Addresses Delivered before the Fifth International Convention of the Student Volunteer Movement for Foreign Missions, Nashville, Tennessee, 1906* (New York: Student Volunteer Movement for Foreign Missions, 1906); W. J. Lhamon, *Heroes of Modern Missions* (New York: Revell, 1899), 33.

62. Charles B. Galloway, "Lessons from Lives of Master Missionaries," in *World-Wide Evangelization the Urgent Business of the Church: Addresses Delivered before the Fourth International Convention of the Student Volunteer Movement for Foreign Missions, Toronto, Canada, February 26–March 2, 1902* (New York: Student Volunteer Movement for Foreign Missions, 1902), 162; A. McLean, *Missionary Addresses* (St. Louis, Mo.: Missionary Publishing, 1895), 203; Henry Otis Dwight, H. Allen Tupper, and Edwin Munsell Bliss, eds., *The Encyclopedia of Missions* (1904; reprint, New York: Gale, 1975), 102, 103.

63. McLean, *Missionary Addresses,* 203; Jessie Brown Pounds, *Pioneer Missionaries: Short Sketches of the Lives of the Pioneers in Missionary Work in Many Lands* (Indianapolis, Ind.: Young People's Department of the Christian Woman's Board of Missions, 1905), 14; Shelton, *Heroes of the Cross,* 66.

64. Shelton, *Heroes of the Cross,* 76, 80; Lhamon, *Heroes of Modern Missions,* 34; Sherwood, "Life and Character," xxiii, xxiv.

65. Gordon, *Holy Spirit in Missions,* 142; C[harlotte] M. Yonge, *Pioneers and Founders or Recent Workers in the Mission Field* (New York: Macmillan, 1890), 42; Hyde, "David Brainerd," 71.

66. Lhamon, *Heroes of Modern Missions,* 19, 35, 36.

67. Sherwood, "Life and Character," xlvii.

68. Robert Wuthnow, *The Restructuring of American Religion: Society and Faith since World War II* (Princeton, N.J.: Princeton University Press, 1988), 35–53; Randall Balmer, "Religion in Twentieth-Century America," in Jon Butler, Grant Wacker, and Randall Balmer, *Religion in American Life* (New York: Oxford University Press, 2003), 364–371.

69. Mark A. Noll, *A History of Christianity in the United States and Canada* (Grand Rapids, Mich.: Eerdmans, 1992), 436–441; D. G. Hart, *That Old-Time Religion in Modern America: Evangelical Protestantism in the Twentieth Century* (Chicago, Ill.: Dee, 2002), 39, 129–132; Mark A. Noll, *American Evangelical Christianity: An Introduction* (Malden, Mass.: Blackwell, 2001), 18–22; George M. Marsden, "Unity and Diversity in the Evangelical Resurgence," in *Altered Landscapes: Christianity in America, 1935–1985,* ed. David W. Lotz, Donald W. Shriver, Jr., and John F. Wilson (Grand Rapids, Mich.: Eerdmans, 1989), 61.

70. On the numbers at the Munich Olympics and insight into the beginnings of one parachurch mission organization, see Loren Cunningham, *Is That Really You, Lord? The Story of Youth with a Mission* (Eastbourne, England: Kingsway, 1984), 96. For the changing face of missions, see Daniel H. Bays and Grant Wacker, "After World War II: Years of Complication," and Grant Wacker, "The Waning of the Missionary Impulse: The Case of Pearl S. Buck," both in *The Foreign Missionary Enterprise at Home: Explorations in North American Cultural History,* ed. Daniel H. Bays and Grant Wacker (Tuscaloosa: University of Alabama Press, 2003), 187–189 and 191–205, respectively; Hutchison, *Errand to the World,* 146–202; Richard V. Pierard, "*Pax Americana* and the Evangelical Missionary Advance," 155–179; James Alan Paterson, "The Loss of a Protestant Missionary Consensus: Foreign Missions and the Fundamentalist-Modernist Conflict," 73–91; Charles E. Van Engen, "A Broadening Vision: Forty Years of Evangelical Theology of Mission, 1946–1986," 203–232, all in *Earthen Vessels: American Evangelicals and Foreign Missions, 1880–1980,* ed. Joel A. Carpenter and Wilbert R. Shenk (Grand Rapids, Mich.: Eerdmans, 1990).

71. Philip E. Howard, Jr., *The Life and Diary of David Brainerd* (Grand Rapids, Mich.: Baker, 1989). The work was originally published by Moody Bible Institute in 1949. Baker Books began to reprint the work in 1989.

72. Howard, "Prefatory Note," *Life of Brainerd,* 8.

73. Publication information in Howard, *Life of Brainerd* and personal communication from Bob Bol, production manager, Baker Books, April 2009.

74. Elliot first noted Brainerd in a diary entry dated July 26, 1949. A letter from Elliot to his wife, Elisabeth, dated October 31, 1949, implies that it was his father-in-law who first placed a copy of the *Life of Brainerd* in his hands. Although there is no way to be certain which edition Elliot was reading, the publication of Howard's work that same year is suggestive. See *The Journals of Jim Elliot*, ed. Elisabeth Elliot (Old Tappan, N.J.: Revell, 1978), 143; and Elisabeth Elliot, *Shadow of the Almighty: The Life and Testament of Jim Elliot* (London: Hodder and Stoughton, 1958), 111.

75. *Journals of Jim Elliot*, 144, 166.

76. *Journals of Jim Elliot*, 173.

77. Elliot, "Preface," in *Journals of Jim Elliot*, 9. For information on the impact of *Shadow of the Almighty*, see Kathryn T. Long, "In the Modern World but Not of It: The 'Auca Martyrs,' Evangelicalism, and Postwar American Culture," in *Foreign Missionary Enterprise at Home*, ed. Bays and Wacker, 223–236.

78. William Thomson Hanzsche, *Forgotten Founding Fathers of the American Church and State* (Boston: Christopher, 1954), 89–115, quotes on 97, 108, 110.

79. Hanzsche, *Forgotten Founding Fathers*, 89, 111, 113–115. Hanzsche was also echoing, knowingly or not, J. M. Sherwood and William Lhamon (see above).

80. Clyde S. Kilby, "David Brainerd: Knight of the Grail," in *Heroic Colonial Christians*, ed. Russell T. Hitt (Philadelphia: Lippincott, 1966), 151–206, quotes on 153, 155.

81. Kilby, "David Brainerd," 180, 185, 190.

82. Richard Hasler, *Journey with David Brainerd: Forty Days or Forty Nights with David Brainerd* (Downers Grove, Ill.: InterVarsity, 1975).

83. Hasler, *Journey with David Brainerd*, 7–9; Ronald M. Enroth, Edward E. Ericson, Jr., and C. Breckinridge Peters, *The Jesus People: Old-Time Religion in the Age of Aquarius* (Grand Rapids, Mich.: Eerdmans, 1972), 15, 239; Erling Jorstad, *That New-Time Religion: The Jesus Revival in America* (Minneapolis, Minn.: Augsburg, 1972), 17–36. Jorstad did not specifically compare the Jesus Movement to the Great Awakening but saw it as a continuation of the revivalist idea, which he traced from the Great Awakening to the Jesus Movement.

84. Hasler, *Journey with David Brainerd*, 20, 21.

85. Hasler, *Journey with David Brainerd*, 48, 49, 114, 115.

86. Hasler, *Journey with David Brainerd*, 53, 78, 79, 94, 95, 97, 115.

Conclusion

1. Mrs. Walter Person, "David Brainerd, 'A Man in a Million,'" in *1949 Program Series, Women's Missionary Federation of the Evangelical Lutheran Church* (n.p.), 56–59.

2. Acts 28:1–6.

3. Joseph A. Conforti, *Jonathan Edwards, Religious Tradition, and American Culture* (Chapel Hill: University of North Carolina Press, 1995), 71.

4. Ranelda Hunsicker, *David Brainerd* (Minneapolis, Minn.: Bethany House, 1999). The Men of Faith series includes such luminaries as C. S. Lewis, Charles Colson, and William Carey.

5. Hunsicker, *David Brainerd*, 139.

Works Cited

Manuscripts

David Brainerd Manuscripts

Beinecke Library, Yale University

Gen. Mss. 214, Brainerd Miscellaneous Diaries and Papers

> Diary Introduction
> Diary Fragments, August 14–19, 1743; April 27–May 11, 1744
> Brainerd to William Bradford, September 20, 1746

Gen. Mss 151, Edwards Collection, series V, box 28, folder 1530

> Brainerd to Joseph Bellamy, February 4, 1743

Yale Divinity Library, RG30

> Manuscript Sermon

Historical Society of Pennsylvania

Gratz Collection

> Diary Fragments, July 20–August 3, 1744; October 24, 1744; November 2, 1744; undated, probably March 1747

Gratz Collection, case 8, box 21

> Brainerd to William Bradford, April 20, 1747

Ferdinand J. Dreer Autograph Collection, 125:1, American Clergy, vol. II

Brainerd to John Sergeant, March 25, 1745

Mission House, Stockbridge, Massachusetts

Diary Fragment, August 8–13, 1743

Morgan Library, New York

Diary Fragment, July 8–15, 1744

New College Library, Edinburgh, Scotland, CM/Appx 20

Diary Fragment, October 21 and 31, 1744

Presbyterian Historical Society, Philadelphia

Brainerd to Joseph Bellamy, March 26, 1743 (transcription)

Eleazar Wheelock Microfilm, Dartmouth College Library

Brainerd to Wheelock (No. 745680)

Lucy Brainard, Genealogy

Diary Fragments, September 1745 (photocopy of original)

Other Manuscript Sources

Bellamy, Joseph. Letters. Presbyterian Historical Society, Philadelphia.
Cleaveland, John. Papers. Phillips Peabody Library, Salem, Massachusetts.
Connecticut Church Records (microfilm). Connecticut State Library, Hartford.
Connecticut Probate Records (microfilm). Connecticut State Library, Hartford.
Dreer, Ferdinand. Autograph Collection, Historical Society of Pennsylvania.
Durham Town Records, Town Clerk's Office, Durham, Connecticut.
East Haddam, Second Congregational Church Records. Connecticut Historical Society, Hartford.
Easthampton, First Church Records. East Hampton Library, New York.
Edwards, Jonathan. Papers. Beinecke Library, Yale University.
Edwards, Jonathan. Papers. Trask Library, Andover Theological Seminary.
Fairfield East Association and Consocation Records. United Congregational Church, Hartford, Connecticut.
Foxcroft, Thomas. Selected Correspondence. Manuscripts Division, Department of Rare Books and Special Collections, Princeton University Library.
Gratz Collection. Historical Society of Pennsylvania.
Ingersoll, Jared. Papers. Library of Congress.
Moravian Mission Records. Microfilm of originals in Archives of the Moravian Church, Bethlehem, Pennsylvania.
Society in Scotland for Propagating Christian Knowledge. Records. National Archives of Scotland, Edinburgh.
Yale University Archives.

Eighteenth- and Nineteenth-Century Newspapers

Boston Gazette, or Weekly Journal (18)
Boston Weekly Newsletter (18)
Boston Weekly Post-Boy (18)
Christian Monthly History (18)
Christian Review (19)
Evangelical Magazine (19)
Glasgow Weekly History (18)
Missionary Herald (19)
Panoplist and Missionary Herald (19)
Panoplist and Missionary Magazine (19)
Pennsylvania Journal, or Weekly Advertiser (18)
Quarterly Christian Spectator (19)

Published Primary Sources

An Abridgement of the Statutes and Rules of the Society in Scotland for Propagating Christian Knowledge. Edinburgh: Robert Fleming, 1732.

Alexander, James, and Robert Hunter Morris. "State of the Facts, Concerning the Late Riots at Newark in the County of Essex, & in Other Parts of New Jersey; December 24, 1746." In *New Jersey Archives* VI:397–418.

Apess, William. *On Our Own Ground: The Complete Writings of William Apess, a Pequot,* edited by Barry O'Connell. Amherst: University of Massachusetts Press, 1992.

Beauchamp, William M., ed. *Moravian Journals Relating to Central New York, 1745– 1766.* 1916. Reprint, New York: AMS, 1976.

Bierhorst, John, ed. *The White Deer and Other Stories Told by the Lenape.* New York: Morrow, 1995.

"Bishop A. G. Spangenberg's Journal of a Journey to Onondaga in 1745." In *Moravian Journals Relating to Central New York, 1745–1766,* edited by William M. Beauchamp. 1916. Reprint, New York: AMS, 1976.

Blair, Samuel. *Short and Faithful Narrative, of the Late Remarakable [sic] Revival of Religion in the Congregation of New-Londonderry and Other Parts of Pennsylvania: As the Same Was Sent in a Letter to the Rev. Mr. Prince of Boston.* Philadelphia: William Bradford, 1744.

Bogue, David. "Objections against a Mission to the Heathen, Stated and Considered. Sermon VI...." In *Sermons Preached in London, at the Formation of the Missionary Society, September 22, 23, 24, 1795. To Which Are Prefixed Memorials, Respecting the Establishment and First Attempts of That Society.* London: Barrett and March, 1797. Evans No. 32384.

Bond, Alvan. *Memoir of the Rev. Pliny Fisk, A.M., Late Missionary to Palestine.* Boston: Crocker and Brewster, 1828.

Bounds, E. M. *Power through Prayer,* 11th ed. New York: Marshall Brothers, n.d.

Brainerd, David. *Divine Grace Displayed; or, The Continuance and Progress of a Remarkable Work of Grace among Some of the Indians Belonging to the Provinces of New-Jersey and Pennsylvania.* Philadelphia: William Bradford, 1746.

Brainerd, David. *Mirabilia Dei Inter Indios; or, The Rise and Progress of a Remarkable Work of Grace among a Number of the Indians in the Provinces of New-Jersey and Pennsylvania, Justly Represented in a Journal Kept by Order of the Honourable Society in Scotland for Propagating Christian Knowledge.* Philadelphia: William Bradford, 1746.

————. Preface to *Meditations and Spiritual Experiences of Mr. Thomas Shepard.* Boston: Rogers & Fowle, 1747.

Buell, Samuel. *A Faithful Narrative of the Remarkable Revival of Religion in the Congregation of East-Hampton on Long Island in the Year of Our Lord 1764.* New York: Samuel Brown, 1766. Evans No. 10250.

Burr, Esther Edwards. *The Journal of Esther Edwards Burr,* edited by Carol F. Karlsen and Laurie Crumpacker. New Haven, Conn.: Yale University Press, 1984.

Bushman, Richard L., ed. *The Great Awakening: Documents on the Revival of Religion, 1740–1745.* New York: Atheneum for the Institute of Early American History and Culture at Williamsburg, Virginia, 1970.

Carey, S. Pearce. *Samuel Pearce, M.A., the Baptist Brainerd.* London: Carey, n.d.

Carey, William. *An Enquiry into the Obligations of Christians, to Use Means for the Conversion of the Heathens. In Which the Religious State of the Different Nations of the World, the Success of Former Undertakings, and the Practicability of Further Undertakings, Are Considered.* 1792. Reprint, London: Baptist Missionary Society, 1934.

————. *The Journal and Selected Letters of William Carey,* edited by Terry G. Carter. Macon, Ga.: Smyth and Helwys, 2000.

Chauncy, Charles. *Seasonable Thoughts on the State of Religion in New-England, a treatise in five parts.* Boston: Samuel Eliot, 1743. Evans No. 5151.

————. "Enthusiasm Described and Caution'd Against." In *The Great Awakening: Documents Illustrating the Crisis and Its Consequences,* edited by Alan Heimert and Perry Miller. Indianapolis, Ind.: Bobbs-Merrill, 1967.

Clap, Thomas. *The Annals or History of Yale-College, in New-Haven, in the Colony of Connecticut.* New Haven, Conn.: John Hotchkiss and B. Mecom, 1766. Evans No. 10262.

A Collection of Letters Relative to Foreign Missions; Containing Several of Melville Horne's "Letters on Missions," and Other Interesting Communications from Foreign Missionaries. Interspersed with Other Extracts. Andover, Mass.: Galen War, 1810.

Dexter, Franklin Bowditch. *Documentary History of Yale University, 1701–1745.* 1916. Reprint, New York: Arno and the New York Times, 1969.

Dwight, Henry Otis, H. Allen Tupper, and Edwin Munsell Bliss, eds. *The Encyclopedia of Missions.* 1904. Reprint, New York: Gale, 1975.

Dwight, Sereno Edwards, ed. *Memoirs of the Rev. David Brainerd: Missionary to the Indians on the Borders of New-York, New Jersey and Pennsylvania: Chiefly Taken from His Own Diary. By Rev. Jonathan Edwards of Northampton.* 1822., New Haven, Conn.: Converse, 1822.

Edwards, Jonathan. *An Account of the Life of the Reverend Mr. David Brainerd.* Boston: D. Henchman, 1749.

————. *The Works of Jonathan Edwards,* 26 vols., edited by Perry Miller, John E. Smith, and Harry S. Stout. New Haven, Conn.: Yale University Press, 1957–2008.

Elliot, Elisabeth. *Shadow of the Almighty: The Life and Testament of Jim Elliot.* London: Hodder and Stoughton, 1958.

Elliot, Jim. *The Journals of Jim Elliot,* edited by Elisabeth Elliot. Old Tappan, N.J.: Revell, 1978.

Fraser, Donald. "Spiritual Prerequisites for the Persuasive Presentation of Christ." In *Students and the Modern Missionary Movement: Addresses Delivered before the Fifth International Convention of the Student Volunteer Movement for Foreign Missions, Nashville, Tennessee, 1906.* New York: Student Volunteer Movement for Foreign Missions, 1906.

Fuller, Andrew. *The Gospel Worthy of All Acceptation; or, The Duty of Sinners to Believe in Jesus Christ,* 3rd ed. New York: Isaac Collins, 1801.

Galloway, Charles B. "Lessons from Lives of Master Missionaries." In *World-Wide Evangelization the Urgent Business of the Church: Addresses Delivered before the Fourth International Convention of the Student Volunteer Movement for Foreign Missions, Toronto, Canada, February 26–March 2, 1902.* New York: Student Volunteer Movement for Foreign Missions, 1902.

Gordon, A. J. *The Holy Spirit in Missions: Six Lectures.* New York: Revell, 1893.

———. "The Spirit in His Work and Preparation for the Missionary Enterprise." In *The Student Missionary Enterprise; or, The World's Conquest: Addresses and Discussions of the Second International Convention of the Student Volunteer Movement for Foreign Missions, Held at Detroit, Michigan, February 28 and March 1, 2, 3, 4,* edited by Max Wood Moorhead. Boston: T. O. Metcalf, 1894.

Green, Ashbel. "An Address Delivered to the Students of the Theological Seminary at Princeton, May 16, 1831." *Biblical Repertory and Theological Review,* n.s., 3, no. 3 (July 1831): 350–360.

Hall, Gordon. *The Duty of the Christian Churches in Respect to Foreign Missions: A Sermon Preached in the Tabernacle, Philadelphia, on Sabbath Morning, February 16, 1812.* Philadelphia: Thomas and William Bradford, 1812.

Hall, Gordon, and Samuel Newell. *The Conversion of the World; or, The Claims of Six Hundred Millions and the Ability and Duty of the Churches Respecting Them.* Andover, Mass.: Flagg and Gould for the ABCFM, 1818.

Hanzsche, William Thomson. *Forgotten Founding Fathers of the American Church and State.* Boston: Christopher, 1954.

Hasler, Richard. *Journey with David Brainerd: Forty Days or Forty Nights with David Brainerd.* Downers Grove, Ill.: InterVarsity, 1975.

Heckewelder, Reverend John. *A Narrative of the Mission of the United Brethren among the Delaware and Mohegan Indians, from Its Commencement, in the Year 1740, to the Close of the Year 1808.* Philadelphia: McCarty and Davis, 1820.

———. *History, Manners and Customs of the Indian Nations Who Once Inhabited Pennsylvania and the Neighbouring States.* 1876. Reprint, Bowie, Md.: Heritage, 1990.

Heimert, Alan, and Perry Miller, eds. *The Great Awakening: Documents Illustrating the Crisis and Its Consequences.* Indianapolis, Ind.: Bobbs-Merrill, 1967.

Hempstead, Joshua. "Diary of Joshua Hempstead." *Collections of the New London Historical Society* 1 (1901).

Hodge, Homer W., ed. *The Life of David Brainerd, Missionary to the Indians.* New York: Christian Alliance Publishing, 1925.

Hopkins, Samuel. *Historical Memoirs Relating to the Housatunnuk Indians.* Boston: S. Kneeland, 1753.

———. *Sketches of the Life of the Late Rev. Samuel Hopkins, D.D., Written by Himself, with Marginal Notes from His Private Diary,* edited by Stephen West. Hartford, Conn.: Stephen D. West, 1805.

Horton, R. F. "The Spiritual Preparation of the Missionary." In *Students and the Missionary Problem: Addresses Delivered at the International Student Missionary Conference, London, January 2–6, 1900.* London: Student Volunteer Missionary Union, 1900.

Howard, Philip E., Jr. *The Life and Diary of David Brainerd.* Grand Rapids, Mich.: Baker, 1989.

Hunsicker, Ranelda. *David Brainerd.* Minneapolis, Minn.: Bethany House, 1999.

Hunter, Henry. *A Brief History of the Society in Scotland for Propagating Christian Knowledge in the Highlands and Islands; and of the Correspondent Board in London; from the Establishment of the Society in the Year 1701, Down to the Present Time.* London: n.p., 1795.

Hyde, P. S. "David Brainerd: The Man of Prayer." In *God's Heroes: Our Examples,* 61–75. Mysore City, India: Epworth League of the Methodist Episcopal Church, [1910].

Janeway, James. *A Token for Children. Being an Exact Account of the Conversion, Holy and Exemplary Lives and Joyful Deaths of Several Young Children. To Which Is Added a Token for the Children of New England.* Boston: Nicholas Boone, 1700. Evans No. 914.

Johnson, Samuel. "Memoirs of the Life of the Rev. Dr. Johnson and Several Things Relating to the State Both of Religion and Learning in His Times. Written 1768–1770." In *Samuel Johnson, President of King's College, His Career and Writing,* edited by Herbert Schneider and Carol Schneider. New York: Columbia University Press, 1929.

Kilby, Clyde S. "David Brainerd: Knight of the Grail." In *Heroic Colonial Christians,* edited by Russell T. Hitt, 151–206. Philadelphia: Lippincott, 1966.

Lhamon, W. J. *Heroes of Modern Missions.* New York: Revell, 1899.

Lindestrom, Peter. *Geographia Americae with an Account of the Delaware Indians,* translated by Amandus Johnson. Philadelphia: Swedish Colonial Society, 1925.

Manwaring, Charles William, ed. *A Digest of the Early Connecticut Probate Records.* Baltimore, Md.: Genealogical Publishing, 1995.

Marsden, Samuel. *Memoirs of the Life and Labours of the Rev. Samuel Marsden,* edited by J. B. Marsden. London: Religious Tract Society, 1858.

———. *The Letters and Journals of Samuel Marsden, 1765–1838,* edited by John Rawson Elder. London: Kierk, 1932.

Martyn, Henry. *Journal and Letters of Henry Martyn,* edited by Samuel Wilberforce. 1851. Reprint, New York: Protestant Episcopal Society for the Promotion of Evangelical Knowledge, 1861.

McCheyne, Robert Murray. *The Works of the Late Rev. Robert Murray McCheyne.* New York: Robert Carter, 1847.

McLean, A. *Missionary Addresses.* St. Louis, Mo.: Missionary Publishing, 1895.

Memoirs of American Missionaries, Formerly Connected with the Society of Inquiry Respecting Missions in the Andover Theological Seminary. Boston: Pierce and Parker, 1833.

Minutes of the Methodist Conferences from the First Held in London, by the Late Rev. John Wesley, A.M., *in the Year 1744.* London: John Mason, 1862.

Mott, John R. *The Evangelization of the World in This Generation.* New York: Student Volunteer Movement for Foreign Missions, 1900.

———. *The Pastor and Modern Missions: A Plea for Leadership in World Evangelization.* New York: Student Volunteer Movement for Foreign Missions, 1904.

———. *Addresses and Papers of John R. Mott.* New York: Association Press, 1946.

Myers, Albert Cook, ed. *Narratives of Early Pennsylvania, West New Jersey and Delaware, 1630–1707.* New York: Barnes and Noble, 1967.

Nissenbaum, Stephen, ed. *The Great Awakening at Yale College.* Belmont, Calif.: Wadsworth, 1972.

Park, Edwards A. *Memoir of the Life and Character of Samuel Hopkins, D.D.* Boston: Doctrinal Tract and Book Company, 1854.

Parsons, Levi. *Memoir of the Rev. Levi Parsons, Late Missionary to Palestine,* compiled by Daniel O. Morton. 1824. Reprint, New York: Arno, 1977.

Pastorius, Francis Daniel. "Circumstantial and Geographical Description of Pennsylvania." In *Narratives of Early Pennsylvania, West New Jersey and Delaware, 1630–1707,* edited by Albert Cook Myers, 353–448. New York: Barnes and Noble, 1967.

Pemberton, Ebenezer. *The Knowlege [sic] of Christ Recommended, in a Sermon Preach'd in the Public Hall at Yale College in New-Haven, April 19th 1741.* New London: T. Green, 1741. Evans No. 4779.

———. *A Sermon Preached in New-ark, June 12, 1744, at the Ordination of Mr. Brainerd, a Missionary among the Indians.* Boston: Rogers & Fowle, 1744.

Pennsylvania Colonial Records. 16 vols. Harrisburg, 1838–1853.

Person, Mrs. Walter. "David Brainerd: 'A Man in a Million.'" *1949 Program Series, Women's Missionary Federation of the Evangelical Lutheran Church.* N.p., 56–59.

Pierson, Arthur T. *The Crisis of Missions; or, The Voice Out of the Cloud.* New York: Baker and Taylor, 1886.

Pounds, Jessie Brown. *Pioneer Missionaries: Short Sketches of the Lives of the Pioneers in Missionary Work in Many Lands.* Indianapolis, Ind.: Young People's Department of the Christian Woman's Board of Missions, 1905.

Prince, Thomas. *The Case of Heman Considered.* Boston: S. Kneeland, 1756.

The Public Records of the Colony of Connecticut, 15 vols., edited by J. H. Trumbull and C. J. Hoadly. Hartford, Conn.: Case, Lockwood & Brainard 1850–1890.

Records of the Town of East-Hampton, Long Island, Suffolk County, N.Y. Sag Harbor, N.Y.: J. H. Hunt, 1937–1957. UMI PS0337.

Reichel, William C., ed. *Memorials of the Moravian Church.* Philadelphia: Lippincott, 1870.

Schneider, Herbert, and Carol, eds. *Samuel Johnson, President of King's College, His Career and Writings.* New York: Columbia University Press, 1929.

Sergeant, John. *A Letter from the Revd Mr. Sergeant of Stockbridge, to Dr. Colman of Boston.* Boston: D. Henchman, 1743.

Shelton, Don O. *Heroes of the Cross in America.* Philadelphia: Westminster, 1905.

Sherwood, J. M., ed. *Memoirs of Rev. David Brainerd, Missionary to the Indians of North America.* New York: Funk and Wagnalls, 1884.

Simmons, William S., and Cheryl L. Simmons, eds. *Old Light on Separate Ways: The Narragansett Diary of Joseph Fish, 1765–1776.* Hanover, N.H.: University Press of New England, 1982.

Speer, Robert E. *Missionary Principles and Practices: A Discussion of Christian Missions and of Some Criticisms upon Them.* New York: Revell, 1902.

Spring, Samuel. *A Sermon Preached at New Haven, Connecticut, before the American Board of Commissioners for Foreign Missions, at Their Ninth Annual Meeting, September 10, 1818.* Boston: Samuel T. Armstrong, 1818.

Stoddard, Solomon. *A Guide to Christ; or, The Way of Directing Souls That Are under the Work of Conversion. Compiled for the Help of Young Ministers: And May Be Serviceable to Private Christians Who Are Enquiring the Way to Zion*. Boston: J. Allen, 1714. Evans No. 1716.

———. *The Duty of Gospel-Ministers to Preserve a People from Corruption*. Boston: Samuel Phillips, 1718. Evans No. 1998.

———. *A Treatise Concerning Conversion Shewing the Nature of Saving Conversion to God and the Way Wherein It Is Wrought*. Boston: D. Henchman, 1719. Evans No. 2072.

———. *Question: Whether God Is Not Angry with the Country for Doing So Little toward the Conversion of the Indians?* Boston: B. Green, 1723. Evans No. 2479.

———. *The Defects of Preachers Reproved in a Sermon Preached at Northampton, May 17th 1723*, 2nd ed. Boston: Kneeland & Green, 1747.

Styles, John. *The Life of David Brainerd, Missionary to the Indians with an Abridgement of Diary and Journal*. Boston: Samuel T. Armstrong, 1812; Evans, 2nd ser., No. 26824.

Tennent, Gilbert. *The Danger of an Unconverted Ministry, Considered in a Sermon on Mark VI. 34*. Boston: Rogers & Fowle, 1742. Evans No. 5070.

Thomas, Gabriel. "An Historical Account of the Province and Country of Pennsilvania; and of West-New-Jersey in America." In *Narratives of Early Pennsylvania, West New Jersey and Delaware, 1630–1707*, edited by Albert Cook Myers, 309–352. New York: Barnes and Noble, 1967.

Tracy, Joseph R. *History of American Missions to the Heathens, from Their Commencement to the Present Time*. 1840. Reprint, New York: Johnson Reprint, 1970.

———. *The Great Awakening: A History of the Revival of Religion in the Time of Edwards and Whitefield*. 1845. Reprint, New York: Arno, 1969.

Wadsworth, Daniel. *The Diary of Rev. Daniel Wadsworth, Seventh Pastor of the First Church of Christ in Hartford*, edited by George Leon Walker. Hartford, Conn.: Case, Lockwood, and Brainard, 1894.

Walett, Francis G., ed. *The Diary of Ebenezer Parkman, 1703–1782*. Worcester, Mass.: American Antiquarian Society, 1974.

Wansbrough, Charles, ed. *Handbook and Index to the Minutes of the Conference: Showing the Growth and Development of the Wesleyan Methodist Constitution from the First Conference, 1744, to 1890*. London: Wesleyan Methodist Book Room, 1890.

Wesley, John. *An Extract of the Life of the Late Rev. David Brainerd, Missionary to the Indians*, 4th ed. Dublin: R. Napper, 1812.

———. *The Letters of the Reverend John Wesley, A.M.*, 8 vols., edited by John Telford. London: Epworth, 1931.

———. *The Works of John Wesley*. 1872. Reprint, Grand Rapids, Mich.: Zondervan, 1958.

———. *The Works of John Wesley*, 36 vols. to date, edited by Frank Baker. Nashville, Tenn.: Abingdon Press and New York: Oxford University Press, 1975–.

Whitefield, George. *George Whitefield's Journals (1737–1741)*. Gainesville, Fla.: Scholars, 1969.

Williams, Daniel. *A True Copy of the Last Will and Testament of the Late Reverend Daniel Williams, D.D.* London: R. Burleigh, 1717.

Williams, William. *A Painful Ministry: The Peculiar Gift of the Lord of the Harvest to Be Sought by Prayer and Acknowledged with Thankfulness.* Boston: B. Green, 1717. Evans No. 1940.

Woods, Leonard. *A Sermon Delivered at the Tabernacle in Salem, February 6, 1812...* Boston: Samuel T. Armstrong, 1812.

Yonge, C[harlotte] M. *Pioneers and Founders or Recent Workers in the Mission Field.* New York: Macmillan, 1890.

Zeisberger, David. "History of the Northern American Indians," translated by Archer Butler Hulbert and William Nathaniel Schwarze. *Ohio Archaeological and Historical Quarterly* 19, nos. 1–2 (January and April 1910): 12–189.

Secondary Sources

Anderson, Owanah. "Anglican Mission among the Mohawk." In *Three Centuries of Missions: The United Society for the Propagation of the Gospel, 1701–2000,* edited by Daniel O'Connor, 235–248. New York: Continuum, 2000.

Andrew, John A. *Rebuilding the Christian Commonwealth: New England Congregationalists and Foreign Missions, 1800–1830.* Lexington: University Press of Kentucky, 1976.

Armstrong, Anthony. *The Church of England, the Methodists and Society, 1700–1850.* Totowa, N.J.: Rowman and Littlefield, 1973.

Atwood, Craig. *Community of the Cross: Moravian Piety in Colonial Bethlehem.* University Park: Pennsylvania State University Press, 2004.

Axtell, James. *The Invasion Within: The Contest of Cultures in Colonial North America.* New York: Oxford University Press, 1985.

———. *After Columbus: Essays in the Ethnohistory of Colonial North America.* New York: Oxford University Press, 1988.

Ayling, Stanley. *John Wesley.* London: Collins, 1979.

Bacon, Leonard. *Thirteen Historical Discourses on the Completion of Two Hundred Years, from the Beginning of the First Church in New Haven.* New Haven, Conn.: Durrie and Peck, 1839.

Bailyn, Bernard, and Philip D. Morgan, eds. *Strangers within the Realm: Cultural Margins of the First British Empire.* Chapel Hill: University of North Carolina Press for the Institute of Early American History and Culture, 1991.

Baker, Frank. *From Wesley to Asbury: Studies in Early American Methodism.* Durham, N.C.: Duke University Press, 1976.

Balsera, Viviana Díaz. *The Pyramid under the Cross: Franciscan Discourses of Evangelization and the Nahua Christian Subject in Sixteenth-Century Mexico.* Tucson: University of Arizona Press, 2005.

Batinski, Michael C. *The New Jersey Assembly, 1738–1775: The Making of a Legislative Community.* Lanham, Md.: University Press of America, 1987.

Bays, Daniel H., and Grant Wacker. "After World War II: Years of Complication." In *The Foreign Missionary Enterprise at Home: Explorations in North American Cultural History,* edited by Daniel H. Bays and Grant Wacker, 187–189. Tuscaloosa: University of Alabama Press, 2003.

Bays, Daniel H., and Grant Wacker, eds. *The Foreign Missionary Enterprise at Home: Explorations in North American Cultural History.* Tuscaloosa: University of Alabama Press, 2003.

Bebbington, David W. "Remembered around the World: The International Scope of Edwards's Legacy." In *Jonathan Edwards at Home and Abroad: Historical Memories, Cultural Movements, Global Horizons,* edited by David W. Kling and Douglas A. Sweeney, 177–200. Columbia: University of South Carolina Press, 2003.

Becker, Marshall Joseph. "The Moravian Mission in the Forks of the Delaware: Reconstructing the Migration and Settlement Patterns of the Jersey Lenape during the Eighteenth Century through Documents in the Moravian Archives." *Unitas Fratrum* 21 and 22 (1987): 83–168.

———. "Native Settlements in the Forks of the Delaware, Pennsylvania, in the 18th Century: Archaeological Implications." *Pennsylvania Archaeologist* 58, no. 1 (1988): 43–60.

Bennett, Christi-Ann C. "John Wesley: Founder of a Missionary Church?" *Proceedings of the Wesley Historical Society* 50, no. 5 (1996): 159–170; and 50, no. 6 (1996): 229–236.

Black, Jeremy. *Eighteenth-Century Britain, 1688–1783.* New York: Palgrave, 2001.

Blackburn, Carole. *Harvest of Souls: The Jesuit Missions and Colonialism in North America, 1632–1650.* Montreal: McGill-Queen's University Press, 2000.

Brainard, Lucy Abigail. *The Genealogy of the Brainerd-Brainard Family in America, 1649–1908.* Hartford, Conn.: Hartford Press, 1908.

Brainerd, Thomas. *The Life of John Brainerd.* Philadelphia: Presbyterian Publication Committee, 1861.

Breen, T. H. "An Empire of Goods: The Anglicization of Colonial America, 1690–1776." *Journal of British Studies* 25, no. 4 (October 1986): 467–499.

Brock, Peggy. "New Christians as Evangelists." In *Missions and Empire,* edited by Norman Etherington, 132–152. New York: Oxford University Press, 2005.

Brown, Callum G. *Religion and Society in Scotland since 1707.* Edinburgh: Edinburgh University Press, 1997.

Brown, Raymond. *The English Baptists of the Eighteenth Century.* London: Baptist Historical Society, 1986.

Brumberg, Joan J. *Mission for Life: The Story of the Family of Adoniram Judson.* New York: Free Press, 1980.

Buell, Lawrence. *New England Literary Culture, from Revolution through Renaissance.* New York: Cambridge University Press, 1986.

Bushman, Richard L. *From Puritan to Yankee: Character and the Social Order in Connecticut, 1690–1765.* Cambridge, Mass.: Harvard University Press, 1967.

Butler, Jon, Grant Wacker, and Randall Balmer. *Religion in American Life.* New York: Oxford University Press, 2003.

Calloway, Colin G. *The Western Abenakis of Vermont, 1600–1800: War, Migration, and the Survival of an Indian People.* Norman: University of Oklahoma Press, 1990.

———. *New Worlds for All: Indians, Europeans, and the Remaking of Early America.* Baltimore, Md.: Johns Hopkins University Press, 1997.

Cannon, William R. "Salvation in the Theology of John Wesley." *Methodist History* 9 (1970): 42–54.

Carpenter, Joel A., and Wilbert R. Shenk, eds. *Earthen Vessels: American Evangelicals and Foreign Missions, 1880–1980.* Grand Rapids, Mich.: Eerdmans, 1990.

Carwardine, Richard. *Transatlantic Revivalism: Popular Evangelicalism in Britain and America, 1790–1865.* Westport, Conn.: Greenwood, 1978.

Cayton, Andrew R. L., and Fredrika J. Teute. *Contact Points: American Frontiers from the Mohawk Valley to the Mississippi, 1750–1830.* Chapel Hill: University of North Carolina Press, 1998.

Chesterman, A. de M. "The Journals of David Brainerd and of William Carey." *Baptist Quarterly* 19, no. 4 (1961): 147–156.

Clyde, John Cunningham. *History of the Allen Township Presbyterian Church.* Philadelphia: Presbyterian Historical Society, 1876.

———. *The Scotch-Irish of Northampton County.* Northampton, Pa.: Northampton County Historical and Genealogical Society, 1926.

Coalter, Milton. *Gilbert Tennent, Son of Thunder: A Case Study of Continental Pietism's Impact on the First Great Awakening in the Middle Colonies.* New York: Greenwood, 1986.

Coffman, Ralph J. *Solomon Stoddard.* Boston: Twayne, 1978.

Cogley, Richard W. *John Eliot's Mission to the Indians before King Philip's War.* Cambridge, Mass.: Harvard University Press, 1999.

Colley, Linda. *Britons: Forging the Nation 1707–1837.* New Haven, Conn.: Yale University Press, 1992.

Collins, Kenneth J. *The Scripture Way of Salvation: The Heart of John Wesley's Theology.* Nashville, Tenn.: Abingdon, 1997.

Conforti, Joseph. *Samuel Hopkins and the New Divinity Movement: Calvinism, the Congregational Ministry, and Reform in New England between the Great Awakenings.* Grand Rapids, Mich.: Christian University Press, 1981.

———. *Jonathan Edwards, Religious Tradition, and American Culture.* Chapel Hill: University of North Carolina Press, 1995.

The Constitution of the Presbyterian Church in the United States of America. Philadelphia: Presbyterian Board of Publication, 1839.

Cook, Edward M., Jr. *The Fathers of the Towns: Leadership and Community Structure in Eighteenth-Century New England.* Baltimore, Md.: Johns Hopkins University Press, 1976.

Cranz, David. *The History of Greenland: Including an Account of the Mission Carried On by the United Brethren in That Country. With a Continuation to the Present Time.* 1767. London: Longman, Hurst, Rees, Orme, and Brown, 1820.

Crawford, Michael J. "The Spiritual Travels of Nathan Cole." *WMQ* 33, no. 1 (January 1976): 89–126.

———. *Seasons of Grace: Colonial New England's Revival Tradition in Its British Context.* New York: Oxford University Press, 1991.

Cray, Robert, Jr. "More Light on a New Light: James Davenport's Religious Legacy, Eastern Long Island, 1740–1840." *New York History* 73, no. 1 (1992): 4–27.

Cunningham, Loren. *Is That Really You, Lord? The Story of Youth with a Mission.* Eastbourne, England: Kingsway, 1984.

Cushner, Nicholas P. *Why Have You Come Here? The Jesuits and the First Evangelization of Native America.* New York: Oxford University Press, 2006.

Custer, Jay F. *Prehistoric Cultures of the Delmarva Peninsula: An Archeological Study.* Newark: University of Delaware Press, 1989.

Daniels, Bruce C. *The Connecticut Town: Growth and Development, 1635–1790.* Middletown, Conn.: Wesleyan University Press, 1979.

———. *The Fragmentation of New England: Comparative Perspectives on Economic, Political, and Social Divisions in the Eighteenth Century.* New York: Greenwood, 1988.

De Jong, James A. *As the Waters Cover the Sea: Millennial Expectations in the Rise of Anglo-American Missions, 1640–1810.* Kampen, Netherlands: Kok, 1970.

Devine, T. M. *The Scottish Nation: A History, 1700–2000.* New York: Viking, 1999.

Dexter, Franklin Bowditch. *Biographical Sketches of the Graduates of Yale College, with Annals of the College History, 1701–May, 1745,* 6 vols. New York: Holt, 1885–1912.

Dowd, Gregory Evans. *A Spirited Resistance: The North American Indian Struggle for Unity, 1745–1815.* Baltimore, Md.: Johns Hopkins University Press, 1992.

Drake, James D. *King Philip's War: Civil War in New England, 1675–1676.* Amherst: University of Massachusetts Press, 1999.

Drewey, Mary. *William Carey, Shoemaker and Missionary.* London: Hodder and Stoughton, 1978.

Dunn, Shirley W. *The Mohicans and Their Land, 1609–1730.* New York: Purple Mountain Press and Fleischmanns, 1994.

English, John C. "The Heart Renewed: John Wesley's Doctrine of Christian Initiation." *Wesleyan Quarterly Review* 4, nos. 2–3 (May–August 1967): 114–192.

Enroth, Ronald M., Edward E. Ericson, Jr., and C. Breckinridge Peters. *The Jesus People: Old-Time Religion in the Age of Aquarius.* Grand Rapids, Mich.: Eerdmans, 1972.

Etherington, Norman, ed. *Missions and Empire.* New York: Oxford University Press, 2005.

Fawcett, Arthur. *The Cambuslang Revival: The Scottish Evangelical Revival of the Eighteenth Century.* London: Banner of Truth Trust, 1971.

Field, David D. *A History of the Towns of Haddam and East Haddam.* Middletown, Conn.: Loomis, 1814. Evans, 2nd ser., No. 31473.

———. *The Genealogy of the Brainerd Family in the United States, with Numerous Sketches of Individuals.* New York: n.p., 1857.

Frazier, Patrick. *The Mohicans of Stockbridge.* Lincoln: University of Nebraska Press, 1992.

Fur, Gunlög. "'Some Women Are Wiser than Some Men': Gender and Native American History." In *Clearing a Path: Theorizing the Past in Native American Studies,* edited by Nancy Shoemaker, 75–103. New York: Routledge, 2002.

———. "Reading Margins: Colonial Encounters in Sápmi and Lenapehoking in the Seventeenth and Eighteenth Centuries." *Feminist Studies* 32, no. 3 (Fall 2006): 491–521.

Garvan, Anthony N. B. *Architecture and Town Planning in Colonial Connecticut.* New Haven, Conn.: Yale University Press, 1951.

Gavaler, Christopher P. "The Empty Lot: Spiritual Contact in Lenape and Moravian Religious Beliefs." *American Indian Quarterly* 18, no. 2 (Spring 1994): 215–228.

Goddard, Ives. "Delaware." In *Northeast,* edited by Bruce G. Trigger, vol. 15 of *Handbook of North American Indians,* edited by William C. Sturtevant. Washington, D.C.: Smithsonian Institution Press, 1978, 213–239.

Goen, C. C. *Revivalism and Separatism in New England, 1740–1800.* New Haven, Conn.: Yale University Press, 1962.

Goodwin, Gregory J. "Christianity, Civilization, and the Savage: The Anglican Mission to the American Indian." *Historical Magazine of the Protestant Episcopal Church* 42, no. 2 (1973): 93–110.

Grant, Charles S. *Democracy in the Connecticut Frontier Town of Kent.* New York: Columbia University Press, 1961.

Gray, Elma E. *Wilderness Christians: The Moravian Mission to the Delaware Indians.* Ithaca, N.Y.: Cornell University Press, 1956.

Greene, Jack P. *Pursuits of Happiness: The Social Development of Early Modern British Colonies and the Formation of American Culture.* Chapel Hill: University of North Carolina Press, 1988.

Greven, Philip J., Jr. *Four Generations: Population, Land and Family in Colonial Andover, Massachusetts.* Ithaca, N.Y.: Cornell University Press, 1970.

Griffin, Edward M. *Old Brick: Charles Chauncy of Boston, 1705–1787.* Minneapolis: University of Minnesota Press, 1980.

Griffin, Patrick. *The People with No Name: Ireland's Ulster Scots, America's Scots Irish, and the Creation of a British Atlantic World, 1689–1764.* Princeton, N.J.: Princeton University Press, 2001.

Grigg, John A. "The Lives of David Brainerd." Ph.D. diss., University of Kansas, 2002.

———. "'A Principle of Spiritual Life': David Brainerd's Surviving Sermon." *NEQ* 77, no. 2 (June 2004): 273–282.

Gunter, W. Stephen. *The Limits of "Love Divine": John Wesley's Response to Antinomianism and Enthusiasm.* Nashville, Tenn.: Kingswood, 1989.

Gura, Philip F. "Solomon Stoddard's Irreverent Way." *Early American Literature* 21, no. 1 (Spring 1986): 29–43.

Gustafson, Sandra M. *Eloquence Is Power: Oratory and Performance in Early America.* Chapel Hill: University of North Carolina Press for the Omohundro Institute of Early American History and Culture, 2000.

Gutiérrez, Ramón A. *When Jesus Came, the Corn Mothers Went Away.* Stanford, Calif.: Stanford University Press, 1991.

Hall, Timothy D. *Contested Boundaries: Itinerancy and the Reshaping of the Colonial American Religious World.* Durham, N.C.: Duke University Press, 1994.

Handy, Robert T. *A Christian America: Protestant Hopes and Historical Realities.* New York: Oxford University Press, 1971.

Harper, Steven Craig. *Promised Land: Penn's Holy Experiment, the Walking Purchase, and the Dispossession of the Delawares, 1600–1763.* Bethlehem, Pa.: Lehigh University Press, 2006.

Harrington, M. R. *Religion and Ceremonies of the Lenape.* New York: Museum of the American Indian, 1921.

Harris, Paul. "David Brainerd and the Indians: Cultural Interaction and Protestant Missionary Ideology." *American Presbyterians* 72, no. 1 (Spring 1994): 1–10.

Hart D. G. *That Old-Time Religion in Modern America: Evangelical Protestantism in the Twentieth Century.* Chicago, Ill.: Dee, 2002.

Hasler, Richard C. "David Zeisberger's 'Jersey Connection.'" *Transactions of the Moravian Historical Society* 30 (1998): 37–53.

Hatch, Nathan O. *The Democratization of American Christianity.* New Haven, Conn.: Yale University Press, 1989.

Hayes, T. Wilson. "John Everard and the Familist Tradition." In *The Origins of Anglo-American Radicalism,* edited by Margaret Jacob and James Jacob. Boston: Allen & Unwin, 1984.

Haynes, William. *The Stonington Chronology, 1649–1976, Being a Year-by-Year Record of the American Way of Life in a Connecticut Town.* Chester, Conn.: Pequot Press for the Stonington Historical Society, 1976.

Hempton, David. *Methodism and Politics in British Society, 1750–1850.* Stanford, Calif.: Stanford University Press, 1984.

Hill, Christopher. "Propagating the Gospel." In *Historical Essays, 1600–1750, Presented to David Ogg,* edited by H. E. Bell and Richard Lawrence Ollard, 35–59. New York: Barnes and Noble, 1963.

Hill, Hamilton Andrews. *History of the Old South Church (Third Church) Boston, 1669–1884.* Boston: Houghton & Mifflin, 1890.

Hindmarsh, D. Bruce. "The Reception of Jonathan Edwards by Early Evangelicals in England." In *Jonathan Edwards at Home and Abroad: Historical Memories, Cultural Movements, Global Horizons,* edited by David W. Kling and Douglas A. Sweeney, 201–221. Columbia: University of South Carolina Press, 2003.

Hiner, N. Ray. "Preparing for the Harvest: The Concept of New Birth and the Theory of Religious Education on the Eve of the First Great Awakening." *Fides et Historia* 9, no. 1 (Fall 1976): 8–25.

History of Suffolk County, New York, with Illustrations, Portraits, and Sketches of Prominent Families and Individuals. New York: Munsell, 1882.

Hoffer, Peter Charles. *Sensory Worlds in Early America.* Baltimore, Md.: Johns Hopkins University Press, 2003.

Hopkins, C. Howard. *John R. Mott, 1865–1955: A Biography.* Grand Rapids, Mich.: Eerdmans, 1979.

Hunter, William A. "Moses (Tunda) Tatamy, Delaware Indian Diplomat." In *A Delaware Indian Symposium,* edited by Herbert C. Kraft, 71–88. Harrisburg: Pennsylvania Historical and Museum Commission, 1972.

Hutchins, Francis G. *Mashpee: The Story of Cape Cod's Indian Town.* West Franklin, N.H.: Amarta, 1979.

Hutchison, William R. *Errand to the World: American Protestant Thought and Foreign Missions.* Chicago, Ill.: University of Chicago Press, 1987.

Isaac, Rhys. "Religion and Authority: Problems of the Anglican Establishment in Virginia in the Era of the Great Awakening and the Parsons' Cause." *WMQ* 30, no. 1 (January 1973): 4–36.

——. "Evangelical Revolt: The Nature of the Baptists' Challenge to the Traditional Order in Virginia, 1765–1775." *WMQ* 32, no. 3 (July 1974): 346–368.

——. *The Transformation of Virginia, 1740–1790.* 1982. Reprint, Chapel Hill: University of North Carolina Press for the Omohundro Institute of Early American History and Culture, 1999.

Jacob, Margaret, and James Jacob, eds. *The Origins of Anglo-American Radicalism.* Boston: Allen & Unwin, 1984.

Jedrey, Christopher M. *The World of John Cleaveland: Family and Community in Eighteenth-Century New England.* New York: Norton, 1979.

Jennings, Francis. "The Delaware Interregnum." *Pennsylvania Magazine of History and Biography* 89, no. 2 (April 1965): 174–198.

——. "The Scandalous Indian Policy of William Penn's Sons: Deeds and Documents of the Walking Purchase." *Pennsylvania History* 37 (January–October 1970): 19–39.

——. *The Ambiguous Iroquois Empire: The Covenant Chain Confederation of Indian Tribes with English Colonies.* New York: Norton, 1984.

——. "'Pennsylvania Indians' and the Iroquois." In *Beyond the Covenant Chain: The Iroquois and Their Neighbors in Indian North America, 1600–1800,* edited by Daniel K. Richter and James H. Merrell, 75–91. Syracuse, N.Y.: Syracuse University Press, 1987.

Johnson, E. Emory, and Hosford B. Niles. "East Haddam." In *History of Middlesex County, Connecticut, with Biographical Sketches of Its Prominent Men.* New York: Beers, 1884.

Jones, Maldwyn A. "The Scotch-Irish in British America." In *Strangers within the Realm: Cultural Margins of the First British Empire,* edited by Bernard Bailyn and Philip D. Morgan, 284–313. Chapel Hill: University of North Carolina Press for the Institute of Early American History and Culture, 1991.

Jorstad, Erling. *That New-Time Religion: The Jesus Revival in America.* Minneapolis, Minn.: Augsburg, 1972.

Kellaway, William. *The New England Company 1649–1776: Missionary Society to the American Indians.* New York: Barnes and Noble, 1962.

Kidd, Thomas S. *The Protestant Interest: New England after Puritanism.* New Haven, Conn.: Yale University Press, 2004.

———. "The Healing of Mercy Wheeler: Illness and Miracles among Early American Evangelicals." *WMQ* 63, no. 1 (2006): 149–170.

———. "Daniel Rogers' Egalitarian Great Awakening." *Journal of the Historical Society* 7, no. 1 (March 2007): 111–135.

———. *The Great Awakening: The Roots of Evangelical Christianity in Colonial America.* New Haven, Conn.: Yale University Press, 2007.

Kimnach, Wilson H., ed. *Three Essays in Honor of the Publication of the "Life of David Brainerd."* New Haven, Conn.: Privately published, 1985.

Kinsey, W. Fred. *Archeology in the Upper Delaware Valley: A Study of the Cultural Chronology of the Tocks Island Reservoir.* Harrisburg: Pennsylvania Historical and Museum Commission, 1972.

Kling, David W., and Douglas A. Sweeney, eds. *Jonathan Edwards at Home and Abroad: Historical Memories, Cultural Movements, Global Horizons.* Columbia: University of South Carolina Press, 2003.

Kraft, Herbert C. "The Miller Field Site, Warren County, New Jersey." In *Archeology in the Upper Delaware Valley: A Study of the Cultural Chronology of the Tocks Island Reservoir,* edited by W. Fred Kinsey, 1–54. Harrisburg: Pennsylvania Historical and Museum Commission, 1972.

———. *The Lenape: Archaeology, History and Ethnography.* Newark: New Jersey Historical Society, 1986.

———, ed. *A Delaware Indian Symposium.* Harrisburg: Pennsylvania Historical and Museum Commission, 1974.

Lambert, Frank. "'Pedlar in Divinity': George Whitefield and the Great Awakening, 1737–1745." *JAH* 77, no. 3 (December 1990): 812–837.

———. *"Pedlar in Divinity": George Whitefield and the Transatlantic Revivals, 1737–1770.* Princeton, N.J.: Princeton University Press, 1994.

———. *Inventing the "Great Awakening."* Princeton, N.J.: Princeton University Press, 1999.

Landsman, Ned C. *Scotland and Its First American Colony, 1683–1765.* Princeton, N.J.: Princeton University Press, 1985.

Le Beau, Bryan F. *Jonathan Dickinson and the Formative Years of American Presbyterianism.* Lexington: University Press of Kentucky, 1997.

Lesser, M. X. "An Honor Too Great: Jonathan Edwards in Print Abroad." In *Jonathan Edwards at Home and Abroad: Historical Memories, Cultural Movements, Global Horizons,* edited by David W. Kling and Douglas A. Sweeney, 297–319. Columbia: University of South Carolina Press, 2003.

Levering, Joseph Mortimer. *A History of Bethlehem, Pennsylvania, 1741–1892.* 1903. Reprint, New York: AMS, 1971.

Leyburn, James G. *The Scotch-Irish: A Social History.* Chapel Hill: University of North Carolina Press, 1962.

Lockridge, Kenneth A. *A New England Town, the First Hundred Years: Dedham, Massachusetts, 1636–1736.* New York: Norton, 1970.

Long, Kathryn T. "In the Modern World but Not of It: The 'Auca Martyrs,' Evangelicalism, and Postwar American Culture." In *The Foreign Missionary Enterprise at Home: Explorations in North American Cultural History,* edited by Daniel H. Bays and Grant Wacker, 223–236. Tuscaloosa: University of Alabama Press, 2003.

Loskiel, George Henry. *History of the Mission of the United Brethren among the Indians of North America,* translated by Christian Ignatius La Trobe. London: John Stockdale, 1794.

Lovejoy, David O. *Religious Enthusiasm in the New World: Heresy to Revolution.* Cambridge, Mass.: Harvard University Press, 1985.

Lovelace, Richard F. *The American Pietism of Cotton Mather: Origins of American Evangelicalism.* Grand Rapids, Mich.: Christian University Press, 1979.

Lucas, Paul R. "Solomon Stoddard and the Origin of the Great Awakening in New England." *Historian* 59, no. 4 (Summer 1997): 741–758.

———. *Valley of Discord: Church and Society along the Connecticut River, 1636–1725.* Hanover, N.H.: University Press of New England, 1976.

Mack, Phyllis. "Women as Prophets during the English Civil War." In *The Origins of Anglo-American Radicalism,* edited by Margaret Jacob and James Jacob, 214–230. Boston: Allen & Unwin, 1984.

Main, Jackson Turner. *Society and Economy in Colonial Connecticut.* Princeton, N.J.: Princeton University Press, 1985.

Mancall, Peter C. *Valley of Opportunity: Economic Culture along the Upper Susquehanna, 1700–1800.* Ithaca, N.Y.: Cornell University Press, 1991.

———. *Deadly Medicine: Indians and Alcohol in Early America.* Ithaca, N.Y.: Cornell University Press, 1995.

Mandell, Daniel. *Behind the Frontier: Indians in Eighteenth-Century Massachusetts.* Lincoln: University of Nebraska Press, 1996.

Marchiando, Patricia. "Bell-Browning Site, 28-Sx-19. In *Archeology in the Upper Delaware Valley: A Study of the Cultural Chronology of the Tocks Island Reservoir,* edited by W. Fred Kinsey, 131–158. Harrisburg: Pennsylvania Historical and Museum Commission, 1972.

Marsden, George M. "Unity and Diversity in the Evangelical Resurgence." In *Altered Landscapes: Christianity in America, 1935–1985,* edited by David W. Lotz, Donald W. Shriver, Jr., and John F. Wilson, 61–76. Grand Rapids, Mich.: Eerdmans, 1989.

———. *Jonathan Edwards: A Life.* New Haven, Conn.: Yale University Press, 2003.

Martin, John F. *Profits in the Wilderness: Entrepreneurship and the Founding of New England Towns in the Seventeenth Century.* Chapel Hill: University of North Carolina Press for the Omohundro Institute of Early American History and Culture, 1991.

Martyn, John R. C. *Henry Martyn (1781–1812): Scholar and Missionary to India and Persia: A Biography.* Lewiston, N.Y.: Mellen, 1999.

Mason, J. C. S. *The Moravian Church and the Missionary Awakening in England, 1760–1800.* Rochester, N.Y.: Boydell Press and the Royal Historical Society, 2001.

McBeth, H. Leon. "The Legacy of the Baptist Missionary Society." *Baptist History and Heritage* 27, no. 3(1992): 3–13.

McConville, Brendan. *These Daring Disturbers of the Public Peace: The Struggle for Property and Power in Early New Jersey.* Ithaca, N.Y.: Cornell University Press, 1999.

McDannell, Colleen. *Material Christianity: Religion and Popular Culture in America.* New Haven, Conn.: Yale University Press, 1995.

McDermott, Gerald R. "Jonathan Edwards and the American Indians: The Devil Sucks Their Blood." *NEQ* 72, no. 4 (December 1999): 539–557.

Meek, Donald E. "Scottish Highlanders, North American Indians and the SSPCK: Some Cultural Perspectives." *Records of the Scottish Church History Society* 23 (1989): 378–396.

Merrell, James H. "'The Customes of Our Countrey': Indians and Colonists in Early America." In *Strangers within the Realm: Cultural Margins of the First British Empire,* edited by Bernard Bailyn and Philip D. Morgan, 117–156. Chapel Hill: University of North Carolina Press for the Institute of Early American History and Culture, 1991.

———. "'Shamokin: The Very Seat of the Prince of Darkness': Unsettling the Early American Frontier." In *Contact Points: American Frontiers from the Mohawk Valley to the Mississippi, 1750–1830,* edited by Andrew R. L. Cayton and Fredrike J. Teute, 16–59. Chapel Hill: University of North Carolina Press, 1998.

———. *Into the American Woods: Negotiators on the Pennsylvania Frontier.* New York: Norton, 1999.

Merritt, Jane T. *At the Crossroads: Indians & Empires on a Mid-Atlantic Frontier, 1700–1763.* Chapel Hill: University of North Carolina Press for the Omohundro Institute of Early American History and Culture, 2003.

Miller, Jay. "The Delaware as Women: A Symbolic Solution." *American Ethnologist* 1, no. 3 (August 1974): 507–514.

Mills, Kenneth, and Anthony Grafton, eds. *Conversion: Old Worlds and New.* Rochester, N.Y.: University of Rochester Press, 2003.

Minkema, Kenneth P. "A Great Awakening Conversion: The Relation of Samuel Belcher." *WMQ* 44, no. 1 (January 1987): 121–126.

Morrison, Dane. *A Praying People: Massachusett Acculturation and the Failure of the Puritan Mission, 1600–1690.* New York: Lang, 1998.

Morrison, Kenneth M. *The Solidarity of Kin: Ethnohistory, Religious Studies, and the Algonkian-French Religious Encounter.* Albany: State University of New York Press, 2002.

Noll, Mark A. *A History of Christianity in the United States and Canada.* Grand Rapids, Mich.: Eerdmans, 1992.

———. *American Evangelical Christianity: An Introduction.* Malden, Mass.: Blackwell, 2001.

———. *The Rise of Evangelicalism: The Age of Edwards, Whitefield and the Wesleys.* Downers Grove, Ill.: InterVarsity, 2003.

———, David W. Bebbington, and George A. Rawlyk, eds. *Evangelicalism: Comparative Studies of Popular Protestantism in North America, the British Isles, and Beyond, 1700–1990.* New York: Oxford University Press, 1994.

Nybakken, Elizabeth. "In the Irish Tradition: Pre-Revolutionary Academies in America." *History of Education Quarterly* 37, no. 2 (Summer 1997): 163–183.

O'Brien, Jean M. *Dispossession by Degrees: Indian Land and Identity in Natick, Massachusetts, 1650–1790.* New York: Cambridge University Press, 1997.

O'Brien, Susan. "A Transatlantic Community of Saints: The Great Awakening and the First Evangelical Network, 1735–1755." *American Historical Review* 91 (December 1986): 811–832.

———. "Eighteenth-Century Publishing Networks in the First Years of Transatlantic Evangelicalism." In *Evangelicalism: Comparative Studies of Popular Protestantism in North America, the British Isles, and Beyond, 1700–1990*, edited by Mark A. Noll, David W. Bebbington, and George A. Rawlyk, 38–57. New York: Oxford University Press, 1994.

O'Connor, Daniel, ed. *Three Centuries of Missions: The United Society for the Propagation of the Gospel, 1701–2000*. New York: Continuum, 2000.

Oden, Thomas C. *John Wesley's Scriptural Christianity: A Plain Exposition of His Teaching on Christian Doctrine*. Grand Rapids, Mich.: Zondervan, 1994.

Olmstead, Earl P. *David Zeisberger: A Life among the Indians*. Kent, Ohio: Kent State University Press, 1997.

Olson, Alison Gilbert. *Making the Empire Work: London and American Interest Groups*. Cambridge, Mass.: Harvard University Press, 1992.

Parker, Gail Thain. "Jonathan Edwards and Melancholy." *NEQ* 41, no. 2 (June 1968): 193–212.

Parker, Michael. *The Kingdom of Character: The Student Volunteer Movement for Foreign Missions (1886–1926)*. Lanham, Md.: American Society of Missiology and University Press of America, 1998.

Pelletreau, William S. "Easthampton." In *History of Suffolk County, New York, with Illustrations, Portraits, and Sketches of Prominent Families and Individuals*. New York: Munsell, 1882.

Pestana, Carla Gardina, and Sharon V. Salinger, eds. *Inequality in Early America*. Hanover, N.H.: University Press of New England, 1999.

Piggin, Stuart. *Making Evangelical Missionaries 1789–1858: The Social Background, Motives, and Training of British Protestant Missionaries to India*. Abingdon, Oxfordshire: Sutton Courtenay, 1984.

———. "The Expanding Knowledge of God: Jonathan Edwards's Influence on Missionary Thinking and Promotion." In *Jonathan Edwards at Home and Abroad: Historical Memories, Cultural Movements, Global Horizons*, edited by David W. Kling and Douglas A. Sweeney, 266–296. Columbia: University of South Carolina Press, 2003.

Piggin, Stuart, and John Roxborogh. *The St. Andrews Seven: The Finest Flowering of Missionary Zeal in Scottish History*. Carlisle, Pa.: Banner of Truth Trust, 1985.

Pointer, Richard W. "'Poor Indians' and the 'Poor in Spirit': The Indian Impact on David Brainerd." *NEQ* 67, no. 3 (September 1994): 403–426.

———. *Encounters of the Spirit: Native Americans and European Colonial Religion*. Bloomington: Indiana University Press, 2007.

Porterfield, Amanda. *Feminine Spirituality in America: From Sarah Edwards to Martha Graham*. Philadelphia: Temple University Press, 1980.

———. *Mary Lyon and the Mount Holyoke Missionaries*. New York: Oxford University Press, 1997.

Potts, Daniel. *British Baptist Missionaries in India, 1793–1837: The History of Serampore and Its Missions*. Cambridge: Cambridge University Press, 1967.

Prime, Nathaniel S. *A History of Long Island, from Its First Settlement by Europeans to the Year 1845*. New York: Robert Carter, 1845.

Purvis, Thomas L. *Proprietors, Patronage, and Paper Money: Legislative Politics in New Jersey, 1703–1776.* New Brunswick, N.J.: Rutgers University Press, 1986.

Rack, Henry D. *Reasonable Enthusiast: John Wesley and the Rise of Methodism,* 3rd ed. London: Epworth, 2002.

Reed, Michael. *The Georgian Triumph.* Boston: Kegan Paul, 1983.

Richter, Daniel K. *Facing East from Indian Country: A Native History of Early America.* Cambridge, Mass.: Harvard University Press, 2001.

Richter, Daniel K., and James H. Merrell, eds. *Beyond the Covenant Chain: The Iroquois and Their Neighbors in Indian North America, 1600–1800.* Syracuse, N.Y.: Syracuse University Press, 1987.

Robert, Dana L. *American Women in Mission: A Social History of Their Thought and Practice.* Macon, Ga.: Mercer University Press, 1997.

———. *Occupy until I Come: A. T. Pierson and the Evangelization of the World.* Grand Rapids, Mich.: Eerdmans, 2003.

Rogal, Samuel J. "John Wesley and the Attack on Luxury in England." *Eighteenth-Century Life* 3, no. 3 (March 1977): 91–94.

Rupp, Gordon. *Religion in England, 1688–1791.* Oxford: Clarendon, 1986.

Salisbury, Neal. "'I Loved the Place of My Dwelling': Puritan Missionaries and Native Americans in Seventeenth-Century Southern New England." In *Inequality in Early America,* edited by Carla Gardina Pestana and Sharon V. Salinger, 111–133. Hanover, N.H.: University Press of New England, 1999.

Schmidt, Leigh Eric. "'A Second and Glorious Reformation': The New Light Extremism of Andrew Croswell." *WMQ* 43, no. 2 (April, 1986): 214–244.

———. *Holy Fairs: Scottish Communions and American Revivals in the Early Modern Period,* 2nd ed. Grand Rapids, Mich.: Eerdmans, 2001.

Schmotter, James W. "Ministerial Careers in Eighteenth-Century New England: The Social Context, 1700–1760." *Journal of Social History* 9, no. 2 (Winter 1975): 249–267.

Schuldiner, Michael. "Solomon Stoddard and the Process of Conversion." *Early American Literature* 17, no. 3 (Winter 1982–1983): 215–226.

Schutt, Amy. *Peoples of the River Valleys: The Odyssey of the Delaware Indians.* Philadelphia: University of Pennsylvania Press, 2007.

Schwartz, Hillel. *Knaves, Fools, Madmen, and That Subtile Effluvium: A Study of the Opposition to the French Prophets in England, 1706–1710.* Gainesville: University Press of Florida, 1978.

———. *The French Prophets: The History of a Millenarian Group in Eighteenth-Century England.* Berkeley: University of California Press, 1980.

Schwartz, Sally. *"A Mixed Multitude": The Struggle for Toleration in Colonial Pennsylvania.* New York: New York University Press, 1987.

Seeman, Erik R. *Pious Persuasions: Laity and Clergy in Eighteenth-Century New England.* Baltimore, Md.: Johns Hopkins University Press, 1999.

Shea, Daniel B., Jr. *Spiritual Autobiography in Early America.* Princeton, N.J.: Princeton University Press, 1968.

Shoemaker, Nancy. *A Strange Likeness: Becoming Red and White in Eighteenth-Century North America.* New York: Oxford University Press, 2004.

Shoemaker, Nancy, ed. *Clearing a Path: Theorizing the Past in Native American Studies.* New York: Routledge, 2002.

Silverman, David. *Faith and Boundaries: Colonists, Christianity, and Community among the Wampanoag Indians of Martha's Vineyard, 1600–1871.* New York: Cambridge University Press, 2005.

Silverman, Kenneth. *The Life and Times of Cotton Mather.* New York: Harper & Row, 1984.

Simmons, William S. "Red Yankees: Narragansett Conversion in the Great Awakening." *American Ethnologist* 10, no. 2 (May 1983): 253–271.

Smith, George. *Henry Martyn: Saint and Scholar.* New York: Revell, 1892.

Sprague, William B. *Annals of the American Pulpit,* 9 vols. New York: Robert Carter, 1857–1869.

Stanley, Brian. *The Bible and the Flag: Protestant Missions and British Imperialism in the Nineteenth and Twentieth Centuries.* Leicester: Apollos, 1990.

Steele, Ian K. *The English Atlantic, 1675–1740: An Exploration of Commerce and Communication.* New York: Oxford University Press, 1986.

Steele, Richard. *"Gracious Affection" and "True Virtue" According to Jonathan Edwards and John Wesley.* Metuchen, N.J.: Scarecrow, 1994.

Stoeffler, F. Ernest. *The Rise of Evangelical Pietism.* Leiden: Brill, 1965.

Stoeffler, F. Ernest, ed. *Continental Pietism and Early American Christianity.* Grand Rapids, Mich.: Eerdmans, 1976.

Stone, Gaynell, ed. *The History and Archaeology of the Montauk.* Stony Brook, N.Y.: Suffolk County Archaeological Association and Nassau County Archaeological Committee, 1993.

Stout, Harry S. "The Great Awakening in New England Reconsidered: The New England Clergy." *Journal of Social History* 8, no. 1 (Autumn 1974): 21–47.

———. *The New England Soul: Preaching and Religious Culture in Colonial New England.* New York: Oxford University Press, 1986.

———, and Peter Onuf. "James Davenport and the Great Awakening in New London." *JAH* 71, no. 3 (December 1983): 556–578.

Stowe, David W. "'The Opposers Are Very Much Enraged': Religious Conflict and Separation in New Haven during the Great Awakening, 1741–1760." *Connecticut Historical Society Bulletin* 56 (1991): 211–235.

Strong, John. "Azariah Horton's Mission to the Montauk, 1741–44." In *The History and Archaeology of the Montauk,* edited by Gaynell Stone, 191–220. Stony Brook, N.Y.: Suffolk County Archaeological Association and Nassau County Archaeological Committee, 1993.

Strong, John A., and Zsuzsanna Török. "Taking the Middle Way: Algonquian Responses to the Reverend Azariah Horton's Mission on Long Island (1741–1744)." *Long Island Historical Journal* 12, no. 2 (1999): 145–158.

Sugrue, Thomas J. "The Peopling and Depeopling of Early Pennsylvania: Indians and Colonists, 1680–1720." *Pennsylvania Magazine of History and Biography* 116, no. 1 (January 1992): 3–31.

Sweet, John Wood. *Bodies Politic: Negotiating Race in the American North, 1730–1830.* Baltimore, Md.: Johns Hopkins University Press, 2003.

Szasz, Margaret Connell. *Indian Education in the American Colonies.* Lincoln: University of Nebraska Press, 1988. Reprint, Lincoln, Neb.: Bison, 2007.

———. *Scottish Highlanders and Native Americans: Indigenous Education in the Eighteenth-Century Atlantic World.* Norman: University of Oklahoma Press, 2007.

Taggart, Norman W. "Methodist Foreign Missions: The First Half-Century." *Proceedings of the Wesley Historical Society* 45 (1986): 157–182.

Tanis, James. "Reformed Pietism in Colonial America." In *Continental Pietism and Early American Christianity,* edited by F. Ernest Stoeffler, 34–73. Grand Rapids, Mich.: Eerdmans, 1976.

Tappert, Theodore G. "The Influence of Pietism in Colonial American Lutheranism." In *Continental Pietism and Early American Christianity*, edited by F. Ernest Stoeffler, 13–33. Grand Rapids, Mich.: Eerdmans, 1976.

Taylor, Alan. *American Colonies: The Settling of North America*. New York: Penguin, 2001.

———. *The Divided Ground: Indians, Settlers, and the Northern Borderlands of the American Revolution*. New York: Knopf, 2006.

Tooker, Elisabeth, ed. *Native North American Spirituality of the Eastern Woodlands*. New York: Paulist, 1979.

Tracy, Patricia J. *Jonathan Edwards, Pastor: Religion and Society in Eighteenth-Century Northampton*. New York: Hill and Wang, 1979.

———. "The Romance of David Brainerd and Jerusha Edwards." In *Three Essays in Honor of the Publication of the "Life of David Brainerd,"* edited by Wilson H. Kimnach. New Haven, Conn.: Privately published, 1985.

Trumbull, James Russell. *History of Northampton, Massachusetts from Its Settlement in 1654*. Northampton, Mass.: Northampton Press of Gazette, 1902.

Tucker, Louis Leonard. *Puritan Protagonist: President Thomas Clap of Yale College*. Chapel Hill: University of North Carolina Press, 1962.

Valeri, Mark. *Law and Providence in Joseph Bellamy's New England: The Origins of the New Divinity in Revolutionary America*. New York: Oxford University Press, 1994.

Van Engen, John. "Conversion and Conformity in the Early Fifteenth Century." In *Conversion: Old Worlds and New*, edited by Kenneth Mills and Anthony Grafton, 30–65. Rochester, N.Y.: University of Rochester Press, 2003.

Virkus, Frederick Adams, ed. *Immigrant Ancestors: A List of 2,500 Immigrants to America before 1750*. Baltimore, Md.: Genealogical Publishing, 1980.

Wacker, Grant. "The Waning of the Missionary Impulse: The Case of Pearl S. Buck." In *The Foreign Missionary Enterprise at Home: Explorations in North American Cultural History*, edited by Daniel H. Bays and Grant Wacker, 191–205. Tuscaloosa: University of Alabama Press, 2003.

Wallace, Anthony F. C. *King of the Delawares: Teedyuscung 1700–1763*. Philadelphia: University of Pennsylvania Press, 1949.

Walls, Andrew F. "The Evangelical Revival, the Missionary Movement, and Africa." In *Evangelicalism: Comparative Studies of Popular Protestantism in North America, the British Isles, and Beyond, 1700–1990*, edited by Mark A. Noll, David W. Bebbington, and George A. Rawlyk, 310–330. New York: Oxford University Press, 1994.

———. "Missions and Historical Memory: Jonathan Edwards and David Brainerd." In *Jonathan Edwards at Home and Abroad: Historical Memories, Cultural Movements, Global Horizons*, edited by David W. Kling and Douglas A. Sweeney, 248–265. Columbia: University of South Carolina Press, 2003.

Walsh, John. "'Methodism' and the Origins of English-Speaking Evangelicalism." In *Evangelicalism: Comparative Studies of Popular Protestantism in North America, the British Isles, and Beyond, 1700–1990*, edited by Mark A. Noll, David W. Bebbington, and George A. Rawlyk, 19–37. New York: Oxford University Press, 1994.

Warch, Richard. *School of the Prophets: Yale College, 1701–1740*. New Haven, Conn.: Yale University Press, 1973.

———. "The Shepherd's Tent: Education and Enthusiasm in the Great Awakening." *American Quarterly* 20, no. 2 (Summer 1978): 177–198.

Ward, W. R. *The Protestant Evangelical Awakening.* Cambridge: Cambridge University Press, 1992.

Warner, Michael. *The Letters of the Republic: Publication and the Public Sphere in Eighteenth-Century America.* Cambridge, Mass.: Harvard University Press, 1990.

Webster, Richard. *A History of the Presbyterian Church in America, from Its Origin until the Year 1760.* Philadelphia: Joseph M. Wilson, 1857.

Weddle, David. "The Melancholy Saint: Jonathan Edwards' Interpretation of David Brainerd as a Model of Evangelical Spirituality." *Harvard Theological Review* 81, no. 3 (1988): 297–318.

Werner, David J. "The Zimmerman Site, 36-Pi-14." In *Archeology in the Upper Delaware Valley: A Study of the Cultural Chronology of the Tocks Island Reservoir,* edited by W. Fred Kinsey, 55–130. Harrisburg: Pennsylvania Historical and Museum Commission, 1972.

Weslager, C. A. *The Delaware Indians: A History.* New Brunswick, N.J.: Rutgers University Press, 1972.

Westerkamp, Marilyn. *Triumph of the Laity: Scots-Irish Piety and the Great Awakening, 1625–1760.* New York: Oxford University Press, 1988.

Wheeler, Rachel. "'Friends to Your Souls': Jonathan Edwards' Indian Pastorate and the Doctrine of Original Sin." *Church History* 72, no. 4 (2003): 736–765.

———. *To Live upon Hope: Mohicans and Missionaries in the Eighteenth-Century Northeast.* Ithaca, N.Y.: Cornell University Press, 2008.

White, Richard. *The Middle Ground: Indians, Empires, and Republics in the Great Lakes Region, 1650–1815.* Cambridge: Cambridge University Press, 1991.

Whited, Milton H. *Durham's Heritage: Men & Homes of Early Durham,* 2nd ed. Durham, Conn., 2004.

Wiebe, Robert H. *The Search for Order, 1877–1920.* New York: Hill and Wang, 1967.

Winiarski, Douglas L. "Souls Filled with Ravishing Transport: Heavenly Visions and the Radical Awakening in New England." *WMQ* 61, no. 1 (January 2004): 3–46.

———. "Native American Popular Culture in New England's Old Colony, 1670–1770." *Religion and American Culture* 15, no. 2 (2005): 147–186.

———. "Jonathan Edwards, Enthusiast? Radical Revivalism and the Great Awakening in the Connecticut Valley." *Church History* 74, no. 4 (December 2005): 683–739.

Woolverton, John Frederick. *Colonial Anglicanism in North America.* Detroit, Mich.: Wayne State University Press, 1984.

Worrall, B. G. *The Making of the Modern Church: Christianity in England since 1800.* London: Society for the Propagation of the Gospel, 1993.

Wuthnow, Robert. *The Restructuring of American Religion: Society and Faith since World War II.* Princeton, N.J.: Princeton University Press, 1988.

Yarwood, A. T. *Samuel Marsden: The Great Survivor.* Melbourne, Australia: Melbourne University Press, 1977.

Youngs, William T., Jr. *God's Messengers: Religious Leadership in Colonial New England, 1700–1750.* Baltimore, Md.: Johns Hopkins University Press, 1976.

Zimmerman, Albright G. "European Trade Relations in the 17th and 18th Centuries." In *A Delaware Indian Symposium,* edited by Herbert C. Kraft, 57–70. Harrisburg: Pennsylvania Historical and Museum Commission, 1972.

Zuckerman, Michael. *Peaceable Kingdoms: New England Towns in the Eighteenth Century.* New York: Knopf, 1970.

Index

Page numbers followed by *f*, *m*, and *n* refer to figures, maps, and notes respectively.